*Praise for Monte Reel's*

# A BROTHERHOOD OF SPIES

"A classic Cold War tale of human bravery, technological bravado, and political skulduggery. Monte Reel tells the story with brio and empathy, marshaling a colorful cast of characters as brilliant—and flawed—as the extraordinary spy plane that changed their lives, for both better and worse. . . . Highly recommended!"
—Michael Dobbs, author of *One Minute to Midnight: Kennedy, Khrushchev, and Castro on the Brink of Nuclear War*

"High above the gray clouds of the Cold War, Monte Reel has discovered a vivid tale of inventors, scientists, spymasters, and the eternal tension between truth and secrecy at the highest levels of American power. Paced like a thriller, *A Brotherhood of Spies* throws new light on famous moments of nuclear brinkmanship and raises troubling questions about the world we live in right now."
—Jason Fagone, author of the national bestseller *The Woman Who Smashed Codes*

"The most riveting tales of history are those where the fate of millions hangs on the actions of a few. The U-2 crisis of 1960 is one such story, and it has never been told with greater verve or closer attention to critical detail." —H. W. Brands, *New York Times* bestselling author of *The General vs. the President*

"A gripping work of narrative nonfiction. . . . This exemplary work provides a wholly satisfying take on a central chapter of the Cold War—a dramatic story of zeal and adventure."
—*Publishers Weekly* (starred review)

"Captivating. . . . A richly detailed, well-researched, and engagingly written book that takes us behind the scenes of one of the twentieth century's most nail-bitingly tense episodes." —*Booklist*

MONTE REEL

A BROTHERHOOD OF SPIES

Monte Reel is the author of two previous books, *Between Man and Beast* and *The Last of the Tribe*. His writing has appeared in *The New Yorker*, *The New York Times Magazine*, *Harper's*, and other magazines. He currently writes for *Bloomberg Businessweek* as part of its Projects and Investigations staff and previously was a foreign correspondent for *The Washington Post*. He lives in Illinois.

ALSO BY MONTE REEL

*Between Man and Beast*
*The Last of the Tribe*

# A BROTHERHOOD OF SPIES

# A BROTHERHOOD OF SPIES

*The U-2 and the CIA's Secret War*

## MONTE REEL

**ANCHOR BOOKS**
*A Division of Penguin Random House LLC*
*New York*

FIRST ANCHOR BOOKS EDITION, MAY 2019

*Copyright © 2018 by Monte Reel*

All rights reserved. Published in the United States by Anchor Books, a division of
Penguin Random House LLC, New York, and distributed in Canada by Random
House of Canada, a division of Penguin Random House Canada Limited, Toronto.
Originally published in hardcover in the United States by Doubleday, a division of
Penguin Random House LLC, New York, in 2018.

Anchor Books and colophon are registered trademarks of
Penguin Random House LLC.

The Library of Congress has cataloged the Doubleday edition as follows:
Names: Reel, Monte, author.
Title: A brotherhood of spies : the U-2 and the CIA's secret war / Monte Reel.
Description: First edition. | New York : Doubleday, [2018] | Includes bibliographical
references and index.
Identifiers: LCCN 2017053819
Subjects: LCSH: Intelligence service—United States—History—20th century. |
United States. Central Intelligence Agency—History—20th century. | U-2
(Reconnaissance aircraft) | U-2 Incident, 1960. | Land, Edwin H., 1909–1991. |
Johnson, Clarence L., 1910–1990. | Bissell, Richard M. (Richard Mervin), 1909–1994. |
Powers, Francis Gary, 1929–1977.
Classification: LCC JK468.I6 R45 2018 | DDC 327.1273047/09046—dc23
LC record available at https://lccn.loc.gov/2017053819

Anchor Books Trade Paperback ISBN: 978-1-101-91042-9
eBook ISBN: 978-0-385-54021-6

*Author photograph © Liz Hansen*
*Book design by Iris Weinstein*

www.anchorbooks.com

Printed in the United States of America
10  9  8  7  6  5  4  3  2  1

*For Sofia and Violet*

# Contents

# A BROTHERHOOD OF SPIES

# *Prologue*

NEW YORK CITY

It's a warm spring day, and about five thousand people—an average crowd for a Tuesday afternoon—swarm across the sidewalks and intersections of Times Square. Near Forty-Second Street, they shoulder past hot dog stands, pause in front of a window display of Stetson hats, and ignore the chattering street vendors with their cheap knives, transistor radios, and miracle powders. A mounted policeman nudges his horse onto Broadway, where the traffic pulses in fits and starts. The sun is bright yellow and still high enough to reach down between the skyscrapers. The clock hands on the "Bond Clothes" sign above Broadway say it's not quite 2:15 p.m.

Electric advertisements beg for attention, flashing from nearly every building, and their collective message is consistent: *the future is right here, right now.* The big TWA sign above the square has a newly installed feature—"Jets," spelled out in bright red neon. The word hasn't been part of the American vocabulary for long, but it's already inescapable, sometimes used as a noun, sometimes a verb, sometimes an adjective, and always jazzing up everything it touches with the silvery sheen of modernity. Just over a year ago, a Pan Am 707 made the first coast-to-coast commercial jet flight, and airlines have been tripping over themselves to inaugurate new routes ever since. "Jets to Africa!" flashes a sign over Broadway. "Jet Your Way to Tel Aviv!"

Speed is the new seduction, and New Yorkers confront it everywhere they turn. In the Willoughbys camera store, there's a sale on Polaroid Speedliner instant cameras, which can spit out prints in less than a minute. At the new Daitch Shopwell grocery store on First Avenue, executives have unveiled a scale model of the "automated supermarket" of the future, with aisles that move on electric-powered conveyor belts, shuttling shoppers past the shelves. At the Horn & Hardart Automat, on Broadway near Forty-Seventh Street, hundreds of shrink-wrapped lunches sit behind a wall of coin-operated windows: drop thirty-five cents into a slot, slide open a window, and pull out today's special—a corned beef and pickle sandwich, ready to eat.

Near the subway stations, the latest front pages are papered to the sides of the newsstands, giving pedestrians an eyeful of headlines as they shuffle past: Senator John F. Kennedy is the predicted winner of today's Democratic primaries in Indiana, Ohio, and the District of Columbia. President Eisenhower, with less than a year left in his second term, is scheduled to tour an army base to inspect America's new "Davy Crockett launcher," a contraption that can fire miniaturized nuclear warheads from the back of a jeep. In sports, the Yankees could jump into first place if they beat the Detroit Tigers.

The clock above Times Square flips to 2:15, and in an instant everything stops.

ON THE OBSERVATION DECK of 30 Rockefeller Plaza, seventy stories above the jostle and throb of the streets, a Chrysler V-8 engine mounted on a platform of riveted steel has just revved to life. The engine powers a high-decibel horn, which has begun spinning on its base. It sends an ear-shattering wail over the city, a tone that rises and falls in pitch. Within seconds, 721 smaller-gauge horns—affixed to streetlamps, to rooftops, to traffic lights—join in to create a warbling chorus, flooding the city in rolling waves of stereophonic alarm.

About ten miles north in Claremont Park, a young girl on a wood-plank swing had been leaning back and kicking her saddle shoes toward the clear blue sky, but when the sirens reach her, she jumps off the swing and abandons the playground. At the Bronx Zoo, an animal handler pushes hard on the hindquarters of an elephant, trying to force it into an indoor shelter. Inside Yankee Stadium, left-hander Whitey Ford is walking off the pitcher's mound, disappearing into the dugout with the rest of his teammates. The stadium's ushers begin ordering spectators out of the sunny bleacher sections, and most of the 10,255 fans in the park huddle together in the dim concourses.

The sirens drone on. At the First National Bank branch on lower Broadway, a manager raises his voice above the din: "Wrap it up!" The tellers slam the lids on their cash trays and hurry them into the vault. Inside the Waldorf Astoria hotel on Park Avenue, the oak-paneled bar—a designated fallout shelter, according to a sign by the door—fills up with about a hundred men, many of whom take the opportunity to order martinis and highballs. Several women also enter and try to get drinks, but they are politely turned away, because ladies are never served at the Waldorf bar. Downtown, on the floor of the New York Stock Exchange, trading stops.

Drivers pull their cars to the curb and abandon them. Hundreds of people stream off paralyzed city buses, and in Times Square a human tide pours down the subway stairwells, out of sight.

A civil defense policeman monitors it all, and when Times Square is empty of people, he checks his stopwatch: the sirens have been wailing for exactly one minute and forty-nine seconds.

THEY'D BEEN WARNED THIS WAS COMING. Operation Alert 1960 had been billed as the biggest civil defense drill in America's history. From New York to Los Angeles, millions of Americans have been instructed to duck for cover as if the country's greatest fear has come true: a fleet of Soviet long-range bombers has penetrated America's airspace, and those jets are about to drop nuclear warheads on the country's biggest cities.

Earlier this year, CONELRAD—a government program that stands for Control of Electromagnetic Radiation—launched an educational drive to teach Americans how to distinguish between the different civil defense sirens. The agency produced an audio play that dramatized a nuclear emergency, distributing it as a vinyl record to households from coast to coast. The recording depicted a prudent family—the Smiths—taking shelter in their basement, which they'd stocked with food, water, flashlights, and a radio.

Now, during the nationwide drill, CONELRAD has commandeered America's airwaves. The country's 566 television stations have gone dark, and all of its 4,335 radio stations have either stopped transmitting or joined the CONELRAD broadcast, which repeats an urgent message to take shelter.

As the drill unfolds, local civil defense officials in lookout points across New York monitor the citizens' response. They estimate that had Soviet jets actually attacked the city, some 3,935,940 New Yorkers, despite their best efforts, would have been killed instantly. Another 1,405,000 would later die from radiation exposure.

The total population of the city is about 7,700,000.

· · ·

THE CITY REMAINS QUIET AND ODDLY STILL, with the exception of a park next to City Hall, where hundreds of people have united in an act of open defiance, refusing to listen to the officials who urge them to take shelter.

Most of them are college students from campuses across the city. One young man sitting next to a tree ignores a policeman's orders, choosing to strum the chords to "We Shall Overcome" on an acoustic guitar. Another student hands out a flyer that says, "Peace is the only defense against nuclear war." Several more carry signs: "Civil Defense Is Futile!" and "Remember, There Will Be No Survivors!" A young man holds a placard over his head that reads, "After Two Weeks in a Shelter, Then What! No Food—No Water—Hot Dust and Death."

A member of the city's auxiliary police—a middle-aged man with a stony expression and grand ambitions—stands on a park bench and announces, "I now place you all under arrest for not obeying the law!" But he's overmatched; there are hundreds of protesters and only two police paddy wagons. "Are we Americans or not?" someone shouts at him.

A sense of empowerment seems to spread among the protesters, forcing the police to shift to a more laissez-faire approach. The scene settles into a relaxed, almost celebratory, vibe. Author Norman Mailer walks among the students, signing autographs. The sirens fall silent, and the participants linger in a pleasant afterglow, telling reporters that they're satisfied with the turnout.

The atmosphere would be different—darker, no doubt—if they had the slightest inkling that a genuine crisis is slowly coming to a head in Washington, D.C. For the president of the United States and his closest advisers, Operation Alert is about to veer wildly off script.

THE MEMBERS OF THE NATIONAL SECURITY COUNCIL were told to ignore the civil defense siren; their signal to take cover would come in the form of a telephone call. To preserve the element of surprise, the call wouldn't coincide with the nationwide drill, but could happen anytime up to three days after the national exercise.

At about seven o'clock on the morning of May 5, the telephone rings inside the Georgetown house of CIA director Allen Dulles. He's instructed to drive downtown and board one of several helicopters that will carry the council to a newly built secret complex about fifty miles outside Washington. He makes it out the door in good time, but his

Cadillac breaks down shortly after he pulls onto Q Street; luckily, he's only about a hundred yards from his house, and he's able to find another ride. Meanwhile, the secretary of defense, Thomas Gates, gets a lift from his wife, who's still dressed in her nightgown as she navigates the morning traffic. When he rushes toward the helicopter pad minutes before takeoff, Gates realizes that he has forgotten his identification documents. He pleads with the marines standing guard; they keep him waiting for a few tense minutes but eventually let him through. Meanwhile, President Eisenhower strolls across the White House lawn to his private helicopter, which whisks him and two aides away at about 7:35 a.m.

The helicopters fly west of the city, across the Potomac, into Virginia. They eventually set down atop the rugged spine of the Blue Ridge Mountains, where a bunker has been hidden within a rocky outcrop. The sprawling underground lair is code-named High Point. But among the select circle of authorities aware of its existence, it goes by another name: the Hideout.

A little more than six years before, the Bureau of Mines determined that the rock inside this mountain was "exceptionally hard and tight," and encouragingly shock resistant. The government decided to expand an old, abandoned mine shaft inside the mountain into a top secret, multiroom tactical center. Beside those rooms, workers created subterranean water pools, which served two purposes: they were emergency reservoirs for drinking water, and they also cooled the air that was circulated to the bunker's two enormous mainframe computers. The roofs were reinforced with twenty-one thousand iron bolts, which were drilled as far as ten feet into the rock to prevent collapse in the event of a nuclear strike. Radiation and chemical contamination detectors were installed near the entrances. Construction was completed in 1959.

Now, a year later, the Hideout employs a full-time staff of technicians, computer engineers, firefighters, doctors and nurses, secretaries, and security guards. Each of them is sworn to secrecy. Three dormitory rooms are available for men and one for women. Only the president, cabinet secretaries, and Supreme Court justices are allotted private bedrooms. There is enough food on-site to feed hundreds of people for a full month.

After scrambling out of their helicopters, Eisenhower and the rest of his team walk toward a check-in station near the "blast gate"—a safety feature built to protect the entrances from any flying debris shaken loose by bombs. Once inside, they file past the chemical-biological radiation sensors and the decontamination chamber, but they don't stop; it hasn't been activated for the drill.

The Hideout isn't fancy, but neither is it rustic. The main "War Room" is outfitted with an Iconorama display system, which can chart the positions of aircraft and missiles on a large screen, and there's also a closed-circuit TV system, several 16 mm projectors, computer monitors, radiotelephones, and a Teletype machine for secure intergovernmental communications.

The president and his Security Council have decided to hold an official meeting in the Hideout; they knew they'd all be together for the drill anyway, so they figured they might as well get something done. Dulles summarizes the first item on the agenda: days before, on May 1, an American U-2 spy jet disappeared after it took off for a high-altitude flight across the entire length of the Soviet Union. The disappearance had been a source of mild worry for Eisenhower and Dulles, but they assume that a crash killed the pilot and destroyed the plane, leaving the Soviets no irrefutable evidence to prove to the world that the CIA had been spying on them from above.

To protect the secrecy of the U-2 program, they've come up with a cover story: NASA lost a high-altitude weather plane, which was monitoring atmospheric conditions in Turkey; the pilot apparently lost consciousness during the flight, and the plane drifted into Soviet territory, where it crashed.

Now, inside the bunker during the civil defense drill, Dulles is handed a Teletype message from the Soviet Union. It says that Nikita Khrushchev, the Soviet leader, is delivering a speech to his governing council and it is being broadcast to the Soviet public. The report includes few details about the content of the speech, and Dulles moves on, shifting everyone's attention toward the latest political upheavals in the Congo.

After the meeting adjourns and some of the helicopters begin shuttling people back to Washington, Dulles and Eisenhower linger in the bunker. Soon, more messages arrive with additional details of Khrushchev's speech. The reports indicate that the Soviet premier is full of righteous indignation, and he's telling a frenzied crowd that his troops have shot down an American military plane flying deep inside Soviet territory. By breaching Soviet airspace, he suggests, the United States is trying to provoke a full-scale nuclear war. "Just think, what would be the reaction of the United States if a Soviet plane flew over New York, or Detroit?" Khrushchev has asked the crowd. "This would mean the beginning of another war. Why then do you not think that we may reply with the same measures should a foreign plane appear over our country? We think that there is no doubt in anybody's mind that we have the ability to retaliate."

The news coming over the wire is troubling, but the CIA's explanation involving the weather plane and the passed-out pilot might still hold. If the Soviets did, in fact, shoot down the plane from a high altitude, then the destruction would likely have been total, wiping out any evidence that could contradict the cover story. They decide to stick by it, and the White House schedules a press conference that afternoon to release more details about the innocent science project that drifted off course.

That decision will turn out to be a mistake. In two days, Khrushchev will reveal that the spy pilot has been captured alive, and he'll show pictures suggesting that many of the plane's components also survived intact. Forced into a corner, Eisenhower will become the first U.S. president to openly acknowledge that the country does, in fact, spy on other nations. He'll also be the first to publicly admit that he has lied to the American people.

Compared with almost all of the other developed nations of the world, the United States was a relative newcomer to the world of institutionalized spying; the American public had never confronted the ethical contradictions inherent in espionage on a broad scale. The U-2 incident pushed those moral conundrums onto front pages and television screens, exposing the CIA—an agency that in 1960 many people could still legitimately claim to have never heard of—to international notoriety.

The U-2 drama is now a central chapter in the Cold War, but many of the behind-the-scenes details did not fully emerge for nearly six decades. The story is an unlikely adventure, driven by four men who together reinvented American espionage and, in the process, were themselves transformed by the secrets that they carried.

THE U-2 WAS THE FIRST LARGE-SCALE technological development project the CIA ever undertook. It redefined both the nature and the scale of the agency, setting it on a course that it would follow into the twenty-first century, when technology and espionage would become inseparable. The plane brought in huge hauls of visual data, spurring the development of new computational and analytical technologies just to process it all. More than forty years after the U-2 debuted, former CIA director George Tenet said of the program, "It constituted nothing less than a revolution in intelligence." Not only was it the single most significant leap forward in the agency's history, he said, but it was possibly the greatest achievement of any intelligence service, anywhere in the world, at any point in history. "Our U-2 revolutionaries got it right," he said. "They were brilliant. They were willing to think big, and think different, and take risks."

Those risks had unintended consequences for the four men at the center of this story. Drawn together into the unfamiliar and disorienting territory of espionage, they were tested in ways they couldn't have predicted. Edwin Land was a brilliant scientist whose inventions had already made him one of the richest men in America; his faith in empirical truth was his bedrock, but the moral ambiguities of intelligence gathering put his ideals to the test. Clarence "Kelly" Johnson was a fiery engineer who, as much as anyone else, had ushered America into the jet age, but his evolution from an aircraft designer to an unofficial CIA operative drove him to sleep with a loaded automatic pistol at his bedside. Richard Bissell was a bookish bureaucrat with an eye for detail and a respect for the power of technology; the U-2 gave him a ticket into the darkest corners of the international spy world, and it led him to push the limits of espionage to deadly extremes. Finally, there was the pilot of the downed U-2, Francis Gary Powers, a soft-spoken coal miner's son with a taste for adventure; his recruitment into the CIA tore his life apart and forced him to face a troubling question: Could any individual—or any nation, for that matter—remain truly uncorrupted by deception?

"Even now at times it doesn't seem real," Powers said years after his plane went down. "You know, it seems more like something I've read in a book."

BOOK ONE

# Icarus Rising

*At last the wings were done and Daedalus*
*Slipped them across his shoulders for a test*
*And flapped them cautiously to keep his balance,*
*And for a moment glided into air.*

—OVID, *THE METAMORPHOSES*, BOOK 8

CHAPTER 1

# *The Idealist*

If you are able to state a problem—any problem—and if it is important enough, then the problem can be solved.

—EDWIN LAND

Just before 3:30 p.m. on April 18, 1954, an American diplomat stepped out onto the rooftop of the new, ten-story U.S. embassy in Moscow. He walked to the white parapet that skirted the perimeter of the roof and looked to the east, across the wide boulevards and rooftops, toward the onion domes and spires of Red Square. In the gray sky above the Kremlin, the dark outlines of dozens of Soviet jets resolved into view, moving like a synchronized flock of birds.

The pilots were practicing for the upcoming May Day Parade, the showy pageant of socialist pride and power held every spring. The highlight of the parade was always the unveiling of the latest breakthrough in Soviet military technology, and the aerial rehearsal gave the diplomat a sneak preview of this year's biggest surprise. He concentrated on the shapes of the planes, counting them as they buzzed in and out of the dense cloud cover. Most of the planes—more than forty, according to his count—appeared to be "Beagles," the Ilyushin Il-28 small bombers that were the workhorses of the Soviet air fleet. But he also spotted an unfamiliar outline among them, a plane that seemed much bigger than the others. To his eye, it looked a little like a Boeing B-52 Stratofortress.

But that surely couldn't be right. The B-52 was an American invention, and although it had been flying test missions for two years, it wasn't scheduled to go into active service for several months yet. The Americans believed they had produced the world's only long-range jet bomber, the only one capable of carrying massive hydrogen bombs between the United States and Moscow. The B-52's debut was expected to give America a clear, exploitable edge over the Soviets in the rapidly escalating Cold War. According to the best American intelligence, the

Soviets wouldn't be able to produce their own long-range bomber for at least another four years.

Yet as the diplomat—who was never identified by name in the secret cables and government reports—stared into the drab Moscow sky, a dispiriting realization sank in: *the best American intelligence was wrong.* For the next week or so, spotters from the U.S. Air Force were assigned stakeout duty on that same embassy roof, just in case the Soviets decided their pilots needed yet another rehearsal before the big show. When one of the huge Soviet bombers buzzed within a mile of the embassy roof, an air force sergeant aimed his camera at the plane and started snapping the shutter as fast as he could. When the prints were developed in an embassy darkroom, all that emerged was a dark blur, frustratingly indistinct. But he and the other spotters had no doubts about what they had seen, and more important they knew exactly what it meant: America's advantage in nuclear strike capability was evaporating before their eyes.

THE EMBASSY CABLE THAT DELIVERED THAT NEWS to Washington hit the State Department the way that gasoline hits fire. It had already been a tense spring, with one major nuclear milestone and lots of smoldering anxieties. Just six weeks earlier, on the Pacific island of Bikini Atoll, the United States tested its new dry-fuel hydrogen bomb—the first hydrogen bomb that could be delivered by aircraft. The atomic bombs that had been dropped over Hiroshima and Nagasaki at the end of World War II were firecrackers in comparison to this colossus, which packed about a thousand times more explosive force, in terms of TNT equivalency, than each of those two bombs. Roughly one second after the test detonation on Bikini Atoll, the mushroom cloud that bloomed over the island measured four and a half miles in diameter. Less than ten minutes later, the cloud's diameter had ballooned to more than sixty miles. The radiation from the blast ultimately contaminated more than seven thousand square miles of the Pacific, an area almost as big as New Jersey. The devastation shocked even the military commanders and nuclear physicists who oversaw the test. The bomb was twice as powerful as they had predicted.

It marked the blinding dawn of a new era. This was the instant—in the chilly spring of 1954—when Americans realized that nuclear weapons were capable of ending not just world wars but entire civilizations. On April Fools' Day, *The New York Times* ran a bold headline at the top of the front page that was anything but a joke: "H-Bomb Can Wipe Out

Any City." Inside the paper, the *Times* reported that news of the test on Bikini Atoll had reduced all those who truly understood its implications to a state of mute awe. "It was symbolic," the article stated, "that this awe—this fear of the tremendous forces that man has unleashed—was most pronounced in cities, in capital cities, which here and abroad are doomed to a common destruction if unlimited atomic war should come." The article emphasized that if the Soviets ever developed the means to deliver such bombs to America, no one was safe. "For the plain truth is there is no 100 per cent defense against piloted enemy aircraft and submarines, much less against guided missiles."

For the Russians, the nuclear race was a game of catch-up from the very beginning. The United States had gotten a head start during World War II, but by 1954 the Americans worried that the Soviets were rapidly gaining ground. Although the Soviets had resolved in 1940 to develop an atomic bomb, they hadn't adopted a full-scale nuclear program until after they learned of the existence of the Manhattan Project, which produced the atomic bombs that were dropped on Hiroshima and Nagasaki in 1945. After the war, the Soviets implemented a fledgling nuclear program that was based almost solely on intelligence stolen from American and German physicists. In 1949, the Soviets tested their first atomic bomb, and by 1953 they'd improved the potency of those explosives tenfold. Now, a mere two weeks after the story in *The New York Times* marveled at the unforeseen power of America's latest H-bombs, the Soviets were spotted flying their own long-range bombers in the overcast skies of Moscow. If those planes were, in fact, equal to the bombers the United States had developed, and if the Soviets' nuclear program continued to develop at its current pace, then the very idea of national security was a sham. New York, Washington, Chicago, Los Angeles—any of them could be vaporized in a matter of minutes.

President Eisenhower was on edge. The specter of a surprise nuclear attack had become, almost overnight, a genuine threat. He confessed his anxiety to a small group of scientific advisers during a breakfast at the White House days after the planes were spotted. One of those in attendance was James Killian, the president of the Massachusetts Institute of Technology. Killian suggested that Eisenhower privately enlist a team of the country's top innovators to sketch out new technologies that might, somehow, eliminate the possibility of a surprise attack. The concept itself—a panel of scientists brainstorming on the government's behalf—wasn't exactly new. Before Eisenhower took office, Killian had been part of a scientific panel under President Truman called Project Lincoln—a group of science and technology experts, many of them pulled from university labs, that had produced a list of recommendations designed to strengthen America's air defense systems. Killian suggested that a similar group of scientists, more narrowly focused on preventing a surprise attack, might come up with solutions that even the most creative military minds could never dream up.

Eisenhower thought about it for a few days and then invited Killian to assemble a small team of innovators—the "surprise attack panel," as it was informally known—dedicated to bringing technological wizardry to national defense.

"I hope very much that you will find it possible to free yourself of your many other heavy responsibilities for a period long enough to undertake this important assignment," Eisenhower wrote to Killian, "and that others whom you choose to be members of your staff will also be able to devote time to the work."

Killian's Rolodex was full of the names of the country's best and brightest, and he quickly got down to work, grabbing the telephone. A good chunk of his recruitment could be done without placing a single long-distance call, because the Cambridge labs at MIT and Harvard were full of world-class innovators in nearly every relevant scientific field, from astronomy to nuclear physics. The man who would become Killian's most prized recruit, however, had just left town, leaving an empty office across the railroad tracks from the MIT campus.

EDWIN LAND WAS THE CO-FOUNDER OF CAMBRIDGE'S Polaroid Corporation, and at forty-five he was probably the most celebrated inventor in America. As a boy, Land had grown fascinated with optical physics and the natural crystal formations that could polarize light waves. While still a teenager, he created a synthetic polarizing sheet of film that could filter out glare—an invention that he believed might be applied to the windshields of cars to save drivers from being blinded by oncoming headlights. As it happened, his technology had much broader applications, revolutionizing the field of optics and eventually finding its way onto camera lenses, sunglasses, binoculars, mirrors, and almost anything else that light might bounce off or pass through.

Had Land stopped with that one breakthrough, his career would have been considered an unqualified success. But his mind never stopped churning out ideas, and he was now on his way to amassing more U.S. patents than anyone except Thomas Edison and Elihu Thomson, another early trailblazer of electric light and power. Land's most famous creation, instant photography, had stunned the world in 1947, and the commercial success of Polaroid's line of Land Cameras, which could develop photographic prints in about a minute, had made him a household name.

That name really should have been Solomonovich. His father, Harry, was born in 1880 near Kiev, then part of imperial Russia. But the year after his birth, a wave of anti-Jewish riots swept through the city and the surrounding villages. Dozens of Jews were murdered, hundreds were raped, and thousands were beaten. The Solomonovich family, fearing for their lives, boarded a ship in Odessa bound for the United States, with young Harry in tow. According to family lore, Avram Solomonovich, Edwin's grandfather, was told that the ship had "landed" at the Castle Garden immigration center in New York; much confusion ensued as he struggled to communicate with an impatient immigration clerk, who entered the patriarch's name in the registry as "Abraham Land."

Abraham, as he was now known, found work in an agricultural colony for Jewish refugees in Connecticut but eventually reinvented himself as a scrap metal dealer. Years later his son, Harry, followed him into the business. In May 1909, Harry and his wife, Matie, had the son that they named Edwin Herbert.

Edwin's youth was quintessentially American. He was a naturally shy boy, but his parents encouraged him to mix with others and fight the instinct to retreat into himself. He joined the Boy Scouts, and after his bar mitzvah in the spring of 1922, he spent most of his summers at Camp Mooween, on the shores of Red Cedar Lake outside Norwich. It was there, between the swimming contests and campfires, that Land's interest in physics took hold. The camp's founder, Barney "Cap" Girden, could often be found inside an old shed—"the Engineering Building"— where he was endlessly tinkering on contraptions that he'd test on his campers (he'd later earn a patent for a snorkel with a periscope attachment, among other things). Girden recognized and kindled Land's creative drive, encouraging him to read everything he could find about optics and giving him free run of the Engineering Building—a privilege other campers didn't have. It was the beginning of a recurring pattern: Land's high school teachers at Norwich Free Academy excused him from required courses so he could conduct experiments; a couple years later, the Harvard physics department granted Land, just an undergraduate, his own laboratory. Eventually, Land grew to associate problem solving with freedom and with America itself. "De Tocqueville enjoyed pointing out a particular characteristic of American democracy," Land later said. "It solves the problems that occur, as they come along, in a new way."

When Hitler's specter loomed during World War II, Land turned himself into a scientific gun for hire, a freelance dreamer who could be called upon whenever America needed a good idea. When General George S. Patton complained that recoil shocks from Sherman tank guns were jamming the sights back into the eyes of his gunners, injuring them severely, Land and his team at Polaroid came up with a larger, fixed-focus lens that solved the problem. When the Coast Guard dogs that guarded the Allies' beaches were plagued with eye problems caused by blowing sand, Land produced customized Polaroid goggles for canines. When American soldiers in the South Pacific began succumbing to malaria—a disease prevented by quinine, which was in critically short supply outside Japan—Land sponsored a team of chemists to search for an alternative. When he revealed the results of their work in 1944, the headline on the front page of *The New York Times* announced, "Synthetic Quinine Produced, Ending Century Search." Even after the atomic bombs in Japan sped the war's end, Land continued to donate ideas to the U.S. military. His team at Polaroid adapted the concepts behind instant photography to create for the U.S. Army a new type of radiation "dosimeter"—a small metal cartridge, to be worn around the necks of soldiers, like a dog tag. The device contained strips of film that would turn a lighter color if exposed to dangerous levels of radiation. "The man is a whirlwind," wrote W. Lewis Hyde, a physicist at Polaroid, in a letter to his parents shortly after he joined the company. "He has about three ideas a minute, and about two of them manage to get tried and tested."

Now, in 1954, Land was back to focusing on his company, and Polaroid seemed perfectly positioned to take advantage of America's renewed obsession with entertainment and leisure. Land decided to leave Cambridge, temporarily moving to the sunny frontier of America's postwar boom, California.

By the time Killian began to assemble his surprise attack panel, it was too late. If he wanted to persuade Land to again put his career on hold for the government, he'd first have to lure him out of Hollywood.

IN EARLY 1954, ALFRED HITCHCOCK had a problem. For more than a year he'd been listening to Hollywood studio executives peddle gloom and doom. Television and home projection screens were destroying the cinema, they kept saying, and if a veteran director really wanted to grab hold of a young audience, he needed to embrace new technologies.

"Home screens are getting bigger all the time," complained Don Hartman, production chief at Paramount Studios. "I run two to three movies at my house every night. My own kids, now, do you think they'd go to a theater to see a movie when they can see anything they want at home? Of course not."

Hitchcock couldn't deny that these were challenging times. The unemployment lines were full of screenwriters, set designers, and production assistants. Warner Bros. Studios, where Hitchcock was under contract, froze production for most of the previous spring and summer because of waning revenues. During that hiatus, the studio's executives urged him to give viewers something they couldn't get on their home screens: a third dimension.

Hitchcock didn't like the idea. He feared 3-D movies were a passing fad, and he'd heard that the oversized cameras were hellishly difficult to move around on set. Even so, he caved. He signed on to direct *Dial M for Murder,* a taut thriller that appealed to Hitchcock because most of the action could be limited to a single room, as in a stage play. A one-room set, he hoped, might minimize the technical headaches.

The 3-D camera turned out to be everything he feared. Hitchcock waddled around studio 20 on the Warner lot in Burbank, jowly and flummoxed. The tool he'd always relied on had become his enemy.

"It's a big, gross, hulking monster," Hitchcock said of the camera. "It's heavy and immobile and frightening."

The script's pivotal scene called for Grace Kelly's character to stab a man in the back with a pair of scissors; then the actor was to fall backward, and Hitchcock wanted to position the camera near the floor, at a low angle, to enhance the 3-D effect of the scissors fatally plunging deep into his back when he hit the ground. But the camera was too bulky, and Hitchcock couldn't position it low enough for the necessary angle. So he had a hole cut into the floor of the stage and lowered the camera into it. It was a devil's bargain, because from then on studio 20 was a danger zone. A luckless carpenter was the first to fall into the pit.

"Tremendous new problems with this medium," Hitchcock grumbled.

Even more challenges waited after shooting wrapped. The illusion of depth in 3-D film required two reels of stereoscopic film to be projected simultaneously, and synchronizing the images was fiendishly tricky. During those months of work on *Dial M,* more new 3-D releases were hitting the theaters, and the audiences kept saying that the films looked blurry. Some viewers complained of headaches. All of the new releases were box office duds. Hitchcock worried that the technology that was supposed to save Hollywood would be his undoing.

Desperate, Warner Bros. called in Land, whose company was heavily invested in the 3-D craze. The viewing glasses that Polaroid developed had become a necessary accessory at every 3-D screening; in 1953 the company had a backlog of seventy million pairs on order, causing it to step up production to six million pairs a week. Land was also working to refine a new 3-D projection system, which he hoped would eliminate the need for twinned projection reels and solve the synchronization problems.

When he arrived in California, Land toured most of the major studios, doing his best to calm the concerns of their executives. "As is the case of any product that has some bugs in it, the thing to do is to get rid of them," Land said. "And I think that will be done."

His optimism was put to a quick test. He attended a special media screening of *Those Redheads from Seattle,* a release that Paramount was hyping as Hollywood's first 3-D musical. The script was an extended cliché, the songs were third-rate, and the reviews were brutal ("a witless and hackneyed trifle," concluded the critic from *The New York Times*). With each subpar release, the 3-D craze dimmed a little more, and Polaroid was in danger of getting smeared by association. Between the second half of 1953 and the first half of 1954, the company's stock fell from $1.56 to $0.54 cents a share. Land believed the public's waning interest in 3-D was behind the slide.

Within the industry, Hitchcock's film was being billed as 3-D's last chance. As the head of a corporation with millions riding on the technology's success, Land should have been fired up by his move west. But his heart wasn't in it.

The devotion to the bottom line, glaringly evident in Hollywood, rubbed him the wrong way. Land was a multimillionaire who cared about his company's financial health, but he was far from greedy; in fact, his occasional ambivalence toward earnings reports had been baffling corporate observers for years. A study by the Harvard Business School published in 1944 portrayed him as that rare corporate specimen who seemed bent on contradicting the "rigid assumption that businessmen act in a coldly rational manner with the sole aim of earning the largest possible profit." Land's driving motivation wasn't money, they wrote, but rather a desire to test himself and contribute to the forward march of human progress, however lofty that might sound.

Hollywood's problems, in the end, simply didn't matter enough to him. Hitchcock's movie turned out to be a commercial and critical success, but it couldn't stop 3-D's slide, and Land's interest in resuscitating the medium waned. He knew his company might suffer from the demise of 3-D, but a brief period of financial stagnation wouldn't be the end of the world.

"My motto," Land said, "is to select things that are manifestly important and nearly impossible."

When Killian reached out to him, Land packed his bags and moved back to the East Coast. His Hollywood days were over.

THE FORTY-TWO MEMBERS of the Technological Capabilities Panel were split into three different study groups. The first concentrated on figuring out how technology might help the United States launch rapid retaliatory strikes on the Soviets in case of nuclear war. The second studied defensive innovations, such as a network of sensors that might detect and destroy incoming Soviet bombers or missiles. The third group's challenge was perhaps the trickiest: come up with technologies that might detect an enemy attack *before* it was even launched.

Killian managed to snag a few rooms for the panel members in the Executive Office Building, a conspicuous heap of granite that occupied a full city block next to the White House. The building was a grab bag of architectural flourishes—pavilions, porticoes, columns, domes, skylights, filigree—united only by a determination to impress. Inside, it was hot in the summer and freezing in the winter, and a movement was afoot among D.C.'s bureaucratic caste to tear the whole thing down and build something more efficient. But the scientists on Killian's panel loved it. Their suite on the second floor, with its high ceilings and ornate fireplace, imbued their conversations with grandeur and gravitas.

Striding through those halls, Land cut a professorial figure. He wore loose-fitting gabardine trousers and herringbone sport coats, the kind with suede patches on the elbows. He wore his dark hair slicked back and parted on the side, and often a rogue lock would curl across his forehead, like Superman in the comic books. He usually showed up a little late, finding the others already seated around a large table in room 274. He'd silently slip into a chair on the outer periphery, his dark eyes heavy-lidded, looking as if he'd just stumbled off an overnight flight.

He'd listen for a while, then suddenly, as if awoken by a turn in the conversation, he'd perk up. Soon he'd be out of his chair, pacing the room, and he'd finally raise his voice, which was measured and steady, but with a trace of New England squawk in it. He was an essayistic speaker, constructing one carefully measured sentence after another to reach a conclusion that seemed as solid as natural law. "Land could overcome his shyness in social and meeting situations and become a very outgoing person," recalled George Ehrenfried, a physicist who'd worked with Land at Polaroid since 1946. "This was hard work for him."

Killian, for one, didn't notice the strain. "Land is an authentic genius," he wrote. "His powers of exposition, his facility in expressing complex ideas in novel, witty, and clarifying ways, can lift a meeting or a report to a higher level of discourse."

Land became the leader of Group Three, the one focused on foretelling a nuclear strike. He told Killian he wanted his group to be the smallest, with no more members than could fit in a single taxicab. That way, Land figured, the discussions could be lively and agile, unencumbered by too many voices. In the end, Land got five scientists who had very little in common, aside from impeccable résumés.

Edward Purcell had shared the Nobel Prize in Physics in 1952 for his discovery of nuclear magnetic resonance. John Tukey was a mathematician at Princeton and a pioneer in the fledgling field of computer science. James Baker was an astronomy professor at Harvard and an expert in telescopic lens design. Joseph W. Kennedy had co-discovered plutonium and had been a team leader on the Manhattan Project when he was just twenty-six years old. Finally, Allen Latham Jr., a former schoolmate of Land's who worked closely with him at Polaroid, was a scientific polymath who, most recently, had developed the centrifugal device used in hospitals to separate blood cells from plasma and platelets, revolutionizing the process of blood transfusions.

Land believed that the team should approach the work in the spirit of intellectual freedom, which also meant he had the freedom to extend their meetings late into the night, or to call them at five o'clock in the morning if that was when an idea seized him. He considered intellectual inquiry an endurance sport, and he believed inspiration was like a runner's high: only after he'd wrung his brain dry through long hours of unbroken concentration would the truly valuable insights begin to surface. The edge of collapse, when the temptation to rest was at its most seductive, was precisely the moment when a thinker's "atavistic competences," as he called them, emerged from some hidden reservoir, pointing the way toward a solution. When a problem truly challenged him, he could stay up for days in a row concentrating on it, fearing that whole braids of thought would unravel, never to be threaded together again, if he relaxed. "You are handling so many variables at a barely conscious level that you can't afford to be interrupted," Land explained. "If you are, it may take a year to cover the same ground you could cover otherwise in sixty hours."

Land declared that Group Three's first order of business would be to take a precise, objective, purely scientific measure of the hard intelligence that America's current network of spies had gathered about the Soviet Union. As it turned out, this particular task didn't require the team to work long into the night. There was almost nothing to measure.

HISTORICALLY, SPYING WASN'T AN AMERICAN STRENGTH, and this was often considered a point of pride, not a shortcoming. A lot of Americans considered espionage an unseemly pursuit that had no place in a democracy that championed the freedom of information and ideas. The other major, industrialized nations of the world—England, France, Russia, China, Poland, Germany, Korea, and Austria among them—had established professional intelligence services years before the United States, which remained a stubborn holdout for most of its first two centuries of existence. In 1908, when President Teddy Roosevelt's attorney general, Charles Bonaparte, asked for funds to establish a small, covert investigative unit within the Justice Department, indignation poured forth from the halls of Congress. "If Anglo-Saxon civilization stands for anything, it is for a government where the humblest citizen is safeguarded against the secret activities of the executive of the government," announced J. Swagar Sherley, a congressman from Kentucky. A couple decades later, in 1929, Secretary of State Henry Stimson affected shock when he learned that others within the U.S. government had intercepted and read Japanese diplomatic correspondence. "Gentlemen do not read each other's mail," Stimson said.

America continued to claim that moral high ground until the exceptionally high stakes of World War II prompted President Franklin Roosevelt to create the Office of Strategic Services, the country's first official intelligence service. Just days after the war ended, President Harry Truman, who'd never been entirely comfortable with the agency, disbanded the OSS and rejected a proposal to establish a peacetime spy service.

Truman changed his mind, however, when the Soviets emerged as America's central postwar threat. In 1947 he created the Central Intelligence Agency, which by 1950 employed about five thousand people. The agency's early failures—such as being taken by surprise when North Korea invaded South Korea in 1950—were far more notable than its successes. The CIA grew quickly, expanding to about fifteen thousand employees by 1955—a staffing benchmark that it would maintain, roughly, for the next twenty-five years.

Despite the agency's growth during the early 1950s, the inner workings of the Soviet Union remained almost as mysterious as they'd been when the CIA was created, and intelligence gathering within its borders was only getting more difficult with time. After Joseph Stalin died in 1953, secrecy became something of a national obsession for the U.S.S.R. The new leader, Nikita Khrushchev, had tightened restrictions at its borders and had placed severe limits on the sorts of contacts its citizens could have with foreigners. About two months before Land's panel met for the first time, a new agency called the Komitet Gosudarstvennoy Bezopasnosti—or KGB—was formed, and its influence was already apparent. In Moscow, Soviet agents seemed to lurk in every shadow. Running American spies and "turning" Soviets to spy on behalf of the United States behind the Iron Curtain had become riskier than ever.

Land's panel examined the technologies currently in use to crack open the U.S.S.R.'s secrets—tiny Minox cameras, electronic eavesdropping bugs, pincers designed to remove letters from envelopes without breaking their seals. As impressive as they were, most of them relied on deep human infiltration. But aside from a few cases, that infiltration wasn't happening. And even when operatives managed to sneak into the corridors of power in Moscow to use those technologies, they almost never emerged with particularly valuable information—just a couple of random jigsaw pieces from a panoramic puzzle. It quickly became clear to Land that the American intelligence system rested on the archetype of the dashing and adventurous spy, and that archetype to him seemed little more than a romantic myth. The American spy was a dud, he believed, and the country's overall efforts to recruit foreigners to spy on its behalf had captured very little information of value.

"It is shocking to learn the extent to which our operations of this kind have to depend upon agents of wholly inadequate training, education, and experience," Land's intelligence group wrote. If the country continued to depend on men and, in some cases, women to steal secrets within an adversary's borders, then it was high time to train them properly, they determined. But therein lay problems. Truly effective intelligence training required years of complex groundwork. "A man who has appeared for years to be a leftist leader in Mexico or Iran can learn more about Russia, and do it more safely," Land's report stated, "than one who slips across the border at night and sends out a message or two before being caught by the Soviet security police." But America didn't have time for that kind of groundwork; the country had let things slide for too long, Land concluded, and the threat was immediate.

How many nuclear weapons did the Soviets have? How many months away were they from producing their own dry-fuel hydrogen bombs? How many Soviet military facilities were currently in operation? How many long-range bombers did Khrushchev already have at his disposal, and how many more were in production? Could the Soviets launch a full-scale, surprise attack that instantly destroyed America's ability to strike back?

No one knew the answers to those questions, and Land's panel concluded that human intelligence wasn't likely to uncover them. They resolved to effectively sketch a blueprint for a new kind of intelligence system that was built on science and technology.

Unfortunately, just as they got down to business, Land's panel clashed head-on with a group of crusaders who viewed America's scientific community not as a valuable resource to be tapped for the common good but as a threat to national security.

YEARS EARLIER, WHEN LAND AND MIT'S KILLIAN had collaborated on Project Lincoln, both of them got to know J. Robert Oppenheimer, who'd also served on the Cambridge-based panel. Oppenheimer had led the Manhattan Project, and if anyone could be considered the father of nuclear warfare, it was him. But since the war, Oppenheimer had been plagued by doubts and misgivings over the technology he'd helped create, and he became an outspoken advocate for disarmament. By the time he joined Project Lincoln, he was arguing that America would be better off suspending its nuclear weapons program altogether. He believed an open exchange of scientific information and technology with the Soviets might be a good thing; secrecy, it seemed, only fueled paranoia and spurred a perilous arms race.

During the Project Lincoln meetings, Oppenheimer stressed that America should overhaul its military budget, spending less on bombers, more on defensive technologies. The panel's summary report included his recommendation that the budget for the U.S. Air Force's Strategic Air Command—the group tasked with carrying out any potential nuclear strike—be slashed in favor of new systems, like an early-warning network of radar sensors.

Killian, Land, and other members of Project Lincoln agreed with Oppenheimer's assessments, and they knew his enemies in the military weren't likely to take the threat to their programs sitting down. "Some people in the Air Force are going to be after Oppenheimer," Killian whispered to another physicist during a panel meeting, "and we've got to know about it and be ready for it."

There was little they could do. Before Project Lincoln's report was submitted to the government, two journalists—the brothers Joseph and Stewart Alsop—got their hands on a copy. The Alsops' newspaper column, published under a joint byline, appeared three times a week in about two hundred newspapers across the country. In March 1953, they wrote that the scientists on Project Lincoln were preparing to challenge the conventional air force wisdom that "offense is the best defense."

The column didn't mention Oppenheimer, but Thomas Finletter, who was just stepping down as secretary of the air force, was convinced that the physicist had leaked the report to the Alsops to drum up public support for his views. Finletter took his suspicions to the Joint Committee on Atomic Energy, the agency that broadly oversaw all matters related to nuclear science. Oppenheimer's loyalty to America was an open question, Finletter told the group; his background deserved greater scrutiny.

The Joint Committee's former director quickly fired off a letter to FBI director J. Edgar Hoover that included an incendiary accusation: "More probably than not J. Robert Oppenheimer is an agent of the Soviet

Union." Joseph McCarthy, the senator from Wisconsin, eventually got wind of the allegations, and in December 1953 he announced that his investigative committee was targeting the scientists who had served on Project Lincoln.

McCarthy had been in the Senate since 1947, but he had forcefully grabbed the national spotlight for the first time in 1950, when he delivered a speech to a women's Republican club in West Virginia in which he claimed that homegrown traitors were causing America to lose the Cold War. Without offering proof, he told the group that the Department of State in Washington was crawling with Communist agents. "While I cannot take the time to name all the men in the State Department who have been named as members of the Communist Party and members of a spy ring, I have here in my hand a list of 205." McCarthy seemed to relish the attention the speech earned him, and since then his paranoid brand of scaremongering had turned him into one of America's most publicized politicians.

His attack against the scientists on Project Lincoln was a classic example of McCarthyism. Dozens of the scientists, McCarthy suggested, might be covert agents plotting against America. He didn't single out Oppenheimer publicly, and he offered no evidence supporting his claim. Instead, he let his vague accusations hang over the entire group. "There's enough to draw a pretty good conclusion the Commies have managed some degree of infiltration," McCarthy assured reporters.

Exactly one week after the senator went public with his suspicions, Oppenheimer's security clearance was revoked. He refused to resign from government work, declaring that he would fight to clear his name.

By the time the scientists with the Technological Capabilities Panel began meeting in the Executive Office Building, McCarthy had commenced his series of exhaustive investigative hearings that aimed to expose Communist infiltration in the U.S. Army. The hearings, which had begun in April, didn't merely attract the public's attention; they dominated it. Each day's testimony was shown live, in its entirety, by two of the country's four main television networks; the other two networks condensed the daily testimony to forty-five-minute highlight reels, which were broadcast each evening.

As a group, Land and the other scientists on the Technological Capabilities Panel despised McCarthy, and they barely followed his three-ring circus, which took place just down Pennsylvania Avenue at the

Capitol. They were far more interested in a closed-door hearing that was under way at the exact same time, inside a temporary building near the Washington Monument.

Oppenheimer was forced to sit in front of a three-man panel while his entire life was picked apart. Like a lot of intellectuals in the United States, Oppenheimer had dabbled in Communist Party politics in the 1930s, though he'd severed all connections to the party before going to work for the government. Several witnesses played on those connections to suggest that Oppenheimer might have passed nuclear secrets to the Soviets or that he'd even served as a spy. Decades later, KGB files released after the Soviet Union's fall would indicate that Oppenheimer had, in fact, rejected repeated attempts to get him to spy on the U.S.S.R.'s behalf, and he had even removed several scientists from the Manhattan Project for having Soviet sympathies. But as the hearing dragged on, the suspicions took on a weight of their own.

Edward Teller, a physicist who after the war led America's effort to develop hydrogen bombs, cast doubt on Oppenheimer's loyalty. Teller, as a nuclear advocate, had often found himself bitterly at odds with Oppenheimer and told the panel that he'd been puzzled by his colleague's recommendations to put the brakes on America's hydrogen bomb production. "If it is a question of wisdom and judgment, as demonstrated by actions since 1945, then I would say one would be wiser not to grant clearance," Teller testified.

Many scientists who knew Oppenheimer were outraged at Teller's comments, which to them smacked of professional jealousy. On behalf of the scientists who'd served with him on Project Lincoln, Killian testified in Oppenheimer's defense. "He impressed me in these meetings as a man deeply devoted to strengthening the security of the nation, and fertile of ideas for promoting the national welfare," Killian said. "Every aspect of his work on this committee sustained my confidence in his loyalty and integrity."

Other scientists echoed Killian's testimony, but it was too little, too late. By a 2-to-1 vote, the panel stripped Oppenheimer of his security clearance, and he was publicly disgraced. The message the decision sent to the scientific community was unambiguous: if you try to challenge the authority of the U.S. military, you do so at your peril.

JOSEPH AND STEWART ALSOP BLASTED the Oppenheimer decision in their columns that summer, and they worried that America's scientists might be scared into submission just when they were most needed. "Not just their talents are required," the brothers wrote. "Their enthusiastic and self-confident collaboration with the government and one another, their dedicated and inspired work against time, are now essentials of American survival."

Killian described an atmosphere of "widespread discouragement" among the members of the Technological Capabilities Panel, and nowhere was the tension more pronounced than inside Land's Group Three. In the weeks after Oppenheimer was shamed, Land and the other five members of his team were forced to interview some of the military's most hawkish leaders, including some who they knew had worked to undermine Oppenheimer. The meetings did nothing to restore Land's confidence in their judgment or abilities. "We would go in and interview generals and admirals in charge of intelligence and come away worried," Land later recalled. "Here we were, five or six young men, asking questions that these high-ranking officers couldn't answer."

An idea had been bouncing around in Land's mind for several years: What if a specialized aircraft, equipped with state-of-the-art, high-resolution photographic equipment and other spy tools, could fly high enough above enemy territory to evade radar detection? He'd discussed this years before with numerous people, both in and out of the military, and he seized on it once again as a way to marry espionage with high-tech innovation.

His team members began to seriously explore the concept, but they weren't the only ones. Air force officials had decided to pursue their own version of a high-altitude reconnaissance plane, and they'd already asked a handful of aircraft manufacturers for designs. Land was convinced a team of scientists could dream up a far more effective spy machine than could a group of military commanders, but the general in charge of the Strategic Air Command, a man who had stood at the front line of the military's campaign against Oppenheimer, wasn't about to let a bunch of lab rats tell him what to do.

GENERAL CURTIS E. LEMAY'S REPUTATION as an unrepentant hard-ass was reflected in his nickname, Old Iron Pants. His cigar—blunt, wet, gnawed to a nub—was an ever-present accessory, so much so that his men speculated he showered with it clamped between his teeth. In World War II he'd been in charge of the bombing campaign in Japan, and if he'd gotten his way, the United States would have dropped a third atomic bomb on the country after wiping out Hiroshima and Nagasaki. His love affair with the nuclear option only intensified after the war, and in 1950, as head of Strategic Air Command, he lobbied for a nuclear strike against North Korea at the outset of the war. Now, in 1954, he seemed to sense that the growing fears over a nuclear showdown with the Soviets might finally give his beloved B-52s an opportunity to prove their power.

LeMay sketched out an air force strike plan against the Soviets that called for 750 atomic bombs to be dropped on the country over the course of a single evening. He calculated that the strike would kill sixty million people and injure seventeen million more. To him, the idea that a civilization might be bombed back to the Stone Age seemed less a dystopian nightmare than a career ambition. "Dawn might break over a nation infinitely poorer than China, less populated than the United States, and condemned to an agrarian existence perhaps for a genera-tion to come," LeMay predicted. He had no patience for handwringers who tried to smuggle concepts like morality into discussions of military strategy. "All war is immoral, and if you let that bother you," LeMay asserted, "you're not a good soldier."

LeMay was an exceptionally good soldier—the youngest since Ulysses S. Grant to wear four stars on his shoulders. As a commander of the Third Air Division during World War II, he personally flew in the lead position on numerous bombing runs to discourage his pilots from aborting missions they might otherwise deem too dangerous. "He was the finest combat commander of any service I came across in war," said Robert McNamara, who served with LeMay in World War II and who years later was appointed secretary of defense by President John F. Kennedy. "But he was extraordinarily belligerent, many thought brutal." LeMay in 1948 took over the Strategic Air Command and had nearly 47,000 personnel under his wing. By the spring of 1954, the nuclear race had pushed that number to nearly 200,000 men, and he didn't want to lose a single one of them. LeMay was particularly wary of a new breed of "defense intellectuals" who he claimed wanted to steal authority from battle-hardened soldiers. Their analytical "gobbledygook," as he termed it, projected weakness, not force, to America's rivals. To LeMay, Oppen-heimer had perfectly represented their eggheaded ethos. Even though he hadn't directly testified against the physicist during the hearings, the general had played an indirect, behind-the-scenes role in his fall: LeMay had personally alerted Edward Teller, whose testimony was considered particularly damaging, that the closed-door security hearings were moving forward. Oppenheimer's fall, in LeMay's eyes, was a victory against people who think too much.

LeMay carried that same aggressive swagger into the spy plane project. If a high-altitude plane was ever going to fly over the Soviet Union, he had a couple of prerequisites for it: the plane had to be armed with guns and missiles, and it had to be fast and powerful enough to engage in combat.

When the air force solicited ideas from aircraft manufacturers for such a craft, two submitted designs were singled out for further study. Both carried twin engines, which would give them enough power to sustain the weight of full battle armaments. Another one, submitted by Lockheed Corporation, was rejected outright. That craft was exceptionally light and looked like a glider, or maybe even a dragonfly, with its unusually long wings and narrow fuselage. Many of the features that weighed down traditional aircraft—such as landing gear—had been eliminated from the Lockheed model, which was designed to skid to a stop on a reinforced underbelly. Its lightness allowed it to soar above seventy thousand feet, which was believed to be the outer limit of Soviet radar detection range.

The Lockheed designer who had sketched the designs and devised its specifications presented his ideas to a group of air force commanders, LeMay among them. In the middle of the presentation, LeMay stood up from his chair, took his cigar out of his mouth, and barked out his verdict.

"This is a bunch of shit," he said.

He allowed no rebuttals. LeMay marched out of the meeting, grumbling that looking at designs for an air force plane that couldn't fire a single gun was a complete waste of his time.

THAT SUMMER, LAND PAID A VISIT to the Central Intelligence Agency's Office of Scientific Intelligence. It was a new bureau within the CIA, and Land discovered that its mission to scientifically assess the Soviet nuclear threat was mostly aspirational; it simply hadn't acquired much hard evidence yet. But the assistant director, Philip Strong, had made it his business to stay abreast of the air force's discussions of a high-altitude plane. Strong slipped Land copies of the aircraft designs that had been submitted to the air force for review.

Land instantly fell in love with the Lockheed proposal. The specific features that LeMay hated about the design—its lightweight frame, its minimalism—were the very ones that convinced Land of its merit. That it was so odd, so defiantly unconventional, didn't bother him at all. The design had earned Land's confidence, and once his confidence was engaged, he was an unshakable force. At Polaroid, he was famously dismissive of all attempts to be led by anything other than innovation. "We don't do market surveys," he once told a colleague who suggested following the advice of a marketing department. "We create the markets with our products." Among his employees, a story went around that traced his intransigence back to a day when he was a child, in the backseat of his father's car when he was forced to visit an aunt he didn't like and declared, "I will never let anyone tell me what to do, ever again."

Just as Land began seriously pursuing the idea for the spy plane, his personal declaration of independence was put to the test. Weeks after Eisenhower had asked the scientists to draft their recommendations for the CIA, he'd assigned the very same task to Jimmy Doolittle, one of America's most celebrated military heroes. Doolittle's classified report, which began circulating around Washington that summer, was a direct challenge to the core philosophical principles upon which Land had built his worldview.

DOOLITTLE WAS ONE OF AVIATION'S TRUE PIONEERS, a pilot whose cross-country flights made international headlines when Charles Lindbergh was just learning how to fly. He was also an innovative engineer who invented "instrument flying," allowing pilots to take off, navigate, and land an aircraft through darkness, dense fog, or any other visual impediment. In World War II he led the first American raid on Japan after Pearl Harbor, making him one of the most publicized heroes of the war. By 1945, he was commanding the air force bombings over Germany while LeMay handled Japan.

When Eisenhower solicited Doolittle's advice in June 1954 for revamping the CIA, the former pilot spent the rest of the summer working on a document that concluded that morality might be an outdated concept in the modern world of spy versus spy. Doolittle wrote,

> It is now clear that we are facing an implacable enemy whose avowed objective is world domination by whatever means and at whatever cost. There are no rules in such a game. Hitherto acceptable norms of human conduct do not apply. If the United

States is to survive, long-standing American concepts of "fair play" must be reconsidered. We must develop effective espionage and counterespionage services and must learn to subvert, sabotage and destroy our enemies by more clever, more sophisticated and more effective methods than those used against us. It may become necessary that the American people be made acquainted with, understand and support this fundamentally repugnant philosophy.

The report seemed to advocate a sort of relativism that repulsed Land, who later said he believed "that there are historic principles of behavior and morality" that should guide all actions, verities as fixed and permanent as the points on a compass. It was true that the Soviet threat was grave—he wasn't going to argue with that—but if victory required a nation to embrace a fundamentally repugnant way of thinking, what sort of victory was it? In Land's mind, the idea for a spy plane became much more than merely a potentially effective tool for intelligence gathering. By pursuing an espionage strategy that avoided dirty tricks and embraced the unique strengths that Land believed defined America— an improvisational ingenuity—the CIA could, perhaps, stay true to the country's ideals and help preserve its moral dignity.

If that wasn't enough motivation for Land to pursue the unconventional, high-flying design, Doolittle had also provided him with a personal challenge. In early 1952, while Land was working on Project Lincoln, he met with Doolittle and several air force commanders to discuss the idea of a high-altitude reconnaissance aircraft—an idea that at the time was a mere seedling in Land's head. At the air force headquarters in the Pentagon on a cold and cloudy morning, Doolittle attempted to douse Land's enthusiasm by saying that the technological leaps that such a project would require were too demanding; Doolittle believed that it would require at least ten years of developmental experimentation—too long of a lead time to be of practical use against an imminent Soviet threat.

But if anyone in America knew how to speed up a development process, it was Edwin Land. In mid-1954, just as Doolittle's dispiriting report was sparking discussion in Washington, the Polaroid executive resolved to prove Doolittle wrong.

Aware that the air force had rejected the Lockheed design, Land nevertheless called James Baker, the Harvard astronomer in Group Three. Earlier he and Baker had discussed the idea of a spy plane, and both were far more optimistic than Doolittle. They'd sketched their own rough idea of what such a machine might do, and the Lockheed design seemed promisingly consistent with their vision, even if LeMay had other plans.

"Jim," Land said into the phone, "I think I have the plane you are after."

# CHAPTER 2

# The Man Who Could See Air

I understood that I was essentially being drafted for the job—
becoming a "spook"—the intelligence community's label for their
agents.

—CLARENCE "KELLY" JOHNSON

The air force rejection letter came as no surprise to Kelly Johnson, Lockheed's chief design engineer. It explained that the reason his design had been nixed had something to do with the proposed aircraft's "safety factor," which struck him as bureaucratic nonsense. Johnson filed the letter away, and in his diary he noted the *real* reason, in his view, that the commanders had hated his plane: "too unusual." The timid souls at the air force were scared to take a chance.

It wasn't that Johnson didn't like air force officers; he worked with them all the time, and he counted many as close friends. But LeMay rubbed him the wrong way. The general was loud, brash, and supremely confident when he believed someone less qualified was trying to assess his performance. But the exact same thing could be said of Johnson. And when it came to aircraft design, Johnson was confident that LeMay was the one who should keep his mouth shut.

The two men had a history. Once, shortly after World War II, LeMay had asked Lockheed to design a nuclear bomber—not a plane that dropped nukes, but rather an aircraft that was actually fueled by nuclear power, with a reactor onboard. The general seemed so entranced by the brute force of nuclear fission that he believed it should be exploited at every possible turn, even if he hadn't fully considered the consequences. Johnson considered the nuclear plane idea impractical, but he scribbled out some calculations anyway. The cockpit alone in such a plane would have to weigh about forty thousand pounds, because a solid lead wall would need to shield the pilot and crew from the radiation generated by the reactor. Nearly every other component would have to be expanded and reinforced to absorb the shocks that all that bulk would generate upon landing. The notion of such a clumsy, graceless flying machine blasphemed pretty much every aerodynamic value Johnson held dear, and he told the air force so, slaying LeMay's monster before it got off the ground. For years afterward Johnson would beam with professional pride when he told the story.

And now General LeMay was the one trying to tell him that *his* idea was weird and unsafe?

If the rejection carried a whiff of payback, it was a shame, because the design was a masterstroke of invention and artistry. Back in February, Johnson had heard from executives at Lockheed that the air force had secretly contacted designers at three aircraft companies—Bell, Fairchild, and Martin—soliciting ideas for a high-altitude reconnaissance airplane. The country's biggest manufacturers, including Lockheed and Boeing, had been purposefully kept out of the loop; the air force commanders believed the smaller companies might consider the project a higher priority, and therefore work faster. Regardless, the Lockheed executives had asked Johnson to play around with some ideas. Spurred by the challenge of designing the highest-flying plane in the world, he ran with the idea, laboring over the design on his own time, turning it into a passion project.

You'd think the air force would have been thrilled to get those unsolicited sketches. Johnson was one of the most innovative and successful aircraft designers in the world, and a generation of air force pilots had grown to revere him. The year before, in 1953, he had designed the prototypes for the F-104 Starfighter, a supersonic jet that would give American pilots an edge over Soviet MiGs in direct aerial combat. Johnson believed the ultra-sleek frame he'd created for the F-104 could be a conceptual building block for a glider-like craft that could sustain altitudes exceeding seventy-three thousand feet.

The new plane wouldn't fly through the air so much as float upon it. Lightness was its virtue. The weight of every nut and bolt was minimized, and anything inessential was eliminated outright. Johnson got rid of conventional landing gear; instead, the plane would rest atop a wheeled dolly for takeoff and skid to landings on its reinforced belly. Instead of two engines, it would sail on the power of just one turbojet. The co-pilot's seat was jettisoned, and there was just enough room for the single seat inside a compact, unpressurized cabin. The wingspan was enormous, about twice as long as the craft's nose-to-tail length.

The whole works would tip the scales at just 13,768 pounds, and that included nearly 5,000 pounds of fuel stored in its wings.

It was like a butterfly—light, frail, beautiful—and LeMay had crushed it. Or rather, as Johnson was about to discover, LeMay had *tried* to crush it.

THE MORE EDWIN LAND EXAMINED the rejected sketches from Lockheed, the more he wanted to call Kelly Johnson right away, fly back to California, and quiz him about the specs. But Land knew he had to tread carefully. LeMay and the rest of the air force brass would throw a fit if they found out he'd ignored their official decision, and the Oppenheimer affair had taught him that they were capable of playing dirty. They might appeal directly to Eisenhower, a military man to his bones, and accuse the scientist of sneaking around behind their backs. It was a delicate operation: he wanted to defy some of America's most decorated officers, but he needed to appear to be working through all of the Pentagon's proper channels.

So Land arranged a meeting with LeMay's boss, Secretary of the Air Force Harold Talbott. He'd just taken over the air force from Thomas Finletter the year before, but Talbott's connections to aviation ran deep (as a child in Dayton, Ohio, he was a customer at Wilbur and Orville Wright's bicycle shop). Land visited Talbott's office with James Fisk, a former research director for the Atomic Energy Commission whom Killian had hired to become the Technical Capabilities Panel's deputy director. If any of the tensions that separated the air force from the scientific community followed Land into the room, Fisk's presence would have done little to ease them; that spring he sat down in front of the Oppenheimer panel to counter the military's assessment of the physicist, saying that he knew of "no more devoted citizen in this country."

The two men joined Talbott in his office, and Land explained to him how much Kelly Johnson's design had impressed him. It was truly innovative, he said, the perfect platform onto which the scientists could graft an array of new, high-tech spy equipment. The aircraft proposal deserved a more thorough review, Land insisted, and he suggested that his panel of scientists—not the air force commanders—should be the ones to do it. He asked Talbott for permission to contact Johnson directly so that together they might bat around ideas for a new kind of spy tool.

Talbott appeared unmoved. He told Land he'd think about it.

Land sensed that Talbott was brushing him off. If the meeting ended at that, Land knew it would be very easy for Talbott to follow the line of least resistance and let the previous rejection stand. Land wanted to force him to make a commitment before he walked out the door. He raised his voice and took a chance.

"All right, Mr. Secretary," Land said, "I guess we'll have to tell the American people all about you!"

Wheels seemed to start spinning in Talbott's head: *What was Land talking about?* It sounded as if the scientist had uncovered some dark secret about him. Had Land been so taken by the spy world that he was collecting dirt on all of his potential adversaries? Talbott held his tongue, opting not to press for elaboration.

This was a lucky break for Land, because he didn't know the first thing about Harold Talbott. Some wild impulse had taken hold of him when he leveled the vague threat, and he was as surprised as anyone by the result.

"I think Talbott may have had a guilty conscience," Land later speculated, "because he immediately picked up the phone and called Lockheed and we got our interview with Kelly Johnson."

PETER AND CHRISTINE JOHNSON HAD IMMIGRATED to America from Sweden, but any genetic traces of the stereotypical Scandinavian temperament (cool, placid, introverted) skipped Clarence, the seventh of their nine children. He was born in 1910, and when he was in second grade in the small mining town of Ishpeming, Michigan, a classmate teased him about his name. "Clara," the boy called him. According to a well-worn story repeated years later, young Clarence walked up to him on the playground, kicked him behind the knee, and pounced on him when he fell. A bone in the boy's leg snapped. The next day, the other kids at school decided that "Clarence" didn't fit him and that he should have "a good fighting Irish name." From then on, everyone called him Kelly.

The family was poor, but his father always found jobs in construction and masonry. Store-bought goods were a luxury, so Peter Johnson often handcrafted his children's toys. Kelly watched closely as his father's callused hands transformed simple, inert materials—a solid piece of birch, fragments of scrap wood, a length of rope—into a sturdy rocking horse that moved with natural grace. Another time, Peter made the boy a wagon, painted green and equipped with a homemade brake system, which Kelly could operate remotely with either his knees or his hands.

In those days, Kelly occasionally wandered to the library in Ishpeming. That's where he discovered the Tom Swift novels. Tom was an inventive, mechanically inclined kid with a taste for adventure, a character custom-made to feed the dreams of boys born in the decade after the Wright brothers first took to the skies. Kelly tore through the whole series of books: *Tom Swift and His Airship, Tom Swift and His Electric Runabout, Tom Swift and His Wizard Camera.* The hero, whose father also happened to work in construction, was everything Kelly wanted to be.

One of the most popular books in the series was called *Tom Swift and His Sky Racer.* The plot starts simply: to compete in a $10,000 airplane race, Tom designs the fastest airplane ever made—"a wonder for lightness and power." The engine "gave a minimum thrust of one thousand pounds at two thousand revolutions per minute," but the book made clear that the plane's genius lay in its simplicity. "In fact, the whole monoplane was so light and frail as to give one the idea of a rather large model, instead of a real craft, intended for service." In the end, Tom wins the race, and in addition to the prize money he lands "a most advantageous contract" with the U.S. government.

At age twelve, Kelly was put to work in a machine shop as a lathe operator so he could contribute $7 a week toward his family's expenses. The following year he entered a model plane contest sponsored by the Kiwanis Club in Flint. He won the $25 prize.

Kelly was still working the lathes after he graduated from high school, but he found time to take classes at Flint Junior College, where he discovered an aptitude for math, physics, and calculus. His years manning the lathe had caused his forearms to bulge with dense muscle, earning him comparisons to Popeye and helping him land a spot on the school's football team. In 1929, he planned to transfer to the University of Michigan, where he was promised a football scholarship, but a car accident wrecked his gridiron dreams. He enrolled in classes anyway, working at a restaurant to cover his tuition costs. By his second semester, the head of the aeronautical engineering department at Michigan had noticed his uncommon drive, and he hired Kelly as his assistant.

Kelly was forever trying to fix design flaws that other students didn't even recognize as problems. That natural vigilance was a valuable tool for a budding aircraft engineer, but he overdid it and turned into a first-class worrier. By his junior year, his gut was riddled with ulcers. He tried to calm his stomach by eating and discovered a curiously effective remedy: two donuts and a glass of milk. Over the course of one semester, he calculated that he'd consumed 647 donuts at a cost of five cents each—a considerable expense, given the fact that the Great Depression had put a squeeze on his already modest finances.

He graduated in 1932 and landed a job making $83 a month working in the tool design department for the Lockheed Corporation in California. The company was an upstart, and it was waging its future on the Electra—a monoplane that was in the late stages of design. Johnson saw the plans and decided that its stability and directional control were flawed. For a green underling in the tool department to pipe up and find fault with the company's veteran engineers seemed like an invitation to unemployment. Hall Hibbard, the company's chief engineer, approached the young man and grilled him. How much math had he studied? Could he draw?

If Johnson thought he could do better, Hibbard said, then he should go ahead and give it a shot. With Hibbard's encouragement, Johnson packed a scale model of the Electra into his car, and he drove all the way back to Ann Arbor, where he planned to test it inside the same wind tunnel he'd used in college. He pinpointed the design flaw that had bothered him and discovered that he could fix it by attaching movable plates to the tail, allowing a pilot to react to wind flows and stabilize the plane. He sent the results to Hibbard, who promptly wrote him back:

Dear Johnson,

You will have to excuse the typing as I am writing here at the factory tonite and this typewriter certainly is not much good. You may be sure that there was a big celebration around these parts when we got your wires telling about the new find and how simple the solution really was. It is apparently a rather important discovery and I think it is a fine thing that you should be the one to find out the secret.

From that day forward, he was the wunderkind. His fellow engineers were stunned by his ability to quickly look at a design element—a wing, a tail, a nose cone—and precisely identify its stress points. He could calculate the amount of drag an external feature would generate, without grabbing a calculator or even a pen and paper. Still in his twenties, he won international design awards for his work on high-speed commercial aircraft, and his reputation among other designers inspired not so much jealousy as awe.

"That damn Swede," Hibbard marveled, "can actually *see* air."

Johnson and Hibbard designed the P-38 Lightning, America's primary fighter plane in World War II. When rumors circulated that the Nazis might be working on a jet-powered fighter, Johnson came up with the P-80 Shooting Star in just 180 days, giving America its first operational combat jet.

He'd ruptured an ulcer doing all that work, but his confidence in his own judgment was bulletproof. Even after General LeMay rejected his high-altitude flier, Johnson couldn't let it go; he kept tinkering with it, though the military considered it dead. He was still working on it when an enthusiastic Edwin Land called and changed his life.

IT WAS THE TIME OF YEAR when fallen leaves spiced the air in Cambridge, and the chill cut through to the bone. As Johnson approached Land's front doorstep, he stood at the threshold of a world he could scarcely have imagined when, as a kid back in Ishpeming, his family heated their house by collecting pieces of coal that had fallen onto the railroad tracks from passing trains.

Land's house, at 163 Brattle Street in Cambridge, sat at the center of one of the most storied stretches of real estate in America, a row of grand old manses that was sometimes called "the King's Highway." George Washington had lived on the same block just before America declared its independence in 1776. The poet Henry Wadsworth Longfellow moved in about fifty years later. Now Land's place—behind a trim wooden fence and a yard full of tall trees—was perhaps the nicest in the neighborhood.

Johnson had always been proud of his own sprawling ranch house back in Encino, with its hilltop view, the wall-to-wall carpeting, the modern kitchen, and the swimming pool out back. But it was nothing like this. If Johnson's house represented the sunny freshness of California, these walls seemed to support history itself. Fine Oriental rugs covered the hardwood floors. In the foyer, a dramatically wide staircase, with sturdy banisters and delicate newel posts, led toward the upper floors. The high ceilings were edged with hand-carved moldings. Everything was tasteful, nothing was showy, but with each step into the house it was clear that Polaroid had made Land very, very rich. In Johnson's house, a portrait of a jet fighter hung over the fireplace; Land preferred Renoir. Johnson would often relax at the end of a hard day with a shot of White Horse whiskey; Land liked wines of good vintage. Johnson would occasionally smoke a cigar; Land puffed on a pipe. Land was trim and always neatly dressed; Johnson's shirttails were forever coming untucked from his pants, and now, in his mid-forties when he walked into Land's house, he looked less like Popeye and more like W. C. Fields.

But when they got down to talking, the two men quickly discovered they had plenty in common. They shared an impatience for small talk, loathed bureaucracy, and considered anyone who worked eight hours a day to be incorrigibly lazy. Johnson's work ethic now meant that he usually spent about as many hours inside his windowless office beside the Burbank Airport as he spent out of it; Land's meant that he had the family cook keep fresh casseroles on hand so he'd always have enough food to fuel his marathon late-night and weekend work sessions.

In recent weeks Land had logged many hours toiling over Johnson's sketches for the high-altitude plane, trying to figure out how to outfit it for espionage. The scientist had transformed one of Polaroid's properties—a nondescript redbrick building on Osborne Street—into a humming command center for the spy plane project, and his enthusiasm for Johnson's design had proved contagious among the other members of Group Three.

No feature of Johnson's sketches excited them more than the wings. In most aircraft, a stabilizing spar stretches from wingtip to wingtip, passing through the fuselage. In fact, the air force required such spars in all of its planes. But the wings of Johnson's hypothetical craft were affixed to the fuselage via several high-tensile steel bolts. By eliminating the spar, Johnson had freed up a sizable area behind the tiny cockpit and another one behind the engine, repurposing the spaces as equipment bays. Land's team wasted no time in devising new gadgets to stuff into them.

James Baker, the MIT astronomer who was an expert in high-powered lens design, resolved to invent a new kind of aerial camera, one with more range and a much higher resolution than any in existence. The best aerial photography systems then available used three cameras—and three separate film tracks—to photograph swaths of the earth below. Baker devised a system that compressed seven exposures onto a single track of film to create a panoramic image. Using an early model IBM card-programmable computer at Boston University and an algorithm of his own invention, Baker was able to efficiently experiment with the three main variables of lens design—curvature, refraction, and the distance between lens components—to capture an image that was also four times sharper than those produced by the best long-range cameras then available. A single flight across the Soviet Union with such an apparatus could photographically capture a strip of land twenty-five hundred miles long and two hundred miles wide.

The very notion of such a vast haul of intelligence was stunning, but it also worried Johnson a bit. He'd worked very hard to keep the plane's weight to an absolute minimum. Any camera expected to photograph such a broad vista would require an enormous amount of heavy, acetate-based film. Hundreds, if not thousands, of pounds of it.

But Land was a step ahead of him. He had rung up Henry Yutzy, who was the resident expert on emulsifiers and film technology for Kodak, and invited him to Group Three's new headquarters. Yutzy told Land's scientists that Kodak had recently experimented with a new plastic called polyethylene, also known by the trade name Mylar. The material was just one-thousandth of an inch thick, and it retained its strength in temperatures that ranged from minus 40 degrees to 120 degrees Fahrenheit, which meant it might be used to create a much lighter, but equally durable, kind of photographic film. Unfortunately, Kodak didn't think Mylar's commercial potential justified the expense of the experiments, and it mothballed the project. Land pounced, appealing to Yutzy's patriotic pride. Kodak had a civic duty, he said, to work on perfecting that film. Soon, Yutzy was doing exactly that.

Land could seemingly speak with fluency about every technical facet of the plane and its equipment, from the chemical properties of the Mylar film, to the camera lenses' refractive indices, to the wind drag coefficients Johnson had calculated. From the moment Johnson stepped inside Land's house in Cambridge to review where things stood, the inventor's restlessness of mind was apparent, though not everyone in that house seemed to experience his hyperactive intellect, and his willingness to delegate responsibility, in the same way. "Oh, it's the bane of my existence," admitted Land's wife, Terre, who oversaw the household for the couple and their two daughters. "He does the same on fixing things. He works on it as long as he doesn't understand it, but as soon as he understands it he wants somebody else to do it."

That approach suited Johnson perfectly: an overseer who understood the challenges and then stepped out of the way to let him attend to the detailed business of keeping a plane in the air. Already his sketches had taken on a life of their own, thanks in no small part to Land's ceaseless enthusiasm, which made the air force rejection seem almost beside the point. As the scientists working with Land continued to refine their ideas, they had even managed to convince some lower-ranking members of the air force, including several officers in the branch's research and development unit, that the Lockheed plan was the only high-altitude project worth pursuing.

One evening in October, MIT's James Killian, who'd put together the Technological Capabilities Panel just six months earlier, stopped by Land's house to speak with the inventor and the aircraft designer. By the time Johnson left days later to fly back to California, the men had come up with an unprecedented strategy to clear the hurdles erected by LeMay and other air force generals. They would try to sidestep the military objections by persuading the CIA, a civilian agency, to run the program by itself.

DAYS LATER, LAND ARRANGED A MEETING with Allen Dulles, the director of the CIA, in Washington. The agency had never developed technology in-house on a large scale, and Land needed to persuade Dulles to broaden the scope of the CIA to make room for modern innovations. A high-tech spy plane, Land suggested, could capture more enemy secrets in one flight than an army of traditional operatives could smuggle home in a year.

It wasn't an easy sell, because Dulles had been a traditional operative himself and his vision of the spy game was one of romance, adventure, and derring-do. As a Princeton undergraduate he'd sailed to India to teach for a term at a Christian school, and on the ship to Asia he'd devoured Rudyard Kipling's novel *Kim*, about an Irish orphan boy reared as a Hindu in Lahore and recruited as a spy by the British in India. Kipling's descriptions of "the Great Game," and the secret agent's place within it, stirred Dulles's imagination. "When he comes to the Great Game," Kipling wrote, "he must go alone—alone and at the peril of his head. Then, if he spits, or sits down, or sneezes other than as the people do whom he watches, he may be slain." The book became Dulles's favorite, and he returned to it regularly (it would be at his bedside when he died, in fact). After he graduated, he landed a post as a junior diplomat in Vienna in 1916. He remained with the State Department until 1926, when he went into private law practice. But when World War II broke out, he was recruited into the Office of Strategic Services, the precursor of the CIA, and served as station chief in Switzerland and Berlin.

After the CIA was formed in 1947, Dulles was recruited by its director, Walter Bedell Smith, to take control of the agency's covert operations. In 1953, the newly elected president, Eisenhower, appointed Smith to the post of undersecretary of state, where he worked for John Foster Dulles, Allen's older brother and the new secretary of state. That opened the door for Dulles to become the director of the CIA, where his enthusiasm for running agents reached full flower. "He might without disrespect be described as the last great Romantic of Intelligence," said Major General Kenneth Strong, a British army officer who served as the head of intelligence for Eisenhower's Supreme Headquarters Allied Expeditionary Force in World War II. Dulles's weakness for swashbuckling also made an impression on Kim Philby, a senior British spy who in 1963 would be outed as a double agent working for the Soviets. Dulles was "good, comfortable, predictable, pipe-smoking, whisky-sipping company," and his boyish love of adventuring was part of his appeal— at least for someone like Philby, whose appreciation for treachery was more brazen than most people's. "Dulles did nothing to play down his legend," Philby observed. "His unprofessional delight in cloak-and-dagger for its own sake was an endearing trait."

It didn't strike Land as quite so charming, because that mind-set was precisely the one that Group Three had diagnosed as a crippling problem. To convince Dulles that the CIA should go into business as a cutting-edge developer of new technologies, Land needed to put on his hat as a master salesman and marketer. At Polaroid, he'd developed a flair for the dramatic and theatrical that would be studied in business schools for decades. When he first tried to market his polarizers for use in sunglasses, for example, he rented a west-facing hotel room and invited executives from the American Optical Company to meet him there in the late afternoon. Before they arrived, Land placed a fishbowl on the windowsill. At the appointed hour, the low-angled sun hit the bowl and created a blazing glare that obscured the goldfish swimming inside. When the executives walked in, Land feigned annoyance, drew their attention to the fishbowl, and asked them to look at it through his polarizing sheet: without the sheet, all was washed out by the sun; with it, they instantly saw the fish. American Optics became the leader in polarized eyewear, eventually supplying specialized lenses to everyone from military pilots to the first men to walk on the moon.

But when it came to selling Dulles on the idea of turning the CIA into a developer of groundbreaking technologies, Land didn't have anything quite so tangible to work with, only ideas. As the meeting came to a close, Land was discouraged. The notion of creating a machine to fly over the Soviet Union and steal secrets seemed to violate Dulles's idea of fair play, Land thought, as if espionage were bound to a rule book written by Kipling and the spy novelists who followed him.

Land left Dulles's office and decided it was time to play the most powerful, and most politically risky, card in his hand. Using James Killian's contacts in the White House, he arranged a personal meeting with President Eisenhower.

THAT SUNDAY MORNING, EISENHOWER AND HIS WIFE, Mamie, walked to St. John's Episcopal Church, just across Lafayette Square from the White House. Every president since Madison had attended a service there, and this was Eisenhower's first. In the pulpit that morning was a guest minister, the Reverend Dr. Charles W. Lowry. Eisenhower settled into pew number fifty-four, the one reserved for the sitting president, and Lowry launched into his sermon.

It was a midterm election week, with voters getting ready to head to the polls that Tuesday, and Eisenhower's Republicans were in danger of losing their majority in the House of Representatives. National security and the Soviet threat had been the dominant themes. Adlai Stevenson—the former Illinois governor whom Eisenhower had defeated to become president—led the national campaign on behalf of the Democrats, and early in the week he had enraged Vice President Richard Nixon by suggesting the Republicans had poisoned the Defense Department with McCarthy-like smears against those who advocated a less aggressive approach to national security. Even here, inside the church, the atmosphere was politically charged and combative. Lowry's sermon was titled "A Strong Offensive," and it centered on two highly topical touchstones: the upcoming election and the recent Oppenheimer hearings.

"Almighty God, the source of all wisdom," Lowry began. "Direct, we beseech Thee, the minds of those now called to elect fit persons to serve in the Congress of the United States." The country, he said, "had been on the defensive long enough," and it was time for America to proactively assert itself against the atheistic Soviets. Second-guessers like Oppenheimer, Lowry said, had undermined the strength of the country by putting science before the fight against Communism, which was a righteous calling. "If by some evil chance our globe is destroyed, this will be the real reason—the tyranny of science and the poverty and defensiveness of the forces of the spirit," Lowry said. "The fact is that

Robert Oppenheimer was symptomatic of a very large number of top flight scientists in the evident vacuum of his soul, in his intellectual naiveté outside of his chosen field of specialization and in his ethical confusion typified by guilt neurosis in the face of success in achieving atomic fission. This guilt neurosis, which is an open secret that a large percentage of Oppenheimer's colleagues shared in a period following Hiroshima and Nagasaki and victory, is the real explanation, along with amazing naiveté, in confronting the whole phenomenon of Marxism, of the corporate hesitancy of American scientists in the face of the challenge of the next discovery—atomic fusion, more powerful thermonuclear weapons."

The president listened to the sermon with the calm, nearly unreadable expression he almost always wore. He was something of a cipher—an amiably unthreatening former soldier who, according to a complaint that had been voiced in the run-up to the midterms, spent a little too much time on the golf course. In recent weeks, "bitterness in Washington had reached a pitch seldom seen short of a Presidential year," according to *The New York Times*. Vice President Nixon raged to reporters that a "fanatical, left-wing clique" was trying to displace the Republican majority in Congress through vicious slander, and he delivered a fiery, nationally televised speech to attack their positions. Eisenhower, by all appearances, remained unfazed. After Nixon's speech, the president remarked to his press secretary, Jim Hagerty, "By golly, sometimes you sure get tired of all this clackety-clack."

But if his critics believed the heaviest burden Eisenhower shouldered was his golf bag, they were underestimating him. Particularly in matters of national security, Eisenhower was an informed leader. Even if everyone from his senior military commanders to the minister at his church was trying to tell him that scientists couldn't be trusted, he had the confidence to make his own decisions.

Eisenhower welcomed Land and James Killian into the White House and listened to Land's overview of Group Three's progress. Land explained how his team had concluded that a high-altitude spy plane designed by Kelly Johnson might solve America's intelligence quandary, but certain air force commanders—not to mention Allen Dulles—were resisting its development. Land told Eisenhower that if the Soviets had lots of long-range bombers, like the ones that had been spotted from the embassy roof in Moscow, this spy plane "could and would find and photograph" the fleet and anything else they were trying to hide. All Land needed was presidential authority to take the project from the conceptual stage to the production line—as well as a funding source to pay for it, of course. "If we are successful," Land told the president, "it can be the greatest intelligence coup in history."

Killian later wrote, "After listening to our proposal and asking many hard questions, Eisenhower approved the development of the system, but he stipulated that it should be handled in an unconventional way so that it would not become entangled in the bureaucracy of the Defense Department or troubled by rivalries among the services." Land couldn't have hoped for a better reaction. The president hadn't formally approved the proposal, but it was clear that he wasn't going to stand in the way of their plan to make an end run around the military. With that endorsement, Land could now go back to Allen Dulles and say that even the president agreed that an agency like the CIA should oversee the program.

Land fired off a letter to the CIA director days later, arguing that civilian control of the project would also prove useful if the Soviets ever found out about it. "The plane itself is so light (15,000 pounds), so obviously unarmed and devoid of military usefulness, that it would minimize affront to the Russians even if through some remote mischance it were detected and identified," he explained to Dulles. Land painted the proposal as a cheap and low-risk way for the CIA to take control of its future. "We told you that this seems to us the kind of action and technique that is right for the contemporary version of CIA: a modern and scientific way for an Agency that is always supposed to be looking, to do its looking. Quite strongly, we feel that you must always assert your first right to pioneer in scientific techniques for collecting intelligence—and choosing such partners to assist you as may be needed. This present opportunity for aerial photography seems to us a fine place to start." Land pulled no punches: if Dulles truly wanted the intelligence agency to reach its highest potential, it could no longer be hamstrung by an outdated dependence on human intelligence. America's ignorance of Soviet capabilities, Land argued, was fueling a headlong rush toward annihilation, because fear had filled the vacuum of knowledge. "This ignorance leads to somewhat frantic preparations for both offensive and defensive action," Land wrote, "and may lead to a state of unbearable national tension."

Dulles couldn't really argue against Land's proposal, because Eisenhower himself had unofficially given it his blessing. The CIA director agreed to back the idea. Land told Dulles that he could build twenty planes within eight months. After the necessary flight tests and modifications, he said the fleet could be flying over the Soviet Union in twenty months, at a cost of just $22 million.

IT WAS UNUSUALLY WARM ON NOVEMBER 18, with temperatures pushing close to seventy by early afternoon and a muggy fog shrouding Washington. John Tukey, the computer scientist assigned to Group Three, sat behind the wheel of his 1953 Ford, peering at the road through the slapping windshield wipers and a fine rain. All six members of the spy panel were crammed shoulder to shoulder on the vinyl bench seats, and the windows kept fogging up. But Edwin Land, who had called an emergency meeting to strategize, insisted that they leave the building for the discussion. Privacy was his concern. LeMay and his allies had somehow found out about the scientist's maneuverings, and the air force's office of research and development had scheduled a meeting to discuss the future of the project with the Technological Capabilities Panel that afternoon. Land suspected treachery. The generals—who still wanted to kill the Lockheed design—might try to sweet-talk the other members of the panel into handing control of the project to the military. Land wanted to defend against that possibility by making sure the scientists spoke up in favor of CIA supervision with a unified voice. Fearing that the generals might connive a way to eavesdrop on the discussion if it were held in the Executive Office Building, Land insisted on speaking in Tukey's Ford, which rolled aimlessly through the wet city streets for two full hours.

When they eventually arrived at the meeting in the Pentagon, the scientists found Johnson there; he had flown to Washington that afternoon to answer whatever technical questions might arise. Harold Talbott, the air force secretary Land had vaguely threatened to expose, was also at the table, and he calmed Land's fears of an ambush. Talbott gave the project his blessing and assured Land that his people would support the CIA however they could. He said he'd even dispatch a few of his generals to speak with Eisenhower and let him know that the air force as a unit—if not all of its generals—was on board with the scientists' plan.

On November 24, 1954, Talbott made good on the promise, accompanying several of his generals to the White House to meet with Allen Dulles and President Eisenhower, who was preparing to fly to Georgia to spend his Thanksgiving at the Augusta National Golf Club. If

Dulles had initially harbored doubts about the spy plane, they had been pushed aside by his desire to exert autonomous control over America's intelligence-gathering systems. If America was going to conduct espionage in the sky, then his department—not the air force—was going to oversee every aspect of it. The generals offered no resistance as Dulles formally requested CIA control over the project, and they remained silent when Eisenhower told Dulles to go ahead and get started on it.

After the meeting, General Nathan Twining predicted that the CIA would fail, having no experience with large-scale R&D. Curtis LeMay agreed with him, and he sniffed an opportunity. "We'll let those SOBs get in," LeMay said, "and then we'll take it away from them."

Johnson had flown back to California before Eisenhower gave the project his stamp of approval. The day after Thanksgiving, the telephone in his Burbank office rang. It was Trevor Gardner, one of the air force research and development staff members, updating him on the whirlwind of activity that had unfolded since he'd flown home. Of all the air force staff, Gardner was probably the friendliest to the designer, and he'd grown convinced that the Lockheed design was both innovative and practical. Gardner explained that he had been assigned as an adviser to the project but that Johnson would be working under the orders of the CIA, not the military. As such, everything about the project should be shrouded in the utmost secrecy, and his work would be unlike any assignment that a government contractor had ever undertaken. One of Lockheed's hangars would be converted into an undercover workshop dedicated solely to the spy plane. The work would push Johnson into uncharted territory: he'd no longer be just an aircraft designer; he'd be an operative.

"Kelly," Gardner said, "begin clearing out that hangar this afternoon!"

# CHAPTER 3

## *The Mysterious Mr. B.*

I took to covert action like a duck to water.

—RICHARD M. BISSELL

On the Monday after Thanksgiving, Kelly Johnson began recruiting a team of about twenty-five Lockheed engineers to be part of his secret project. "It is extremely difficult to pull these engineers from other projects at this time, particularly in that I cannot tell anyone why," Johnson confided in his daily log. Yet he managed to persuade their supervisors to surrender them for several months and to trust him when he said it would be worth it. One by one, engineers began filing into his office, curious to find out what kind of work they'd be doing.

The thermodynamics specialist he recruited was Ben Rich, a twenty-nine-year-old who'd been working with the company for four years. "Rich," Johnson said, "this project is so secret that you may have a six-month to one-year hole in your résumé that can never be filled in. Whatever you learn, see, and hear for as long as you work inside this building stays forever inside this building. Is that clear?"

Johnson slid a piece of paper across his desk—a nondisclosure form. After Rich signed it, Johnson's production supervisor, Dick Boehme, unveiled the preliminary designs for the secret plane. When Rich looked up from the drawing, Boehme was holding a finger to his lips. "You've just had a look at the most secret project in the free world," he said.

The team set up shop in an old hangar on Lockheed's Burbank campus. The place had all the charm of a bomb shelter: the walls were thick with asbestos stuffing, and the windows were blacked out. The open floor was a minefield of hazards: ladders, tangles of wires, parts assemblies, drill presses, oil slicks on the concrete. On the second level of the building, the engineers sat side by side in windowless offices.

They called the shop the Skunk Works—a recycled nickname that had first been applied to the production tent Johnson used when developing the P-80 during World War II. Back then, a nearby plastics factory filled the tent with noxious fumes, an eye-watering stench that made one of the engineers think of the *Li'l Abner* comic strip; in the comic, a stinking factory on the edge of the fictional town of Dogpatch was called "Skonk Works." Johnson hated the name at first, but it stuck, and it followed him to the hangar where he was now beavering away on the CIA project, worrying his guts sore about the deadline. Eight months, twenty planes. And he didn't even have the design finalized yet.

The place hummed with the raw energy and shambolic disorder of a frat house. "We don't dress up for each other," Boehme explained to the new engineers, telling them to save their coats and ties for church. Everywhere you looked, another cigarette was being lit, the smoke massing in the dense gloom. If anyone tried to air the place out by opening the big hangar doors for more than a minute or two, birds would swoop in, and sooner or later they'd befoul the engineers' precious sketches with a sloppy imprimatur. The hangar was so secretive that even the company's janitors were barred from entering, which meant the engineers were responsible for keeping the place clean, a task that proved to be outside their skill set. The crudeness that pervaded the place extended to the jokes, and also to the casual chauvinism that went unchallenged. They tacked pictures of swimsuit models on the walls, and if ever Johnson brought in a distinguished guest—a CIA officer, for example—someone would yell, "Present ducks!" and they'd flip the pictures around, revealing portraits of waterfowl. When the CIA suggested that the engineers come up with security aliases for themselves, the opportunity for juvenile punning wasn't squandered. Ben Rich, for one, decided his alias would be "Ben Dover."

Yet they made progress, each day cranking out new ideas and solving problems. Johnson was intolerant—*volcanically* intolerant—of horseplay if it got in the way of work. "Be quick, be quiet, be on time"—that was his motto. Eight months, twenty planes. Nothing else mattered.

At first, Johnson put the engineers on forty-five-hour workweeks, but he soon upped the load to sixty-five hours, and then to a hundred hours. He'd convene morning meetings at seven o'clock sharp. "Working like mad on airplane," Johnson wrote in his log on December 20, less than a month after Eisenhower had okayed the project. "Initial tunnel tests successful." By January 10, production on the parts for the first aircraft had begun. Johnson would stomp around the premises, his short-sleeved shirt untucked, his suspenders crooked, vigilant for any sign of loafing. "I actually observed guys flushing and breaking out in a nervous sweat every time they had to deal with him—even several times a morning," Rich later recalled.

The engineers noticed one man who seemed immune to Johnson's wrath, however. He was pale, tall, and lanky, with horn-rimmed glasses—the kind of guy who was born to wear a gray suit. But inside Skunk Works, he made a spirited, if not altogether successful, attempt to relax his standards and blend in: he wore an open-collared shirt, gray slacks, a lurid checkered sport jacket, and tennis shoes. He quietly stuck his nose into everything, and Johnson, who was always harping about security, didn't seem to mind. The man peeked at production schedules, traced design drafts, asked tough questions about the tensile strength of metal sheeting, and gazed into the gills of jet engines. When an engineer finally asked Dick Boehme, the production supervisor, who the mysterious man was, Boehme played blind. "What guy?" he deadpanned. "I don't see a soul."

During those early months, it was said, only Johnson knew the man's true identity. To everyone else, he was simply "Mr. B."

RICHARD BISSELL WAS BORN WITH CROSSED EYES, and he got his first pair of glasses when he was a six-month-old baby. For the first eight years of his life, until corrective surgery solved the problem, he was unable to see well enough to make out words on a page. His mother would sit at his bedside and read to him. One poem she read—the one that would leave the deepest, boldest mark on him—was Rudyard Kipling's "White Man's Burden."

*Take up the White Man's burden—*
*Send forth the best ye breed—*
*Go bind your sons to exile*
*To serve your captives' need;*
*To wait in heavy harness*
*On fluttered folk and wild—*
*Your new-caught, sullen peoples,*
*Half-devil and half-child.*

The poem was Kipling's message to America, which in 1899 had just begun to wage a war in the Philippines. The United States had taken possession of the country after the Spanish-American War, but Filipino revolutionaries fought for their independence. The war sparked a fierce debate: Should America cast itself as a new empire, entangling itself in far-flung conflicts, or should it mind its own business and turn inward, toward its own political concerns? Kipling advocated empire. He believed that impoverished, undeveloped, and occupied nations—those "new-caught, sullen peoples"—needed a guiding hand to lead them toward progress and civilization. To Kipling, imperialism was sort of like missionary work, and those who dedicated themselves to it should only expect hardship and resentment in return for their thankless, farsighted struggle. Kipling believed it was the price that those born to privilege at the dawn of the twentieth century—white men, in other words—simply had to pay.

The poem became something of a political litmus test in America, dividing people on one side or the other. Teddy Roosevelt was a fan of Kipling's viewpoint, even if some of the verses were too crude for his taste, believing the writer made "good sense from the expansion point of view." Mark Twain, on the other hand, despised everything about it. From his chair as the recently elected vice president of the Anti-imperialist League of New York, he penned an acidic essay in response titled "To the Person Sitting in Darkness." It was strange, Twain observed, that the condescending brand of "civilization" that Kipling extolled seemed a product deemed fit only for export, not domestic use.

Bissell's mother might have leaned toward Kipling's side, but Twain's influence was never far from the boy; Bissell's father had bought the family house in Hartford, Connecticut, from Twain himself, who had built it and spent his most productive decades there, writing *The Adventures of Tom Sawyer, The Adventures of Huckleberry Finn,* and *Life on the Mississippi,* among other books. It was an airy castle of red brick, with peaked roofs and turreted balconies. Louis C. Tiffany & Company had designed the soaring entrance hall. The library was a snug refuge of dark wood, and in the conservatory an artificial stream burbled between the ferns. Each Christmas Eve, a large tree stood in the downstairs hall, and it was lit with real candles; a servant, armed with a pail of water and a long rod with a sponge attached to the end, stood by in stoic vigilance, in case of fire.

He went to Groton, the elite boarding school in Massachusetts. He was nervous, gangly, and uncoordinated. During the afternoons ("the most disagreeable part of the day"), when everyone was sent to the baseball and football fields, he endured humiliating indignities, until he learned that his teachers would excuse him from competition if he spent an hour and a half briskly walking the school grounds. Soon he found himself falling in step with another boy, a fellow athletic outcast who would come to consider Bissell his only friend at the school. The boy was Joseph Alsop.

Together they took refuge in the library. As a hobby, Bissell developed an obsession with trains, model and otherwise. He memorized railroad timetables between cities and, drawing upon his uncanny gift for logistics, would draw up maps for new rail networks that could more efficiently move people around the country. As they got older, both he and Alsop recognized they possessed a quickness of mind, and the dominant trait they shared was no longer physical awkwardness but intellectual assertiveness. As debate stars in high school, they staged a mock trial in front of the rest of the student body: Bissell, the prosecutor, made a case against Napoleon for war crimes; Alsop defended the French revolutionary. Bissell won, but the school yearbook lightheartedly alleged that he "stole the defense's papers and references before trial, made accurate copies, and returned only part of the stolen property" (Alsop, incidentally, was on the yearbook staff).

The two of them—along with Joe's younger brother Stewart—remained close friends for the rest of their lives. They went to different colleges (Joe Alsop to Harvard, Bissell to Yale) but visited each other regularly. At Yale, Bissell studied history and took a Twain-like delight in rebelling against stuffy establishment traditions. One day, a young man in a dark suit tapped him on the shoulder and said, "Go to your room"— the well-known signal among undergraduates telling them they'd been chosen for membership in the exclusive secret society known as Skull and Bones. Bissell surprised the young man by declining the offer, and he wrote an editorial in a school paper against such clubs, declaring himself opposed to arbitrary coronations of a social elite.

Next came the London School of Economics, then back to Yale for a job as a professor of economics. In 1940, as America debated whether to enter the war in Europe, Bissell joined the America First Committee, which campaigned against foreign intervention. It wasn't a popular stand among many of his friends, particularly Joe Alsop, who was a staunch interventionist (Teddy Roosevelt happened to be Alsop's great-uncle) and described the members of the America First movement as being "open to charges of serious irresponsibility." Yet Bissell went so far as to organize a rally at Yale and invited America's most famous isolationist, Charles Lindbergh, to speak. Bissell stood on a stage, buttoned into a sharp double-breasted suit, and introduced Lindbergh to an overflow crowd of nearly three thousand. It was, in Lindbergh's judgment, "by far the most successful and satisfying meeting of this kind in which I have ever taken part."

Bissell's mind seemed made up: he'd rejected the White Man's Burden outright. But as Hitler continued his brutal march across Europe and into Russia in 1941, Bissell's faith in isolationism wavered. Pearl Harbor turned him against it for good.

His conversion was dramatic. During World War II, Bissell moved to Washington, where his extraordinary logistical skills earned him the important job of coordinating the Allies' cargo shipping network. He created his own database using three-by-five index cards and a hand-cranked calculator; it allowed him to match up the storage capacity of ships with the equipment demands of military units scattered across the globe. The work wasn't glamorous, but a lot of people in important positions considered it heroic. One of his fans was James Killian, who persuaded Bissell to join the MIT economics faculty after the war. He moved into a house just down Brattle Street from Edwin Land in Cambridge and lived there until he took the job as an administrator for the Marshall Plan, the massive American aid program that distributed over $12 billion to help the countries of Western Europe rebuild after World War II.

Bissell had lots of friends in the CIA who kept trying to persuade him to join the agency. He resisted until one evening in 1953, when he was invited to the home of the journalist Stewart Alsop, his old friend, in Washington. Another guest was Allen Dulles, whom Stewart had met during the war when both Dulles and Alsop worked for the Office of Strategic Services, the precursor of the CIA. As the dinner party wound down, Bissell mentioned to Dulles that he might be looking for another job soon. Dulles told him to stop by his office.

Bissell became Dulles's "special assistant," a purposely vague title that gave him the flexibility to search for a niche. His first major operation was a heady one: inciting a military coup in Guatemala to overthrow a Soviet-friendly government. Working alongside just a handful of colleagues, Bissell helped supply a rebel air force with black-market airplanes. On May 1, 1954—the same day the new Soviet Bison bomber made its official debut in Moscow—Bissell helped launched a disinformation campaign against the Guatemalan government via the Voice of Liberation radio station. By the end of summer, the Guatemalan president was gone and the CIA was riding high, having also secretly intervened to topple the Iranian government the year before. He'd made a 180-degree turn. The young man who'd argued against foreign intervention was now the hidden hand helping the American empire hold and gain territory abroad. Was he callously toying with the fates of native populations, trespassing on their right to figure things out for themselves? Or did he have a duty to help stop the spread of Soviet-style Communism and lead those same populations to a more rewarding way of life, whether they realized it now or not? It depended which side you were on:

> *Take up the White Man's Burden—*
> *The savage wars of peace—*
> *Fill full the mouth of Famine*
> *And bid the sickness cease.*

ALLEN DULLES CALLED BISSELL INTO HIS OFFICE on the Tuesday after Thanksgiving and handed him a pack of classified documents. Eisenhower had approved the development of a high-altitude spy plane, Dulles told him, and the president had put the CIA in charge of it. "I want you in a meeting at four o'clock this afternoon at the Pentagon," Dulles said. Bissell had done well with Guatemala, and this—the freedom to oversee a new covert project on his own—was his reward.

Bissell hopped in one of the CIA's black cars and was driven across the Memorial Bridge and into Arlington, where he made his way to the Pentagon. He soon found himself sitting at a large conference table, staring out the window at the Potomac River. The table filled up with air force officials, who explained to Bissell that this project was unlike any they'd ever heard of—a new kind of multimillion-dollar partnership between the government and the private sector. They seemed to doubt that the CIA could pull it off.

"Where is this money going to be found?" someone asked.

Good question, Bissell thought; he'd been wondering the same thing. He looked to his right to see if anyone on that side of the table was going to offer an answer. No one said a word. He looked to his left—more silence. Then he realized that everyone was staring directly at him.

Somehow, they'd sniffed out one of Bissell's greatest gifts: he knew where the money was hidden in Washington, and he was an expert at navigating the labyrinthine culs-de-sac of bureaucracy that kept most people away from it.

He'd gotten quite an education in that sort of thing when he was put in charge of administering the Marshall Plan. He had steered billions of dollars in aid abroad, helping to decide which foreign industries America would support, which it would let die. By 1951 some politicians were arguing that "foreign aid" was nothing more than charity and during a Senate hearing charged that Bissell and his colleagues were "trying to support the whole free world" by mindlessly tossing American cash to the winds. "You fellows who spend all of your time spending the government's money never think where the revenues come from," grumbled Tom Connally, a senator from Texas.

Bissell listened calmly, but inside he boiled with contempt. To imply that he mindlessly threw money around was absurd; no one thought more about where the money came from, where it went and, above all, *why*, than Richard Bissell. Almost none of the congressmen realized, for example, that the Marshall Plan legislation included a provision that 5 percent of the local currency that participating countries contributed to the European Recovery Program could be spent on "administrative costs" by the U.S. government. Bissell knew that, and he knew that much of that money went to the CIA's newly established Office of Policy Coordination, a unit whose charter described it as focusing on covert operations overseas including "propaganda, economic warfare, preventative direct action, including sabotage, anti-sabotage, demolition and evacuation measures; subversion against hostile states, including assistance to underground resistance movements, guerillas and refugee liberation groups, and support of indigenous anti-communist elements in threatened countries of the free world." Bissell didn't go into any of that during the congressional hearing. He explained to the committee that the Marshall Plan didn't dole out profligate charity, but directed strategic investments around the world. If some of the funds supported industrial production in a certain country, for example, it was because the economic power resulting from the investment would help the country resist the spread of Soviet-led Communism. "When future historians look back upon the achievements of the Marshall plan," Bissell told the legislators, "I believe they will see in it the charge that blasted the first substantial cracks in the centuries-old walls of European nationalism—

walls that once destroyed will clear the way for the building of a unified, prosperous, and above all, peaceful continent."

The work earned Bissell the reputation as one of the brainiest people in Washington, a technocrat who usually had a good answer for any question thrown at him. It's ultimately what persuaded Dulles to hire him, and it was why he was now sitting at this Pentagon conference table, surrounded by air force officials who were stumped to silence, unable to figure out how this spy plane project could ever get the money to get off the ground. They couldn't have been too surprised when Bissell, staring back at them, cleared his throat to speak.

"Well, the Director of Central Intelligence has access to a special reserve fund which he may tap for unforeseen projects."

FOR WEEKS, STRANGE PACKAGES—BIG AND BULKY— were arriving from all over the country to a newly opened post office box inside the Sunland Post Office, in the foothills of the San Gabriel Mountains. The parcels were addressed to CLJ Manufacturing, but none of the local business associations had ever heard of such a company. Every time a new package arrived, anonymous men would collect it, load it into the back of an unmarked truck, and drive away. The postmaster's suspicions were piqued, and a postal inspector was sent to follow the truck and figure out what this CLJ Manufacturing outfit was all about.

He tailed the truck as it left Foothill Boulevard and continued down Sunland Boulevard. The truck threaded through the streets of Sun Valley and south to Burbank, finally entering the industrial sprawl around the airport. When it entered a closed gate, the postal inspector was spotted, surrounded by guards, and forced to explain himself.

The inspector didn't see anything beyond the security perimeter, but still he was questioned, sworn to secrecy, and released. The new security measures that Bissell had established for the project had faced their first real challenge, and they passed the test.

From the beginning Bissell had obsessed over ways to keep the secrecy of the project intact. Two weeks after Dulles put him in charge, Bissell summoned Kelly Johnson to Washington for a meeting. "We discussed at length problems of security and method of dealing with each other," Johnson noted in his diary. "Large amount of time taken on the optimum cover story for the project."

They borrowed Johnson's initials—CLJ—to create a fake company that could be used as a front. They bought letterhead, stationery, and drafting paper emblazoned with the CLJ logo. All of the new design tweaks that his engineers drew up were sketched on CLJ paper, and all parts and supplies that had to be ordered from other companies were sent to its post office box in Sunland.

The CIA's Los Angeles office took over the security detail at Skunk Works in January 1955. In February the agency briefed J. Edgar Hoover on the existence of the project, and three members of the FBI's field office in Los Angeles, including the head of the bureau's Espionage Squad, were enlisted to help keep everything under wraps.

To communicate by telephone, the CIA first installed multiple unlisted telephones in Johnson's office, then, a few months later, installed an even more secure Teletype system that could be used to communicate directly with Bissell's office at the CIA. Bissell's staff acquired eight post office boxes in four different cities across the country that the agency used to communicate with parts suppliers and air force liaisons. Incoming mail to the CIA from Lockheed and its suppliers was directed to one of several P.O. boxes scattered around Washington.

By February 1955, Johnson submitted his first voucher to try to get a reimbursement for the progress Lockheed had made on the project. Lockheed had entered into sensitive contracts with the military before, but the work with the CIA was something completely new, and it inspired some highly improvised bookkeeping. Johnson's project was an invisible line item in a black budget, a government expense that almost no one aside from a select few souls with the proper security clearances had any idea existed. One day, Johnson walked outside his house in Encino to check the mailbox, and he was pleasantly surprised to discover that his reimbursement had come through. Inside, he found two personal checks, made out to his name, totaling $1,256,000.

EDWIN LAND WATCHED THE PLANE TAKE SHAPE inside Skunk Works, paying particular attention to the Q-bays behind the wings, where the cameras would sit. A single flight would last about nine hours, during which time about a mile of film—hundreds of pounds of it—would be threaded through the three-part camera system. With so much film moving from one spool to another, the engineers realized that the weight shifts could throw off the balance of the lightweight plane. So Land and his team redesigned the camera system to use two simultaneously moving film spools that moved in opposite directions, to keep everything balanced. Jim Baker, the Harvard astronomer working with Land on the camera's design, mentioned to Johnson that to accommodate the 240-inch focal length lens, six more inches of cargo space would be ideal. "Six more inches?" Johnson replied. "I'd sell my grandmother for six inches!" The cameras already weighed about 750 pounds, which gave Johnson fits whenever he thought about it. Land reminded Johnson that the whole point of the plane was to take pictures. "Let me remind you," Johnson snapped back, "unless we can fly this thing, you've got nothing to take pictures of."

Johnson was whittling everything down to bare essentials. The aluminum that encased the frame was so thin—about 0.02 inch—that some of the engineers worried it might simply peel off in flight. The plane's enormous, fuel-bearing wings weighed only four pounds per square foot—about a third of the weight of conventional wings. The idea to land the plane on a skid had, in the end, been scrapped, replaced by the lightest landing gear ever designed—a two-hundred-pound bicycle-style unit featuring only two wheels, one in front and one in the back, instead of the standard three. The tail assembly was attached to the fuselage by only three small bolts, instead of being studded with heavy rivets. Johnson calculated that each pound saved added approximately a foot onto the plane's maximum altitude.

His guts were knotting up again. In March the executives at Lockheed issued an interdepartmental directive, drafted on the advice of Johnson's doctors, suggesting that his workload be kept to a minimum. Johnson had "suffered from the unusually heavy work load pressures his position has forced him to carry," the memo stated, and shouldn't take on new work. But he couldn't afford to let up on the spy plane. The deadline loomed, and throughout the spring his workdays stretched to twelve hours, fourteen, sometimes more. He tore open another ulcer worrying over problems like "aerolastic divergence"—a dirty trick of aerodynamic physics that could cause light and large wings to actually *flap* while in the air, which raised the possibility they might tear clean off the fuselage.

"Having terrific struggle with the wing," he complained to his journal.

He worked out a solution, recalibrating the wing flaps to relieve more pressure from potential wind gusts. But on the heels of that, he discovered that keeping the engine supplied with fuel was more complicated than previously thought. At seventy thousand feet, the air was so thin that the intake systems had to be superefficient to feed enough oxygen to the engine for compression and fuel burning—sort of like the cardiovascular challenges a high-performance athlete faces when competing at altitude. Johnson and his team tinkered with the alternator, the oil coolers, and the hydraulic pump, optimizing each. But because the outside air temperatures would be about minus seventy Fahrenheit and the atmospheric pressure so low that standard military airplane kerosene would simply freeze or boil away, Johnson called friends at Shell Oil for some help, and the company's chemists came up with a solution: a special low-vapor kerosene that incorporated several petroleum by-products, including those used in commercial insect sprays. It smelled like lighter fluid, but the engineers at Lockheed determined that you could hold a match to it and it still wouldn't easily catch fire. It was just what Johnson needed.

The prototype that was taking shape on the floor of Skunk Works still needed a name. The engineers called it "the Angel," but that wouldn't work as an official designation. Because secrecy was paramount, Bissell and Johnson believed the name should be so generic, so uninspired, that if anyone outside the tiny circle of those with security clearance accidentally stumbled across a document with the name listed, his eyes might pass right over it.

Normally, experimental aircraft were tagged with the prefix X, like the X-1, which Chuck Yeager had piloted during the first supersonic flight in 1947. Since then the X tag had become shorthand for "cutting edge," and it drew too much attention to itself. Alternatively, the Canadian aviation company de Havilland had used the prefix U—for "utility"—in 1951 during the development stages of its decidedly unsexy DHC-3 Otter propeller plane. It was the airborne equivalent of a pickup truck, and during development the Otter was called the U-1.

The exotic bird that Land, Johnson, and Bissell were trying to get off the ground, therefore, got a name that was designed to misdirect people into thinking it was thoroughly unremarkable, barely worth a second thought. They called it the U-2.

IN THE SPRING OF 1955, Joe Alsop would rise in the morning, slip on a colorful silk kimono, and pad from his bedroom to the table in his "breakfast room," where his live-in cook, Maria, would pour his tea into a large porcelain cup that he had collected in China. As he read the morning papers, warm light streamed in through the transom windows that ringed the room's ornate, domed ceiling. Through sliding glass doors, he could gaze out onto his patio and across the interior courtyard, which he'd filled with azaleas, nine varieties of boxwoods, wisteria, and the most exotic tropical plants he could find.

The house at 2720 Dumbarton Street in Georgetown was pure Joe Alsop—determined to stand out among the staid and traditional. He had designed most of it himself, and his neighbors had watched with gaping mouths as it took shape in 1949. Almost all of the houses in the neighborhood conformed to the Federal style—red brick, white window frames, black shutters—which Joe casually dismissed with the back of his hand ("Charming," he judged those houses, "if somewhat insipid"). His house was defiantly modern, with sharp, clean angles and an exterior of cinder block and stucco. It was painted yellow ("*Ochre*," Joe insisted), and the idiosyncratic front door was on the top floor of the three-level house, accessible by a metal staircase covered in creeping ivy and flowering clematis. He lovingly described the house as a "heinous outrage against 'Georgetown charm.'" Soon after he moved in, the Citizens Association of Georgetown passed a municipal ordinance to prevent anyone else from trying to build another house that wasn't classically styled. Joe was delighted; it meant that his house would forever be unique.

He lived alone, aside from Maria and Jose, the Filipino husband-and-wife team he'd hired to be his cook and butler. On the ground floor, he kept an office with two Underwood typewriters sitting side by side—one for himself, and one for his brother and journalistic partner, Stewart, who lived with his wife and kids in the neighborhood of Cleveland Park.

Joe's place was a landmark, perhaps *the* landmark, of Washington's social scene. He'd regularly host dinners within the red-lacquered walls of his dining room, and the invitation list was always studded with high-ranking officials and government insiders. The alcohol would flow freely, and so would the conversation, which Joe directed with the authority of a field marshal. To enliven these "gen-con" (general conversation) sessions and stir up juicy bits of gossip and inside information, he'd apply what became known as "the Alsop Method": he'd make a bold assertion regarding a topic a guest knew something about, loading the statement with absolute conviction and zero basis in fact. Then he'd listen intently as the person elaborated a denial, spilling privileged information in the process.

As Alsop's oldest friend, Richard Bissell was a regular attendee along with his wife, Annie. Alsop, the Bissells, and a handful of other couples were the core members of a Sunday night supper club, which would convene in a different house on the circuit each week. Often, the same group dined together on Monday evenings as well, because on Monday afternoons Julia Child—the soon-to-be-famous chef who'd been an OSS clerk during World War II—hosted a small cooking club in her home with Annie Bissell and a few other Washington wives. After their husbands got off work for the day, they—plus Joe Alsop—gathered to sample that week's culinary experiment, washing it all down with plenty of wine and cocktails.

Bissell spent about as much time with Stewart, whose son had become the best friend of Bissell's oldest child, Richie. The boys shared a passion for electronics, and they had gone so far as to connect their houses via a makeshift telephone line; armed with spools of wire and ladders, they'd traipsed up and down the alleys of Cleveland Park and rigged their own secure communications network across ten city blocks.

The close connections between the two families hadn't gone unnoticed by the CIA. The Alsops consistently broke news in their columns, and a lot of it was sensitive. In one column the Alsops penned in the spring of 1955, they claimed the Pentagon was worried that the Soviets might soon launch a satellite into space that could be of "enormous military value in reconnaissance, missile guidance and other fields." In fact, the day before the column came out, the members of the National Security Council had met to discuss that very threat. Someone had tipped the Alsops off. Eisenhower was incensed.

Bissell had been planning to spend the upcoming weekend with both Alsop brothers in Maryland at the family farm of Frank Wisner, a mutual friend and a CIA veteran. But after the column appeared, Dulles barred Bissell and Wisner from socializing with the Alsops that weekend.

Joe blew up. He stormed into Dulles's office and banged on the table, shouting something about his First Amendment rights. Bissell looked on, amused. "A tempest in a teapot," he thought.

Bissell knew that perhaps he should be more discreet around the Alsops and that maybe he occasionally let slip a few tidbits that might technically be considered classified. But he was also confident in his own ability to keep his mouth shut when it came to the big stuff, like the U-2. Even though he was spending almost all of his time working on it, he never breathed a word about it to the Alsops.

•   •   •

KELLY JOHNSON CALLED SKUNK WORKS' best test pilot, Tony LeVier, into his office in April 1955. "Close the goddam door," he said. LeVier sat down. "Listen, you want to fly my new airplane?" "What is it?" the pilot asked. He hadn't heard a thing about it. "I can't tell you," Johnson said. "Only if you say yes first."

LeVier agreed, and Johnson gave him the rundown, explaining that before the prototype was ready to fly, the CIA needed to find a place to test it in total secrecy. Normally when the military tested experimental aircraft, the pilots took off from an airbase like Edwards or Palmdale. But not this time; the risk of arousing curiosity was too great. Bissell had instructed Johnson to try to find an untouched, remote location with a hard, flat surface—a dried-out salt lake in a desert somewhere, maybe. Johnson asked LeVier to spend a couple days flying the company's little Beechcraft Bonanza around Southern California and Nevada in search of possibilities.

For two days, LeVier buzzed over Death Valley and the Mojave Desert, squinting down through the wavy heat, jotting coordinates. He returned to Burbank with a short list, but Bissell rejected every one of them. Too risky, he said. Bissell's deputy in the CIA, a former air force pilot named Osmond "Ozzie" Ritland, remembered a remote test range in Nevada where B-29s used to drop nuclear bombs years earlier; next to it, there was a dry lake bed that was long and flat. If the CIA could get permission from the Atomic Energy Commission to take a look at it, the site might prove ideal.

LeVier found it, and it looked good—if the ground was as solid as it seemed. Afraid that the surface might be covered by a layer of soft sand, he packed two sixteen-pound shot puts in his plane, flew over the lake bed, and dropped them out the window to see if they sank. They bounced. The ground was baked hard and didn't give an inch.

Bissell and Johnson, along with Herbert Miller, a CIA officer specializing in the Soviet Union, decided to take a look themselves. On April 13, LeVier flew them to the spot in the Bonanza. Johnson sat in the back, with geological maps spread out on his lap, and told LeVier he wanted to check out a spot just northeast of Death Valley, near the California-Nevada line, on the way. It wasn't bad, but when they approached the dry lake bed near the atomic testing range, about seventy-five miles northwest of Las Vegas, they instantly agreed that they had found their hideaway.

In geological terms, it was an endorheic basin measuring about six miles across, with barely a bump on the salt-pan surface. The surrounding terrain couldn't have been more desolate: mile after mile of barren plain, flanked by hills sparsely stubbled with spiky yucca, flowering creosote, and the occasional Joshua tree. The snowy peak of Bald Mountain shielded the valley to the north, and to the south it was hemmed in by a range called the Papoose. The only trespassers seemed to be scaly reptiles and tumbleweeds borne on a hot, dry wind. Elated, the men started to fly back to Burbank, but LeVier couldn't resist making a pass over the AEC's proving ground ("very illegally," Johnson noted in his diary); there, they spotted an atomic bomb sitting atop a tower, awaiting detonation scheduled for nine hours later.

Bissell hustled back to Washington and did some quick research on government land rights, and he discovered that the dry bed—called Groom Lake—wasn't included in the property controlled by the AEC. So he got Eisenhower's approval to extend the boundaries of the AEC's real estate holdings by about 10 square miles. After that, the federal government declared 575 square miles of airspace above the site off-limits to private and commercial aviators.

Within days, Bissell was casting around for trustworthy construction companies to build a makeshift camp in the deserted valley. He found several that had previously done work for the AEC at the testing ground. On April 26, Bissell's office sent a memo to the contractors that laid out some of the challenges: "Physical security of this site probably cannot be equaled, but the fact that it is so remote raises a number of problems which must be settled well in advance in order to properly plan the base." Consequently, the memo stated, the entire base had to be designed and planned in less than three weeks. "Barracks and mess hall will be airconditioned, but no provision is made for any airconditioned working space. A need for a small airconditioned work space may be filled by a trailer."

The electricity would come from diesel generators, and to control all the dust blowing around the site, they'd need lots of water. The contractors reopened an old well that had been dug before the war, and they discovered that it could pump up to fifteen gallons of water a minute. But it wasn't really enough. To conserve water, the workers labored at night with headlamps attached to their heads and high boots covering their shins—protection from rattlesnakes. They built wooden platforms on the ground, which served as the foundations for canvas barracks. The mess hall went up, as did a crude hangar. Overnight thunderstorms would occasionally dump an inch of standing water on the lifeless hard-top, but all that water would almost instantly evaporate when the relent-less sun peeked over the eastern hills at dawn. In the afternoons, the temperatures could soar to 120 degrees.

It was a godforsaken patch of desolation, but it was shaping up nicely. "Mr. Bissell pleased," Johnson noted in his diary. "He enjoyed my pro-posed name for the site as 'Paradise Ranch.'" The nickname, dripping with irony, stuck among the engineers at Lockheed and the officers at the CIA. But in Washington, on the classified maps drawn up by the AEC in the summer of 1955, the site was labeled, simply, "Area 51."

IN 1955, JOE AND STEWART ALSOP BECAME America's most vocal proponents of an idea dubbed "the bomber gap"—the notion that the Soviets were outpacing the United States in the produc-tion of jets capable of carrying hydrogen bombs across the world. Some American officials were skeptical, pointing out that only a handful of Soviet long-range bombers had actually been seen firsthand—such as the Bison prototype that had first been spotted in the air a year earlier from the embassy roof in Moscow. Secretary of Defense Charles Wil-son, for example, speculated that the Soviets had only produced a few prototype bombers—just enough to frighten the Americans during the annual May Day parades.

Did the Soviets have four Bisons, or four hundred? Could they launch a devastating attack against U.S. cities and military installa-tions that would overwhelm the country's defenses and instantly wipe out America's ability to launch a counterattack? Eisenhower's entire national security strategy depended on the answers, but they remained hidden behind an Iron Curtain that American spies still couldn't effec-tively penetrate.

Amid the uncertainty, millions of Americans considered the Alsops' conjectures the closest approximation to the truth available. In the summer of 1955, Stewart Alsop traveled to Moscow and spotted sev-eral Bisons at an air show staged by the Soviet government. The display didn't definitively shed any light on the size and nature of the Soviets' long-range bomber fleet, but the Alsops concluded that the planes were likely being mass-produced on a grand scale. If the United States didn't ramp up its production of bombers, Joe Alsop wrote, the gap between the United States' modest intercontinental strike force and Russia's more impressive fleet would only widen. By the summer of 1955, thanks largely to Alsop's insistence, the bomber gap had become a national preoccupation.

One newspaper reader who paid close attention to everything Joe Alsop published was FBI director J. Edgar Hoover. Unlike many critics who considered Joe and his brother defense hawks whose military conservatism was unforgivably strict, Hoover despised Joe as a left-winger of weak, and perhaps debased, moral character.

The animosity was mutual. As early as 1946, the Alsop brothers had been painting Hoover as a power-hungry schemer, a dictatorial agency head who wanted to control all of America's intelligence gathering himself and therefore never passed up a chance to try to undercut the CIA. In the early 1950s, when the brothers began their sharp attacks on Joseph McCarthy's purges, Hoover and the Wisconsin senator joined forces in what would become a furtive, long-running campaign to dig up dirt on the Alsop brothers and their tight circle of friends.

It started in 1950 when a column published under the brothers' joint byline appeared in the *Saturday Evening Post*. It cast McCarthy as a deluded crusader, a scourge whose paranoia had begun to contaminate the capital. To illustrate how McCarthy's contagious influence was spreading, the Alsops cited "the spectacle of the Minority Leader of the Senate, Kenneth Wherry, attempting to elevate the subject of homosexuality to the level of a serious political issue, on the grounds that sexual perversion presents a clear and present danger to the security of the United States. Examples of this sort of vulgar folly could be extended *ad nauseam*." The headline of the column was "Why Has Washington Gone Crazy?"

McCarthy wrote a letter to the editors to attack the Alsops, but instead of sending it to the magazine, he recited it on the Senate floor. McCarthy bristled at the suggestion that rooting out "perversion" was anything but admirable; the Roman Empire fell, he said, when its ruling class became "morally perverted and degenerate." McCarthy addressed his speech to the editors of the magazine: "I know some of your editorial staff and frankly can't believe Sen. Wherry's attempt to accomplish the long overdue task of removing perverts from our government would be considered either 'vulgar' or 'nauseating' to them. I can understand, of course, why it would be considered 'vulgar' and 'nauseating' by Joe Alsop."

Joe, in the discreet phrasing of the day, was a committed bachelor. His homosexuality wasn't public knowledge, and even some of the members of his own family would have been shocked to know that he was gay. Many of his friends considered him almost asexual, and romantic relationships were rarely discussed in his presence ("We were brought up in a very sort of restrained family," Alsop would say, "and we didn't go in for discussing our inmost feelings, and it still makes me uncomfortable"). Richard Bissell, for one, had noted Joe's "almost ladylike interest in people's clothes and things of that nature," but the subject of his sexuality was never broached. But Stewart once had to make an emergency trip to San Francisco to bail out Joe and suppress a police report after he'd been arrested in a sweep of a popular gay gathering spot. Even so, McCarthy's thinly veiled threat to expose Joe did nothing to discourage the Alsops' criticisms; if anything, it inflamed them. Stewart wanted to fire off an immediate rebuttal to McCarthy in the magazine's next issue, but the editors rejected the idea.

Hoover, of course, was also a committed bachelor, and his relationship with the FBI's associate director, Clyde Tolson, would later spark all sorts of questions; they dined together, drove to work together, took vacations together, and when Hoover died, Tolson inherited Hoover's estate and played the role of bereaved spouse, accepting the flag that had covered his coffin during his funeral. Whether Hoover himself was gay or not, he was an almost maniacal pursuer of people he labeled "perverts" and "deviants," running after whispers of homosexuality with a terrier-like zeal. A few months after McCarthy's tirade on the Senate floor, the FBI sent a report to an aide to President Harry Truman suggesting that Hoover had evidence Alsop was gay. From that point on, McCarthy and Hoover formed a shadowy alliance to undermine Alsop's Georgetown set.

In 1953, Chip Bohlen was nominated by Eisenhower to become the new ambassador to the Soviet Union. Along with the Bissells and the Alsops, Bohlen and his wife had been a part of the Sunday supper club, which allowed the career diplomat to indulge his considerable gifts for conversation and drinking. Bohlen liked to tell the story about the physical examination he underwent in preparation for his Moscow post. When a State Department doctor asked him how much he drank, Bohlen was taken aback by the doctor's response to his answer: "All I can say is, Mr. Bohlen, you must be one of those rare persons for whom alcohol is food." Somehow, Bohlen passed the physical, but his Senate confirmation hearing was more of a challenge, thanks to the combined efforts of McCarthy and Hoover.

Before the confirmation hearings, McCarthy had asked Hoover whether he'd be willing to tell him, in complete confidence, "just how bad" Bohlen might be. "Senator McCarthy asked whether I thought he was a homosexual and I told him I didn't know," Hoover explained in a memo to Tolson and two other aides. Homosexuality was hard to prove, Hoover said, "but it is a fact, and I believed very well known, that he [Bohlen] is associating with individuals of that type . . . and certainly normally a person did not associate with individuals of that type." McCarthy was disappointed Hoover had no proof that could be shared on the Senate floor. But that didn't stop McCarthy from trying to railroad Bohlen's appointment and feeding reporters vaguely incriminating and unsubstantiated innuendos for their daily reports. "I know what's in Bohlen's file," McCarthy told reporters. "I have known what's in his file for years." When a reporter asked McCarthy if that file suggested Bohlen was a security risk, McCarthy cryptically replied, "That's putting it too weak." Despite the efforts to cloud Bohlen in suspicion, his nomination was upheld.

Bohlen's confirmation drama had unfolded around the same time Richard Bissell was considering joining the CIA, an agency that also had come under McCarthy's suspicious gaze. As Bissell considered Dulles's offer, Cord Meyer, another CIA recruit, was targeted by the Wisconsin senator as a possible Red. Dulles was incensed. He refused to let the FBI interview Meyer, and somehow Dulles forced Hoover to show him his file on Meyer, which was full of baseless innuendo. As Bissell watched the episode play out, he admired Dulles's principled stand in defense of his recruit. Bissell later said, "There is no doubt in my mind that Allen's strong stand against McCarthyism and his very able leadership were the key reasons the agency was able to attract so many capable people during the midfifties." Bissell likely had no idea, however, that Hoover had also started a file on *him*.

HOOVER DIDN'T IDENTIFY WHAT ABOUT BISSELL bothered him specifically, but his suspicions probably rested on three unrelated things. The first was his friendship with Alsop. The second was his past affiliation with the America First Committee. The third was the fact that Bissell had once testified on behalf of an economist named William Remington, who had served as his assistant during his days with the Marshall Plan.

Remington was accused of being a Soviet spy by a Russian defector who claimed the young economist had passed her secrets about U.S. military aircraft. In 1948, Bissell had testified that when they worked together, Remington often took staunchly conservative positions—opposing policies favored by labor unions, for example—that a liberal Democrat, much less a Communist, would never support. Remington was cleared by the Loyalty Review Board and successfully settled a libel suit against NBC for broadcasting the claims he had committed treason. But two years later, both the FBI and the House Un-American Activities Committee reopened investigations, and Remington was eventually convicted of perjury and sentenced to three years in prison. In November 1954, on the same day that Eisenhower approved the U-2 project, Remington died in prison after being bludgeoned by a fellow inmate, a man who confessed that he killed him because he hated Communists.

Before Bissell joined the CIA, Hoover had asked an aide to look into Bissell and several other "economists of the ultra-liberal, reformist trend." The economists previously held government positions but had recently "gone underground," according to an FBI memo. "These men are believed to be in close personal association while awaiting an opportunity to rise again to a position of dominance in U.S. economic policy."

After Bissell joined the CIA, Hoover's suspicions must surely have been inflamed, particularly because Bissell's relationship with Joe Alsop had only grown stronger during that time. When Joe published a column in 1955 referencing "The Killian Report"—the document produced by the Technological Capabilities Panel, for which Killian had recruited Edwin Land—it was clear that someone had leaked the classified document to the journalist. Hoover targeted Alsop for an investigation to determine who was feeding him top secret information.

The leaking of classified materials was still a relatively new phenomenon in the mid-1950s. President Truman had established the federal government's classification system in 1951 via an executive order that created four different labels that could be applied to sensitive documents: "Top Secret," "Secret," "Confidential," and "Restricted." Almost immediately, Washington's bureaucrats began abusing the labels, slapping them on even the most mundane correspondence. By 1955, about 1.5 million government employees were authorized to classify materials. The following year, the Pentagon estimated that about 90 percent of its classified documents could be made public without risking any harm to the general population, but the government's mania for confidentiality continued apace. All of this newfound secrecy exerted a profound and lasting influence on the way information flowed to the public, fueling a brand of political journalism that relied on inside access to sources and to classified leaks.

Hoover's investigation into the Alsop leak ultimately proved fruitless. But Alsop's close connections to important officials, particularly those inside the politically suspect CIA, made him an ongoing target for Hoover's off-the-books domestic spying operation, and the FBI director often sent agents to Georgetown to keep an eye on the journalist.

As Bissell and his friends would converge on Joe's house for drinks and dinner, FBI agents lurked in cars on Dumbarton Street, keeping an eye on everyone who came and went. In Cold War–era Washington, if one person in a social network was touched by suspicions, simple proximity was enough to taint the whole group.

IN EARLY JULY, KELLY JOHNSON EASED his car into an intersection in Encino, and a drunk driver ran a red light and broadsided him. Johnson cracked four ribs.

The wreck couldn't have come at a worse time. Back in November, he'd promised to finish the first planes within eight months, by July 25. That was a little more than three weeks away. Taking time off for recuperation was out of the question, so he gritted it out. On July 15, he noted in his journal, "Airplane essentially completed. Terrifically long hours. Everyone almost dead."

On July 24, in the predawn darkness, Lockheed workers began packing the disassembled components of the first U-2 in separate shipping containers. The large pieces—the wings, fuselage, and tail assembly—were wrapped in tarpaulins. It took about three hours to load everything into the rear hatch of a massive C-124 cargo plane.

When Johnson called Paradise Ranch to let everyone know the plane was almost on its way, the man in charge of overseeing Area 51 got cold feet. It had rained, and the lake bed was too soft for a landing. A paved landing strip had recently been completed, but workers hadn't yet had time to apply sealant and armoring to the surface. He worried that the cargo plane, freighted with yet *another* plane inside its belly, would ruin the landing strip, and possibly the cargo plane itself. Johnson improvised a solution: they'd partially deflate the cargo plane's tires, which would widen the landing footprint, spreading out the force of impact over a larger surface area. The controller at the base was nervous; the technique wasn't part of any standard operating procedure that he'd ever heard of, and he told them he was sorry but he couldn't allow them to land.

Johnson was flabbergasted. He'd nearly killed himself meeting the deadline to build the plane, and now some nervous airstrip overseer was forcing them to land off-site. That would force them to put the storage containers in trucks, then haul the plane piecemeal over desert roads and paths that were barely passable. They'd miss the target flight date by as much as a week. Johnson put a few calls into Washington, reduced the air pressure in the cargo plane's tires, and took off for Nevada. At 8:30 a.m., they made a soft landing on the runway, carving indentations into the fresh, untreated pavement that measured one-eighth of an inch deep.

For the next two days, inside a hangar that wasn't even completely built yet, they began bolting the pieces of the first U-2 back together.

TONY LEVIER, THE LOCKHEED TEST PILOT, strapped himself into the tight, single-pilot cockpit and checked the controls. Everything looked good. He flashed a thumbs-up to Johnson and Bissell, who stood together on the lake bed.

This wasn't a test flight, just a taxi run—a quick roll to check the engine. Johnson told LeVier to try it out at a speed of fifty knots, or roughly fifty-eight miles per hour.

LeVier hit the throttle. The speedometer wound up to fifty, and he applied the brakes, which felt a little unresponsive. Johnson and Bissell followed him in a jeep, and when they caught up with him, LeVier mentioned that the brakes felt funny. Johnson told him not to worry; they just weren't broken in yet. Johnson told him to taxi across the lake bed again, this time to seventy knots. LeVier accelerated to the requested speed, heading southwest. Everything felt fine, and he let up on the throttle. He then thought he'd test the ailerons—the hinged flaps on the surface of the wings—just to see how the controls worked. He felt the plane jerk when he moved them—a strange response, because the ailerons shouldn't move a plane that's on the ground. That's when he realized he was airborne. "I almost crapped," he later recalled.

Because the lake bed was so bright and smooth, he had no depth perception. Not knowing exactly where the ground was, he simply tried to keep the plane level and ease it down. But he slammed down with a jolting thump. Both tires, front and back, blew on impact.

Johnson and Bissell raced after the plane, which continued to roll on its flat tires for almost a mile before stopping. Seeing the U-2 accidentally fly at about thirty-five feet off the ground was scary, but now they spotted something far worse: the brakes, which were located just under the fuel lines, had burst into flames. When the plane finally stopped, Johnson and Bissell jumped out of the jeep, gesturing to LeVier to warn him about the fire. An emergency crew roared up with extinguishers and put out the blaze.

"Goddam it, LeVier, what in hell happened?" Johnson asked.

"Kelly, the son of a bitch took off and I didn't even know it."

The damage wasn't serious, and the brakes were quickly repaired and improved. Bissell wired a cable back to CIA headquarters to let everyone know how the plane fared. "No ill effects," the cable stated, "except to Tony's ego."

A few days later, on August 4, they decided to take the plane up to eight thousand feet for its first real test flight. LeVier once again climbed into the cockpit, and Johnson got into a C-47 "chase plane" that would tail the U-2 in the air.

LeVier took off a little before 4:00 p.m. and leveled at the target altitude. He spent about forty-five minutes testing the flaps and the landing gear, checking the temperatures and exhaust pressure, and practicing engine stalls and restarts. No problems. "Kelly, it flies like a baby buggy," LeVier said over his radio.

Landing, however, was the challenge. "Remember," Johnson radioed to LeVier, "I want you to land it on the nose wheel."

He tried to. The wheel touched and bounced back into the air, forcing him to ascend again. The U-2 simply didn't want to stay on the ground. "Take it around and come in even lower than last time," Johnson said. LeVier did as instructed and got the same result. His next three attempts were similarly unsuccessful, even the one in which he forcefully jammed the control wheel down to try to drive the front wheel into the runway.

Johnson, frustrated, kept shouting instructions into his radio headset. The sun was about to disappear, and he could see that a rainstorm was gathering force. Desperate, LeVier brought it low to the ground and went into a controlled stall, and the two wheels—front and back—hit the ground at the same time. He adjusted the gust control flaps on the wings, which helped keep the plane down.

Within minutes after touchdown, the skies opened, flooding the runway with two inches of rain.

That night, everyone celebrated with beers in the mess hall. "Tony, you did a great job today," Johnson said. As he downed more beers, Johnson seemed to absorb the fact that he'd actually managed to deliver a flyable plane to the government within his eight-month deadline, and he did it under budget. He buzzed with manic energy, and before the night was over, he was challenging everyone to arm-wrestling contests. When it was LeVier's turn to lock hands with Johnson, the designer slammed the pilot's arm down on the table with a sudden, painful, thwack.

The next day, a bleary-eyed Johnson spotted LeVier with a bandage wrapped around his wrist.

"What the hell happened to you?" Johnson asked.

Johnson must have been a happy man, LeVier decided, if he'd partied so hard that he now couldn't even remember the party.

THE BISSELL HOUSE ON THE CORNER of Newark and Thirty-Fourth in Cleveland Park was big and comfortable, and Richard and Annie made no effort to disguise the fact that they shared the space with four children and a dog. If Bissell had grown up the scion of wealth and a stuffy sort of privilege, he'd lost the desire to prove it somewhere along the way. Laundry, toys, and generalized calamity seemed to spill from every corner, except from the third floor; a sign on the stairway leading to it read, "Parents Only." On the second floor, young Ann, in her early teens, had converted a broom closet into a darkroom, where she indulged her passion for photography. Downstairs, her brother Richie tinkered with radios and tape machines, taking them apart and spreading the pieces on the floor (Richie once dangled a homemade listening device inside the family fireplace; a few years after that, his father got him a summer job as a technician at the CIA, where he helped record language-learning tapes for foreign officers). When someone knocked on the front door, the dog would bark, the kids would race down the stairs, and everyone converged in the front hall, eager to see who was there.

If the kids saw Edwin Land standing at the door, it was a cause for silent celebration; he'd hand out the latest cameras and accessories from

Polaroid as gifts. Kelly Johnson was greeted like a fun-loving uncle: he was loud and animated and never failed to turn on the charm when Mrs. Bissell emerged, gallantly presenting her with another bottle of perfume ("*real* perfume," Ann Bissell later recalled, "not eau de toilette"). The kids knew the rules: before dinner, they were free to mingle, but they would be expected to make themselves scarce afterward. During those predinner chats, Land was unfailingly polite and curious about the kids' hobbies, while Johnson picked around the mischievous edges of things. Once, he piqued young Ann's curiosity about photography by telling her he'd heard that someone had come up with a camera that could take a picture of a parking lot from miles away and the prints were so clear you could pick out a golf ball sitting on the pavement. The girl was astonished; she'd never heard of such a thing.

Bissell manned the bar, which was always topped with dozens of bottles. For Land, he might offer one of the first-growth Bordeaux wines he regularly bought down at Pearson's Wine & Spirits. For Johnson and Annie, it was usually bourbon or scotch. For himself, he'd mix Campari, vermouth, and soda water in a tall glass.

When the three men finally kicked back to talk shop after dinner, they relaxed into an easy familiarity. In less than a year, the trio at the center of the U-2 project had become more than just colleagues; they were genuine friends. They'd come from totally different backgrounds, but their similarities were striking. They'd been born within nine months of one another. None of them had served in the military, yet each of them had made significant contributions to the war effort during the 1940s. All of them could rattle off a list of enviable achievements, yet they seemed to assume that their most important work was ahead of them. And all three of them shared a bedrock faith that the force that would shape their careers, and the future of their country, was the transformative power of technology.

Perhaps it's not surprising that a physicist and an engineer would be technophiles, but an agency bureaucrat? Yet Bissell had become something of an evangelist for science and technology, so much so that some of his colleagues in the CIA had begun to suspect that he might be secretly plotting to replace a whole staff of foreign operatives with "technological solutions," machines that could secretly trespass into forbidden territories and record huge caches of raw data, leaving it to the specialists in Washington to sort through it all.

Even if Bissell's technological bent was starting to feel "unsettling in its coolness," as one colleague in the CIA described it, it wasn't as if he, Land, and Johnson believed they could completely eliminate living, breathing spies in their quest to invent a more efficient model of intelligence gathering. Yet they did envision a new kind of spy, one who was, essentially, purpose-built. In the past, tools were developed to help spies do their jobs, but they wanted to try doing it the other way around: choose and develop the spies based on their ability to use the tools. Now the technology came first.

CHAPTER 4

# The Human Element

I have never thought of myself as a spy, yet in a certain sense this
attitude is probably naïve.

—FRANK POWERS

About four miles south of Albany, Georgia, at the end of a curving driveway that meandered off Highway 19, the Radium Springs Casino sat on the sandy banks of a deep natural spring. The name of the place was a little misleading—no games of chance were ever played at the casino—but since it opened in 1927, Radium Springs had earned a reputation as one of the classiest resorts in the southern half of the state. The eighteen-hole golf course attracted some of the best players in the Southeast. On weekends, the casino—with its tiered sunporches and its fifth-floor cupola—was often filled with wedding parties, and during the week the crowd was split between tourists and conventioneers. The resort's brochures said that the waters in its natural bathing stream maintained year-round temperatures of sixty-eight degrees. A miniature locomotive, which could carry up to twenty passengers, ran on tracks between the resort's various buildings, which by the 1950s included a motor lodge that advertised reasonable rates "for the discriminating traveler and vacationer." The guests stayed in cottages—single-room, ranch-style units with yellow siding and limestone trim.

Around seven o'clock on a late winter's evening, it was already dark when Lieutenant Frank Powers, a reservist in the 468th Fighter Squadron, drove through the magnolias and longleaf pines toward the motel. The lights were on inside cottage 1, which sat at the end of the row. He got out of the car and approached the door.

Earlier in the day, his squadron commander had pulled him aside to tell him that as one of the best pilots on the base he might have the opportunity to serve his country on a special mission. The commander couldn't tell him anything about it, but he said if Powers was interested in hearing more, he should drive down to Radium Springs, about fifteen minutes south of their headquarters at Turner Air Force Base, and knock at cottage 1 at precisely seven o'clock.

The man who answered was in his mid-thirties, about five ten, of medium build, with black hair, and Powers noted that he was dressed in civilian clothes—as if he'd been cut out of the same mold as the two other men in the room behind him. All of them stood in silence, waiting for Powers to say the first word.

He felt a little awkward. "I was told to ask for a Mr. William Collins," Powers said, the words stretching slowly. His voice was soft and southern, with the sort of shy drawl that sometimes led others to suspect he was less complicated and quick-witted than he actually was.

"I'm Bill Collins. You must be . . ." Again, he waited for Powers to fill the silence.

"Lieutenant Powers."

Collins ushered him into the room. "I suppose you're wondering what this is all about?" he said. "I'm afraid there's not much I can tell you, at least at this time."

Collins was holding two typewritten sheets of paper in his hand, and he consulted them periodically as he spoke, as if following a script. Everything about this meeting—the man's caginess, the silence of the others who stood behind him, even the woodsy darkness that cloaked the motel—heightened a sense of mystery. Powers began to wonder if the effect was intentional, a strategy designed to arouse his curiosity.

"What I can say," Collins continued, "is this. You, and several other pilots, have been picked to be part of an organization to carry out a special mission. It will be risky, but patriotic. Should you decide to join us, you'll be doing something important for your country. The pay will be more than you are now receiving."

So far so good, Powers thought. But Collins refused to elaborate. "That's about all I can tell you now. What we'd like you to do is think about it overnight. Then, if you're still interested, call me here at the motel tomorrow. We'll arrange another meeting."

Although it had fought with the air force to retain control of the U-2 program, the CIA was still dependent on the air force's assistance; without the military, the agency wouldn't have anyone to fly its new planes. Luckily for Bissell, not every air force commander was as antagonistic as Curtis LeMay. Weeks before the meeting between Collins and Powers,

Bissell persuaded a few cooperative air force officials to wade through America's roster of pilots, searching for those who might be suited to join the CIA and fly the U-2. The pilots had to be between twenty-five and thirty-five years old, with at least five hundred hours at the controls of a jet, with experience using celestial navigation, and with stellar physical and psychological assessments. Bissell's office, with help from the air force, interviewed the squadron commanders of the pilots on the list, quizzing them about each pilot's ability to get along with others, his trustworthiness, and his ability to handle pressure. Eighteen of the pilots who made the initial cut, including Powers, were stationed at Turner Air Force Base in Albany, and Collins had come here to subject each of them to three interviews over three successive days. He made it clear during the initial interviews that the project wasn't a military one, but he didn't mention the CIA or elaborate on the organizational structure. An interagency memo written by Bissell laid out early guidelines for recruitment and predicted that "if properly approached," enough qualified young pilots would volunteer for hazardous duty without being told who, exactly, would be employing them. "The pilots would be told that this was an organization backed by a group of American philanthropists, organized with at least tacit approval of the United States Government," the memo stated.

Six of the potential recruits, frustrated by Collins's unwillingness to answer their questions, pulled themselves out of contention immediately, saying they weren't interested in hearing more; they signed secrecy agreements, and Collins wished them well, assuring them it would have no impact on their air force careers.

But Powers was intrigued, and he leaned into the conversation, eager for details. His interest shouldn't have come as a surprise to Collins. The pilot's squadron commander had raved about the twenty-six-year-old, who was a member of the unit's air gunnery team and flew F-84 Thunderstreaks, turbojet fighters that had just become operational in 1954. In the four years since he'd entered basic training, Powers had performed well in advanced survival training, had aced his lessons in how to resist brainwashing, and had earned a top secret clearance that allowed him to learn about nuclear weapons, which one day he might be asked to launch from a fighter jet. He was a good athlete and during the previous year's pentathlon competition, which mixed fast-paced obstacle courses with a ten-mile "escape and evasion" drill, finished third out of the hundreds of airmen at Turner. He'd once been forced to bail out of a plane in midair, which the CIA recruiters interpreted as a good sign: his mettle had been tested in a pressure situation, and he'd kept his head. In an assessment of his military record, he was labeled "possibly counterphobic," a term used to describe people who embrace risk and are often attracted to, rather than repelled by, the things that scare them most. On top of all that, Powers had even been trained as a military photographer, and at Lowry Air Force Base in Colorado he'd worked as a photo lab technician.

In short, he was perfect for the U-2.

Except for one thing, an aspect of the job that Collins had saved for last. The work would require Powers to be apart from his family for eighteen months or more, and he wouldn't be able to tell anyone—not even his closest family member or friend—what exactly he was doing, or even where he was living. In an early interagency memo, the recruitment guidelines stipulated that the pilots must be single. Eventually, however, that prerequisite had been dropped, and it was decided that each pilot's aptitude for secrecy would be evaluated individually.

Powers, who'd been ready to accept the assignment on the spot, wilted when Collins mentioned the forced separation. He told Collins that he believed he'd have to turn down the offer. He'd been married for less than a year, he said.

Collins said he was sorry to hear it but urged Powers to sleep on it. In the notes he typed up after the meeting, the officer wrote of Powers, "Was not sure at time of first interview just how wife would feel about the separation and he asked permission to discuss this one factor with her." Collins told him that would be fine: he could mention the job offer to her, and he could explain that it would provide them with more money than he currently made, but no further details should be discussed.

BARBARA GAY MOORE WAS A FORCE of nature. She'd grown up fast, bouncing with her family from one dirt-road town to another in northern Florida and southern Georgia. Her uncle Joe Beck—"gallus-snappin', snuff-dippin', moonshine-lovin' Uncle Joe," as she remembered him—had put her to work driving a two-ton watermelon truck when she was just twelve years old. No one thought much of it, because even at that age Barbara didn't *seem* young; she'd skipped two grades of grammar school and was set to graduate from Albany High School at fourteen. When she was fifteen, she enrolled in a business college for women, and about two and a half years later she was working as a stenographer at the Marine Corps Depot of Supplies in Albany. She possessed a rare, unembarrassed confidence and exuded spiky down-home sass. She was also considered pretty, with short black hair and big, dark eyes that she'd narrow playfully, as if she were looking out at the world from some mischievous inner core that was always cooking up trouble.

Often, after she'd get off work, she would drive over to Turner Air Force Base, where her mother worked as a night cashier in the cafeteria. One night in August 1953, she was reading a book when she saw an athletic young officer with coal-black hair walk into the cafeteria. Frank Powers, who'd arrived on base just a month earlier, noticed her, too, but seemed too shy to talk to her. Barbara's mother helped him out. "That's my oldest daughter," she told him.

He thought she was funny, whip smart, and as good-looking as any girl in Albany. He'd grown up among the coal mines of rural Virginia, and they swapped stories of their backcountry roots. Her acid wit, unfiltered by even the slightest desire to appear a demure southern belle, could be a bracing shock to some, but he was smitten. He'd always been addicted to adventure—exploring caves, parachuting from planes, hiking in forests—and she seemed up for anything. On weekends they'd drive to the Florida coast, where she'd water-ski right alongside him, and they'd retreat to a bar together to drink rum punches. They laughed loud, hard, and often. But they fought the same way.

Powers lived with three other pilots in a small house on the edge of Albany. In his roommates' eyes, Barbara was often the life of the party, and her no-holds-barred approach struck them as anything but conventional in small-town America in the 1950s. While other girls struggled to appear restrained and self-controlled, Barbara didn't seem to regard either as a virtue, and some people didn't trust her as a result. They talked about her—about her drinking, about how she seemed a little too comfortable in the company of men. Powers's roommates assumed he must surely have heard some of the talk, but he seemed to ignore it. He said he planned to marry her, and his friends silently waited for the whole thing to fall apart. And it did. Several times.

Once, Barbara lost her temper and threw the ring that Powers had given to her into the Flint River. They split up but soon got back together, establishing a cycle they'd repeat constantly during their engagement. He often had to travel, once as far as Japan on a flying mission, and resentments grew during those absences. But they always fell in love again. Once, during one of his trips, he wrote a poem to her:

*Could you be patient, dearest one,*
*And could you go along*
*If all the world were upside down,*
*And everything seemed wrong?*

*Could you contain your temper*
*If you thought I were to blame?*
*Or, would you just ignore me*
*And forget my humble name?*

*How much would you believe in me*
*If nothing turned out right?*
*How long would you remain with me*
*To wage a desperate flight?*

*The answer to each question, dear,*
*Is solely up to you,*
*And my own love depends upon*
*Whatever you would do.*

*Unless your faith and promises*
*Could last forever more,*
*It would be better, darling, now*
*If we just closed the door.*

They were married on April 2, 1955. Barbara Powers later remembered a moment when they stood together at the altar: she leaned over to kiss him, biting him on the neck and telling him, "Now don't you keep flying away from me."

And here he was, less than a year later, arriving home late from work and telling her that they needed to have a serious talk. He mentioned their finances. Their combined take-home pay was about $700 a month, they were falling behind on their car payments, and if things continued on this same path, they'd eventually be buried in debt. He told her he'd been recruited to participate in an important mission that would earn him more money, perhaps quite a bit more. The only catch, he explained, was that they would have to live apart for a while.

They talked for much of the night, debating the pros and cons. The next day, he called Collins back and told him he was still interested. He returned that afternoon to the Radium Springs Casino for a second round of interviews.

Collins fed him a few more details. If Powers got into the program, his salary would be set at $1,500 a month during his initial training period in the United States; then it would jump to $2,500 when he was deployed overseas. Powers could hardly believe what he was hearing; that was more money than he ever dreamed of making in the military, and it was almost as much as a senior captain for one of the big commercial airlines could expect. And there was more. Collins told him that he would be asked to fly a plane that was unlike any that he'd ever seen, one that would carry him higher into the stratosphere than any human had ever gone before.

His imagination caught fire. "I'm in," Powers said.

It wasn't that simple. The vetting process, Collins explained, had only just begun.

PRESIDENT EISENHOWER EYED ALLEN DULLES with skepticism. The CIA director was talking about the U-2 recruitment efforts, explaining that each prospective pilot would decide for himself whether the world of covert operations suited him. "You won't have many volunteers to fly over Russia," the president predicted. It was simply too dangerous for an American. What if a U-2 was forced down in Soviet territory? Even if the plane had no markings or identifying tags connecting it to the United States, how could Eisenhower deny his involvement and knowledge of the overflight when the pilot was obviously an American?

"It would seem that you would be able to recruit some Russians or pilots of other nationalities," Eisenhower suggested.

Dulles promised him he'd give it a try.

He assigned the task to Bissell. "In order to have a second string to our bow," Bissell explained in an internal memo, "we have recruited and are carrying out the basic training of some six to eight non-U.S. [pilots] who could be used if political circumstances dictated." The foreign recruits included Greek and Polish pilots, and none of them spoke English well—a complication that tested Johnson's patience. "It's been decided to use only American pilots from now on," Johnson noted in his journal, "thank God." The foreign pilots were reassigned to other training missions and kept in the United States for more than a year after their dismissal, "because of the extensive knowledge of the whole operation they had acquired," according to a CIA report.

One of the reasons it was easy to get rid of the foreign pilots, despite Eisenhower's urgings, was that their presence complicated the cover story that Bissell was drafting. During the plane's development phases in Burbank and Area 51, he determined that if any unauthorized personnel found out about the program, the CIA's involvement could be hidden by telling them that the U-2 was a joint air force and Atomic Energy Commission project designed to test the air quality of the upper atmosphere. But if the CIA ever deployed the planes at U.S. bases overseas, as it planned to do, additional explanations would be necessary. Early in 1956, the CIA concluded that the U-2's cover story would be that the plane was an experimental craft of the National Advisory Committee for Aeronautics used to compile global weather data, "cloud atlas photography," and air samples to help assess worldwide weather patterns. Because interception over hostile territory was a concern, additional meteorological equipment, such as air-sampling filters, was added to the planes' Q-bays.

Bissell held a meeting with senior air force officials to finalize the cover story in the spring of 1956. In May, a press release titled "NACA Announces Start of New Research Program" was drafted in Bissell's office. It read,

The need for more detailed information about gust-meteorological conditions to be found at high altitude, as high as 50,000 feet, has resulted in the inauguration of an expanded research program to provide the needed data, Dr. Hugh L. Dryden, Director of the National Advisory Committee for Aeronautics, announced today.

"Tomorrow's jet transports will be flying air routes girdling the earth," Dr. Dryden said. "This they will do at altitudes far higher than presently used except by a few military aircraft. The availability of a new type of airplane, which is one of several that will be used in the program, helps us obtain the needed data in an economical and expeditious manner." . . .

Among specific research goals will be more precise information about air turbulence, convective clouds, wind shear, and the jet

stream. Richard V. Rhode, Assistant Director for Research of
the NACA, said that as a result of information so to be gained,
tomorrow's air travelers might expect degrees of speed, safety and
comfort beyond the hope of the air transport operators.

"The program would not have been possible," Mr. Rhode said,
"without the ability of American scientific efforts to join forces."

Edwin Land didn't like what he was reading. Why such elaborate
deception? He urged Bissell to accompany him and James Killian to a
meeting at the White House, where they could go over the cover story
one more time with Andrew Goodpaster, who was Eisenhower's staff
secretary and defense liaison.

The president, Goodpaster said, generally approved of the current
plans. Even so Land recommended changing those plans and coming
up with a new, more honest cover story in case a plane was lost over
enemy territory—"a much bolder action by the U.S. involving admission that overflights were being conducted to guard against surprise
attack." It was a matter of principle to Land: err on the side of truth,
not lies. Bissell didn't seem convinced. In his notes after the meeting,
he wrote, "It was left that we would think further about this matter and
perhaps suggest several alternative courses of action which would be
discussed with someone in the Department of State and among which a
choice could be made on short notice." No records exist suggesting that
changes to the cover story, or a plan to tell the truth in case of disaster,
were ever considered.

Kelly Johnson dove headfirst into the cover story, perhaps because
he'd considered Skunk Works a monument to subterfuge from the start.
Lockheed's Burbank campus during World War II was as thoroughly
enveloped in pretense and pantomime as any Hollywood studio lot.
Worried about the possibility that Japanese bombers might reach the
West Coast and target the facility, camouflage experts with the U.S.
Army Air Corps teamed with crews from the big studios—Paramount,
Disney, 20th Century Fox—to erect tall wooden scaffolds between the
Lockheed buildings and spread massive swaths of camouflage netting
over the works. Employees from the studios' prop departments painted
images onto the dense netting—make-believe subdivisions, quiet streets,
harmless residential rooftops—and stretched them over the equivalent
of several city blocks. The netting was green, which meant that creating front yards was easy, yet the artists sometimes took the extra step

of painting some of the "lawns" brown, to suggest the residents had neglected to water them. Some of the illusory houses and public buildings were constructed using flimsy frames and canvas coverings. They also created realistic shrubs and bushes using chicken wire and burlap. Trees were made from wire molds, then covered with tar and chicken feathers before being sprayed green—a process that gave them a natural leafy look from the air. Inflatable automobiles were positioned on top of the netted screens to appear as if they were parked along the "streets," and the workers changed their positions every few days; if the Japanese were to send bombers on successive weeks to search for military factories, the seemingly dynamic streets of that Burbank neighborhood wouldn't raise suspicions. Everyone who worked at Lockheed during that time, Johnson included, learned that pretending to be something you weren't wasn't just part of the job; it was a patriotic duty.

The report that war hero Jimmy Doolittle had submitted to Eisenhower—the one that said "hitherto acceptable norms of human conduct do not apply" to the CIA in a covert war with the Soviets—made a certain amount of sense to Johnson. He had known Doolittle since the 1930s, when the celebrated pilot was flying a Lockheed Orion and needed the engineer to design new landing gear for him, and their friendship solidified early in World War II when Doolittle flew Johnson's P-38 Lightning on missions. Johnson never offered an opinion of the Doolittle Report for the record, but everything he said and wrote suggested that he believed defeating the Soviets *by whatever means necessary* was itself a morally righteous purpose. If outright deception was what it took to keep America safe from a nuclear attack, he was willing to throw himself headlong into the effort.

Johnson and Bissell decided that the pilots brought into the CIA's fold would be disguised as Lockheed employees, complete with aliases, false IDs, and bogus contracts identifying them as "Flight Test Consultants." To Johnson, devising secret strategies might have felt like something that came straight out of the pages of *Tom Swift and His Sky Racer,* a childhood favorite. In that story, Tom's arch nemesis tried to foil his quest to win a $10,000 airplane race by stealing his plans and copying his design. In the end, Tom burned his rival, winning the money and a government contract, in part because he created a fake set of plans. "I've put in a whole lot of wrong figures and measurements, and scores of lines and curves that mean nothing," Tom says in the novel. "I have marked the right figures and lines by a secret mark, and when I work on them I'll use only the proper ones. But any one else wouldn't know this. Oh, I'll fool 'em this time!"

At Lockheed, Johnson assigned four engineers to create a fake flight manual for the U-2, something that might be placed in Soviet hands, if the need ever arose. According to the manual, the plane could reach a maximum altitude of about fifty thousand feet. Its Q-bays were equipped solely with meteorological equipment. The phony manual included photographs of the instrument panels, but the gauge markings had been altered to convey false speed, altitude, and load-factor limits. To make it appear as if the manual had been passed around among pilots and mechanics, copies were marked with grease, coffee stains, and cigarette burns.

INSIDE THE DUPONT PLAZA HOTEL IN WASHINGTON, a young man signed the guest registry, using a signature he'd never tried out before: Francis G. Palmer. It was the name on his new driver's license and on the work contracts he'd been given in case anyone asked him too many questions.

Everything felt strange—the new identity, the civilian clothes, the slightly disquieting notion that his wife had no idea where he was or what he was doing. He turned the key to his room and waited inside until the phone rang. When he picked up the receiver, he was greeted by the familiar voice of Collins, who gave him his own room number and told him to stop by.

The other four pilots from Turner were already there. The room looked unremarkable—a small Pullman kitchen, a radio on a bureau, an air conditioner, a black dial phone, thick drapes, venetian blinds, a separate bedroom—but the CIA's security man was treating it like some sort of crime scene. He took the picture frames off the walls, examined every inch of a chest of drawers, peeked under the bed. Collins, meanwhile, appeared more relaxed than he had in Georgia. He put a little music on the radio and pulled a photograph out of his briefcase.

It was the first time Powers or any of the others had seen the U-2. "What do you call it?" one of them asked.

"No one calls it anything publicly yet," Collins said. "This project is so secret . . ."

Powers was struggling to hear Collins over the radio music, so he turned it off. But as soon as the music stopped, so did Collins; he shot Powers a hard, silent stare. The message was clear: the music was a security protocol, something to mask their voices in case the security officer had failed to notice any hidden listening devices during his sweep. Powers, embarrassed, turned the music back on.

One by one, the pilots were called into the bedroom, and the door was closed behind them. A machine that looked like a large tape recorder, with lots of buttons and a roll of paper, sat on a table. A man Powers had never met told him to take a seat. "Ever see one of these before?" he asked. It was a polygraph machine, and Powers was terrified. "While I'm strapping you in," the man said, "you can look over this list of questions."

If Powers harbored any embarrassing secrets—the kind that an enemy might exploit to blackmail him—the questions and the machine were supposed to pull them out into the open. He knew he had nothing serious to hide, but that didn't mean the ordeal wasn't humiliating. His loyalty, his integrity, his fundamental human decency—all of it felt as if it were under attack. When it was over, the man simply unhooked the sensors and acted as if nothing out of the ordinary had happened.

He must have passed the test, because the next day he and the other pilots were told they'd undergo extensive physical examinations in Nebraska. When Powers traveled to Omaha for the exams, he found Collins waiting for him at the airport. The CIA man had a surprise for him: the examinations wouldn't take place in Nebraska. Collins handed Powers a series of plane tickets that sent him backtracking to St. Louis and then on to New Mexico. Powers assumed his maddeningly indirect journey was designed to shake anyone who might have been following him; it seemed unnecessarily elaborate—comically so—but he didn't question it.

Eventually, he landed at the city airport on the lonely outskirts of Albuquerque, New Mexico. About a mile from the airport, down a windblown road surrounded by khaki-colored desolation, sat the Lovelace Clinic, where the limits of the pilots' tolerance for pain and fatigue would be measured, challenged, and at times overwhelmed.

THE PLACE WAS RUN BY William Randolph Lovelace II, a man everyone called Randy. In the 1930s he'd been a pioneer of oxygen deprivation research at the Mayo Clinic, and in World War II he'd been put in charge of the U.S. Army Air Force Aero Medical Laboratory in Dayton. After the war, Lovelace returned to his native Albuquerque and transformed his father's medical clinic into a foundation for medical research. In 1951, the clinic won a grant from the Atomic Energy

Commission to evaluate the "biodynamics" of nuclear detonations. The clinic's specialists conducted field and laboratory experiments with more than a dozen different kinds of mammals—guinea pigs, rabbits, dogs, sheep, monkeys, cows—and quantified the unnatural damage that nuclear shock waves from bomb tests had inflicted on them. They counted the scars inside the lungs of exposed dogs, devised "lethality-time curves" for small versus large animals, and sketched diagrams with labels like "Accumulative Percent of Mortally Wounded Animals Dying over the 24-Hour Period Following Whole-Body Impact." The work, grim as it was, earned Lovelace the trust of AEC bureaucrats who were always on the lookout for contractors who knew how to keep secrets.

A year earlier, in 1955, Bissell's office had reached out to the clinic to see if its specialists might be able to help the CIA evaluate the strain that extraordinarily high altitudes might put on U-2 pilots. Randy Lovelace tapped Dr. Donald Kilgore, who'd joined his staff less than two years earlier, to visit the CIA officials running the program for a briefing. Kilgore hopped on a TWA flight to Burbank, where he waited inside the airport with his black medical satchel on his lap—a sign that would allow his contact to identify him. Sure enough, a stranger eventually approached Kilgore where he sat, telling him to return to the Lockheed gate at the airport the next morning at 5:30. By the time dawn rolled around, he was aboard a plane that eventually landed on a dry lake bed in what looked like the dead center of nowhere. That's where Kilgore learned about the U-2 and got the job to oversee the medical evaluations for the program's recruits.

At the clinic, Kilgore welcomed the four pilots to Albuquerque—"the brownest, dustiest place in the country," as he called it. Kilgore couldn't promise them that all of the tests they'd soon undergo would be *enjoyable,* but if anyone among the thirty or so specialists could put the pilots at ease, he was the man to do it. He spoke their language and knew something of their world; Kilgore was a pilot himself, and a good one. Before he'd even turned twenty-three, he'd flown more than eighty combat missions in the South Pacific, earning himself the Distinguished Flying Cross. Now, at thirty-four and with a soft smile and kind eyes, he didn't seem that much older than they were.

That's not to say that *all* of the specialists in Lovelace put them at ease. The clinic's leading authority on the physiological effects of high altitude was a tall, stern, redheaded German named Ulrich Luft. Like Kilgore, Luft knew something about adventure, but his experience was darkly tragic. In 1937, Luft attempted to climb the 26,660-foot summit of Nanga Parbat in the Himalayas to conduct physiological tests on the members of a seventeen-man expeditionary team; an avalanche devoured the group, killing every last person except Luft, whose story of lone survival made newspapers around the world. During the war, he had continued his physiological research, but on behalf of a research unit in Hitler's Luftwaffe that was later denounced for being involved in human medical experiments—immersing people in freezing water, exposing them to extreme air pressures—at the Dachau concentration camp. Luft himself was never implicated in those crimes, but his presence at the clinic did little to calm the pilots' nerves.

By the end of a full week at Lovelace, Powers and the other pilots were ready to fly as far from Albuquerque as they could get. For eight hours every day they were poked, penetrated, measured, and manhandled. Electrodes were attached to their scalps. Their arms were plunged in buckets of ice, just to see how long they could stand it. They were made to ride a stationary bike while breathing into a bag, which drained the oxygen from their cells until they doubled up with a stiffness that let them know what rigor mortis must feel like. They were jammed into tight, hot, dark spaces as the doctors tried to squeeze the slightest vestige of claustrophobia out of them. They were pushed past the edge of exhaustion while the doctors calmly jotted their vitals on their ever-present clipboards. In one of the most puzzling experiments for the pilots, they were told to sit on a chair in a silent room for two hours. Nothing happened. Powers believed it might have been the only test he failed. When the doctors came to check on him, he had fallen asleep.

FROM THE AIR, THE BASE at Area 51 now looked like a tiny, rectilinear city constructed of children's blocks. Three airplane hangars stood side by side, and dozens of silver trailers sat a short walk away, where up to 175 people—4 to a trailer—could sleep. Another trailer contained the "classroom" where the recruits could attend ground school and study their preflight checklists, and nearby was a mobile photography unit complete with air-conditioning and dehumidifiers. An air control tower was erected near the runways, and a water tower doubled as a security guard perch. At night, most everyone gathered in the mess hall, where a pool table and 16 mm movie screenings provided the nightly entertainment.

Kelly Johnson spent much of his time at the base, arriving in a C-54 transport shuttle that made daily flights to and from Burbank. Even after the initial test flights, he continued to tinker with critical components of the plane. It quickly became clear that the engine was leaking oil, which would vaporize and enter the cockpit through the high-pressure compressor. The windshield would fog over with an oily film, which meant the pilot would have to wipe it clean with a swab mounted on the end of a stick. Some of the engineers worried that even a little bit of hot oil in the cockpit could be an explosion risk, given that the pilots would be breathing highly volatile pure oxygen inside their helmets. On top of that, the air from the cockpit was recycled to pressurize the Q-bays, which meant the glass surfaces on the equipment might also be clouded in greasy fog. The images from the cameras could be spoiled and, along with them, the plane's entire reason for being.

One of the mechanics at the site heard a Lockheed engineer complaining about the problem and suggested a quick fix. "Why don't we just stuff Kotex around the oil filter and absorb the mess before it hits the windshield?" The idea bounced around the base until it reached Johnson, who figured it was worth a try. One of Johnson's engineers in Burbank was soon calling the techs stationed at Paradise Ranch, telling them to "stand by for a delivery of industrial-size cartons of sanitary napkins."

Johnson's knack for improvisation made some people connected to the program nervous. They worried his tendency to "grab the ball and run without waiting for signals," as one CIA report phrased it, might prove contagious. Someday, one of those balls might be dropped. One too many corners would be cut. Everyone knew the mechanics often smoked cigarettes on the job, even when they were refueling the planes. It might not have seemed like a big deal to them—you could practically hold a blowtorch to U-2 fuel and the stuff wouldn't burn—but what if one of those mechanics wasn't thinking and mindlessly fired up a Marlboro when he was gassing up the C-54 shuttle? The whole project, and people's lives, might be jeopardized.

It was the C-54 shuttle to Lockheed, in fact, that soon showed everyone just how costly human error could be. On a morning about three months after the first test flights started, the daily shuttle from Lockheed failed to show up on time. The pilot, it was later discovered, had ignored several of the standard protocols before he took off that morning. He didn't fill out the preflight forms correctly. And when he saw that a storm was pushing in behind him as he crossed the state line into

Nevada, he decided to change his route and veer off the normal flight path, without informing anyone else.

In addition to the pilot, the shuttle carried thirteen passengers— camera specialists, aeronautical engineers, and CIA officers. Among them was William H. Marr, whom Bissell had put in charge of overseeing all security surrounding the U-2 project. The flight was rocked by heavy winds, and any passengers looking out the windows could see mountainous peaks looming close. The pilot yanked on the yoke as he approached Mount Charleston, about forty miles west of Las Vegas. Just fifty feet below the mountain's crest, at about 11,300 feet, the left wing clipped the snowy slope and snapped off. The nose pancaked into the rocks, the fuselage snapped in half, and the passengers were hurled against the mountainside.

When a cable reached Bissell's office informing him of the plane's disappearance, everyone scrambled. The news that five CIA men were aboard, personal friends to many, "added an emotional overtone to the crisis atmosphere prevailing at Project Headquarters," according to a CIA report.

The wreckage was spotted later that day. Curious residents near Mount Charleston and journalists who tried to drive closer to the scene were stopped at the entrance of Highway 158 and told to turn around. As the *Las Vegas Review-Journal* reported, "A complete veil of secrecy was clamped on information on the ground. All questions were countered with a grim shake of the head."

The air force tried to deploy paratroopers to the crash site, but the winds were too strong. Instead, a recovery team strapped on snowshoes and hiked up the mountain with seventeen horses, which would help them carry the bodies and the victims' personal belongings down the mountain. An amphibious military airplane kept constant watch on the team and maintained radio contact with the air force colonels leading the mission. When they finally reached the crash site, the horses' legs were bloodied from plunging through the hard, encrusted snow. They loaded the frozen bodies onto the horses, and among the items they bagged was a wristwatch that was stuck at 8:19—perhaps the precise moment of impact.

One item they failed to find was a briefcase that William Marr had carried with him on board the plane. As the project's security chief, he had access to its most classified, most sensitive details, and many of them were inside that briefcase. After a supervisor with the U.S. Forest

Service—who wasn't told anything about the U-2 project, the classified work of the passengers, or the briefcase—mentioned that thousands of weekend hikers climbed the mountain every spring and summer, the CIA decided some follow-up was necessary. In the spring of 1956, the air force dispatched another crew to the site. The crew rooted around on the ground for hours, but they still didn't find the briefcase.

The crew placed explosives around the remaining wreckage and blew it to bits.

THE FLIGHT CREW WHEELED THE PLANE out of the hangar, and Powers struggled to compare it to anything he'd flown before. It looked like some fragile, mutant fowl. Its thin aluminum skin shone like polished chrome in the strong Nevada sun. Its proportions were all wrong.

He couldn't wait to fly it.

First, though, he needed to log a week or two in the classroom trailer getting up to speed on some basics. Because he would be flying so high, one of the biggest risks he'd face was a sudden loss of air pressure in the cockpit. If that happened in the thin air above fifty thousand feet, the gases existing naturally inside his bodily fluids would rapidly expand; this would cause the blood to "boil," and his skin would inflate like a balloon. For him to survive in such an emergency, a steady force of air would need to press against the skin, counteracting the swell. The air force partnered with a clothing manufacturer in Massachusetts to create a full-body pressure suit—a rubberized, body-hugging garment with an inflatable bladder under the fabric that could apply about three pounds of pressure against every square inch of the pilot's body.

It was the most god-awful thing Powers had ever squeezed into. The fabric was stiff, with almost no give in it. If he tried to bend his arms or legs more than a couple inches, his skin would bruise. Long underwear made things a little more comfortable, but he had to be careful: a wrinkle or seam would leave painful indentations. The suit wasn't ventilated, so if Powers wore it for more than a few minutes—and he was told he'd eventually have to wear it for up to *twelve hours* at a time—his long underwear would get so waterlogged that he'd have to wring it out afterward. The glass-faced helmet they gave him fastened into a hermetic seal around the suit's neck, which Powers thought felt "exactly like a too-tight tie over a badly shrunk collar." As he sat there suffocating inside his new uniform, Powers experienced an epiphany: *this* must have been what those claustrophobia tests were all about at Lovelace.

In the classroom trailer, he was also taught how to "pre-breathe." Before every flight at full altitude, he would have to be hooked up to a tank of pressurized pure oxygen for up to two hours. This helped drain nitrogen out of his blood, which would help him avoid the bends. To anyone watching him undergo this ritual, it might have looked as if he were relaxing, without a care in the world. But it took some getting used to. Normally, inhaling feels as if it requires a tiny bit of effort, whereas exhaling feels like an involuntary relaxation, a letting go. When he was hooked up to the pressurized oxygen, the sensation was the opposite: exhalations required a small push, and the lungs filled up with oxygen automatically when they relaxed. After an hour or so of it, his head sometimes throbbed with pain.

Before he reported to Paradise Ranch in April 1956, eight other recruits had already begun their flight training. In just over three months, they'd collectively logged more than nine hundred hours in the air, sometimes going up for as long as nine and a half hours at a time. The first time Powers watched one of them take off, he knew that all of the discomfort he might have to endure before climbing into that snug cockpit would be worth it.

The plane required an absurdly short stretch of runway, less than a thousand feet, because almost as soon as it started rolling, it caught air. As soon as that happened—whoosh. It was swept away on a sudden tangent, the nose knifing upward at a forty-five-degree angle, and it simply vanished.

The other pilots warned him that the Angel could be a cantankerous machine, but the lessons he learned on the ground could only do so much. There were no flight simulators. Because the U-2 was a single-seater, he couldn't ride along with someone else to get a feel for it. In this plane, flying solo was simply the only way to fly.

His first runs were quick buzzes around the base at low altitude, without the pressure suit, so he could get the hang of landing it. It felt almost intangibly light. A normal plane can land with the engines running, but if he tried that in the U-2, the plane would never stay on the ground. He had to bring the plane in low and keep it level, taking care that the delicate wings didn't kiss the ground. When he was just about two feet off the ground, he had to kill the engine. If he stalled the plane too high, by even a foot or two, a hard landing could damage the plane; if he stalled it too low, the U-2 would lightly skip against the ground and bounce right back up in the air.

After mastering these touch-and-gos, he was allowed to take it up to altitude. His first quick ascent felt so steep that he was afraid the plane might flip over backward. When the U-2 steadied out at about forty-five thousand feet, the engine coughed and banged, and then it stalled. The other pilots had warned him about this. The engine had flamed out, but because the air was so thin at that height, it couldn't be relit. After a flameout, he had to carefully control his descent to thirty-five thousand feet or lower, then try to reignite it. Johnson's team was working on a new and improved engine to solve the problem, but Powers began his test flights with the original, problematic version. Sometimes he experienced as many as three flameouts in a single flight.

Perhaps the trickiest part of flying a U-2, and something that the new engine wouldn't fix, was a phenomenon the pilots called the "coffin corner." At altitudes above sixty-five thousand feet, the maximum speed the U-2 could safely fly was only 10 knots (about 11.5 miles per hour) higher than its *minimum* limit. If the speed exceeded that narrow range, the plane's nose would pitch down; that momentum would automatically cause the plane to pick up more speed as it plunged down into thicker air, exerting pressures that could tear the wings off the fuselage. If the speed dipped *below* that 10-knot safety range, the engine would stall—a problem that got harder to control at altitudes above sixty-five thousand feet and could send the plane into a dangerous spin. The aluminum encasing the plane was only 0.02 inch thick in many places, and if Powers thought about it too much, the margin between life and death felt even thinner.

After a few flights, his instructors allowed him to take the plane up to heights that no human—other than his fellow U-2 pilots—had ever reached. It was like entering another world, above the wind, above the weather. To look below him, he peered through an upside-down periscope, which he could swivel 360 degrees and set to different magnification levels. When he looked through the cockpit windows, his gaze could stretch across four hundred miles of landscape. The horizon, which seemed a flat line from most airplanes, appeared curved from the U-2. Because the nearest objects—the clouds and the earth—were so far away, there were no reference points up there to give him the sensation of speed. Even when he was cruising along at hundreds of miles per hour, it felt almost as if he were hanging suspended in the sky, motionless.

On the ground, his tranquillity might be scattered by a thousand distractions; here, it coalesced. After several hours in the air, some of the pilots wrote letters, or read books, or struggled mightily to keep from going numb in their seats. As some of the recruits complained, "You run outta ass before you run outta gas."

To Powers, the long flights were strangely satisfying. The silence was profound, meditative. He felt "a special aloneness" above seventy thousand feet, he said. Nothing could touch him up there.

According to newspapers around the world, a British pilot named Walter F. Gibb had recently set a new world altitude record in a Canberra jet, which for a brief instant reached 65,859 feet before descending back to safety.

Powers secretly broke that record and stayed above that milestone for hours at a time, nearly every time he climbed into the cockpit.

ON APRIL 14, 1956, RICHARD BISSELL picked up the phone in his office and got an earful of stress: A U-2 pilot recruit, Jake Kratt, had taken off from Paradise Ranch that morning on a long, routine training flight, and somewhere above the Mississippi River his engine flamed out. He descended to thirty-five thousand feet to restart it and managed to get it going for a little while. But it soon died again, and now he couldn't coax any life at all out of it.

As Bissell listened, Kratt was floating about six miles over the middle of America, steadily losing altitude, with no chance of getting back to the secret base.

The CIA had already decided that if any pilot was ever forced to make an emergency landing, he should try to come down at the nearest Strategic Air Command facility. Even without power, a U-2 could drift for hundreds of miles. In this case, the nearest base happened to be in Albuquerque, practically next door to the Lovelace Clinic. Kratt checked his coordinates and began gliding in its direction.

Bissell and others on his staff hurriedly began placing calls on secured lines. Bissell quickly got ahold of Albuquerque's base commander and said a "special aircraft" would be landing there in the next half hour or so, and he told him to quickly dispatch a military police crew to the runway. Before hanging up, Bissell tacked on a few more instructions that made it clear this was no ordinary forced landing: *Find a big tarp, throw it over the plane as soon as it comes to a standstill, and station guards beside it to make sure nobody peeks underneath.*

Within half an hour, the plane was on the runway, and Kratt—nerves a-jangle, but otherwise fine—was popping the roof on the cockpit. The puzzled military police on the ground had no idea what to make of him; in the pressure suit, he "looked like a man from Mars," one of the officers said. Another incredulously observed that the aircraft *wasn't even a real plane;* it was just a glider. Kratt was perfectly happy to let that assumption go unchallenged. Within minutes the U-2 was hidden under the tarp, Kratt was ushered into the commander's office, and plans were already under way to discreetly get him back to Area 51. Bissell's beleaguered heart, meanwhile, recovered from yet another averted crisis.

On that day, he was working out of "Quarters Eye," a two-story building near the Reflecting Pool and the Lincoln Memorial, close to the Potomac River. The structure was hurriedly built during World War II as a temporary barracks for the WAVES—Women Accepted for Volunteer Emergency Service with the U.S. Naval Reserve—but a shortage of federal office space after the war kept it in use. During the early months of 1956, the U-2 project headquarters kept outgrowing its offices. First, Bissell moved it out of the CIA headquarters on E Street to the third floor of a small, redbrick building a few blocks down the street that was, according to agency lore, a former whorehouse. The floors sagged, and Bissell was warned against bringing in any new furniture bigger than a typewriter. Conditions in Quarters Eye weren't dramatically better, but at least he had more space. By the middle of 1956, he was splitting his time working "down on the river" at Quarters Eye and in a new, larger office at 1717 H Street, about three blocks from the White House. The U-2 program was his primary responsibility, and it kept him and a growing staff very busy.

He ran the program, in his words, as if it were his own "private duchy," keeping a close eye on everything from personnel files, production schedules, payroll, flight testing, technical hiccups, and, of course, maintaining secrecy. He lobbied Dulles to remove the entire project from the CIA's own classified organizational chart; it was, in effect, a secret inside a secret. It was the only office within the agency that had its own communications office and that maintained its own, dedicated network of cable traffic. Normally, every CIA cable sent to or from any agency station around the world—even the most sensitive ones—was copied and delivered to Dulles's office. But not the ones that passed

Bissell's desk. "No one saw copies of cables except on my release," he recalled. By the end of 1956, the U-2 project was generating about one-fifth of the CIA's total cable traffic.

To the people who worked for him, he seemed to be coping incredibly well with the workload. His knack for untangling complex logistical challenges was a wonder to behold, and the way he consistently extinguished crises earned him an unusual level of trust from those who worked under him. He was their general, and the nicknames that started bouncing around Quarters Eye and the headquarters building nicely captured his newfound authority. The guys at Lockheed still called the plane the Angel, but around the CIA it became "Bissell's Bird." His office was "the Bissell Center." The shuttle service that flew between Burbank and Paradise Ranch was "Bissell's Narrow-Gauge Airline." Officially, the U-2 project was code-named Aquatone, but as it grew to include a fleet of more than a dozen planes and nearly twenty pilots, they started calling it the RBAF—Richard Bissell's Air Force.

Curtis LeMay—a *real* general, in the *actual* air force—bristled with contempt. Even though Bissell took pride in the smooth working relationship he'd established with the air force officers who effectively served under him, he couldn't help feeling a little twinge of delight at LeMay's expense. Eisenhower had made it clear that civilians should be in charge of the program; if something ever went wrong, he didn't want the Soviets to be able to say that the U.S. military had invaded their airspace. To LeMay and General Nathan Twining, the two who'd plotted to snatch control of the program after the CIA started it, Eisenhower's decision to keep the program in civilian hands felt like a betrayal by a military brother. But some of LeMay and Twining's colleagues, once they saw how things were shaping up under Bissell's direction, quietly supported the CIA. "Amusingly enough," Bissell later recalled, "at least two other very senior Air Force commanders found occasion to say to Allen Dulles, privately, that LeMay shouldn't be allowed, and I quote, 'to get his cotton-picking fingers on the U-2 project.'"

Tweaking LeMay appealed to an iconoclastic streak that had run through Bissell's core since he was a kid, leading him to defy orthodoxy at almost every turn. Back at Groton, the Reverend Endicott Peabody, an august Episcopal priest who'd founded the school in the 1880s, once called Bissell into his office after he'd planted a powerful stink bomb in Joe Alsop's room. Peabody judged Bissell's deed "not evil but mischievous" and let him off with some light punishment. Far more serious in Peabody's eyes, however, was another matter that later came to his attention: at one of the most prestigious Christian schools in America, designed to instill devotion in the hearts of young men, Bissell had begun to declare that he was an atheist. A few years later, he and a group of friends at Yale would smear black greasepaint on their faces and climb the roofs of campus buildings, dropping into the windows of friends for drinks (a pastime that he later judged "criminally dangerous and potentially fatal"). When he studied at the London School of Economics, he became a Keynesian—a defiantly unfashionable stance, at the time. Even Bissell's admiration for Rudyard Kipling fit a pattern of playing the contrarian, because, as Stewart Alsop said, by the time they came of age admitting to that "marked a man a fuddy-duddy."

One day, he was driving his secretary, Doris Mirage, to an office party in a quiet Washington neighborhood and turned the wrong way onto a one-way street. She looked on in horror, but Bissell told her not to worry, he was only going one block. "Why bother with the rule," he said, "when there are no cars on the street?"

That's what it was like inside the walled-off kingdom he'd constructed within the CIA: there were no other cars on the street. "Allen Dulles knew less of what went on in that component of the Agency than he did about any of them," Bissell later said. "There were an awful lot of details that never came to anybody else's attention." He'd been given enormous freedoms, but the pressures to prove himself and the CIA worthy of a big project—and to prove doubters like LeMay wrong—seemed heavier every day. Sometimes he'd call staff meetings at ten o'clock at night. His hands were constantly in motion—twisting paper clips, digging into his pockets, tapping on the desktop, wadding Kleenex into tight little balls. They called him "the mad stork"; he'd walk with such ferocious purpose from one office to another that Doris would often have to skip into a trot behind him just to keep up. Somehow, though, he never seemed overwhelmed. His ability to juggle so many different things at the same time produced an almost frightened awe among his subordinates. It wasn't that he made them feel stupid or doubt their own abilities; it's just that it seemed that somewhere within that enormous brain of his he saw a bigger picture than they did, and he seemed to have an aesthete's appreciation for the tiniest details within it. His reputation as a sophisticated thinker who stayed several mental steps ahead of everyone else led some of them to ascribe complex motives to nearly everything he did. He had a chronic sinus problem and was forever sniffing loudly through his blocked nose. To some of his aides, it seemed that he saved his most dramatic snorts for the moments when they were taking too long to explain something or when they were telling him something he already knew—as if he were warning them that his patience was running out. But they were probably reading too much into this. In truth, he did very little to mask the limits of his patience, particularly when someone tried to tell him bureaucracy was getting in the way of his goals. As his workload increased, his temper flared. Sometimes he threw pencils at the bearers of bad news. If ever he let loose with a long and loud "Sweet Jesus!" his aides knew it was best to leave him alone for a while.

The one thing that seemed to calm him down in those moments, however, was a phone call or visit from Edwin Land, whose flair for innovation seemed to be able to solve any technical complication. "It's going to be better," Doris would assure colleagues who nervously tried to judge Bissell's mood. "He's talking to Land, he's always better after he talks to him."

EDWIN LAND WAS SPENDING A LOT OF TIME in Quarters Eye, because that's where all the photos from the U-2 test runs ended up. The CIA had decided to establish a new photointerpretation department, and Quarters Eye, near the Lincoln Memorial and the Reflecting Pool, was the only place available with enough water hookups. Inside the old barracks, the water spigots were close to the ground—faucets designed for mopping the floors—and the new team of interpreters would have to bend low to fill buckets for photo processing. The CIA code-named the office HTAutomat, a reference to the coin-operated Horn & Hardart Automat in New York. Art Lundahl, the office's director, hoped the department would function like the self-serve food emporium: "open twenty-four hours a day, seven days a week, with a variety of products available around the clock and at a moment's notice." If Edwin Land wanted to see a specific image from the latest U-2 test flight, or if he wanted to compare images from the plane with photos taken on the ground, it was HTAutomat's job to get him that information, on demand.

The U-2 pilots were secretly flying all over the country. On one early flight, Lundahl's office requested that a pilot fly over President Eisenhower's farmhouse just outside Gettysburg, Pennsylvania, so they could demonstrate the plane's potential by displaying some images at the White House.

Eisenhower was impressed. He had reviewed plenty of reconnaissance photos during World War II, but none like this. He could see the new porch addition he'd had built, spotted his Angus cattle, and could even pick out the bull in the herd. When they showed him shots taken over major American cities, he was astonished at the level of detail. Eisenhower wrote, "On these we could easily count the automobiles on the streets and even the lines marking the parking areas for individual cars." On a picture taken of Washington, D.C., Bissell noticed that he could discern the particular makes of the cars parked beside the Capitol.

Any ethical concerns Land continued to wrestle with concerning the program's bogus cover stories and various deceptions were pushed to the background by the daily rush of technical challenges. When Land reviewed the test photos, he recognized that the sheer volume of visual data that the U-2 would produce could overwhelm analysts, and he sought a technical solution. He knew that Arthur Tyler, a leading optical scientist at Kodak, was working on something he called the Minicard. The system consisted of cards, each measuring less than one square inch, that could hold miniaturized images up to sixty times smaller than the originals. As many as two thousand cards were slotted onto a "stick" (the photointerpreters called them "shish-kabobs"), and these could be placed into searchable punch card sorters like those manufactured by IBM. Because the Minicards also contained coding, the analysts could enter a variety of search terms into a typewriter-like device and sort through the images at a rate of eighteen hundred cards per minute.

Kodak didn't have much interest in spending money on developing Tyler's idea, but Land spearheaded an effort to get the CIA involved. On March 1, 1956, the agency began negotiations to develop the system with Kodak, and shortly thereafter the photointerpreters in Quarters Eye began experimenting with it. A CIA memo predicted that the new system would be "capable of a level of information manipulation and a degree of coding sophistication" that could radically augment the agency's handling of data.

Richard Leghorn, a former air force reconnaissance specialist and Kodak executive who consulted closely with Land and Bissell, quickly began working to launch a corporation built around Minicard, and Tyler joined as a partner. The tycoon Laurance Rockefeller provided funding, and within months they had created Itek Corporation, which within two years would be making headlines when its stock prices spiked from $2 to $345. The *Boston Globe* dubbed it "the wonder child of space-age industries" and reported that Itek's aim was nothing less than to "make a new science." The *Wall Street Journal* commented on the company's "cryptic name," which was an abbreviation for the term that the company had coined to represent this new field: "information technology."

IT WAS SHOW-AND-TELL TIME in Mrs. Myra Montgomery's third-grade class at Maplewood Elementary in Austin, Texas. Eight-year-old Jimmy Rose raised his hand. He had a story to tell.

"My daddy was killed yesterday in an airplane crash."

Mrs. Montgomery and the rest of the class fell into a stunned silence. "My mother told me to be brave and not to cry. She said that is what daddy would have wanted me to do." The teacher stared at him, tears starting to well in her eyes. "But mother cried a lot," Jimmy said.

Mrs. Montgomery struggled to maintain her composure and excused herself. She found the school principal in his office, and they placed a call to Bergstrom Air Force Base, where Jimmy's father, Wilburn Rose, had last been stationed. The base confirmed it: Mr. Rose had recently left the air force and had begun working as a test pilot for Lockheed Corporation, and his former commanders had been informed that he had been killed in Nevada. Days later, the newspaper obituary offered no further details.

Rose had taken off in a U-2 from the lake bed at Paradise Ranch on May 15, 1956, for what was supposed to be an extended test flight. One of the pogo stabilizers affixed to the ends of the wings didn't automatically detach as intended—more of an inconvenience than a safety problem—and Rose made a loop around the base in hopes it would fall off. He banked too sharply on a turn, and the right wing, heavy with fuel, dipped too far and he lost control.

"The aircraft disintegrated over a wide area," the CIA later reported.

His family got a payout from the life insurance that had been part of the recruiting package for all the pilots. But the board of directors for the Government Employees Health Association quickly realized that whatever those new CIA recruits were doing out in the desert, it probably wasn't something they should be insuring. Two weeks after Rose's crash, they canceled all of the policies. Bissell scrambled to try to come up with a solution, and eventually the CIA ponied up the money to underwrite its own insurance policies. But it took months to sort that out, and during that time a second pilot crashed and died. Then a third.

Powers tried not to think too hard about how ridiculously dangerous this business of being a test pilot was. One grim reminder came when the pilots were told Johnson's team of engineers had added a new piece of equipment to the planes: a self-destruct mechanism.

The idea was that if the pilot encountered a problem over the Soviet Union and it was clear the plane was going down, the spying equipment—the cameras, the film, the radar, and the radio intercept units—should be destroyed. Johnson's crew designed a simple detonator and three-pound charge that was meant to obliterate the Q-bays and everything in them. Inside the cockpit, the pilot flipped a switch marked "ARM," and this activated the device; if he flipped a second switch marked "DESTRUCT," a timer began ticking, giving the pilot seventy seconds to bail out. If the timer was set longer, the CIA feared there was a chance the device would detonate after the plane fell to earth—not ideal, because the ground could cushion some of the explosion. When the pilots began simulating detonations and bailouts on the ground, they discovered that some of the timers had been calibrated wrong and ran at varying speeds—some hit the "seventy" mark a full five seconds before seventy seconds had actually elapsed.

That didn't reassure the recruits, who were already getting the feeling that their safety and well-being might not be the CIA's number one priority. Bissell sent a CIA lawyer to Paradise Ranch to try to iron out the insurance policy problems, and the recruits greeted the man with a litany of complaints.

In a cable to Bissell's office the lawyer reported, "They were particularly concerned with the possibilities of escape and evasion if they were to go down. For example one man said that he was under the impression that the Government would not acknowledge him and, therefore, he was wondering if he were able to make his way to a U.S. embassy whether he would be barred from admittance. I attempted to reassure them on this point generally that certainly the organization was giving considerable thought to the subject of escape and evasion and I was sure they would be briefed specifically and in great detail on this." Before the lawyer added his signature line to the bottom of the page, he tacked on one more point: "I might add slightly on the personal side that most of these men came up to me after the final meeting and expressed the view that I was the first person who had talked to them on a factual basis and on a man-to-man basis. In fact, it was clear they felt they were being treated in some respects like children."

Bissell got the message. "The pilots' equipment, preparation, and briefing should be designed to contribute in every way possible to high morale without increasing the grave dangers inherent in the loss of a U-2 behind enemy lines," he responded. He arranged for them to undergo a specialized training regimen in escape and evasion. In Bissell's mind, this was a simple morale-building exercise for the sake of the pilots' psychological—not necessarily physical—well-being. He still believed that no pilot could ever survive a U-2 crash, no matter how many survival skills they might possess. Was he manipulating them for the sake of his program? Perhaps, but his confidence in the U-2 was such that he found it difficult to imagine a catastrophe. No one was more invested in the pilots' success and safety than he was, after all.

If he might be accused of low-grade duplicity when it came to assuaging his pilots' fears, he believed the stakes of the Cold War justified it. Bissell had come to agree with Jimmy Doolittle's controversial code of ethics in espionage: the normal rules of human conduct do not apply. If keeping the pilots in the dark about their own chances of survival was required to ensure their cooperation, he had no problem doing it.

Bissell arranged for the pilots to leave Area 51 to undergo a rigorous— and likely pointless—survival training program.

He was sending them to the Farm.

A FARM IN VIRGINIA—THAT WAS SOMETHING Powers could relate to. He'd been born in rural Kentucky, the son of a fifth-grade dropout who scratched out a living as a coal miner and shoe cobbler, but Powers spent most of his youth in the tiny burg of Pound, Virginia, tucked among the hills in the southwest corner of the state. His family did its cooking on a wood-burning stove, and goats nosed around the yard. But when he arrived at the heavily guarded property near Williamsburg, Virginia, he quickly realized this was a different kind of farm.

"The Farm" was the nickname for a training facility where the CIA trained covert officers in the paramilitary arts. During World War II it had been used as a prisoner-of-war camp for captured Nazi soldiers. To Powers, it looked a little like a country estate—nearly ten thousand acres surrounded by deer-filled woods and the occasional open field. But a few of the buildings were surrounded by fourteen-foot-high electrified fences. Some of the open fields were laced with land mines. He saw jump towers and shooting ranges.

The training was relatively short—just five days, from July 30 to

August 3, 1956—and centered on survival and escape techniques inside
a Communist country. The Farm featured a simulated border zone that
replicated conditions in the Soviet Union. The "border fences" were
electrified and mined, and the fields stretching from them were cleared
in exactly the same way the Communists plowed their borders. Powers
was taught how to spot land mines and how to walk across the plowed
ground—where to step, how to vary his stride—so that his footsteps
couldn't be tracked and followed. He was confronted by a man playing
the role of a Soviet guard, who pointed a pistol at him. Powers practiced disarming him and turning the gun back on him. He was shown
numerous types of Soviet-style handguns and instructed on their use.
He was issued his own handgun—a High Standard .22-caliber pistol
with a silencer attachment—and he practiced with it for nine hours on
the range. He also got a hunting knife, and he was taught how to use it
to shave firewood from trees and how to cut up his parachute to make
a tent.

Another item to be packed in his "survival kit" was something called
an "L pill," a small glass ampoule containing a deadly dose of prussic
acid (the *L* stood for "lethal"). One week before Powers arrived at the
Farm, the CIA's counterintelligence division had shipped ten of the pills,
packed in chopped cork and locked in a Protectall safe, to the U-2 program. They came with the following label:

> *Instructions for use:* When the ampoule is required to be used it
> should be put in the mouth and held tightly between the teeth,
> with the lips tightly shut. The ampoule should then be crushed
> between the teeth. The user should then inhale through the mouth,
> shut the mouth again, and hold the breath as long as possible.
> Unconsciousness will follow in a short time, probably in about 30
> seconds.
>
> It is expected that there will be no pain but there may be a feeling
> of constriction about the chest.
>
> Death will follow without consciousness being regained.
>
> If the ampoule held in the mouth is swallowed it will be excreted
> unchanged and no harm will result.
>
> One ampoule will be quite effective unless the man concerned is
> particularly resistant to prussic acid, as happens from time to time
> (this applies to all drugs). If, however, two ampoules are used the
> effect *may* be slightly more rapid.

His trainers told Powers that the use of the L pill was up to him. But if for some reason he was captured by the Soviets and outed as a spy, who knew what would happen? Torture, brainwashing, and, after all that, execution—everything was on the table. The pills had been tested for their ability to withstand the extreme temperature fluctuations of high-altitude flight and were considered sound if kept between minus 95 degrees and 120 degrees Fahrenheit. They had also been exposed to simulated altitudes of seventy-five thousand feet and sudden drops in air pressure without suffering damage. However, a note in Bissell's office cautioned that this didn't mean they should be roughly handled. "It should also be mentioned that the contents of the ampoule being highly volatile, are dangerous even if released within the confines of a closed room. One ampoule, if broken in an average sealed room, ten feet by ten feet, is lethal." The memo helpfully added that the ampoules should always be transported to and from mission sites in a Protectall safe and "should never be carried by an individual traveling commercial air."

TELL ME AGAIN, EISENHOWER WAS SAYING, *what are the chances a pilot could survive a crash in Soviet territory?*

Allen Dulles repeated what he'd been saying all along: if a plane went down, the pilot wouldn't survive, no matter how much training he underwent. "It would be impossible, if things should go wrong, for the Soviets to come in possession of the equipment intact—or, unfortunately, a live pilot," Eisenhower later recalled being told. "This was a cruel assumption, but I was assured that the young pilots undertaking these missions were doing so with their eyes open and motivated by a high degree of patriotism, a swashbuckling bravado and certain material inducements." One of the only members of Eisenhower's staff allowed to attend the U-2 briefings was his son and assistant staff secretary, John Eisenhower. Dulles gave his father "absolutely categorical" assurances that no pilot would survive. This notion, he said, was "a *complete* given, a *complete* assumption."

Even so, Eisenhower had a hard time pushing the possibility out of his mind, and he seemed hesitant to fully embrace the U-2. If, somehow, one of the planes went down, a pilot was captured, and the program's cover was blown, he'd be the one in the hot seat. "I'm going to catch hell," Eisenhower predicted.

Throughout that spring and early summer of 1956, as Bissell continued to make preparations for the U-2's maiden missions, the release of transcripts of a series of air force hearings prompted the Alsop brothers to publish a series of columns revisiting the idea of the bomber gap. "The recently released testimony of Gen. Curtis LeMay and Earle Partridge ought to be required reading for every policy-making official of the Eisenhower administration," the Alsops wrote, "conspicuously including President Eisenhower himself."

Partridge, another four-star general in the air force, said the Soviet bomber and missile programs were outpacing America's defense capabilities, and LeMay estimated that within four years the United States might be perfectly helpless to avoid outright annihilation against Soviet might. "If Partridge and LeMay, in a fit of hysterical parochialism, are simply misinterpreting the meaning of the national estimates, why are they kept on in their immensely responsible positions?" the Alsops asked. "If, on the other hand, their interpretations are correct, and their testimony substantially correct, what becomes of the twin doctrines of massive retaliation and mutual deterrence which supposedly form the basis of American defense policy?"

According to the Alsops, the testimony of the generals was yet another argument suggesting Eisenhower should make the narrowing of the bomber gap his top priority. But Eisenhower knew as well as anyone that LeMay's testimony was built mostly on guesswork. The U-2 might have been ready and waiting to provide him photographic evidence to turn the speculation into something more solid, but the risks of a botched spy flight were enormous. "We've got to think about what our reaction would be if *they* were to do this to *us,*" Eisenhower warned.

Behind Eisenhower's caution was the knowledge that the potential consequences of blundering into a war had never been higher. In late November 1955, the Soviets conducted a series of nuclear bomb tests that culminated in the detonation of their most powerful hydrogen bomb yet—one that was about a hundred times more powerful than the first atomic bomb the Soviets had tested in 1949. If there had been any doubt that Khrushchev's nuclear program could compete with America's, that doubt had disappeared into the mushroom cloud over the test site in Kazakhstan.

In response to one of Joe Alsop's columns, a friend wrote to Eisenhower urging him to follow the journalist's advice and confront the Soviet threat aggressively. Eisenhower wrote back, "Suffice it to say here that I doubt that any columnist—and here I depend on hearsay as I have no time to read them—is concerning himself with what is the true security problem of the day. That problem is not merely man against man or nation against nation. It is man against war."

The leaders of the U-2 program appreciated the president's caution, but they believed the nuclear advances in the Soviet Union intensified the need for overflights, and they grew more frustrated with each passing week. Bissell, Land, and Johnson had invested years in the spy plane, and they had convinced themselves that it was one solution that could satisfy both action-oriented hawks like the Alsops and more cautious types who had grown to dread any possibility of nuclear war. To Bissell, Land, and Johnson, it seemed as if Eisenhower were dragging his feet, and his inaction was threatening to undermine all of their hard-won innovations. Around this time, Bissell and Johnson came up with a new nickname for the president: Speedy Gonzales.

WHEN HER HUSBAND LEFT for his new job, Barbara Powers was given a typewritten note with instructions detailing how she could send him messages:

MAILING ADDRESS—
Mr. Francis G. Powers
c/o Mr. Calvin E. Mundell
P.O. Box 4054
Valley Village Station
N. Hollywood, California

EMERGENCY PHONE NUMBER—
Mr. John E. Donaldson
Office: Jackson 5-5166
Home: Jackson 2-3768
Arlington, Virginia

Her letters, at first, trickled into Paradise Ranch. Powers and the other pilots hated the CIA's mail service; it made them feel as if they were living behind the Iron Curtain, not in America. The pilots complained to the CIA that the delivery of letters was painfully slow and they were "deeply resentful of the censorship of both incoming and outgoing mail." No one else at the base—not the Lockheed engineers, not the mechanics, not the air force officers—was subject to "such an indignity," they said.

Barbara, too, was fed up with the way the government—she didn't even yet know he worked for the CIA—seemed intent on putting up walls between her and her husband. She decided "to fight this insidious, mysterious thing" that was pushing them apart and tried to flood the CIA's postal system with paper, mailing two letters a day to the California post office box. Eventually, responses from Frank starting coming back, and his letters finally revealed some information she could use: He would soon be transferred from a base in the United States to another one overseas. He was moving, the letter said, to Athens, Greece.

Barbara decided to take action. She quit her job at the Marine Corps Supply Center and persuaded her boss, a Marine Corps major, to write her a glowing letter of recommendation: "Mrs. Powers was a very cooperative employee in that she always accepted any additional duties assigned to her in a cheerful manner and carried them out conscientiously." She packed her luggage, traveled from Georgia to New York, and bought an airline ticket on Air France to Greece, where she hoped to find a job and move into an apartment close to her husband's new base.

But Powers wasn't being transferred to Greece. That was just more CIA cover. He was moving to southern Turkey.

THE PILOTS WERE SENT OVERSEAS in two separate groups. The first group, Detachment A, went to the Wiesbaden Air Base in West Germany. Powers's group, Detachment B, went to Adana, Turkey. Each group consisted of six pilots, four U-2s, and dozens of support staff from the CIA and the air force.

The group in Germany was ready first, and on June 20, 1956, a U-2 flew over East Germany and Poland. Everything went smoothly, and when the pictures got back to the analysts in Quarters Eye, they looked great. To Bissell, the flights reinforced his faith in the U-2, and he was eager to launch another mission, one that actually flew over the Soviet Union, as soon as he possibly could. Eisenhower, however, told him that he couldn't send any plane deep into Soviet territory until the German chancellor, Konrad Adenauer, agreed to allow an overflight to depart from his country. On June 26, Bissell flew to Germany and personally cleared the mission with the West German leader.

Days later he was back in the White House. Eisenhower had recently undergone bowel surgery to remove an obstruction in his small intestine, and he was still recovering; Bissell spoke with his staff secretary,

Andrew Goodpaster, who relayed his messages to the president. Bissell explained that he wanted to fly over some of the U.S.S.R.'s major military airfields and installations, all the way to Leningrad and back, to try to compile an inventory of the Soviet fleet of Bison bombers. Bissell said the pilots were "ready and eager" to get in the air. Upon receiving the reports, Eisenhower lingered solemnly over the decision. According to Goodpaster's notes, Eisenhower labeled it "one of the most soul-searching questions to come before a President." The next day, Goodpaster told Bissell that he had a ten-day window to do the flyover, but after that all bets were off.

The same morning, Bissell sent a coded message to Wiesbaden alerting the team of the possibility of a flight, weather permitting. At six o'clock that evening, after reviewing the weather reports, Bissell sent another signal to communicate a "high likelihood of a mission." He continued to monitor weather reports throughout the evening, and just before midnight in Washington—or at about six o'clock in the morning on the Fourth of July in Germany—Bissell delivered a one-word message over a secured CIA line.

"Go."

# BOOK TWO

# *Icarus Soaring*

*By this time Icarus began to feel the joy*
*Of beating wings in air and steered his course*
*Beyond his father's lead: all the wide sky*
*Was there to tempt him as he steered toward heaven.*

—OVID, *THE METAMORPHOSES*, BOOK 8

# CHAPTER 5

# In Plain Sight

One of the best ways to keep a great secret is to shout it.

—EDWIN LAND

The morning of the Fourth of July was hot and sticky, but traffic in Washington was mercifully light—except in the immediate vicinity of CIA headquarters. The complex sat at the nucleus of the holiday picnic rush, and by ten o'clock thousands of people, armed with blankets and coolers, were already stalking the most coveted patches of lawn near the Washington Monument and the Lincoln Memorial. Allen Dulles for years had pleaded with the government to move the agency away from all that tourist traffic, and now, finally, all of his complaining was paying off: starting the very next day, the CIA would take its first real step toward building a new, comfortably isolated complex in Langley, Virginia. A contract had already been drawn up, and the agency's lawyers planned to present it to an architectural firm the next morning, on July 5. To allow the firm's designers and engineers to get started, more than forty secret clearances had to be finalized. To catch up, Dulles ignored the national holiday and reported to the office, where he found Richard Bissell.

"Well, Allen," Bissell said, "we're up and running."

Dulles had given Bissell free rein, letting him handle all of the U-2 planning, and even though the first flight was enormously important to the CIA, Dulles hadn't stayed on top of the details.

"Where is it running?" Dulles asked.

"It's flying first over Moscow, then over Leningrad, then home," Bissell told him.

Dulles seemed a little uneasy. "Was it really wise to do that the first time?"

"The first time is the safest," Bissell said. "We should hear within another hour."

His confidence was built upon everything the CIA's analysts had taught him about radar systems. The best aerial tracking machine available—the American-made SCR-584—could consistently monitor aircraft at heights up to fifty-five thousand or sixty thousand feet. Detecting anything above that was just dumb luck—sort of like casting a bare hook in the ocean and hoping to blindly snag a fish while reeling it in. Broad, constant sweeps at those heights were practically impossible. Even if a crack team of technicians were able to jury-rig a cluster of SCR-584s together and set one of them to monitor a higher-elevation sector, the machine would likely burn out if they left it running for more than a few minutes.

The analysts said the American radar systems were getting stronger every day, and they warned that the Soviets probably weren't far behind. For that reason, Edwin Land and others sometimes referred to the U-2 as a "wasting asset" or a "melting technology" in interagency memos, which meant that its effectiveness would likely erode with time. The window for spy flights was lowering a little more every day, and although they didn't think it was dangerously close to shutting yet, Bissell believed the sooner the planes got in the air, the safer they'd be.

At least, Bissell *hoped* that was the case. Despite his outward calm, he'd been nervous in the days before the flight. But late on that holiday morning a message came over the wire from Germany that dissolved his unease, filling him with a weightless sort of elation: the U-2 had returned to the base without problems, and all of its equipment had worked as planned.

Bissell saw an opportunity and seized it; he checked the weather forecasts for Eastern Europe and the Soviet Union and ordered two additional flights over Russia for the next day.

Hours later, clouds massed over Washington and rained out that evening's fireworks. The same thing happened the next night, and the next, but the weather didn't bother Bissell, because the skies over Russia were clear.

IT WAS THE PERFECT DAY for a garden party: sunny, mild, and the rose blooms lining the patio couldn't have been brighter. Spaso House, the elegant yellow and white mansion where U.S. ambassador Chip Bohlen lived with his family in Moscow, sat on a quiet side street, but it wasn't particularly quiet on this day. Hundreds of people—

diplomats, military attachés, and embassy staff—crowded onto the front lawn to celebrate America's independence.

When Nikita Khrushchev arrived, a tight cluster of aides steered the Soviet leader through the crowd toward Bohlen, who stood under a shady linden tree.

Bohlen extended his right hand. He was overseeing the event with the flowing ease of a model diplomat—handsome and relaxed, buttoned into a trimly elegant dark suit, the silk handkerchief perfectly squared in the pocket, a tall glass of scotch in his left hand. Bohlen's grandfather had been a U.S. ambassador to France, and putting people at ease in social situations seemed to come naturally to him. Khrushchev, in a lumpy gray suit that was still wrinkled from the car ride over, challenged that skill, because the two men had so little in common. Khrushchev had come from a family of peasants, and as a young man he'd worked as a metal fitter, fixing pipes and fixtures in Russia's underground mines. When he cast capitalistic Americans as children of privilege who exploited their underclass, the American ambassador might have been his poster child. Bohlen's father, in fact, had never really had a career; instead, he'd lived off an inheritance and considered himself a "man of leisure."

Yet here on the Spaso House lawn, the ambassador and the Soviet leader seemed to be getting along perfectly. Bohlen steered a scotch into the hands of both Khrushchev and Nikolai Bulganin, the Soviet prime minister, whose tongue loosened up when he drank—or so Bohlen had been advised. While the men chatted casually about President Eisenhower's recent bowel surgery, Dag Hammarskjöld, the secretary-general of the United Nations, joined their circle.

"We're all armed here," Bulganin said, noting that Hammarskjöld wasn't holding a glass, "but you're not."

"Well," Khrushchev jumped in, "that's because the Swedes are neutral. Yours is the best position."

Bohlen remedied the oversight, commandeering another drink, and someone suggested that the Soviets, as the guests of honor, might offer a friendly toast to mark the American holiday. Bulganin seemed to be in an expansive mood: "On behalf of all of us present, and on behalf of the Soviet government, we send greetings to the American people and we raise our glasses to the health of President Eisenhower."

The toast sounded warm and genuine, and Khrushchev lifted his scotch toward Bohlen. To the hundreds of people on the lawn whose eyes were glued on them, everything seemed happy and hopeful—a friendly respite in the tense relationship between the two superpowers. But both Bohlen and Khrushchev were playacting. Bohlen was pretending that a U-2 hadn't just flown over the Soviet Union for the first time, potentially tilting the balance of the Cold War decisively in America's favor. And Khrushchev was pretending he didn't already know all about that flight.

Soviet radar operators, using systems they'd recently improved, had spotted the mysterious aircraft over Soviet airspace at about 9:35 that morning. Beneath his smile and friendly toasts, Khrushchev seethed with a white-hot anger. To secretly fly into the country's airspace was an act of war, he believed, and a provocation for retaliation. America liked to present itself in the international arena as an honorable and honest broker, but in Khrushchev's eyes this flight revealed Eisenhower's hypocrisy.

After the embassy reception, Khrushchev returned to the Kremlin and summoned some of his top air defense commanders and engineers, asking them to reconstruct exactly what had happened. Their radar systems hadn't been able to track the entire flight, but they guessed that the plane had flown over Minsk, Vilnius, Kaunas, and Kaliningrad. The new S-25 missile system that the Soviets had developed to protect urban Moscow was not yet operational, and none of the other anti-aircraft missiles positioned throughout the country could reach that high.

Some of the engineers suggested that the plane was likely a twin-engine medium bomber, but Andrei Nikolayevich Tupolev, probably the greatest aircraft designer in the country, told Khrushchev that was unlikely. Tupolev believed the plane was most likely an extremely lightweight, single-engine glider. He quickly sketched a drawing on a piece of paper: a dragonfly-like design, with a thin body and long, thin wings.

Whatever it looked like, Khrushchev hated it, and he hated the idea that it could fly over his country at will. "We have to create air defenses capable of reaching that altitude," he said, "but in the meantime . . ."

He let the sentence hang there, as if he didn't know what more to say.

ABOUT THIRTY THOUSAND FEET of undeveloped film—the product of the first five U-2 flights over Russia flown between July 4 and July 10, 1956—was wheeled onto cargo planes and flown from Wiesbaden, Germany, to Dover Air Force Base in Delaware, stopping in the

Azores on the way. The film was then trucked to Rochester, New York, where it was developed at a secured facility operated by Eastman Kodak. Bissell's assistant, Herb Miller, accompanied the processed film back to Washington, where an unmarked 1956 Chevrolet Suburban drove it to an alley behind a Ford auto repair shop at Fifth and K Streets. An armed guard stood watch as couriers hauled the parcels through the back door of the auto shop building, then trudged up four flights of stairs to the clandestine headquarters of the CIA's brand-new Photointerpretation Department.

The photointerpreters had gotten permission to move out of Quarters Eye and into offices above the auto shop just days before, on July 1. There was plenty *not* to like about the new digs. The neighborhood was awful: crime was rampant; the alley was littered with broken bottles and abandoned cars; there was nowhere to park; and finding somewhere to grab lunch was an exercise in frustration. The building itself was nearly as bad: grease-splattered mechanics roamed around the ground floor; the exterior was pocked and cankered; inside, crumbling particles of pressed fiber rained down from the decomposing ceilings. But what it *did* offer was space, and plenty of it—about fifty-five thousand square feet spread over four floors. Bissell thought it provided excellent cover; no one would guess that the most advanced photo-intelligence center in the world sat above all those junked cars. Art Lundahl, who supervised the operation, figured things could be worse. "Where a choice be necessary," he quipped, "give me good men in poor ships rather than the converse."

Sitting at light tables, armed with six-power magnifiers, rulers, and grease pencils, the interpreters bent over the images and went to work. A few of the interpreters zeroed in on the pictures of Poznan, Poland, a city that the U-2 passed over on its way to Russia on July 4. They'd never seen anything like this; they could clearly pick out the city's Communist Party headquarters, which just days before had been ransacked when more than 100,000 protesters rioted. Other interpreters could barely contain themselves as they gazed down onto a military base in Minsk and then followed the successive images into Moscow and Leningrad, where they could count the boats inside the country's most secured naval base. At the Saratov-Engels Airfield, they spotted several Bison bombers sitting wing to wing on the grass.

The interpreters were overwhelmed with visual data, but few complained. They considered themselves lucky: they were the chosen ones, witnesses who'd been present at the exact moment their profession was transformed, radically and permanently.

Within days, the interpreters were able to isolate some of the best images from the flight, enlarging them into eighteen-by-twenty-inch prints and mounting them on captioned presentation boards. They carefully cloaked the boards in sheets and smuggled them out of the building and into the unmarked Suburban in the alley, which ferried them to Richard Bissell inside CIA headquarters on E Street.

Bissell and Dulles stood in front of a long table, marveling at the clarity of the prints. They counted the cars in the streets of Leningrad—not because it was valuable intelligence, but just because they could. Bissell was amazed that he didn't even need a magnifying glass to pick out the Bisons at Saratov-Engels. He and Dulles couldn't help themselves; staring down at the pictures, they broke out in delighted laughter.

The CIA knew that the Soviets had spotted the plane. Leo Geary, the air force liaison assigned to the U-2 project, had already informed Bissell that American technicians in Eastern Europe had intercepted radio chatter indicating that the U-2 had been detected early on the morning of July 4, even before it entered Soviet territory. "East German radar picked it up and passed it on to the Soviet radar, fully expecting that it would never come back," Ritland told Bissell. Later that day, the East Germans spotted the plane again when it returned, no doubt shocked that it hadn't been shot down. The intercepts suggested that the radar operators had estimated that the U-2 was flying at forty-two thousand feet—a whopping thirty thousand lower than its actual height. It seemed clear to Bissell that the radar systems never got a good fix on the plane. The fact that the U-2 was spotted, therefore, didn't worry Bissell and Dulles so much as it encouraged them. Their plane seemed absolutely untouchable.

Lundahl showed Bissell and Dulles several images that revealed several Soviet fighter planes—MiG-19s and MiG-17s—flying tens of thousands of feet below the U-2 early in its flight, apparently trying to shoot it down. The MiGs would rise and rise, then lose control when they exceeded their altitude limits, sometimes flipping over as they tumbled into chaotic descents. As many as twenty Soviet fighters chased the U-2, and all failed, spectacularly.

Frank Wisner, the head of covert intelligence, joined the men as they examined the images. He was just as impressed as they were, and he didn't have to state the obvious: there was more solid intelligence in one of those images than any of his officers could ever hope to coax out of an informant on the ground. Dulles turned to Wisner and asked him, "How much would you have paid for the information in this photography?" Wisner considered the photo again, which was just one of thousands the U-2 had captured in less than a week of operations.

"About a million dollars," he said.

DULLES, BISSELL, AND LUNDAHL HURRIED the presentation boards to the West Wing of the White House, eager to gauge the president's reaction.

Eisenhower dove right in; he took his glasses off to peer in at the details and put them back on again to take a broader look. The president had a keen eye for aerial photography—he'd planned many a battle in his day using reconnaissance maps—and he immediately quizzed Lundahl about the scale and altitude parameters. With his bearings firm, he had no problem picking out details from the airfields and naval yards. After a good long look, he turned from the boards and flashed the men a look that they all interpreted the same way: *Good job—well done.*

But if Eisenhower possessed a single, overriding trait, it was prudence; he was not one to let himself get carried away in premature celebration. The Soviets had spotted the plane, which meant this mission could never be considered an unalloyed success, no matter how much information it might yield. When Bissell showed him the pictorial sequences of the MiGs falling from the sky in hapless pursuit, the familiar cautious pall seemed to return to Eisenhower, and he seemed to share little of the delight that Bissell felt. It almost seemed as if, to the president, those MiGs were bad omens.

LATER THAT DAY, SOVIET AMBASSADOR Georgi Zaroubin showed up at the State Department, accompanied by an aide. The men plopped themselves into two of the stuffed chairs in the waiting room and demanded an audience with John Foster Dulles, the secretary of state and Allen's brother. Next to the ashtray on the table in front of them, Zaroubin laid down a typed message that he planned to deliver to Dulles on behalf of Khrushchev. It read,

According to precisely verified data, on July 4 of this year, at 8:18 a.m. Moscow time, a twin-engined medium bomber of the United

States Air Force appeared from the American Zone of Occupation in Western Germany and flew over the territory of the German Democratic Republic, entering the air space of the Soviet Union from the direction of the Polish People's Republic at 9:35 in the area of Grodno. The aircraft which violated the air space of the Soviet Union flew on the route Minsk, Vlnyus, Kaunas, and Kaliningrad, penetrating territory of the Soviet Union to the depth of 320 kilometers and remaining over such territory for one hour and thirty-two minutes.

That wasn't all. Additional U-2 missions that Bissell had authorized, flown on July 5 and July 9, had also been spotted:

It must be underscored that these gross violations of the air space of the Soviet Union took place at a time when, as a result of the efforts of the Soviet Union and other peace-loving governments, a definite lessening of international tensions has been achieved, when relations between governments are improving, and when mutual confidence between them is growing. . . . The Soviet Government expects that steps will be taken by the Government of the United States to punish those guilty for the said violations and to prevent such violations in the future.

The press found out about the complaint, and the State Department issued a reply to the Soviet embassy; it was an outright denial. Drafted with input from the CIA and the White House, the response stated that "the invented overflights" amounted to nothing more than a Soviet scheme to undermine America's image abroad. "These remarks, which are as obviously out of place as they are unwarranted, indeed of themselves have the effect of hindering the improvement of international relations."

The New York Times repeated the U.S. view that the Soviet complaint was a "pure fabrication," and the article suggested the accusations would quickly fade into the irrelevance they deserved.

Eisenhower wasn't so sure. His point man, Goodpaster, called Bissell and told him to suspend all further flights of the U-2 immediately.

BISSELL WAS AFRAID THAT THE ENTIRE PROJECT might be mothballed for good. He assigned his assistant, Herb Miller, to write a memo to convince Eisenhower that the spy plane wasn't merely a machine; it was a paradigm shift.

Edwin Land had predicted the U-2 might eventually transform the CIA; Bissell and Miller wanted to convince Ike that it already had done so after less than a week in operation over the U.S.S.R. The U-2 wasn't just a technological substitute for the eyes and memory of a spy, Miller wrote; it was an *improvement* on them. No human could ever see, or retain, nearly so much vital information. Through just a handful of flights, the U-2 had presented Eisenhower with strong evidence that America had overestimated the Soviet inventory of Bisons; the "bomber gap," it seemed, was likely a fiction. That contribution to America's intelligence—an invaluable one in itself—was merely the tip of the iceberg. The U-2's potential wasn't limited to prying the lid off a few military installations; it could pry the lid off *an entire culture*. Already, the U-2's initial images had revealed the structure and working conditions at Soviet farms and factories; the routes and traffic patterns of railroads, roadways, and ports; the condition of agricultural harvests. By the U-2's covering as much as 400,000 square miles of land—at least 15,000 square miles of which was photographed in fine-scale detail— America now had "a cross section of a part of the entire Soviet way of life." Miller explained,

> Airfields previously unknown, army training bases previously unknown, industrial complexes of a size heretofore unsuspected were revealed, and so on down through a long list of various types of significant activities. More than 130 airfields can be identified inside the Soviet Union and more than 60 urban areas can be examined from photographs now available from AQUATONE. Yet there is a huge area included in the Urals and beyond about which we know even less from other intelligence sources and which may really hold the key to the understanding of the Soviet Union that we seek.
>
> To bar the United States from reaching this understanding through overflights of the critical regions of the Urals and eastward could well be tragic.

If the memo was meant to prevent Eisenhower from scrapping the program, it worked—sort of. Eisenhower told Allen Dulles that if any new missions would be flown, he would personally have to sign off on each and every one of them, and he was in no mood to do so at the moment. The program wasn't condemned to oblivion, but neither had it earned the president's full blessing.

To try to get out of maddening purgatory, Bissell summoned Edwin Land and Kelly Johnson back to Washington.

THE FIRST BOTTLE OF SCOTCH sat on the table, empty. So Bissell, Johnson, and Land cracked open the second one and just kept working.

It was a brainstorming session for the ages. Land had invited two friends of his to join them: Ed Purcell, the Nobel Prize–winning physicist who'd worked with him in Group Three, and Stewart Miller, a specialist from Bell Labs who'd later pioneer the development of fiber-optic communications. That day, Bissell had defined their objective succinctly enough: come up with some sort of upgrade to the U-2 to help it evade detection by Soviet radar.

They batted around some ideas, then some more, and before they knew it, the second bottle was empty and it was 1:30 a.m. They adjourned until the next morning, when all of them reconvened at 7:00. "By noon," Johnson noted in his diary, "we had program 'X' going. My biggest job now."

Program X was quickly renamed Project Rainbow. Land and Johnson would spearhead it, and they began compiling names of scientists and engineers who might join the effort. Together, they would test radar-absorbing materials that might be applied to the U-2's exterior— perhaps a wallpaper-type covering imprinted with a circuit pattern that could disperse incoming radar pulses. They would also explore a theory that Purcell had outlined during the brainstorming session, which he called "the Trapeze." It involved placing small bamboo or plastic poles on the surface of the plane, then extending small-gauge wires between those poles, effectively encircling the entire airframe. Attached to those wires would be small, precisely spaced ferrite beads. Purcell believed that the wire and bead contraption might capture 70 MHz radar pulses and trap them in a loop, or at least weaken them so much that they wouldn't register back on the ground.

Land and Johnson together took the lead of Project Rainbow, and although they couldn't have known it, they were also taking America's first step toward another technology that was so advanced it didn't yet have a name: stealth aviation.

· · ·

THE LINCOLN LABORATORY IN CAMBRIDGE was a defense research facility that had sprung from the recommendations floated by Project Lincoln, the study group that Edwin Land and J. Robert Oppenheimer, among others, had helped organize back in 1950. Now, six years later, Land visited the lab's sprawling campus to try to recruit a small team of radar researchers to be part of Project Rainbow. In the years since he'd served on Project Lincoln, Land's intimate involvement with the CIA had thoroughly initiated him into the world of spycraft, and upon his return to the Lincoln Lab it showed.

When Land summoned three radar systems researchers into the office of the lab's director, he didn't immediately explain to them why he'd called them together. Instead, he ushered them out of the building and into a convertible parked outside. He drove away from the lab and parked in an empty parking lot beside a construction site. It was a little after ten o'clock in the morning, but the August heat was already stifling. Land, however, didn't roll down the windows or drop the top of the convertible. Instead, as the researchers sweated in the backseat, he turned around and challenged them with a simple question: Could they make a plane perfectly invisible to radar?

Land doled out a few relevant details. "For the past six weeks the U.S. has been flying a reconnaissance aircraft over Russia at altitudes far above the reach of their air defenses," Land said. "The good news is that we have been able to go anywhere we wish without fear of being shot down. The bad news is that their radars have been able to track us continuously from border to border."

The scientists didn't really know if they could engineer a radar-resistant aircraft or not. But they agreed to try, and days later they were summoned to another meeting, this time at Land's Polaroid office on Osborne Street. There, the scientists were joined by a couple of new faces. One was Ed Purcell, the physicist, whom they all knew by reputation. The other was a tall man with glasses who was introduced to them only as "Mr. B."

While they spoke, Land reached for his desk telephone. He turned the phone's rotary dial, then instead of releasing it he jammed a pencil through the ring, holding it in place.

They watched, confused. Land explained that it was a simple precaution, a trick he'd learned to disable one common type of bug.

A sneaking suspicion that had first dawned on the researchers in the back of that sweltering convertible hardened into something closer to a certitude: Edwin Land was a lot more complex than his public persona, as one of America's most successful entrepreneurs, had led them to believe.

ADANA, IN SOUTHERN TURKEY, was a bustling city of more than 200,000 people, but to the pilots it felt like the last outpost at the end of the world. Horse-drawn buggies raised dust on unpaved roads, and vendors who looked as if they'd stepped out of another century hawked silver, pottery, leather, and bread in the center of town. The stone bridge leading across the Seyhan River was about seventeen hundred years old, and when they crossed it, the pilots could look down and watch women scrub clothes and men watering their horses. In the vast tracks of flat desert on the other side of the bridge, camel caravans followed the same routes that traders bound for Persia traversed around the time of Christ. Tarsus, the birthplace of Saint Paul, was about thirty miles away. The waters of the Mediterranean Sea weren't much farther.

To call the new home of Powers's U-2 detachment an air force base was a stretch. When he arrived in that hot summer of 1956, it was little more than a way station for U.S. Air Force planes that needed more fuel on their way to somewhere else. At the south end of a ten-thousand-foot runway sat a few Quonset huts and tents, where the strip's skeleton crew of local Turks slept. Bissell's office had picked the site mostly because of its geography: it was far enough away from the Soviet Union to be out of radar range but close enough so that the pilots wouldn't have to burn all their fuel just to get to the border.

The detachment was designed to appear like a normal air force squadron. About 130 men accompanied the seven CIA pilots as members of the ground crew, radio operators, medics, and support staff. They settled into tents and small trailers, while Lockheed mechanics pieced together five U-2s, which had been disassembled at Area 51 and shipped to Adana in C-130s.

Those first weeks were tough. The base's commanding officer, Colonel Edward Perry, quickly began firing off a long list of complaints to Bissell: "delayed completion of facilities, poor sanitation, substandard mess, electrical failures, low quality indigenous help, and extreme heat." The detachment's medical officer, air force major William Marriott, who shared a trailer with Powers, also outlined the "unsatisfactory and unsanitary" condition of the mess hall in his own letter to Washington.

His letter found its way to Bissell's office and eventually sparked corrective actions: the Turkish food service staff was fired, the mess hall was cleaned and painted, the windows got new screens, and the air force flew in a new supply of dishes, glasses, silverware, and watercoolers.

Because Eisenhower had suspended the flights over the Soviet Union, the pilots had plenty of time to acclimate. On base and off, they looked like vacationers, dressed in Bermuda shorts and short-sleeved sport shirts, with argyle socks (a mid-1950s trend most of the pilots embraced) and sneakers or loafers. As the summer dragged on, their sunburns darkened into deep tans. They were wary of the local men, and they'd been warned to stay away from the women at all costs, so they spent most of their time inside the base's wire fence. At night they screened movies outdoors near the base snack shack and played marathon games of poker. One of the pilots bought a donkey and tied it next to his trailer, and its raspy, hee-hawed braying became an inescapable element of the Adana soundscape.

At first, they took the U-2s up only for test flights and for periodic missions over the countries of the Middle East, where tensions surrounding the control of the Suez Canal were rising. They also flew close to the Soviet border, but not inside it, making sweeps in the hopes that the U-2's radar-sensing equipment might intercept Soviet signals.

At the end of one of those early flights, Powers crawled out of the U-2 and walked back toward the detachment's hangar, where Colonel Perry, visibly annoyed, handed him a message. Powers started to read it, but he was exhausted from spending hours in the cockpit and struggled to make heads or tails of it.

"Your wife," Perry explained, "called the Washington number you gave her, Powers. To tell us she's on her way to Athens, determined to see you."

THE MORNING BEFORE BARBARA LEFT NEW YORK, she called the number Frank had given her and informed whoever was on the other end of the line—a Mr. Donaldson, she was told—that she was heading to Athens. He sounded more than a little concerned. Did she really think that was a good idea? She did, and there was nothing he could do to stop her.

He asked her to report to the King George Hotel as soon as she landed, and Frank would be waiting for her there. The hotel was the favorite for foreign dignitaries in Athens, sitting in the center of the city, just across the street from Constitution Square. From under the striped canvas awning on the terrace, she could lounge in a wicker chair at a marble-topped table and gaze at the columned ruins of the Parthenon atop the Acropolis. Frank found her shortly after she arrived, and they both checked into the hotel.

She freshened up in the bathroom, they went out to dinner, and he *still* wouldn't tell her where he was really stationed—just that it wasn't in Athens. He pleaded with her to understand that all of the secrecy was part of his job and to trust him that it was for a good cause. Even so, guilt nagged at him. He supported her idea to find an apartment and get a job in Greece. He'd already bankrolled some vacation time, he told her, and he could travel to Athens as often as twice a month.

And that's exactly what he did. She rented a place not far from the U.S. military headquarters, and when he came into town, they burned whole days exploring the city—the Arch of Hadrian, the statues and masks at the National Archaeological Museum, the Theater of Dionysus at the foot of the Acropolis. At night, they hit the tavernas, sampling the stuffed eggplant, the lamb skewers, the avgolemono soup. Then he'd head back to Adana, wait a couple weeks, and fly back to do it all over again.

With the help of the CIA, Barbara landed a job as a stenographer and clerk for the staff judge advocate of the U.S. Air Force. Her boss was a thirty-three-year-old captain from Texas named Reuben Jackson, a former bombardier who after the war graduated from law school at Southern Methodist University. His wife and two children weren't fond of Greece, and they had recently moved to Ramstein, Germany, with plans to return to the States.

Jackson and Barbara, geographically separated from their spouses, often dined together near the base, and Jackson persuaded Barbara to be the "hostess" at the cocktail parties he'd host when dignitaries visited from the States or from other bases abroad. Speculation that their relationship might be something more than professional began to circulate, but those rumors didn't spread outside Athens. For the moment, the threat posed by Barbara to the CIA was contained.

LATE IN THE SUMMER OF 1956, a Boy Scout troop from Nevada marched up the rocky slope of Mount Charleston, and one of the hikers spotted a briefcase beside the trail. Their scoutmaster opened the case, rifled through some of the papers, saw all sorts of "Top Secret" stamps, and decided that someone whose rank was quite a bit higher than his should figure out what to do with it.

He took the briefcase to Nellis Air Force Base just outside Las Vegas and handed it over to the special agent in the Office of Special Investigations, who discovered it had belonged to William Marr, the security agent in charge of the U-2 program who'd been killed in the plane crash months before. The agent forwarded the briefcase to his regional headquarters in Los Angeles, and the officers there, in turn, handed it over to the California CIA liaison. "The compromise of the project's security was contained," a CIA memo reported, "by debriefing those involved and stopping up all possible leaks therefrom."

The Soviets might know the U-2 flights were happening, but they didn't know important details: how high it could fly, what equipment it carried, what it could see. The KGB still worked feverishly to find out as much as they could about the U-2, but so long as Khrushchev's planes and missiles couldn't stop the overflights, he had an incentive to keep them secret from the Soviet public; he couldn't afford to appear weak to his own people. Similarly, if the American public found out about the nature of the flights, Eisenhower would face political pressure to reveal the photos and the CIA would forever lose its most valuable tool. Two hostile powers, therefore, effectively conspired to keep their respective citizenries in the dark.

If the briefcase had gotten into the wrong hands, it could have blown the lid off the entire project. These were the sorts of complications that drove Bissell mad, and they were proving very difficult to eliminate.

THE PHOTOINTERPRETERS INSIDE HTAUTOMAT on K Street were still pulling new details from the U-2 images more than a month after the initial examinations, and Allen Dulles had to admit that technology was, in fact, ushering in a new era in spying, just as Edwin Land had promised. Even so, Dulles couldn't resist delivering a bittersweet eulogy to the old era. "You're taking all the fun out of intelligence," he told the photointerpreters. But if Dulles believed that the U-2 was killing the cloak-and-dagger game, he was wrong; it was simply providing new targets.

From a high window above the Ford shop, Art Lundahl spotted a suspicious-looking car parked across K Street. The photointerpreters had noticed it there before, because it seemed a little too big, too black, and too nice for the neighborhood. The office was full of optical equipment, and Lundahl grabbed a Questar telescope to get a closer look. Two men were sitting in the front seat. He got a camera and telephoto lens and took a picture of the men and the car's license plate.

Henry Thomas, who oversaw security of the building for the CIA, ran the plates. They were registered to the embassy of the Soviet Union.

Somehow, the Russians had figured out that something secretive was under way in the decrepit building. Thomas's team had initially believed the auto shop—"augmented by an ancient and completely irrelevant directory in the lobby"—provided near-impenetrable cover for their operation. However, a CIA report later noted that just before the photo-interpreters moved into the building that July, a sign was posted on the door that read, "Rented to the CIA."

WORRIED THAT THE SOVIETS IN WASHINGTON might infiltrate the photointerpretation center above the Ford shop, Bissell explored the idea of moving HTAutomat abroad, closer to the U-2 bases. Wiesbaden seemed like the obvious choice, but when CIA personnel traveled to Germany in the fall of 1956 to assess its prospects, they didn't like what they found. The foreign nationals working on the base seemed to move around with little supervision, but that was just the first of many challenges. "More difficult to cope with were the potential hazards presented by the Valhalla, a night spot favored by base personnel," a CIA report concluded. The Valhalla, according to the agency, was full of dangerous types, particularly "the unattached females who frequent the place." It was exactly the sort of dive where the Soviets might bait a "honey trap," wherein an unsuspecting American is lured into an illicit affair with an undercover Communist agent, thus making him vulnerable to blackmail.

Adana seemed a safer bet. In October 1956, construction crews began assembling a new photographic analysis center there, and Bissell got on a plane to visit the fledgling operation. That wasn't his only business in Turkey. After reporting to the base, he specifically sought out Frank Powers, who had been flying numerous missions in the U-2 over the Middle East. Bissell wanted to speak with Powers about a potential security problem that, he feared, might compromise the U-2 project— his wife.

Athens was a powder keg. Several months before, riots had erupted in Greece after the British government executed members of a guerrilla group in Cyprus that sought to undermine regional British authority. Since then, anti-Western sentiment had been on the rise. Americans had been threatened on the streets of Athens. Who knew what might happen if Barbara got tangled up in an international incident and had to explain her presence in the country; the fact that her husband was a pilot involved in a secret program might spill out. On top of all that, Barbara's presence in Greece wasn't necessarily good for morale, Bissell suggested, because the other pilots had been discouraged from moving their wives overseas.

The explanations to Powers sounded contrived. The CIA had gone to the trouble of finding Barbara another job—as a clerk at Wheelus Air Force Base, in Tripoli—and the agency would help her move to Libya. Powers couldn't help feeling that there was another motive behind the decision, something Bissell, for whatever reason, didn't want to tell him about.

Shortly after Bissell's visit, one of the T-33 training planes stationed at Adana was in need of service, and the maintenance crew from the U-2 detachment decided to fly it to Wheelus, where it would receive a complete checkup. Powers grabbed a spare seat on the flight so he could surprise Barbara with an unannounced visit.

The plane landed at Wheelus, and Powers went directly to the women's barracks, where Barbara was living. It was a modest dormitory: a bare lightbulb dangled from the bedroom ceiling over her bunk, and flies buzzed around the windows. When she let him in the door, he discovered that she had been preparing to go out for the evening and seemed caught off guard by his arrival. He spotted her purse and a letter that was jutting out from it; when he ventured near it, she grabbed the letter. Suspicious, he made a move to take it from her, and she ran with it toward the bathroom. He intercepted her before she could flush the letter down the toilet.

The letter was from Reuben Jackson, her former boss in Athens. The opening sentences were benign: the whole crew in Athens missed her, he said, and he hoped she was doing well in her new home in Libya. Then came the bombshell: he was going to ask his wife for a divorce. He wrote that his marriage had been an unhappy one, and he guessed that surely Barbara must have been unhappy too, with her husband so far away and so incapable of giving her what she needed. He wanted to know if there was any chance that she, too, might end her marriage. He loved her, he wrote.

Barbara insisted that the letter was a complete surprise to her; she had never been involved with Jackson, she said, and she couldn't help it that he'd fallen for her. She swore she'd done nothing wrong, but Frank didn't believe her. He flew into a rage.

In the middle of much shouting and slamming of doors, one of the women living in a nearby room called the military police. The officers arrested Frank, and they confiscated the letter that he held in his hand. Barbara accompanied them to police headquarters, where both she and Frank were questioned. After the police read the letter, it was no use lying about the exact nature of the argument. Barbara's new boss was called, and after hearing both of them out, he said he was going to deliver "an official reprimand" to Captain Jackson.

Afterward, Barbara found Frank in the Officers' Club. She continued to insist that she and Jackson had had no relationship. He'd bought her dinner on a couple of occasions, but that was all. His romantic feelings had come as a complete surprise, she said. Frank wanted to believe her, and so he did.

THE SECRET U-2 PHOTOS HAD EXPOSED the bomber gap as a fiction to those in the know, yet during the late summer of 1956 Joe Alsop continued to insist America was falling behind in the arms race. This presented Bissell with a choice: he could set Alsop straight by revealing the classified information, which showed that the Russians weren't mass-producing long-range bombers; or he could protect the secrecy of the U-2 program and risk letting his friend—and the readers of his newspaper columns—believe that America was losing the Cold War.

Bissell kept his mouth shut, protecting the most valuable technology the CIA had ever developed. Alsop, meanwhile, continued to suggest the president was neglecting America's national security and lulling the country into a benumbed, self-satisfied trance.

"One of the ways that Dwight D. Eisenhower has restored concord among us has been to convince most Americans that the danger is not there any longer," he wrote during the summer of 1956, when Ike was accepting his party's nomination for reelection. "Yet it is there, none the less."

The idea that Eisenhower was putting Americans at risk contributed to a depression that had seized Alsop, a malaise that resembled a midlife crisis. As a kid he'd been overweight, but he forced himself to drop sixty-five pounds after college; now, at forty-five, the weight was creeping back on. Immediately after the Republican convention, he checked himself into a health spa, managing to lose three inches off his middle, but he couldn't drop his ennui. When he returned to Washington, it felt to him as if the entire capital had been corrupted by Eisenhower's complacency. "There is something rancid about this city now," he wrote to his friend Chip Bohlen, the American ambassador in Moscow.

Alsop decided he needed to get out of the country for a while. He'd move to Paris, he decided, and from there he'd try to visit the Soviet Union so that he could better witness and describe America's biggest threat. He knew it wouldn't be easy to get a visa; *Pravda*, the state-controlled newspaper in Moscow, regularly mocked the Alsop brothers as "atom-happy" and "troubadours of the most aggressive circles of the USA." Given that notoriety, there were only so many strings Ambassador Bohlen could pull for him. Yet that August, Joe launched a charm offensive against the Soviet embassy in Washington. In his visa application letter to Georgi Zaroubin, the Soviet ambassador, he conceded that "you and your government may well hold that my political viewpoint is unsound, to put it rather mildly." But Joe challenged him to prove him wrong by letting him experience the Soviet Union for himself. He wrote that his primary motivation for traveling centered on "the fear that I may have misjudged the Soviet Union's present world role." To hammer that message home, he invited Zaroubin and his embassy colleagues to his house on Dumbarton for drinks.

The Russians took him up on the offer, stopping by one evening for drinks and dinner. As they chatted, one of the ambassador's aides, a man named Sergei Striganov, drained a quarter bottle of brandy *after* finishing a bottle of red wine, another bottle of white, and a stiff cocktail. "The rest of this long conversation, which was floated, as you might say, on a considerable quantity of wine and brandy, was chiefly episodic in interest," Alsop wrote in a letter to a friend. But by the time Zaroubin and his party stumbled out of the door, Joe was optimistic about his chances for a visa. "He was very forthcoming about my proposed expedition to the Soviet Union," Joe wrote, "and promised that I could go almost anywhere except the atom-plant cities."

When the Soviet officials walked, or staggered, across the darkened Georgetown sidewalks to their car, FBI agents stationed outside the house witnessed their departure, which they noted in a memo they later delivered to J. Edgar Hoover.

JOE ALSOP GOT HIS SOVIET VISA and traveled from Paris to Moscow in January 1957. Chip Bohlen had invited him to stay with his family at the ambassadorial residence in the Spaso House, but Joe declined, explaining to him that his "CIA friends"—a small group that included Bissell and Frank Wisner, the CIA's chief of covert operations—had strongly advised him against that idea. They believed that Joe's reputation as an ideological enemy to the Kremlin might cause the ambassador unnecessary headaches, and it would be wiser for Joe to travel independently. For that reason, Alsop checked into the Hotel National, which sat across from the Kremlin and was managed by Intourist, the state-run tourism monopoly.

Alsop had always imagined Moscow as a monochromatic eyesore, a charcoal sketch where all distinctions were drawn in shades of gray. But the colors jumped out at him—the "rich, dark strawberry red" of the Kremlin's walls; the "bright butter yellow" of the Grand Kremlin Palace; the "happy riots of colored and gilded domes" at St. Basil's Cathedral. The ornate white plaster inside St. George Hall made him feel as if he were inside a giant, beautifully decorated wedding cake.

He toured Siberia, sheltered from the cold by an enormous fur hat and a coonskin coat that made him the center of attention nearly everywhere he ventured. When he returned to Moscow, he was invited by Ed Stevens, a Moscow-based journalist, to join him for dinner with Chester Bowles, a former U.S. diplomat who happened to be one of Bissell's closest friends from Yale. Alsop accepted the invitation, joining them in the dining room of the Grand Hotel. As they chatted, another friend of Stevens's—a reporter for TASS, the Soviet news agency—approached them and graciously invited the group to join him at his table. They did, and Alsop found himself seated next to a man who introduced himself as Boris Nikolaievich.

Boris, a young and athletic blond, told Alsop he was a teacher of literature visiting from Leningrad, and they launched into a discussion, in French, about Soviet letters. After a single vodka, Boris's political filter seemed to abandon him. He incautiously revealed that he didn't care for the social realism championed by the Soviet apparatchiks, and instead preferred poets like Boris Pasternak and Anna Akhmatova, both of whom were considered politically suspect by Kremlin hard-liners. As they got deeper into the discussion and the vodka, Boris risked an even more daring confession: he liked men, he said.

Alsop didn't bat an eye, and Boris seemed to read a subtext beneath his composure. He asked Joe if he might want to continue their conversation after dinner in his hotel room upstairs. When it was time for Alsop to bid adieu to Bowles and the rest of the party, he and Boris retreated to room 219.

They spent a passionate hour together. Before Joe left to walk back to his hotel, he agreed to see Boris again the next afternoon—"to say goodbye" before Boris returned to Leningrad. As they embraced inside Boris's room, the door flew open and three men burst into the room.

Joe, shocked and terrified, scrambled to collect himself. One of the men was a militia officer, who pulled out a confession that he ordered Alsop to sign. Joe refused, because he couldn't read the document, which was written in Russian. Soon two more men entered the room, and they dismissed the others, saying that they'd handle everything from that moment on.

The older of the two men was the very picture of a Soviet apparatchik—early fifties, portly, eyes narrowing behind steel-rimmed glasses, a muskrat *chapka* on his head. He plopped down behind a small table and lit an imitation Turkish cigarette. Eyeing Joe, he drummed his fingers on the tabletop, and then he opened a red dossier. He pulled out a photograph, which had apparently been taken in that very room less than an hour before: Alsop and Boris, in the throes of passion.

The KGB officer—at least that's what Alsop assumed he must be— mentioned that sodomy was a very serious crime in the Soviet Union. But considering that he and his countrymen were a merciful people, the man suggested he was willing to offer Joe the benefit of absolute secrecy, but only if Joe agreed to give *them* something in return for it.

What that *something* might be, the man didn't say. Instead, he instructed Joe to meet him for dinner the next evening at the Praga Restaurant, one of the most popular establishments in the city. There, he told Joe, they would discuss options to "try to find a way out of your problem."

Joe was stunned, and he walked back to his hotel in a daze. If Bissell and the rest of his friends with the CIA had worried that Alsop's cozy relations with some in the agency were potentially tricky before, what would they say about *this*?

This, Joe realized, was what it felt like to get caught in a devilishly sticky honey trap.

# CHAPTER 6

## Rocket Men

You can't put your foot in your mouth if you keep your mouth shut.

—CLARENCE "KELLY" JOHNSON

Before Joe Alsop arrived at the Praga Restaurant to meet his KGB blackmailers, he had worked out a plan: he'd suffer through the dinner, lead them to believe he would cooperate, return to his hotel, write a detailed confession of his tryst with Boris, slip it under the door of another journalist staying at the same hotel, and, finally, kill himself.

At the Praga, the two KGB agents were waiting for him. They led him to a private room where a table had already been prepared for them. The spread looked delicious, the best Moscow had to offer, but when he sat down to directly confront it, Alsop failed to summon an appetite. They offered him vodka, but he surprised them by refusing it, blaming his abstinence on an upset stomach and a case of hepatitis.

The conversation was maddeningly indirect, as if they were trying to torture him by pretending he had nothing to worry about. Joe found it hard to concentrate. The small talk—mostly about politics, with occasional questions about America's military budget—seemed to never end. Finally, at close to 11:00 p.m., they returned to the subject of how Joe might be able to solve his "problem."

They suggested that he return to the United States and his role as Washington's most well-sourced journalist, the close friend of CIA insiders, the man who left no string unpulled. He could write whatever he wished; the Soviets didn't care. "You and your brother do not write nearly so badly about the Soviet Union as many other people," the portly KGB agent told Joe, "and in any case you must carry on your career."

There was just one tiny catch.

From time to time, the agent said, the Russians would expect Joe to share "advice that would assist the cause of peace."

To the KGB, the prospect of a beholden source who regularly shared cocktails with the men who kept the nation's most valuable secrets was priceless. Joe heard them out, and he played along. He told them it seemed like a reasonable arrangement.

The agent knew Alsop planned to travel to Leningrad in two days, and he told Joe they would catch up with him there to work out some more details. As a show of goodwill, they promised that someone in Leningrad would give him a special tour of the restricted Special Collections room at the Hermitage, the grand museum of art and antiquities that Catherine the Great had founded more than two hundred years earlier.

Joe returned to his room at the Hotel National that night and reconsidered his initial plan. The idea of ending it all, of leaping out the window and landing hard in front of the stunned proletariat on Mokhovaya Street, had lost its melodramatic appeal. A trip to Leningrad and the Hermitage didn't seem so bad. He could make the trip and *pretend* to go along with his new Soviet handlers—a ruse that would allow him to leave the country without a problem. From the relative safety of Paris, he could come clean about everything. If he publicly confessed his homosexuality, he might render himself worthless to the Soviets as a blackmail target. His journalistic career would go down in flames, needless to say, but at the moment that seemed like the least of his problems.

He'd need to survive for at least a few days in this country and endure any tests of loyalty the KGB might subject him to. Even if the worst happened—an execution, a gulag, a smear campaign—he figured that the American government should know that he went down fighting and that he never betrayed his country's trust. So he sat down and wrote out a detailed confession, transcribing everything that had happened in the hotel room with Boris and admitting that he'd been a closeted gay man his entire life. He folded the confession into a sealed envelope and gave it to a friend whom he deemed trustworthy; if there was any hint that something bad had happened to him, Joe said, then the note should immediately be delivered to Chip Bohlen at the U.S. embassy, who could forward it to his friends at the CIA. On the other hand, if nothing suspicious happened to him within two weeks, the friend could open the letter at that time; by then, Alsop would be back in Paris, where he would already have confessed the whole truth to whomever it concerned.

Alsop called Bohlen that Friday to say good-bye before he boarded the night train to Leningrad. Joe sounded calm and gracious, same as always. He gave no hints of distress; he didn't want to burden his old friend with worry.

In Leningrad, Alsop reported as requested to the Hermitage, where he was treated to a three-hour tour of the Special Collections. He killed a few anxious hours during the afternoon pretending to write a column that he never intended to file. At about 5:00 p.m., a hotel maid knocked on his door to deliver an unexpected telegram. It was from a diplomat in the American embassy in Moscow. It read,

> JOSEPH ALSOP C/O ASTORIA HOTEL OR EVROPEISKYA LENINGRAD—
> HAVE URGENT PERSONAL MESSAGE FOR YOU WHICH AMBASSADOR
> SAW BEFORE DEPARTURE. HE SUGGESTS YOU RETURN IMMEDI-
> ATELY MOSCOW. PLEASE CALL ME ON RETURN.

Alsop's friend—the "trustworthy" soul to whom he'd entrusted the confession—must have succumbed to curiosity. Apparently, he had opened the sealed envelope, panicked, and delivered the letter to Bohlen immediately.

Joe called the number at the top of the telegram and hurried to the Intourist ticketing agency, where he hoped to reserve a seat on the 8:00 p.m. flight to Moscow. After an agonizing delay at the ticket counter— the phone lines were all tied up, they said—he got the ticket and hurried back to his hotel room to pack his bags. In the lobby, he caught a glimpse of his two KGB blackmailers, and the woman who had secured his seat on the plane regretfully informed him that she'd made a mistake: there were no available seats on the plane, as it turned out. Exasperated, Joe hustled back to his room to call his contact at the American embassy again, but before he got through, a knock rattled his door. It was one of the KGB agents.

Alsop was desperate. He told the agent that he'd received a telegram suggesting that something terrible had happened to someone in his family, and it was simply imperative that he return to Moscow to find out what it was. Joe assured the agent that he'd gladly meet with him again in Moscow and they could talk there for as long as necessary.

The KGB agent considered him for a moment, then agreed. When Joe returned to the Intourist ticket counter, one seat on the eight o'clock flight had mysteriously become available.

. . .

WHEN HE ARRIVED BACK IN MOSCOW, Joe Alsop wrote, in longhand, a more complete version of his confession. He gave it to Chip Bohlen, who quickly whisked Alsop onto another airplane to Paris, via Prague, and forwarded the confession to the CIA. The document was long and achingly detailed:

> I have been an incurable homosexual since boyhood. Very early, I sought medical advice, especially from Doctor Adolf Mayer at Johns Hopkins, but the doctor I consulted only confirmed my own diagnosis. It is a curious thing, but it is a fact, that the vast majority of homosexuals who have honestly faced the nature of their predicament, somehow end by accommodating themselves to it, shocking though this may seem. Most simply say, as I have said, "If I do no harm to anyone, if I am no trouble to anyone, I should not be too much troubled myself." I have always been deeply troubled, however, by one aspect of my predicament—by the concealment of the truth from my family and friends. Circumstances have now arisen which make further concealment impossible and while those circumstances are disturbing and painful in the last degree, there is still a certain inner relief at being forced to tell the whole truth at last.

Alsop stayed in Paris for a few weeks awaiting the fallout, which never seemed to come. He was unaware that his confession was briskly wending its way through Washington's power circles. Allen Dulles had sent a copy of the handwritten confession to the FBI's J. Edgar Hoover, who wasted little time in spreading the news. After a meeting at the White House, Hoover spilled the details of the confession to Eisenhower's chief of staff, Sherman Adams. Hoover also told Attorney General William Rogers, who in turn informed Secretary of Defense Neil McElroy. In an internal FBI memo, Hoover stated that the information should probably be shared with Gordon Gray, a newly appointed national security adviser whom Alsop had repeatedly criticized for chairing the panel that stripped J. Robert Oppenheimer of his security clearance in 1954.

Alsop soon moved back to Washington and continued to write his columns, unaware of these machinations. Bohlen had advised him to hold off on going public with his homosexuality, so Alsop simply pretended nothing out of the ordinary had happened. On the same day that Dulles had informed Hoover of the honey trap, Alsop wrote in a letter to a friend, "The Russian trip was an immense success from every standpoint."

THE BOMBER GAP WAS DEAD. By early 1957, the U-2 photo-interpreters concluded that the Bison bomber—the linchpin of the Soviets' long-range nuclear threat—had *not*, in fact, been produced on a mass scale. Instead, it appeared likely that only a couple dozen or so of the bombers existed, far fewer than the most recent estimates from the air force and from the Alsop brothers, who had reported that the Soviets' production of bombers likely outpaced America's by three to one. The U-2 evidence suggested that the few Bisons the Soviets had displayed during the past two May Day parades and at the Moscow air show accounted for almost the whole fleet. Updated government estimates were released, but the source of the information—the U-2—wasn't divulged.

Right on cue, the bomber gap found a worthy successor among America's most hawkish military observers: the missile gap.

In January 1957, about three hundred scientists and military officials gathered in San Diego for the first National Symposium on Space Flight. Major General Bernard Schriever, who oversaw the air force's ballistic missile program, told the audience that the Cold War between America and the Soviets would soon spread to a new battlefield—outer space. "In the long haul, our safety as a nation may depend on our achieving 'space superiority,'" Schriever told the crowd. The space race, he predicted, could decide the victor of the Cold War.

The first step for both sides would be the perfection of intercontinental ballistic missiles, or ICBMs—nuclear bombs that could soar above the earth's atmosphere to strike an enemy target on the other side of the world. The second step, he predicted, would be the launch of unmanned satellites that could orbit the planet and perform a variety of tasks, from gathering intelligence to guiding the flight paths of the aforementioned ICBMs.

Schriever's speech impressed the editors of *Time* magazine so much that they put his face on its cover. Within a matter of weeks, the space race had become an American priority. "The United States has one leg up in the world race for supremacy in rocket weapons and space ships," crowed an article in the *Chicago Tribune* in early 1957. "And military strategists say the nation that is first into outer space with rocket vehicles will be able to dominate the earth."

Sixty-seven different countries around the world planned to participate in a scientific forum called the International Geophysical Year, which was scheduled to run from July 1957 to the end of 1958. Both the United States and the Soviet Union were already announcing that they planned to try to launch experimental satellites in honor of the event. The U.S. satellite, according to preliminary reports, would consist of a small, twenty-one-pound ball that would require a mechanism weighing twenty thousand pounds to launch it into space. "The Soviets have been cagey about their plans beyond announcing they are 'actively engaged in developing a rocket which will carry a vehicle into outer space,'" *The Washington Post* reported. Whatever the Russians were cooking up, it was probably nothing to worry about, Americans were assured. The assistant director of the Pentagon's research unit, Clifford Furnas, told *The New York Times* that the Russians were "still a long way behind" the fledgling U.S. space program. In fact, Furnas said, if America continued to press hard, it might be able to send a man to the moon as soon as 1982.

The U-2 photos, however, began to raise suspicions about the Soviet space program. One image, taken over a rural area about seventy-five miles west-southwest of Moscow, caught the interpreters' attention. It was a strange-looking compound of about three square miles, surrounded by a double fence and a ten-foot-wide strip of cleared land. Inside were all sorts of odd structures: buildings with massive walls measuring ten feet thick; two large, earth-covered domes with what appeared to be detachable roofs; other structures that appeared to be buried as much as twenty feet underground.

Early in 1957, the CIA summoned to Washington several rocket and nuclear experts and described the site to them, hoping the scientists might be able to guess at its purpose. Wernher von Braun, a former Nazi scientist who immigrated to the United States after World War II, suggested that it might be a launch site for long-range nuclear missiles.

Von Braun was one of the most respected rocket scientists in the world, and he was credited with inventing the V-2 rocket—the first long-range guided missile ever made. His suggestion sent the photointerpreters into a frenzy of analysis, and in the first three months of 1957 the team concentrated much of its work on the enigmatic compound.

In February, the CIA called von Braun in for an all-day meeting. Considering his Nazi past, the agency wasn't sure it could fully trust him, so it hid the truth about how it had gathered its intelligence. Art Lundahl told von Braun that the detailed models of the site that the interpreters had constructed were based on a photo snapped by a 35 mm camera, which spies had secretly affixed to a commercial airliner flying over Moscow. Lundahl showed von Braun the "original" photo—a blurred and degraded shot that he'd concocted from the much clearer, much more comprehensive U-2 images.

"You get all this information from one picture like this?" von Braun asked, looking at the faked photo. "You must have the world's greatest photo interpreters. I never saw anybody who could do such a thing as this. How you all do that?"

Von Braun's conclusions were, alas, inconclusive. The interpreters decided that they needed *more* U-2 photos to determine what, exactly, the Soviets were doing at the site.

THE TECHNICIANS WHO'D BEEN ASKED TO MAKE the U-2s invisible to radar believed that Kelly Johnson's security measures were a little over the top. "Nobody's to know who you are or why you're here," he said when they met in his office in Burbank. He motioned to one of them—"You're going to be Mr. Brown"—and then to another: "You're going to be Mr. Smith." Considering that "Mr. Smith" was ethnically Japanese, Johnson's tactics didn't strike the group as particularly convincing. But he might have been forgiven a little paranoia, because the secrecy surrounding Skunk Works and the demands the CIA was putting on Johnson were reaching all-time highs.

In 1956, the CIA had reported that a Soviet physicist named Pyotr Leonidovich Kapitsa had recently been "rehabilitated"; he'd been living under house arrest since 1945 after falling out of favor with Stalin, and now he'd been reinstated as the head of the Institute for Physical Problems, the country's most prestigious physics lab. Kapitsa was a known expert in the use of liquid hydrogen as fuel, and some aerospace experts in the United States speculated that he might have been released to work on an aircraft propelled by that kind of rocket fuel—one that might fly high and fast enough to catch the U-2. Johnson, who had experimented with hydrogen as fuel when he was designing the U-2, decided he'd try to use the same propellant to create a next-generation, supersonic spy plane that could outpace any fighter Kapitsa might be working on.

Johnson's venture was code-named Suntan and was classified as *above* top secret, which meant that the twenty-five people authorized to know about it had to keep their work a secret even from the other engineers who'd been cleared to work in Skunk Works.

Keeping track of all those layers of secrecy was difficult enough, but Johnson's engineering task was even harder: create an aircraft that could fly at altitudes of 100,000 feet and at speeds of Mach 2.5. By the second half of 1957, Johnson had begun to realize that he wasn't going to get there with the plans he'd drawn up. The team encountered all sorts of problems surrounding the storage and transport of the liquid hydrogen fuel, and by the late summer he'd lost his enthusiasm for the project, turning instead to Project Rainbow, the effort to retrofit the existing U-2s with radar-deflecting material.

The first radar-camouflaged U-2s—nicknamed "Dirty Birds" because of the dark, wallpaper-like material that covered them—took to the skies that summer, and the images they brought back from Russia were embedded with clues that would be confirmed months later: Kapitsa hadn't been released from house arrest by the Soviets to work on a hydrogen-fueled plane; rather, he'd been released to assist them in their effort to beat the Americans into space.

BISSELL TOLD THE WHITE HOUSE that the newly outfitted Dirty Birds would be virtually invisible to Soviet radar. They were not; the Soviets were able to track some of them over Russian territory despite their low radar profiles. But it didn't really matter. The series of flights that Eisenhower approved in mid-1957 "produced a veritable bonanza of scientific and technical information," images that would keep the photointerpreters busy for more than a year.

When the planes flew over compounds where chemical and biological weapons were produced, for example, the interpreters were able to identify where the trucks supplying the facility came from; they pinpointed the electrical station that powered the factory; they even spotted the animals that would be sacrificed during experimentation. At multiple nuclear testing sites, they inventoried new missiles under development; they were able to estimate how powerful those missiles were by measuring the dimensions of the burn marks they left on the testing pads.

One of those testing sites, located near Tyuratam, merited particular attention. An unusually large launch stand had been built there, and the analysts guessed that it was probably designed for long-range ICBMs. Any rocket-powered contraption that used that stand, the analysts decided, would have to be enormous—perhaps twice as large as any of the American rockets under development. Some analysts, believing that the technology simply didn't exist yet to launch such a large object into space, guessed that the site was probably more aspirational than operational.

But five weeks later, *Sputnik* blasted off from that very spot.

"LADIES AND GENTLEMEN, we are bringing *to you the most important story of this century.*"

That was how the announcer on NBC Radio News broke the news of the launch of the first man-made earth satellite to the American public. The *New Republic* magazine expanded *Sputnik's* significance by a few hundred years more, comparing it to the discovery of America by Christopher Columbus. Newscasters tracked its progress through space and over cities like New York and Washington, and amateur ham radio enthusiasts tuned their dials to pick up the chirpy beep-beep-beep the satellite emitted as it circled the earth. The Soviets had revealed that the 184-pound metal sphere carried a radio transmitter, batteries, and temperature-measuring instruments, but it was also full of symbolism and portent. If the Soviets could launch a satellite that high and far, then they could surely do the same with a nuclear warhead. "The Russians can now build ballistic missiles capable of hitting any chosen target anywhere in the world," the *Guardian* claimed. *Time's* conclusion sounded a note of defeat: "The Russians are now on their own."

The national mood darkened even more a few weeks later, when America responded with its own satellite—the comparatively modest, twenty-eight-pound *Vanguard*. On national television, the dramatic countdown to blastoff was broadcast live from Cape Canaveral. At the critical moment, the rocket thrusters flared in a fiery storm of exhaust, and the craft, very slowly, began to rise from the launch stand.

Then, just as slowly, it began to sink back down.

*Vanguard* made it about four feet off the ground before collapsing into its own fire. As if that weren't humiliating enough, the satellite's radio equipment somehow remained intact inside that blazing conflagration of burning fuel, and the grounded satellite continued to transmit its signal, a mournful chirp that was broadcast to viewers across the world. A syndicated columnist for the *New York Journal American,* Dorothy Kilgallen, spoke up for an embarrassed nation: "Why doesn't somebody go out there and kill it?"

Eisenhower played down the failures, claiming Russia's triumph didn't really *mean* anything. It wasn't as if *Sputnik* were a nuclear bomb or anything, he said; it was just a harmless hunk of metal. His dismissals did little to calm an anxious nation. "Let's quit acting as if nothing has happened," complained Hubert Humphrey, the Democratic senator from Minnesota, "because something has happened and it has embarrassed us throughout the world." Eisenhower was getting slammed in the press: he was old, tired, complacent, out of touch. Facing mounting pressure to do something—*anything*—to counter *Sputnik,* he fell back on a plan that had worked pretty well the first time he'd tried it: he called a select group of the nation's most prominent scientists to the White House, and he asked them if they had any bright ideas.

At 11:00 a.m. on October 15, the nuclear physicist I. I. Rabi, who'd won a Nobel Prize in 1944, called the meeting to order. After a few introductory remarks, Rabi introduced Edwin Land, who delivered an impassioned manifesto that skewered all of the American politicians and bureaucrats who, in his eyes, had conspired to wage an undeclared war on science, undercutting its role in American life. He challenged Eisenhower to take a firm, unequivocal stand in support of the sorts of innovators whom people like McCarthy had tried to silence. Andrew Goodpaster, the president's secretary, scribbled notes on a yellow legal pad, trying to keep up with Land's racing oratory:

He said that the country needs a great deal from science. But he felt that science, to provide this, needs the President acutely. The Soviets are now in a pioneering stage and frame of mind. They regard science both as an essential tool and as a way of life. They are teaching their young people to enjoy science. Curiously, in the United States we are not now great builders for the future but are rather stressing production in great quantities of things we have already achieved. In Russia science is now being pursued both for enjoyment and for the strength of the country. He asked if there is not some way in which the President could inspire the country— setting out our youth particularly on a whole variety of scientific adventures. If he were able to do that, there would be tremendous returns. At the present time scientists feel themselves isolated and alone, but all of this could change.

Eisenhower responded by creating a new position—the presidential science adviser—which Killian, still president of MIT, accepted. Shortly after the White House meeting, Major General Bernard Schriever, the head of America's ballistic missile program and recent *Time* cover subject, traveled to Cambridge to discuss potential satellite projects with Jerome Wiesner, a former Los Alamos researcher at MIT's Radiation Laboratory. Shortly after they got together, they decided to call Land, and that same morning they drove over to Polaroid to meet him at his lab. For several hours, Land walked them through ideas for a recoverable spy satellite, one that would be equipped with cameras much like those used in the U-2. Wiesner later wrote, "By the end of the afternoon, we had a recoverable satellite!"

It was an exaggeration, of course, but Land's ideas had dramatic consequences. Before the end of the month, the Pentagon quadrupled the budget for a new spy satellite program, then tripled it again a few weeks later. Early the next year, Land and Killian outlined the spy satellite proposal to Eisenhower. They agreed that the rockets powering the satellite could be provided through a new defense agency called the Advanced Research Projects Agency (ARPA, which later became known as DARPA), which was tasked with brainstorming new technologies and was officially formed that same day. Eisenhower agreed that the CIA should control the project, just as it had for the U-2.

Land walked into the CIA building on E Street and found Bissell's office. Doris Mirage, the secretary, each night would tidy up Bissell's desk, protecting him from the agency security men who handed out demerits to employees, no matter their seniority, who left classified documents out in the open, or forgot to lock their safes, or didn't empty their trash cans. And each morning, within minutes after Bissell arrived, his desktop reverted to its natural state: a chaos of papers, teetering folders, and tortured paper clips.

Land informed him that he'd just talked to the president, and they'd decided that he—Bissell—would oversee America's new satellite program.

That meant a lot more paperwork, Bissell knew. But if Doris could handle it, so could he.

. . .

NO  ONE  EMBRACED  LAND'S  CHALLENGE  to push science into new frontiers with more enthusiasm than Bissell. Less than six weeks after the launch of *Sputnik,* he delivered a presentation at the CIA that he called "The Stimulation of Innovation." He proposed a new CIA position, a special assistant for planning and development, that would concentrate not on merely developing tools for spies but on encouraging "major break-throughs" that could transform intelligence gathering in much the same way the U-2 had. Already, he said, new developments in infrared and acoustical sensing devices promised to push surveillance into new territories and open the possibility of "gray activities"—surveillance that the CIA may or may not actually have the jurisdictional right to pursue. But that shouldn't discourage the CIA from pursuing every new technique it could dream up. Furthermore, he said, the agency shouldn't limit itself to pursuing revolutionary break-throughs in intelligence collection but also explore innovation in covert political action or, as he phrased it, "the art of political warfare."

The reaction within the CIA was mixed. Dulles seemed to like the idea, and he seemed willing to adopt Bissell's suggestions, including the establishment of an innovation director, as a matter of course. But the CIA's internal note taker attending the meeting noted that "it was quite clear that Frank Wisner and Dick Helms had serious reservations" about some of Bissell's ideas.

Wisner was the agency's longtime spy runner, the head of covert operations. If Bissell wanted to rebuild the CIA on a technological foundation, did that mean he was tacitly rejecting everything Wisner had built his career around? Helms, for one, suspected it might. He respected the value of the intelligence the U-2 had brought in, but he believed Bissell was threatening to turn the agency over to "gadgeteers," technophiles who would reduce covert officers to a secondary role. "You just can't do away with the human side," Helms told colleagues.

Bissell would never have described his intentions that way. He knew how important CIA officers and contract employees were to the agency; he was reminded of it all the time. That fall, for example, Frank Powers and several of the other pilots who'd been recruited to the U-2 program said they were considering quitting. Powers's contract was set to expire in November, and he'd begun to question whether the job was worth the strain on his marriage.

Bissell came up with an idea to keep him and the other pilots with the program. He told them their wives would be allowed to join them at their overseas bases, which would be renovated with "both residential and recreational" upgrades, he said.

The strategy worked. Powers signed an extension to his contract, and Barbara was allowed to live with her husband again. Maybe things would be smoother between them if they were together, they said. "We could at least give it one more try," Powers decided.

CHAPTER 7

## To the Sun

In this age, in this country, there is an opportunity for the development of man's intellectual, cultural, and spiritual potentialities that
has never existed before in the history of our species.

—EDWIN LAND

When Barbara Powers arrived in Adana, she and Frank moved
into a simple sandstone house that the CIA had rented from
a group of Turkish teachers. "We offered them such high
rent that they were happy to move out," Frank explained to Barbara on
her first day in Turkey.

He gave her a tour of the base, which had changed a lot in the past
few months. New buildings were springing up along the gravel road that
ran through the center of the compound, and instead of crude Quonset
huts several of them were two stories tall with metal siding and proper
windows. One housed the Oasis Theater, showing first-run movies
nightly, and another was a library building. Frank and Barbara liked the
new, six-lane bowling alley, which was staffed by young Turkish men
who worked as pinsetters.

A blue Mercedes shuttle bus would rumble down the main road three
times a day, offering rides to and from the center of the city. The air
force enlistees on the base often spent their free time at the Mar Mar, a
bar where local musicians plucked ouds and dragged their bows across
*kemenches* and men formed circles for folk dancing. The U-2 pilots generally avoided the bar and most everything else in the city. Instead they
went trout fishing in the nearby rivers and hunted for duck and partridge in the deltas. Frank and Barbara got the CIA to ship their Buick
to Adana, and they used it to explore the countryside on the weekends. They bargained for silks and textiles in Bursa and Diyarbakir;
they explored the temples of Ankara; they crawled through the ancient
Phoenician caves near the village of Magaracik and toured the crusader

castles and Roman aqueducts scattered throughout southern Turkey. They visited Beirut—"the Paris of the Middle East"—where they bought a camel saddle and copper trays as souvenirs. The CIA bought the pilots their own boat, which they took water-skiing at a newly dug reservoir a few miles from the base. They also played lots of poker, and seven nights a week the seven pilots and their wives took turns hosting a cocktail hour (actually, it usually lasted two hours). Their drink of choice was the gin martini—"Beefeaters," they called them. Barbara could usually be found at the center of the action, and she was elected "social director" of their circle. If the pilots had to work during the weekends, she sometimes led the women on excursions out of town; one of those excursions stretched for fifteen days, during which the ladies saw Paris, Rome, Pompeii, and Naples.

Most of the time, their husbands' work schedule, like nearly everything else, was relaxed. Eisenhower continued to insist on personally approving each and every overflight into Soviet territory, so long flights were rare throughout most of 1958 and 1959. When they did fly, it was usually around the Soviet borders and into Iran or Afghanistan for an hour or two, where they conducted ELINT (electronic intelligence) sweeps, fishing for Soviet radar signals.

Like everyone else in Adana, Barbara was told her husband and the other pilots were monitoring weather and atmospheric conditions. She had no idea they sometimes flew above the Soviet Union, much less that enemy planes were desperately trying to blast them out of the sky. When the CIA allowed the wives to visit the U-2 hangar as a group, Barbara remarked that the plane looked like a big black crow. "Its wings actually do flap on takeoff," Frank told her. She wasn't sure whether to believe him or not.

The wives were not allowed to take a long look inside the cockpit, where a new piece of equipment—an ejection seat—had recently been installed. Johnson's crew added the device to help pilots avoid getting pinned to their seats by gravitational forces if the plane were to go into a spin and they needed to bail out. The way it was designed, the top of the rigid seat back was supposed to strike the cockpit's plastic canopy first and instantly break it apart; the pilot would then fly out and away from the craft, and the parachute would automatically activate. But the designers hadn't realized that in the subzero temperatures of the stratosphere, that cockpit canopy would freeze into a nearly shatterproof shell. So they added sharpened points to the top of the seat, along with a small explosive charge. The pilots didn't like the ejection seats, just as they didn't like the self-destruct button, on philosophical grounds. Plus, they feared that if they activated the seat, the bottom halves of their legs, which were tucked snugly under the instrument panel, would be severed at the knees when they were launched out of the cockpit.

Frank tried not to waste too much energy worrying about such things. To both him and Barbara, life in Adana felt like a lucky break, an incredibly *good deal*. The CIA upgraded the pilots' living quarters, moving them out of the sandstone houses and into new, three-bedroom house trailers on the base that were each fifty-five feet long. When Frank and Barbara moved into theirs, they discovered that they had also been assigned two maids, a butler, and a gardener.

With most of their living expenses paid for by the CIA, they could afford to throw a little of Frank's salary around. During a jaunt to West Germany, Frank bought a German shepherd that had been trained by police, and Eck von Heinerberg, as they named the dog, became part of their household. Around the same time, Frank got rid of their old Buick and splurged on a brand-new charcoal-gray Mercedes-Benz 220SE, a convertible with red leather seats. With the dog perched between them in the front, they'd speed along the dry desert roads, the top turned down and the radio turned up, the Technicolor image of a perfectly happy couple.

BISSELL FELT RESTLESS AS THE PRESS BEGAN hammering away at his CIA colleagues, threatening to expose the agency's most valuable program. In the summer, Hanson Baldwin of *The New York Times* pieced together most of the relevant details of the U-2 program—the plane's design specs, the cameras, the nature of its flights over the Soviet Union. He met with Robert Armory, the deputy director of intelligence for the CIA, at the Hay-Adams hotel and told him that he'd actually glimpsed one of the U-2s during a recent trip to Wiesbaden. "I'm afraid I've got to publish it because I was in an unclassified position and it's a great story," Baldwin said.

Armory left the hotel and huddled with Dulles, who quickly placed a call to Arthur Hays Sulzberger, the publisher of the *Times*. Sulzberger agreed to hold the story, but he told Dulles all bets were off if he found out *The Washington Post* had gotten wind of the story. As it happened, the *Post* soon found out, but its editors also agreed to sit on the news. So did Cleveland's *Plain Dealer*. The security officers in Bissell's group scrambled to keep things under control, like men spread-eagled in front of a leaky dike, stretching to plug all the new holes.

Inevitably, they missed one. On page 34 of the March 1958 issue of *Model Airplane News*, tucked between ads for Uhu glue and X-Acto knives, was an illustrated feature titled "Planes Worth Modeling—Lockheed U-2." The article included several scale diagrams, and the physical details of the craft—from the undercarriage doors to the pogo supports on the wings—were too accurate to be coincidental. Someone had leaked the exact specs. The text stated that the U-2 was built for upper-atmosphere research, but the article didn't merely leave it at that. "The aircraft has no announced military application—but could possibly be used for long-range photographic reconnaissance missions. An unconfirmed rumor says that U-2s are flying across the 'Iron Curtain' taking aerial photographs—or probing radar defenses. At least one U-2 has been reported crashed in Eastern Germany!"

The story didn't send the Washington press corps into a frenzied game of catch-up, perhaps because the reporters at the *Times* and the *Post* didn't closely monitor *Model Airplane News* for scoops. The White House, meanwhile, was preoccupied with another leak it considered far more worrisome. Somehow, Joe Alsop had gotten his hands on a classified document that suggested the frightening concept of a missile gap might be a verifiable reality.

THE SECRET DOCUMENT LEAKED TO ALSOP was the National Security Estimate, which had been drafted by the Pentagon. He likely got it from Stuart Symington, a Missouri Democrat on the Senate Armed Services Committee, who in the coming months tried to capitalize on the so-called missile gap to benefit St. Louis–based defense contractors.

"It is time to say quite bluntly that the Eisenhower Administration is guilty of a gross untruth concerning the national defense of the United States," Alsop wrote. According to the Pentagon's document, the Soviets were expected to produce at least a hundred intercontinental ballistic missiles within a year; the Americans, meanwhile, hadn't produced a single one. Things would only get worse in the coming years, he reported. "Massive orders for hardware must be placed immediately—indeed, they should have been placed last winter—if we are going to make the feeblest pretense of 'keeping abreast' during the years of the gap."

Bissell, once again, could have helped set Alsop straight and nipped the very concept of a missile gap in the bud. The numbers in the National Security Estimate had been calculated without the benefit of the information collected in the most recent U-2 flights, which showed no evidence that Soviet ICBM production had begun. But again, to correct Alsop would have required Bissell to betray the most highly classified information the government possessed, and it would have undermined the future of the project he'd spent the past four years nurturing.

Eisenhower and his closest aides, too, felt as if their hands were tied. "We had the dope," Thomas Gates, the deputy secretary of defense, later recalled, "but we couldn't say we were flying the U-2." Instead Eisenhower's aides watched helplessly as the president threw newspapers across the Oval Office and cursed Joe Alsop as "about the lowest form of animal life on earth."

The White House's anger boiled over at a reception for reporters in 1959. Jim Hagerty, the press secretary, cornered one of Alsop's colleagues from the *Herald Tribune*, Robert Donovan, in an anteroom of the White House.

"We're fed up," Hagerty said. "We can't stand the guy any longer."

Donovan had nothing to do with Alsop's reporting, and he tried to tiptoe away from the subject, but Hagerty reeled him back in.

"I'm going to lift his White House pass," Hagerty insisted. "I'm going to lift his pass, and I can do it."

Donovan was skeptical. Alsop was one of the most powerful and widely read journalists in Washington, and he'd surely raise all sorts of hell if he were barred from official events. "How are you going to do that, Jim?" Donovan asked.

"He's a fag," Hagerty said, "and we know he is."

On January 3, 1959, an item tucked inside the *National Review* proved that Alsop's enemies in America were willing to play almost as dirty as those in Russia. "A prominent American journalist is a target of Soviet blackmail for homosexuality. U.S. authorities know it. His syndicate doesn't—yet." The column strongly suggested the CIA might have helped the journalist cover up the incident. "The feverish activities of Washington's internal security personnel suggest that a major scandal may be under an intelligence agency's rug."

EDWIN LAND HAD COME to the Oval Office to brief Eisenhower on the satellite program, but before he could get down to business, the president needed to empty his spleen. The leaks to the press were driving him batty, and it was the military hawks in Congress—not necessarily the reporters—who *really* ticked him off. Senator Symington, particularly, continued to pounce on the supposed missile gap to try to bully him into more defense spending, and Eisenhower deeply resented it.

"The munitions makers are making tremendous efforts toward getting more contracts," Eisenhower told Land, "and in fact seem to be exerting undue influence over the Senators."

Eisenhower was just beginning to articulate a new concept that he'd later tag with an enduring label—"the military-industrial complex." Before World War II, the concept didn't exist, because the country didn't have an industry dedicated solely to the weapons of war. Now it did, and those companies had learned that fear was good business. For a man who'd earned his reputation as a military commander, Ike was in a strange position: he deeply respected military institutions, yet he lamented the rise of a class of permanent war hawks who seemed to think the solution to all of America's ills was to spend more on defense. It was his vast military experience, he believed, that allowed him to see through their arguments and prevented the senators from taking advantage of him through crude patriotic appeals. "God help the nation when it has a President who doesn't know as much about the military as I do," he said.

Land empathized with him. Hard information was the key to putting the brakes on an unnecessary arms race, and the U-2 was the way to get it. Science and technology, therefore, represented the country's best hope for peace. During a series of meetings in the Oval Office in 1958 and 1959, Land told Eisenhower that he'd sensed a change in the country after *Sputnik,* a scientific reawakening among members of the younger generation. He shrewdly credited Eisenhower for that, thanking him for "making science as popular as baseball." But now, Land told the president, was the time to do even more. At a meeting of the President's Science Advisory Committee, Land "stressed the president's prestige would be an invaluable aid in supporting efforts toward arms control, especially in discussions with military personnel," according to the meeting notes of one person present. "He asked that Eisenhower make this scientific effort at arms limitation a part of the American mission, not only by providing funds, but also by broadly promoting the idea."

It was an astonishingly bold suggestion, and it illustrated just how far the scientific community had come in the four or five years since McCarthy and others attempted to wage their undeclared war on science. McCarthy's fall in the intervening years had been swift and severe. The public turned on him after 1954, tiring of his scare tactics, and the Senate censured him late that year. His political career fizzled, and he began to drink heavily. In May 1957, McCarthy died at age forty-eight. The cause of death was officially hepatitis, but many assumed alcoholism was to blame. And now, in the wake of McCarthy's demise, the fortunes of the senator's many enemies—Oppenheimer among them—seemed on the ascent.

Here was Land, advancing many of the same ideas that Oppenheimer had championed, and instead of getting run out of town for them, he was holding court in the Oval Office. The U-2 had an awful lot to do with that; the success of the spy plane program had earned Land the president's trust, as well as the sort of influence in Washington that few others enjoyed. As far as the public knew, Land was simply a businessman, but to Eisenhower he was a silent partner. In 1959, for example, the White House approached Land with a request: Would he consider giving the president a shipment of Polaroid cameras so the president could take them on his trips overseas and give them to his foreign counterparts as gifts? Land agreed, sending the White House a hundred full photo kits, which included cameras, flashbulbs, and other accessories. Eisenhower eagerly received them, according to an aide, and his staff composed a letter that would go to "every king and princeling receiving the camera, which would explain that the gift was being made by Polaroid and the President jointly, and would express the hopes of Dr. Land and the President that the recipient would enjoy its use."

Around the same time, Land and his wife, Terre, received a telegram from Western Union: "The President and Mrs. Eisenhower hope you can come to dinner at the White House on Tuesday, February 4, at eight o'clock. Stop. White tie. Stop. Please wire reply. Mary Jane McCaffrey, Social Secretary."

It wasn't an intimate gathering but a gala state dinner. Land saw plenty of familiar faces in the room: James Killian was there, as were James Fisk and Edward Purcell from the original panel that dreamed up the U-2. He also saw I. I. Rabi, and Wernher von Braun, both of whom Land had worked with as part of Eisenhower's new science advisory group. There were plenty of uniformed military types in attendance as well, and at one of the tables, decorated with red carnations in gold tureens, sat Curtis LeMay, who still held a grudge against Land, the CIA, and their U-2s.

*The Washington Post* ran an article about the event the following day, and the headline suggested that if the dinner was any indication, Washington's power structure was undergoing a significant shift: "At White House Dinner, Outranked Scientists Outnumber Military."

BY THE SECOND HALF OF 1958, Richard Bissell was able to estimate that a full 90 percent of the CIA's hard intelligence on the Soviet Union was a direct result of the U-2. Edwin Land's initial prediction—that the plane could be the greatest intelligence coup in history—had come true. Bissell's private air force was, within the CIA, considered an unqualified success; in his office, Bissell kept an "R.B.A.F." coffee mug that his colleagues had emblazoned with the words "OUR LEADER." As a reward for his work on the spy plane, Dulles offered Bissell a promotion—the director of all of the agency's covert operations.

He considered the offer for ten days, then accepted the post on the condition that he'd continue to oversee the U-2 and satellite programs. The workload was absurd—he would be directly managing virtually every significant CIA program that existed—but the subtext of the appointment was easily legible to everyone in the office: Bissell was being groomed to take over as the head of the agency when Dulles retired. Richard Helms, who had been considered the other main contender for that role, started referring to Bissell by a nickname drenched in jealousy: Wonder Boy.

These were long, hard days. When Bissell got home from work, often late at night, he'd sink into a chair, thoroughly drained. At the same time his responsibilities at work were ratcheting up, his home life was getting more complicated by the day. His son William, then about six years old, was struggling with a cognitive disability; the doctors had labeled him mentally retarded and his behavior seemed increasingly erratic (today he would probably be diagnosed as severely autistic). Richard and Annie tried to learn as much as they could about his condition, going to lectures and attending weekly group therapy sessions with the boy. But after William smeared feces all over the walls of his room, they decided that his special needs had exceeded their capacity to meet them. It was an agonizing decision, but in 1959 William was sent to a group home, where he remained for the rest of his life (several years later, William would kill another patient in a New Jersey group home; for years after that tragedy, the family wasn't allowed to visit him, because the staff at the institution feared their presence might trigger another violent episode).

Bissell coped with the stress, it seemed, by diving deeper into his work. There was no shortage of it; on the same day Bissell officially took the reins as the head of covert operations—January 1, 1959—the U.S.-backed dictator in Cuba, Fulgencio Batista, was driven out of the country by Fidel Castro's rebels. Weeks later, Allen Dulles appeared before the Senate Foreign Relations Committee to share his agency's intelligence, collected from spies on the ground, in a closed-door hearing. "We do not think that Castro himself has any communist leanings," he said. "We do not believe Castro is in the pay of, or working for, the communists. We believe, however, that this is a situation on which the communists could capitalize if there is not a move to get control of the situation more fully than Castro has control of it now." Within months, the CIA's assessment changed. Bissell's chief of the Western Hemisphere Division, J. C. King, sent him a memo late in 1959 that warned Castro had established a left-wing dictatorship in Cuba and was eager to spread the Communist ideology to his neighbors. "It is my personal opinion that if Castro is successful in consolidating his position and remaining in power for two more years, lasting damage may occur to the United States' already weakened position of leadership in Latin America." King recommended that the new director of covert operations pursue a bold objective: "the overthrow of Castro within one year, and his replacement by a junta friendly to the United States which will call for elections six months after assumption of office." To help make it happen, King offered a suggestion: eliminate Fidel. "None of those close to Fidel, such as his brother Raul or his companion Che Guevara, have the same mesmeric appeal to the masses. Many informed people believe that the disappearance of Fidel would greatly accelerate the fall of the present Government."

NO SOVIET LEADER HAD EVER VISITED the United States, but when Eisenhower invited him to come to America in 1959, Khrushchev jumped at the chance. He landed in Washington on September 15 and thus began one of the strangest media circuses of the decade: a twelve-day, coast-to-coast tour that CBS's Walter Cronkite took to calling "The Khrushchev Road Show."

In the motorcades that paraded him through the streets of Washington and New York, he was all smiles and waves. The fire-breathing dragon that Americans had been primed to fear, it seemed, looked like a warm, jolly cubby bear of a man, and one who was having the time of his life. In Los Angeles, he attended a luncheon with everyone who was anyone—Marilyn Monroe, Bob Hope, Judy Garland, Elizabeth Taylor, Gary Cooper, Henry Fonda, and dozens of other A-listers—and visited the set of *Can-Can,* a musical starring Frank Sinatra and Shirley MacLaine.

Everyone seemed to be having a great time, at first. Then his trip to Disneyland was canceled, for security reasons, and Khrushchev got a little sour. His mood darkened more when Los Angeles mayor Norris Poulson, a staunch conservative, decided that his fellow Americans had been treating Khrushchev far too kindly. "Everybody else has been nice to him," Poulson told a TV reporter, "but I'm not going to be." The mayor proved to be a man of his word. At a dinner in the ballroom of the Ambassador Hotel, the mayor introduced Khrushchev with what sounded like a threat. "We do not agree with your widely quoted phrase, 'We shall bury you,'" Poulson said. "You shall not bury us, and we shall not bury you. We are happy with our way of life. We recognize its shortcomings and are always trying to improve it. But if challenged, we shall fight to the death to preserve it."

The "we shall bury you" line was something Khrushchev had said at a diplomatic reception in 1956, and it was clear to everyone who'd actually been there that what he'd been *trying* to say, metaphorically, was that Soviet Communism would eventually triumph over capitalism in the long run of history—not that he'd engulf the United States in smoldering heaps of radioactive ash. But clarity wasn't one of Khrushchev's strong suits, and many Americans interpreted it as a military pledge. Khrushchev more than once had already tried to clarify the remark during his visit, and he was getting tired of explaining himself.

When Khrushchev took the podium, he started by reading a few anodyne remarks, but he cut himself short, folding up his speech and pocketing it. He looked at Poulson, whose face was fixed in a satisfied smile. The we-shall-bury-you line had struck a nerve.

"Why did you mention that?" he asked the mayor.

The crowd chuckled, not immediately comprehending that Khrushchev's blood pressure was spiking and that he was working himself up into a genuine, fist-shaking lather. "The unpleasant thought sometimes creeps up on me," Khrushchev said, "that perhaps Khrushchev was invited here to enable you to sort of rub him in your sauce and show him the might and strength of the United States so as to make him shake at the knees." His face was turning an angry shade of red. "If that is so," he continued, "it took me about twelve hours to fly here, I guess it will take no more than ten and a half hours to fly back." When the interpreter translated the remarks to the crowd, the ballroom hushed. Was he really threatening to cut his historic visit short because of *this*? "If you want to go on with the arms race, very well," Khrushchev told the audience. "We accept that challenge. As for the output of rockets—well, they are on the assembly line."

After that dinner, Khrushchev's son, Sergei, asked his father what he'd meant by that last part—*the rockets are on the assembly line*? Sergei was, as it happened, a rocket scientist, and he often sat in on military meetings with his father. He knew of no ICBMs in production. His father told him, "It's not important how many missiles we have. Americans just have to *believe* we have them."

Khrushchev had calmed down somewhat by the time he returned to the East Coast, where he spent a day with Eisenhower at his Camp David retreat. The two leaders, accompanied only by an interpreter, took a stroll in the woods around the compound, and Eisenhower broached the subject of the arms race and military spending. "My military leaders come to me and say, 'Mr. President, we need such and such a sum for such and such a program,'" Eisenhower told Khrushchev. "'If we don't get the funds we need, we'll fall behind the Soviet Union.' So I invariably give in. That's how they wring money out of me. They keep grabbing for more, and I keep giving it to them. Now, tell me, how is it with you?"

"It's just the same," Khrushchev said.

Eisenhower seemed to sense an opening. "You know, we really should come to some sort of agreement to stop this fruitless, wasteful rivalry."

They made no promises, but they agreed to give it a shot. They promised each other they would speak again during a summit in Paris the following spring. Along with the leaders of Great Britain and France, they would attempt to untangle some of the knottier problems of the Cold War. After that summit, Eisenhower would travel to the Soviet Union, where Khrushchev would offer him quid pro quo—a deluxe, cross-country tour of Mother Russia.

Later, after he got back to Moscow, Khrushchev told the Supreme

Soviet that his visit to the United States had convinced him it was time to make some cuts in the Soviet military. "The clouds of war," Khrushchev said, "have begun to disperse."

THE SPRING THAW ALONG THE ATLANTIC SEABOARD gave Bissell the chance to reacquaint himself with one of the enduring passions of his life—the *Sea Witch*, a fifty-seven-foot yawl that he'd had since his days at Yale. His co-owner was Herman "Fritz" Liebert, the director of the Rare Book Room at Yale's Sterling Library, who often served as the ship's cook while Bissell took the helm.

Bissell almost always appeared plagued by an excess of energy, and in Washington he'd burn it off by walking for an hour or two at a time around the National Mall. But nothing relieved him quite like a day aboard the *Sea Witch*.

The boat seemed to heighten every part of his personality. With his sons, for example, he was never more fatherly than when on the boat; they bonded over lines and anchors, depth charts and safety inspections. Among his friends, the boat intensified the same personality traits that were surfacing with increasing frequency in his professional life: an impatience with inaction, and a persuasive confidence that led others to trust him to take risks on their behalf, even when a little caution was in order.

Bissell might have *seemed* like an unusually open-minded thinker, always listening to the advice of others and willing to debate a point, but by watching him on the boat, Liebert grew to recognize that Bissell was almost always in control of those conversations, whether anyone else realized it or not. He'd entertain the dissenting views about charting navigational courses, for example, but things always seemed to end the same way: with Bissell steering others toward his position. He'd exhibited the same sort of commandeering influence when he devised the cover story for the U-2; he'd allowed Edwin Land to voice concerns on ethical grounds, but in the end it didn't matter: Bissell's idea prevailed. In his private life, his persuasiveness rarely came across as didactic or heavy-handed. But if Liebert stopped to analyze Bissell's behavior aboard the *Sea Witch*, he couldn't deny that there was something dictatorial in his personality.

"My friends," Bissell once admitted, "question my commitment to democracy."

He was a skilled navigator and fantastic with charts. Yet if he was able to maneuver the boat out of trouble nine times out of ten, he could never seem to resist tempting fate that tenth time. Once, in a predicament that Liebert described as perfectly illustrative, a fog stranded them in a harbor on the rocky and turbulent Nova Scotia coast, and Bissell grew impatient for the weather to clear. "Goddammit," he said, "we'll go anyway." The others were terrified, but went along with him, because they were convinced his reading of the waters was more insightful than their own.

The yawl ran aground.

Bissell directed operations at the CIA much as he helmed the *Sea Witch*. The success of programs like the U-2 had inflated his confidence in his ability to get out of jams, and it persuaded others to put their trust in him.

As he eyed Castro strengthening his relationship with Khrushchev, Bissell chose Cuba as the place where he'd push his luck.

IN MARCH 1960, IAN FLEMING ARRIVED in Washington to stay for a few days at the home of Henry Brandon, the Washington correspondent for London's *Sunday Times,* the paper where Fleming had worked as the foreign news chief from 1945 to 1959. Fleming didn't much like Washington ("It reminds me of one enormous Greek mausoleum," he said), but he had some good friends there, including a well-known socialite named Marion "Oatsie" Leiter, whom he'd known since the 1940s (Fleming would lend her last name to the fictional character Felix Leiter, the CIA agent who worked with James Bond on numerous assignments). They arranged to meet for a Sunday lunch, and as Leiter was driving him in her white Chrysler through Georgetown, she spotted John and Jackie Kennedy, who were friends of hers, on the sidewalk. She stopped the car and asked if she might bring a guest over for dinner at their house that evening. When Leiter introduced the Kennedys to the man in her passenger seat, they immediately said yes; Leiter had introduced both John and Jackie to Fleming's James Bond novels five years before, and the couple had become big fans of the series ever since, snatching up each of his new installments as soon as it was released. Jackie, in fact, had gotten Allen Dulles hooked on the books in 1957, when she gave him a copy of *From Russia with Love,* which he devoured. A few months later, during a trip to London, Dulles got in touch with

Fleming and shared dinner with him. "We talked of new tools that would have to be invented for the new era," Dulles later recalled. "The U-2 was already making its top secret flights, but Fleming's imagination could go even higher."

Dulles was out of town and couldn't attend dinner that evening, but the Kennedys did invite Joe Alsop, who they guessed would fall into easy conversation with Fleming. If Joe continued to suffer any residual stress from his drama in Moscow, he showed no sign of it when he was engaged in social banter, a drink firmly in hand.

Alsop and Fleming, as predicted, got along well. At one point in the evening, Joe decided to test the author's imagination with a real-world hypothetical: How would James Bond deal with the problem of Fidel Castro?

"Ridicule, chiefly," Fleming replied.

For example, he suggested, the United States could spread rumors, via aerial leaflet drops, that the island had been contaminated with radiation. The leaflets would inform the Cuban citizenry that radiation can make men impotent and the contamination lingers longest in facial hair. Perhaps, Fleming suggested, Castro would shave his beard and thus be stripped of much of his revolutionary swagger. Everyone, Kennedy included, seemed sufficiently entertained by the answer.

The next morning, John Bross—a CIA officer who'd been a schoolmate at Groton with Bissell and Alsop and who'd also attended the dinner at the Kennedys' house—repeated the story in the office. Bross didn't know it, but that very day Bissell had scheduled a meeting to review the agency's anti-Castro plans, which he and Dulles planned to present to the National Security Council that week, and he had compiled some ideas for bold schemes in a memo he titled "A Program of Covert Action Against the Castro Regime." After hearing about Fleming, Dulles telephoned both Leiter and Brandon that morning, saying that he'd heard the author had "developed some interesting ideas of how to deal with Castro," and said he wanted to quiz Fleming about them. Dulles was too late; Fleming had already left Washington, they said.

According to an "Eyes Only" report drafted by the CIA's inspector general seven years later, it was at this same time—March 1960—that Bissell's staff began experimenting with unconventional techniques primarily aimed at "discrediting Castro personally by influencing his behavior or by altering his appearance." One of the ideas was "to contaminate the air of the radio studio where Castro broadcast his speeches with an aerosol spray of a chemical that produces reactions similar to those of lysergic acid (LSD)." The plan ultimately went nowhere "because the chemical could not be relied upon to be effective," according to the report. Another idea centered on a cigar that would be treated with a similar chemical: "The thought was to somehow contrive to have Castro smoke one before making a speech and then to make a public spectacle of himself," according to the report. A third scheme that the CIA pursued in early 1960 targeted Castro's facial hair:

> [Name redacted] recalls a scheme involving thallium salts, a chemical used by women as a depilatory—the thought being to destroy Castro's image as "The Beard" by causing the beard to fall out. The chemical may be administered either orally or by absorption through the skin. The right dosage causes depilation; too much produces paralysis. [Name redacted] believed that the idea originated in connection with a trip Castro was to have made outside of Cuba. The idea was to dust thallium powder into Castro's shoes when they were put out at night to be shined. The scheme progressed as far as procuring the chemical and testing it on animals. [Name redacted]'s recollection is that Castro did not make the intended trip, and the scheme fell through.

Bissell continued to oversee the U-2 program, and he and Dulles pestered Eisenhower for additional flights over the Soviet Union that spring. The president agreed that a couple more missions might help definitively disprove Khrushchev's claim that he had assembly lines of ICBMs. But Ike had one condition. "No operation is to be carried out after May 1," he said. The Paris Summit with Khrushchev was set for May 16, and Eisenhower worried that if the Soviets detected an overflight so close to that date, Khrushchev would consider it an unforgivable provocation and might call the whole thing off.

Bissell's office began making plans for the flights. The first one was tentatively slated for early April, and the second one for late in the month. Bissell hoped the second flight would transit the entire Soviet Union; all previous flights had penetrated no more than halfway across the country before they turned back, returning the same way they had come.

As Bissell's office charted the desired course for that flight, they code-named it Operation Grand Slam—the name that Ian Fleming had invented for the plot to break into Fort Knox in *Goldfinger*.

KELLY JOHNSON WAS OBSESSING ABOUT ALTITUDE again. For several months, Soviet MiG-19 and MiG-21 interceptor planes had been pursuing the U-2s, trying to shoot them down, and they seemed to be getting closer with each mission.

The Soviets, it seemed, had been working on a flying maneuver called "zoom climbs" or "snap ups." The MiG pilots would latch onto the same compass heading as the U-2 and follow the plane at an altitude about ten thousand to fifteen thousand feet below. Then the MiG would go into a shallow dive, which would cause the plane to suddenly pick up speed, and at maximum velocity the MiG pilot would yank back his stick to wildly heave the plane upward. Under the right conditions, the MiGs could—for the briefest of instants—reach an altitude that was close to the U-2. The MiG pilots, however, had absolutely no control of their planes when they tried this. A few U-2 pilots saw the stunt play out underneath them: the MiGs would dart up, fail to reach them, then spin helplessly back toward the earth. Some of the U-2 pilots feared that one of these days, one of those MiG pilots was going to get lucky and crash into one of them.

Johnson tested some ideas to try to prevent that possibility. By early 1960, he had hatched a plan to retrofit the entire U-2 fleet with a more powerful Pratt & Whitney engine. The new jet generated 4,200 more pounds of thrust while adding only 2,050 more pounds in weight. The engine's strength allowed the plane to more quickly pass through the tropopause—the space between the troposphere and the stratosphere at 45,000 to 55,000 feet—which significantly reduced the U-2's contrails and made it tougher for enemy spotters to get a bead on the planes before they reached maximum altitude. The new engine also gave the planes an extra 2,500 feet in altitude, permitting the U-2s to cruise at a maximum of 74,600 feet.

Lockheed didn't have time to retrofit all of the U-2s by April 1960, but it had installed the new engine in two of the planes at Adana. One of those U-2s was selected to fly over the Soviet Union for Operation Grand Slam. That particular plane had made a crash landing the previous September, and some of the pilots dismissed it as a "hangar queen"; it always seemed to be in need of repairs. But before the Grand Slam flight, it was outfitted with every bell and whistle in the CIA's shop, including a new System-IXB, which had been designed to communicate false angle readings in response to radar pulses used to control some Soviet air-to-air missiles.

To fly the plane, the CIA chose its most experienced pilot, a man who'd completed twenty-seven operational U-2 missions. Six of those flights had been along the Soviet border, but it had been more than three years since he'd flown his one and only mission inside the U.S.S.R. Frank Powers was itching to go.

ON THE MORNING OF APRIL 27, Powers got up early to find Barbara in the kitchen, moving slowly. At a party with some of the other couples a few weeks before, another pilot had twirled her around and sent her flying across the improvised dance floor. She landed wrong and broke her leg, which was now encased in a plaster cast. The leg bothered her, but it didn't prevent her from packing Frank a lunch to take on his upcoming U-2 mission. She poured some potato soup in a thermos and filled another one with hot coffee. She made six sandwiches, spreading tuna, pimiento cheese, and Spam on bread, and packed them in a red-plaid lunch case along with some pickles, olives, and cookies.

Before he said good-bye, Barbara asked him if he thought he'd be back in time for the going-away party that had been planned for the base's communications director. It was scheduled for the night of May 1. He told her it shouldn't be a problem.

For this mission, the CIA wanted Frank to take off in the U-2 from Peshawar, Pakistan, instead of Adana, just in case the Soviets had figured out where previous flights had originated. So he and a crew from the detachment boarded a transport plane and flew to Pakistan, where he planned to take off the next morning at dawn. But when he got to Pakistan, the weather was bad, and the skies didn't clear for three days. Finally, he was given the go-ahead to fly the morning of May 1—the last possible day before Eisenhower's deadline.

He got up at 2:00 on the morning of the flight, downing a breakfast of eggs, bacon, and toast. A doctor gave him a routine once-over, and another pilot, a backup who'd come with him from Adana, helped him squeeze into the pressure suit. He was hooked up to the pre-breathing machine, and as he inhaled pure oxygen for about two hours, he checked the weather reports. There was a slight wind change, so the navigational details had to be adjusted—nothing drastic. He grabbed the maps and reviewed his route: he'd enter the Soviet Union via Afghanistan, and his first target—marked in red—was the Tyuratam Missile Test Range. Then he'd cross over Kyshtym and Sverdlovsk, head northwest toward Kirov, continue north to Yur'ya and Plesetsk, proceed to Severodvinsk, Kandalaksha, and Murmansk, then finally exit the country to the west. He was instructed to fly to Bodø, Norway, where Colonel Stanley Beerli, his previous detachment commander in Adana, would be waiting for him.

Powers finished up with the oxygen and Colonel William Shelton, the new commander at Adana, stopped by to wish him well.

"Do you want the silver dollar?" Shelton asked.

The silver dollar was a new suicide device, invented to replace the L pill. Inside a hollow coin, which could be screwed apart, a sharp needle was hidden. It was full of a highly lethal dose of shellfish toxin. Powers thought about it for a moment and figured he might as well. He stuck it in the outer pocket on the right leg of his pressure suit and zipped the pocket shut.

At 5:20 a.m., about forty minutes before the scheduled takeoff, Powers climbed a ladder beside the plane and the backup pilot helped him settle into the cockpit. His seat pack, connected to his folded parachute, bulged with supplies: a collapsible life raft, heavy-duty hunting clothes, arctic boots, a compass, signal flares, matches, chemicals to help damp wood catch fire, water-purification tablets, and other first-aid gear. It also contained a large silk American flag poster with a message printed on it that was translated in fourteen languages: "I am an American and do not speak your language. I need food, shelter, assistance. I will not harm you. I bear no malice toward your people. If you will help me, you will be rewarded." In the bottom of the pack rested seventy-five hundred Soviet rubles, twenty-four gold Napoleon francs, and a selection of wristwatches and gold rings that could be used for barter. His .22-caliber High Standard pistol and a hunting knife were packed snugly alongside.

Powers checked the oil, fuel, hydraulic pressure, and exhaust gas temperature gauges. The backup pilot stood on the ladder outside the cockpit, watching for Shelton to flash the signal okaying the takeoff. Minutes ticked by, with no sign of Shelton. The sun was rising in the eastern sky, shining directly on Powers, whose long underwear was already soaking wet with perspiration inside the snug pressure suit. The backup pilot stripped off his shirt, closed the canopy, and draped the shirt over it, to shield Powers from the rays.

Shelton, it seemed, was having a problem communicating with

Washington. For a solid half an hour beyond the anticipated departure time, Powers sat on the runway waiting. Finally, Shelton jumped out of a van and ran across the airfield, flashing them the all clear.

Takeoff was smooth, and the ascent was fast. Powers's flight instructions called for a steady altitude of seventy thousand feet over Soviet territory, but he couldn't race up to those heights right away; he needed to burn about half an hour's worth of fuel out of the wings and make sure all was well with the jet. After almost thirty minutes, not yet in Soviet territory, he was up to sixty-six thousand feet, and he clicked a switch on his radio two times in rapid succession—a signal back to Shelton and the others in Peshawar saying everything was working well. Soon, he heard a single click in response, which was his cue to break all radio contact and continue in silence for the remainder of the nine-hour flight.

He soared over the peaks of the Hindu Kush, and when he neared the Soviet border, he checked the view below in the drift sight. The weather here was "undercast," which meant that dense clouds blocked most of the mountainous topography. His first real target on the map was a rocket range just east of the Aral Sea, and when he approached it, the clouds seemed to cooperate below him, breaking apart. He flipped a switch to turn the cameras on.

He was cruising at seventy thousand feet now. On his maps, clear lines delineated the river network that was supposed to vein the land below him, but spring floods had caused the waters to spill over their banks. He wasn't sure if he was on course or veering slightly off it. He reached for his sextant, thinking he might try to get a line on the horizon and the sun, but the thirty-minute delay at takeoff had rendered his settings inaccurate. Finally he spotted a field of tanks through his drift scope and got his bearings. As he corrected his course, he saw the contrails of planes streaking the sky below him. That meant the Soviets had spotted him. But the planes—MiGs, probably—were thousands of feet below him. They posed no threat, and Powers didn't waste any anxiety over them. He imagined how frustrating it must be for those pilots who seemed to be struggling so hard, and ultimately failing, to reach these heights.

Those MiGs disappeared after he passed the military installation, and for the next couple hours, as he traveled deeper into Soviet territory, he saw no signs of more. The plane's vitals were good: the temperature gauge was safely below max, the light on the camera control indicated all was working well, his oxygen was fine. The one thing that did worry him, just a little, was the pitch-control component of his autopilot system. Every now and then it would blink off, causing the nose to dip slightly. After correcting it a couple times, he decided to shut the system down and fly manually. If he had decided to turn around and abort the rest of the mission, no one would have faulted him.

But he was already four hours into the flight, nearly halfway across the Soviet Union. Behind him, the skies were mostly undercast; ahead, everything looked clear. He'd get good pictures, and if the Soviets hadn't been able to bring any of the U-2s down yet, why should their luck, and his, change now?

He felt calm and secure as he continued to fly straight ahead, following his charts, not turning back.

BOOK THREE

# Icarus Falling

"Icarus, where are you, Icarus,
Where are you hiding, Icarus, from me?"
Then as he called again, his eyes discovered
The boy's torn wings washed on the climbing waves.

—OVID, *THE METAMORPHOSES*, BOOK 8

## CHAPTER 8

# Fallen Angel

It was like a poker game. Each side with its hole cards, hopefully unknown to the other.

—FRANCIS GARY POWERS

At six o'clock in the morning, the telephone next to Nikita Khrushchev's bed rattled to life, rousing him from sleep. It was his emergency line, a special connection that each night was rerouted from his office in the Kremlin to his family's two-story residence in east Moscow. On the other end of the line was Rodion Malinovsky, the defense minister. Soviet radar operators had spotted a high-altitude aircraft crossing the southern border, he said. The intruder appeared to be heading north, toward the heart of the country.

Khrushchev dragged himself out of bed. This was no way to start May Day, the most festive holiday on the Soviet calendar. He washed up, put on a suit, knotted his tie, and trundled downstairs to the dining room, his face locked in a scowl. He sat down at the table to a cup of tea, stirring it silently.

The Americans were trying to intimidate him, he thought. He knew he was being spied upon, and he considered the flight an overt act of aggression, but it was the *shamelessness* of it that really infuriated him. The Americans were trying to assert some sort of technological advantage over him, to rub his nose in their ability to fly just out of reach, taunting him as if he were a child. The fact that they'd pulled this stunt on May Day surely couldn't have been an accident, he thought. It had to be a calculated insult. He took an impatient sip of tea. When his son, Sergei, slipped into the room to join him for breakfast, Khrushchev didn't even bother to acknowledge him.

Sergei was now a twenty-four-year-old rocket scientist and a trusted adviser. He was also an expert judge of his father's moods, and right now he knew better than to pry. When Khrushchev rose to head out the door, Sergei got up and followed him to the gate in front of the house, where a line of cars waited to take the Soviet leader and a small entourage to the annual parade in Red Square. Patriotic music was blaring out of the loudspeakers that flanked the road in front of the residence. Finally, Khrushchev spoke to his son.

"They flew over again."

Sergei understood what he meant; in April, an American spy plane had been detected over Soviet skies, and now the plane—or several of the planes—must have returned. "How many?" Sergei asked.

"Like before—one," Khrushchev said. The plane was detected crossing the border just after 5:30 that morning. Several pilots were being dispatched to try to intercept it, and he'd ordered the military to prepare its S-75 Dvina missiles—a new and powerful ground-based rocket—to try to shoot the plane down.

"But where is it now?" Sergei asked.

"In the area of Tyura-Tam. He took a direct course there after the border, but who knows where he'll go after that." Khrushchev climbed into the back of a boxy ZiL limousine, and before Sergei could squeeze in another question, the car's door closed, silencing the conversation.

Sergei climbed into another car, and when they arrived at Red Square, thousands of people were already filling the streets in preparation for the holiday festivities. In front of the Kremlin, the stepped facade of Lenin's Tomb had been converted to a grandstand reserved for Communist Party leaders, military generals, and Khrushchev himself. Sergei scanned the crowd and found Ivan Dmitriyevich Serbin, the head of the Central Committee's Defense Industry Department. Serbin told him he'd just received an update on the American spy plane from Sergey Biryuzov, the head of the country's air defense forces: the U-2 had successfully flown over Tyuratam, and now it appeared to be headed toward Sverdlovsk. "Biryuzov is at his command center," Serbin told Sergei. "After Sverdlovsk, he'll come and let us know what has happened."

Sergei looked up on the grandstand and saw the crowd making way for his father. Khrushchev was glowering, as if watching a parade were the last thing in the world he wanted to do.

THE AIR COMMAND CENTER was a short car ride from the Kremlin. Inside, Biryuzov had spent much of the morning staring at a floor-to-ceiling map of the Soviet Union printed on a partially translucent screen. Behind that screen, an air defense sergeant held a toylike airplane icon against the back of the map. Every few minutes the sergeant, holding a telephone receiver in his other hand, was fed updates on the plane's coordinates, and he'd reposition the icon against the back of the screen. On the other side of the map, Biryuzov and the commanders sitting beside him at a large table watched the icon inching toward Sverdlovsk.

For the past couple of hours the commanders had been trying to harass the plane with both MiG-19s and ground-based missile fire, without success. But as the U-2 neared Sverdlovsk, where a battery of S-75 Dvina missiles were positioned, they knew they'd have their best chance yet. A commander ordered another formation of MiG-19s to try to chase the U-2 down as ground crews readied the missiles for launch.

The commanders in Moscow couldn't appreciate how confused the situation was at the missile stations in Sverdlovsk, where everyone labored frantically amid shouts and curses. Only one of the three guided missiles successfully fired; as the other two revolved on their bases to take aim at the U-2, a parked truck blocked their paths, causing the launches to automatically abort.

As chaos reigned, the Soviet radar operators monitoring the U-2 noticed that the image of the plane on their screens seemed to disappear, replaced by green "snow"—scattering flecks of light. This could signify that the pilot had ejected chaff to confuse the Soviet radar systems, or it could mean that the plane had been hit by the missile and was breaking into pieces.

Meanwhile, up in the air, the MiG-19s continued their pursuit of the U-2, trying to visually track it above them. One of the Soviet pilots, Captain Boris Ayvazyan, saw something explode in the sky and watched debris shower down around him. It didn't look like the parts of an airplane. He assumed the missile had self-destructed, and he believed the debris was its shattered remnants. He radioed to his commanders on the ground, telling him what he'd seen.

A senior Soviet radar officer got his message and telephoned a report to his superiors in Moscow, updating them on the U-2's status. "The target has discharged chaff and is performing an evasive maneuver," he said. He was mistaken.

AS HE APPROACHED SVERDLOVSK, Powers had peered down through his drift sight and spotted his next target to photograph: a cluster of big buildings that looked like a military barracks of some sort. As he performed a routine check on the oxygen levels feeding into his helmet, he sensed an odd buckle in the air, as if a strong gust had pushed his plane from behind. At the same time, the sky around him turned a brilliant orange.

He felt the plane's right wing dip, and he struggled to correct the imbalance. But just as the plane leveled, the nose began to drop. He pulled back on the stick, and it felt loose, as if the connection between the controls and the tail had been severed. Helpless against the worsening dip, the U-2 nosed straight down and then did a somersault. The force of the sudden maneuver tore one of the wings off the fuselage.

The plane continued soaring through the air upside down, with the nose pointing up at an angle that must have been close to forty-five degrees. Powers was strapped tight by his seat belt as the plane started into a violent spin. In the center of the whirl, his mind was still; he had to get out fast.

He struggled to focus on the altimeter: thirty-four thousand feet and unwinding fast. His pressure suit began to inflate, squeezing him tight, and strong gravitational forces pressed him forward in the seat. His knees were jammed under the control panel, and if he activated the ejection seat, he feared his legs would be cut off. It dawned on him that he could simply unlatch the canopy roof from inside, then unfasten his seat belt, and jump into the open air.

He popped the canopy latches, and the plastic roof was instantly ripped off by the roaring wind.

Powers unlatched his seat belt. He was in a hopelessly vulnerable position, exposed to the violence of forces far beyond his control. His body jerked upward, to an almost standing position. He was now tethered to the plane only by the hose that had been feeding him oxygen throughout the flight. He looked for the self-destruct timer switch, but he couldn't reach it. With the plane continuing to hurtle downward, he pressed his feet against the seat and jumped, tearing his oxygen hose free and thrusting himself out into the shockingly cold air.

He didn't pull the rip cord on his parachute, because he didn't have to; the chute opened instantly and tugged him away from the rapidly falling plane. Suddenly his vision blurred; the faceplate on his helmet was freezing over. He clawed at it to pry it free, and when he succeeded, the world around him resolved with piercing clarity. He hung suspended within a bright blue sky. He looked up and saw the orange-and-white-paneled parachute billowing. Peering down, he saw the fields and forests of the Soviet Union, all spread out in greens and browns underneath his dangling boots.

INSIDE THE SOVIET COMMAND CENTERS in Sverdlovsk and Moscow, so many calls were being radioed back and forth that no one could stitch together an accurate picture of what was going on.

The facts, however, would eventually emerge. That first S-75 Dvina missile that was guided toward the U-2 was a near miss; it exploded behind Powers's plane, but the force of the blast was enough to throw the plane out of balance, and the sudden, unusual stresses on the U-2's frame caused it to break apart. But neither the MiG pilots nor the radar operators realized that this was what had happened, and they misinterpreted the evidence. In the moments after the blast, the MiG-19s continued to soar through the sky, searching for the U-2 that had just been shot down. Meanwhile, a second battalion of missiles was prepared for launch, and the ground-based crews scanned their radar screens for signs of the American craft. Amid all the confusion, some of the missile operators were unaware that the MiGs were racing through the same skies they were searching.

Inside one of those MiG-19s, Lieutenant Sergey Safronov received clear instructions from his commanders: "Radar operators report that the target has released chaff and has descended to an altitude of 12,000 meters. Find it!"

As Safronov and other pilots searched in vain, several more missiles were launched. Radar operators spotted a plane flying just under forty thousand feet—roughly twelve thousand meters—and they guided one of the missiles toward it. The missile hit Safronov's MiG-19, and the luckless pilot was automatically ejected from his plane.

Like Powers, Safronov drifted down toward a village west of Sverdlovsk. A group of villagers saw Safronov's parachute and ran toward him when he landed.

Safronov, who at thirty was the same age as Powers, was bleeding profusely from a deep gash in his side. He was already dead by the time the villagers reached him.

STILL FALLING SLOWLY THROUGH THE SKY, Powers tried to gather his scattered wits and figure out what he might do when he hit the ground. He reached around himself, feeling for the pack that contained all of his emergency supplies. It was supposed to be tethered to him, but he couldn't find it. He began to do a mental inventory of everything in the pockets of his flight suit, recalling all the items others might find if he was captured. There was a paper map, which showed aerial routes leading back into Pakistan and Turkey. He took off his gloves, pulled out the map, and ripped it up into tiny pieces, scattering it like confetti. There was also the silver dollar in his pant pocket. He pulled it out and decided that the coin might attract attention. He unscrewed the silver dollar, removed the poison pin, and let the coin fall to the ground. A thin sheath covered the pin's sharp tip; he put it back in his pocket, figuring it now looked inconspicuous, like a sewing needle. The thought of suicide never crossed his mind. If he was captured and things got dire, he thought, he might use the pin as a weapon.

He surveyed the landscape below him. A lake gleamed like a puddle of chrome beside a village of ten or twenty houses and farms. Beside those clearings sprawled a forest, and he pulled on the parachute's shroud lines to try to steer himself toward it. If he landed in dense tree cover, he figured, he might stand a better chance of making an undetected escape.

But where would he escape *to*?

He had no idea what kinds of people he might eventually find, or how he would communicate with them. He didn't speak Russian. He'd never really even *met* a Russian. He might as well have been a Martian, hurtling toward Earth.

As much as he tried, he couldn't seem to make the parachute go where he wanted it to; he was headed for a plowed field next to the village. That wasn't the worst of it. On a road that ran alongside that plot of land, he spotted a car that seemed to be trying to follow his course. He also caught a glimpse of a farmer on a tractor, and another man who appeared to be piling up brush.

As he descended, it felt as if the ground were now rising up faster to meet him. He narrowly avoided getting clipped by a power line. He hit the ground about a hundred yards from the village.

His helmeted head slammed against the dirt, and he skidded across the ground. Behind him, the parachute was still billowing out, catching the wind and stubbornly yanking him backward.

The two farmers ran toward him; one of them helped him to his feet, and the other worked to try to collapse the chute. As Powers struggled to find his balance and wriggle out of his harness, he noticed that a crowd was quickly forming around him. They were children, maybe thirty of them. They had raced out of the village school to witness the spectacle after spotting his parachute in the sky. Some of the grown-ups now arriving joined the farmers in trying to help him get his helmet off. Everything was happening so fast Powers didn't even have time to panic.

Finally they pried the helmet free. Through his ringing ears, Powers listened as a man peppered him with questions, but he couldn't understand a word. The villagers didn't seem angry, just genuinely puzzled by his inability to speak their language.

AT THE COMMAND CENTER IN CENTRAL MOSCOW, Marshal Biryuzov finally got a report from Sverdlovsk that aimed to cut through the confusion, but it only added to it. An officer said that the enemy plane had likely been shot down—as well as a Soviet MiG-19.

Biryuzov struggled to process the information. "What do you mean, one of ours? How many planes did you shoot down? Can't you tell the difference between ours and theirs?"

The news about the Soviet casualty was distressing, but Biryuzov didn't let it overshadow the central point: the Soviets had finally shot down an American intruder. This was a clear military victory, a triumph against the brazen Americans that was worthy of celebration. But then, of course, there was the matter of the MiG-19. Biryuzov and the other commanders decided that the exact cause of Lieutenant Safronov's death didn't necessarily need to be included in the official write-ups. Safronov, they decided, crashed in a valiant pursuit of the American violator. He was lauded as a hero, and for decades the true circumstances of his death would remain unreported.

With the plane shot down, Biryuzov needed to get the good news to Khrushchev. Biryuzov was dressed in military combat gear, and if he showed up at the parade wearing anything but his ceremonial formal uniform, he'd look out of place. He briefly considered rushing home to change clothes, but that would take too long. So he proceeded to Red Square and found Khrushchev atop Lenin's Mausoleum.

The military portion of the parade had just ended, and in the streets below him a float designed in the shape of a giant dove rolled by; women waved sprigs of flowers, and men hoisted Communist banners; troupes of ballerinas danced on tiptoe, and thousands of marching citizens smiled and sang, peering up at the mausoleum where Khrushchev waved at them approvingly. Biryuzov made his way up to the Soviet leader and leaned down toward his ear to tell him the news.

Khrushchev beamed.

ONE OF THE MEN WHO HAD RUN to meet Powers and helped him to his feet saw the gun attached to his flight suit. When the man moved to grab it, Powers didn't stop him. Soon, Powers saw that someone else had located the pack of emergency supplies that he failed to find as he drifted down; apparently, the pack had been attached to the parachute. The villagers motioned for him to get in the front seat of a small car. Powers squeezed in next to the driver, and the man who now had his pistol sat on the other side of him. A few more men piled into the back. They began to drive through the village, and Powers motioned to his throat, struggling to communicate that he was thirsty. They eventually stopped at a house and brought him a glass of water. One of the men pulled out a pack of cigarettes, and Powers accepted a smoke. As he lit up outside the car, Powers noticed that the man with the pistol had slipped it out of the holster and was examining an engraving on it: "Made in the USA." With his finger, the man traced the letters—USA—in the dust on the dashboard and looked to Powers for an explanation.

It seemed useless to deny it. Sooner or later, they'd find the cloth flag in his emergency pack, if they hadn't already.

He nodded his head—yes, he was an American.

They seemed to brighten, as if they couldn't believe their luck.

They drove over muddy roads until they came to another village, bigger than the first. A man in uniform greeted them, and he searched Powers, patting down his flight suit. He found a pack of Kent cigarettes and a lighter but missed the poison pin. Soon more uniformed men arrived, from the military apparently, and Powers was given a brief medical examination. His shin was scraped up, and his head ached; a female doctor rubbed his leg with antiseptic and gave him two pain pills.

More people began arriving at the site, many of them carrying pieces of the U-2 wreckage they'd collected. They hustled Powers into a military truck, and with a machine gun trained on him, they drove him into Sverdlovsk, the fourth-largest city in Russia. A man dressed in civilian clothes—a KGB agent, Powers guessed—searched him again, and this time he found the poison pin. The agent gave it a quick look and slipped it into a briefcase.

Powers's ears were still ringing. He stuck a finger into one of them to try to clear the clogged canal, but the agent swiftly slapped his hand down. Powers didn't understand why he was being so brusque. When Powers's finger again went into his ear, the agent slapped it away a second time. An idea formed in Powers's mind: the man had figured out what the poison pin was, and now he suspected him of trying to push some sort of poison capsule into his ear canal. Whatever the truth might have been, Powers stopped touching his ears.

"Are you an American?" the agent asked in stiff, accented English.

Powers answered that he was, and he remembered the cover story that the CIA had provided him: he was a civilian pilot whose navigational equipment had conked out on him, he said, and he'd gotten lost. Powers knew it must have sounded far-fetched; he was, after all, in the center of one of the largest countries in the world, some thirteen hundred miles from the border. When he saw that a giant reel of 70 mm film had been recovered from the wreckage, he figured his cover was probably blown.

When the man showed Powers a wallet that had been found among the debris, Powers silently cursed his own foolishness. He'd forgotten he'd brought his wallet, which contained all sorts of awkward material—his international driver's license, a Social Security card, pictures of Barbara, and a Defense Department identification card describing him as a civilian employee of the air force—into the plane.

Powers pointed out the word "civilian" printed on the military ID, but the man seemed far more interested in the words "Air Force." The agent kept insisting that Powers was a U.S. fighter pilot on a mission of aggression. Powers sensed that his life was in serious danger and nervously scanned the room: the briefcase with the poison pin inside it was out of reach, and a guard was standing directly in front of the unbarred windows. He was trapped with no means of escape.

To try to convince the man he wasn't on a military mission, Powers abandoned his cover story and admitted that he was an employee of the Central Intelligence Agency. Judging by the way the agent eyed him, Powers got the distinct impression that he had heard of the CIA before.

LUBYANKA, A HUGE BUILDING in Moscow that housed the Soviet secret police headquarters and a prison, had an international reputation as a place where spies were tortured. Sidney Reilly, accused of spying on behalf of the British Secret Service, was imprisoned there in

we knew he would take care of it—the president, the U.N., or anything else."

It was, in fact, partly an act. Bissell was gripped by a sense of impending doom, as if his career—and, perhaps, the free world itself—were now infinitely less secure than they'd been earlier that morning. The program that had done so much to revamp American intelligence gathering was in danger of complete, dramatic collapse; worse, it now threatened to spark a diplomatic crisis that could push the Cold War to dangerous new extremes. But he tried not to let his imagination get ahead of itself. If Powers had been shot down, it meant he was almost certainly dead. His loss was a tragedy, but death had always been an unstated possibility, and the truth was it made things much simpler. The cover story the CIA had worked out years before—the one that said the U-2 was designed to collect weather data at high altitudes—might yank them out of this entire mess. Inside his office, aides dug the cover story out of the files and began drafting a statement that NASA or the State Department might be able to release to the American people.

IN CALIFORNIA, KELLY JOHNSON GOT THE CALL that Powers was missing shortly after midnight.

This wasn't the first time he'd lost a pilot, and his previous experience had taught him to fear the worst. Twenty-three years before, shortly after he'd earned his reputation as Lockheed's precocious superstar, he had been Amelia Earhart's technical adviser as she prepared to try to fly around the world in a Lockheed Electra 10E. Johnson would go up in the plane with Earhart on test flights, and together they'd fill the cockpit with different weights, fly at different altitudes, use different engine settings—all in an effort to figure out how she might squeeze more miles out of the plane's fuel tanks.

Earhart and her navigator, Fred Noonan, plotted a west-to-east course that started in Hawaii. But on that first attempt, she lost control of the plane on takeoff and stripped the landing gear; the Electra had to be shipped back to California by boat for repairs. For her next attempt, begun in the late spring of 1937, she decided to fly east. This course required her to land briefly in several strategically selected locations for refueling. Johnson kept in touch with her via telegrams sent to her refueling stations, offering reminders about the proper use of the wing flaps and tips on how best to execute her climbs after takeoff to maximize efficiency. Her second-to-last refueling stop was Howland Island,

ABOVE: Edwin Land in 1947 at the Optical Society of America, where he publicly unveiled his "instant" photography process. The success of his instant cameras would help make Polaroid Corporation one of the most successful companies in America.

BELOW: Francis Gary Powers in 1956, the year he left the air force and secretly joined the CIA, where he was given the alias Francis G. Palmer.

ABOVE: Clarence "Kelly" Johnson with models of some of the airplanes he designed for Lockheed. In addition to the U-2, Johnson was the lead designer for numerous aircraft, including the P-38 Lightning, the P-80 Shooting Star, the Super Constellation, and the SR-71.

BELOW: Richard M. Bissell in the early 1950s, shortly before Allen Dulles recruited him into the CIA. Bissell's administration of the U-2 program helped establish him as one of the agency's most powerful senior leaders.

ABOVE: General Curtis E. LeMay, the head of the U.S. Strategic Air Command, was an early and energetic opponent of Kelly Johnson's design for the U-2. After the Lockheed design was approved, he fought to prevent the CIA from taking control of the spy-plane project, believing that the military should administer it.

RIGHT: Joe Alsop (seated) is pictured with his brother and journalistic partner, Stewart, in Joe's Georgetown home in 1955.

BELOW: Allen Dulles was the director of the CIA from 1953 to 1961. "His unprofessional delight in cloak-and-dagger for its own sake was an endearing trait," said British spy and Soviet double agent Kim Philby.

ABOVE: For years the Burbank campus of Lockheed was obscured by overhead camouflage netting. Movie-studio crews helped design some of the nets, painting housetops and street grids on them and planting false shrubs and bushes on top of them using chicken wire and burlap.

BELOW: Kelly Johnson with Tony LeVier, the Lockheed test pilot who was the first person to fly a U-2 during tests at Area 51 in 1956.

LEFT: Soviet leader Nikita Khrushchev (right) shakes hands with Dag Hammarskjöld, the secretary-general of the United Nations, as Nikolai Bulganin, the Soviet prime minister (far left) looks on. U.S. ambassador Charles Bohlen, standing between the two men, hosted the leaders at the American embassy for a party on July 4, 1956. Earlier the same morning, the CIA flew the first U-2 spy mission over the Soviet Union.

BELOW: President Dwight Eisenhower with Nikita Khrushchev at Camp David in 1959. Khrushchev became the first Soviet leader to visit the United States, spending twelve days on a well-publicized, coast-to-coast trip.

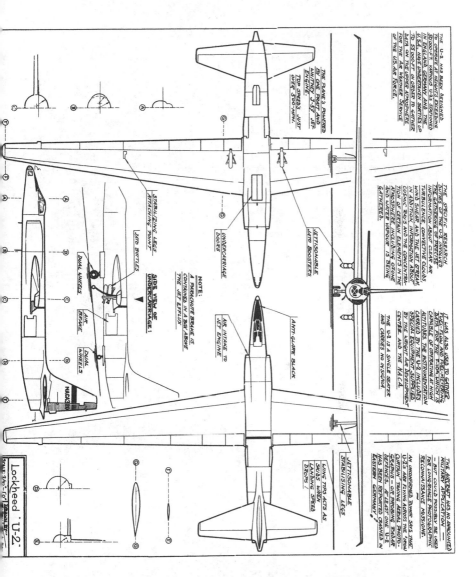

Even before Powers was shot down, the CIA struggled to keep details of the U-2 program secret. In 1958 the magazine *Model Airplane News* published a remarkably accurate design overview for hobbyists. "An unconfirmed rumor says that U-2s are flying across the 'Iron Curtain' taking aerial photographs—or probing radar defenses," the magazine stated.

ABOVE: Among the pieces of evidence displayed at Powers's trial in Moscow was the three-inch-long "suicide pin" the pilot had carried in his flight suit. When the plunger tip of the pin was pressed, a lethal poison was injected into the bloodstream.

RIGHT: Powers in 1960, after he was captured in the Soviet Union and imprisoned in the Lubyanka building in central Moscow.

BELOW: After Powers was shot down in May 1960, Khrushchev's government displayed the remnants of the U-2, along with articles that Powers was carrying, to the Soviet public in Moscow.

RIGHT: Barbara Powers arrives amid a throng of reporters in Moscow in August 1960 for her husband's trial. Barbara blamed the CIA for much of the stress she endured before and after her husband's capture and imprisonment.

BELOW: Powers testifying before a Senate committee in 1962. Upon his release from prison, Powers was dismayed at the number of people who believed he might have been an agent for the Soviets.

BELOW: Edwin Land's success with Polaroid made him a celebrity of the business world. Here he is shown on the cover of *Life* magazine in 1972, when the company's SX-70 instant camera was unveiled. Throughout his years in the public eye, however, his work on the U-2 and other intelligence-gathering projects remained secret.

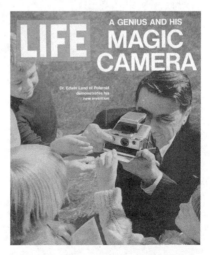

Kelly Johnson with Powers in late 1962. After his return from the Soviet Union, Powers moved to California to work as a test pilot for Johnson at Lockheed.

a tiny dot in the Pacific less than two miles long that rose only a couple feet above water. The skies around Howland Island that day were heavily overcast, which would have made it difficult for Earhart to fly high enough, above twenty thousand feet, to spot the sun—a requirement for accurate navigation. She didn't arrive at Howland Island, and she was never heard from again.

After Earhart went missing, some people held out hope that she might have survived, perhaps by landing on a different island. But Johnson never doubted she was gone. The hard numbers—the distances to other islands, the miles per gallon of fuel the Electra could achieve—added up to disaster. No amount of wishful thinking could change the math.

When he arrived at Skunk Works the morning after he'd been told the U-2 was missing, Johnson's mood was one of resigned dejection. He had met Powers back in 1956 at Area 51, and he'd gotten to know him as a well-trained pilot. Johnson was in mourning—for the assumed loss of Powers, and also for the assumed loss of a project that he'd poured his soul into for four years. "That's that," he told a small group of engineers. "We're dead."

ABOUT FORTY MILES SOUTHEAST OF ISTANBUL, inside a barbed-wire enclosure near the Sea of Marmara, technicians employed by the National Security Agency manned America's most important "listening post" of the Cold War. There, the NSA's operators could intercept some of the high-frequency Morse communications of the Soviet air and naval services, as well as signals emitted by Soviet radar defense systems. Each time a U-2 flew over the Soviet Union, NSA operators monitored this electronic chatter, and they relayed it via encrypted messages to the agency's headquarters in Fort Meade, Maryland.

While Powers was flying toward Sverdlovsk, the head of the NSA's Soviet Air Defense Branch, Henry Fenech, was monitoring the operators' reports as they came into Fort Meade. The transmissions indicated that the Soviets had plotted Powers's altitude as somewhere above sixty thousand feet for the duration of his flight. But shortly after his plane passed over Sverdlovsk, the Soviets reported that Powers had descended to an altitude between thirty thousand and forty thousand feet and reversed course, inexplicably turning back in the direction from which he'd just come.

The Americans poring over the radar and Morse signals were baffled. Why had Powers turned back and descended? They had no idea, of course, that the Soviets had been thoroughly disorganized in their pursuit of the U-2 and that their own internal communications were corrupted by disinformation. The NSA didn't know that Soviet radar operators had apparently confused Powers's plane with Safronov's lower-flying MiG-19, which they had shot down.

Lacking this context, Fenech shared the intercepts with CIA analysts. At Quarters Eye and in Bissell's office, the analysts couldn't come up with a good explanation—one that wasn't alarmingly suspicious, that is—for why Powers would radically change his flight plan just before he disappeared in Soviet territory.

EISENHOWER WAS WRAPPING UP A WEEKEND of shooting skeet and hitting golf balls at Camp David when he got the call from Andrew Goodpaster, his staff secretary. "One of our reconnaissance planes on a scheduled flight is overdue and possibly lost," Goodpaster said.

The president flew back to Washington that afternoon, landing on the South Lawn of the White House at 4:26, but he didn't directly deal with the missing plane until the next morning, when Goodpaster walked into the Oval Office wearing an expression that told Eisenhower the news wasn't good. "Mr. President," Goodpaster said, "I have received word from the CIA that the U-2 reconnaissance plane I mentioned yesterday is still missing. . . . With the amount of fuel he has on board, there is not a chance of his being aloft."

Goodpaster handed Eisenhower the draft of the cover story that Bissell's office had prepared for public release. It read,

A NASA U-2 research airplane being flown in Turkey on a joint NASA-USAF Air Weather Service mission apparently went down in the Lake Van, Turkey, area at about 9:00 A.M. (3:00 A.M. E.D.T.) Sunday, May 1.

During the flight in eastern Turkey, the pilot reported over the emergency frequency that he was experiencing oxygen difficulties. The flight originated in Adana with the mission to obtain data on clear air turbulence.

A search is now underway in the Lake Van area. The pilot is an employee of Lockheed Aircraft under contract to NASA. The U-2 program was initiated by NASA in 1956 as a method of making high-altitude weather studies.

Eisenhower's skepticism about the U-2 had proved well-founded, but all he could do now was to try to minimize the fallout. He handed the page back to Goodpaster and nodded his approval.

IT WAS FIVE O'CLOCK IN THE MORNING in Adana, and Eck von Heinerberg, the German shepherd, began barking loudly when two men approached the trailer where he was tied up. Barbara awoke, hoisted herself onto her crutches, and hobbled to the front door.

The men introduced themselves as employees of the Central Intelligence Agency. Barbara knew what the spy agency was, but she still wasn't aware that Frank worked for it, and the introduction only thickened her early-morning fog. They told Barbara that she should gather some clothes and toiletries for an emergency return to the United States. The rest of her possessions—and Frank's—would be packed and shipped stateside by the government. She wouldn't have to worry about a thing, they said.

But she did worry, of course. Had something happened to Frank? They wouldn't give her any details, just generic assurances that everything would be okay.

She argued with them for a while, trying to extract a straight answer as she struggled to collect not just her belongings but also her wits. She'd been living abroad for more than three years now. When she got back to the United States, where would she go? What would happen to their Mercedes? And what about the dog? "I just can't leave him here," she told them.

She could bring the dog with her on the plane, they said, but they had to leave now. They drove her and Eck to the runway and her waiting plane.

During the flight across the Atlantic, they served her liquor to calm her nerves, but they still wouldn't tell her what had happened to her husband.

AFTER POKING HIS SILVERWARE AT AN UNAPPETIZING lunch of potatoes and cabbage soup, Powers was told by his prison handlers that they would take him on a tour of Moscow that afternoon. A change of scenery sounded welcome after three days of interrogations inside Lubyanka.

They led him to a car, which drove out of the prison grounds and steered through the streets of Moscow. Powers drank in the scenery:

the Kremlin, Moscow University, a large stadium, a man-made ski slope near the center of the city. His tour guides seemed to enjoy the outing, as if they were proud of their city and liked showing it off.

They wanted to impress him, he thought, and maybe that meant they weren't going to kill him after all. When he returned to his cell, a fantasy took root in his imagination: What if the Soviets were detaining him as part of a big public relations stunt? Maybe, he thought, Khrushchev was planning to take him to the Paris Summit, where he'd hand him over to Eisenhower as the international media looked on. The Soviets would brag about how humanely they had treated him, portraying his stay with them as if it were a vacation, complete with hot meals and guided tours of Moscow—all in spite of the fact that Powers and his government had so willfully mistreated them by trying to spy on them. This way, Khrushchev would be able to claim a moral advantage when he began negotiations with the United States, France, and Britain.

He held on to the daydream for hours, turning it over in his mind like a sparkling jewel as he fell into a light sleep.

His optimism didn't last. The next morning, the *real* interrogations began—tense sessions that stretched for eleven hours at a time, convincing him that the questioning he'd endured during the first three days of captivity were mere warm-ups. Five people loomed over him: an interpreter, a stenographer, two military majors, and a colonel. Afterward, he was led back to his cell, where he fell into bed, only to wake up and endure the same interminable ordeal yet again the next morning.

His interrogators niggled at the smallest of details. Where was he based? How many planes were stationed there? How many pilots? What were their names? Did any high-ranking officials visit the base while he was there? Who ordered the flight? Who was in charge of planning it? Who marked the route on his maps? Did he radio his base when he went down? Where did he learn to fly the U-2? What was the name and rank of his commanding officer? Where did he grow up, go to school, what did he study? When was he recruited into the CIA? How? By whom? How fast could the U-2 fly? How high?

Perhaps the interrogations wouldn't have drained him so thoroughly if he had felt free to answer everything truthfully, without shading the details. The Soviets already knew some of the answers to these questions, he assumed. They had the film, as well as pieces of the plane. Lying about the nature of his mission, which was obvious, would be the equivalent of begging for an execution. He resolved to truthfully admit what he believed they already knew, but nothing more.

He figured there was a good chance that Soviet intelligence already knew about the base in Adana, and perhaps they'd surveilled it. He revealed that the numerical designation for his detachment was "10-10," because that number had been printed on his ID card and also on a radio channel chart in the cockpit. He tried to protect the names of everyone who'd ever worked on-site, but he let it slip that both General Thomas White, the air force chief of staff, and General Frank Everest, the commander in Europe, had visited Adana—a safe admission, he thought, because their tours of the base had been written up in *Stars and Stripes*.

From some of their questions, it became clear to Powers that the Soviets had detected the overflight that had taken off on April 9, the mission that had flown before his own. Powers had been the backup pilot that day, and he knew everything about it—the pilot, the flight plan, the targets. But when asked where he'd been that day, he played dumb.

"Probably in the club," Powers answered. "Drunk."

They kept hammering at him, trying to get him to give up the names of his superiors in the CIA who ran the program, but he purposefully shielded Bissell and his team, claiming he'd had little contact with agency higher-ups. When they pressed him for the name of the officer who'd recruited him, Powers was quick with his answer.

"Bill Collins," he said.

In the years since their first meeting at the Radium Springs Casino, Powers had gotten to know the man who'd introduced him to the CIA, and he had learned his real name. But he fed the Soviets his pseudonym. If that name somehow ever made it back to America, Powers thought, then the government would realize that he was still loyal and still guarding its secrets.

MAY 5 GOT OFF TO AN ODD START for Llewellyn "Tommy" Thompson, the new U.S. ambassador in Moscow, and it grew increasingly bizarre as the day progressed.

That morning, a Soviet guard led him into the vast auditorium of the Supreme Soviet to hear a special address by Khrushchev. Instead of depositing Thompson within the sea of heads on the floor, where a relatively new member of the foreign diplomatic corps was expected to sit, the guard ushered him to a prime seat, in a box in the front row, close to the main podium and in full view of the twelve hundred Soviet deputies chattering in the crowd.

Khrushchev was greeted with thunderous applause, which he allowed to continue for a moment before he silenced it with a clap of his hands. "Comrade Deputies!" he said. "This session of the Supreme Soviet has convened in the spring, a wonderful time." Khrushchev was in fine spirits, his voice resonating throughout the hall. He talked, and talked some more—a rambling, patriotic address that didn't really reach its central point until more than two hours into the speech, when he finally broached the subject of the upcoming Paris Summit.

American officials, he announced, had apparently given up on all hopes of a negotiated peace. "Lately influential forces—imperialist and militarist circles, whose stronghold is the Pentagon—have become noticeably more active in the United States," he said. "These aggressive forces stand for the continuation of the Cold War and the arms race. And they have been going in for *downright provocation.*"

Thompson was already feeling the hot glare of unwelcome attention when Khrushchev raised his voice and revealed that an American spy plane had illegally entered Soviet territory. "The plane," Khrushchev thundered, "was shot down!"

The hall erupted. Several people shouted "Down with the aggressors!" as Khrushchev continued to heap scorn upon the "bandits" who invaded sovereign territory. He turned toward Thompson, a sitting duck as all eyes turned on him. "What *was* this?" Khrushchev asked him. "A May Day greeting?"

Thompson endured another hour of Khrushchev's theatrical contempt and, after delivering several "no comments" to reporters in the hall, made his way back toward the embassy. American news reports were already hitting the wires, and Thompson picked up the phone to expand on the embassy's initial bulletin with more details, but he was having trouble reaching his bosses in Washington. At that moment, the civil defense drill called Operation Alert 1960 was under way; the members of the National Security Council were on their way to High Point, the secret government bunker hidden in the Blue Ridge Mountains. He sent a cable to the State Department informing them of Khrushchev's speech, which eventually made its way to the president and others in the bunker.

In the early evening, Thompson made his way to the stately Sovietsky hotel, where the Ethiopian ambassador was hosting a reception. Thompson knew that most of Moscow's diplomatic community would turn out for the event and representatives from the Kremlin would join them. They'd all be buzzing about Khrushchev's explosive speech, no doubt.

Shortly after Thompson arrived, he spotted Jacob Malik, Khrushchev's deputy foreign minister, chatting with the ambassadors from Sweden and India. Thompson made sure he was close enough to overhear the conversation. One of the men asked Malik which article of the UN charter the Soviets would cite in their complaint about the American incursion? Malik said they hadn't yet decided. "The pilot hit the silk," Malik said, "and we are now interrogating him."

*Hit the silk?* It was military slang for deploying a parachute. Thompson couldn't believe what he was hearing, and he hurried back to the embassy and sent a rush cable to Douglas Dillon, the acting secretary of state, informing him that he'd heard Powers might still be alive and talking to the Soviets. The words "MOST URGENT" were printed boldly at the top of the cable.

It arrived at the State Department at 1:34 p.m., which was exactly four minutes too late.

AT 1:30 P.M. INSIDE THE MADISON HOUSE on Lafayette Square, Walter Bonney, NASA's press officer, entered the ballroom and greeted the assembled journalists. Armed with a script prepared for him by Bissell's office, he offered additional details concerning the high-altitude weather plane that was reported missing two days earlier.

The plane had taken off from Adana and was studying "gust-meteorological conditions," he said, when it disappeared over the Lake Van region of Turkey. "About one hour after takeoff, the pilot reported difficulties with his oxygen equipment," Bonney said. "Using emergency radio frequency, he reported he was heading for the Lake Van beacon to get his bearings, and that he would return to Adana."

At the State Department, spokesman Lincoln White was conducting his own press conference. Like Bonney, White was unaware that Powers might still be alive. He referenced Khrushchev's speech to the Supreme Soviet and suggested that the Soviet leader's misinformed outburst must have had something to do with the missing weather plane. "It is entirely possible that having failure in the oxygen equipment, which could result in the pilot losing consciousness, the plane continued on automatic pilot for a considerable distance and accidentally violated Soviet airspace," White said.

By the time White and Bonney had ended their conferences, the news from Thompson's telegram was spreading through the upper echelons of the CIA. If Powers truly was alive, he would likely contradict nearly every detail that the government had just sold to the American people. All that stuff about Lake Van, and wind gust, and oxygen problems, and using an emergency radio frequency—Powers didn't know any of it. If the rumor Thompson had heard was true and Powers was alive, then the Soviets would certainly have enough evidence to prove the pilot had been on a spy mission and the Americans had lied. Eisenhower could, of course, claim ignorance of the U-2 flight, and he could even say he'd had nothing to do with the cover story, but it would make him appear woefully disengaged. And that impression—that he was more interested in golf than running the country—was already chum to his political enemies.

If Eisenhower privately told members of Congress the truth, many would be angered that they hadn't been informed of the project earlier and would attack both Eisenhower and the CIA. But Bissell and Dulles believed they might be able to manage the political fallout. On the morning of May 6, Bissell walked to the White House and urged Eisenhower to take a select few lawmakers into his confidence and tell them the whole story—"to prevent the building up of indignation in Congress, which would only pour more fuel on the fire."

Eisenhower didn't like that idea. The information that Thompson had passed along was, after all, still only a rumor; no one had confirmed that Powers was still alive, and Khrushchev hadn't said a word about capturing the pilot during his speech to the Supreme Soviet the day before. If Powers was dead—the assumption they'd worked on all along—then it would be foolish to spread the classified truth around to too many people. "These Congressional fellows will inevitably spill the beans," Eisenhower said.

Lincoln White held another press briefing that afternoon and doubled down on the lie.

"There was absolutely no—N-O—no deliberate attempt to violate Soviet airspace," he said. "There never has been."

And that same afternoon, a press release was issued by the State Department that read, in part, "The name of the American civilian pilot is Francis Gary Powers."

. . .

KHRUSHCHEV WAS OFTEN PORTRAYED IN AMERICA as a blustery clown, angry and red-faced, an unhinged fanatic with his finger trembling over the nuclear button. In fact, he was the best potential partner for peace, by a wide margin, that America had yet encountered in the Soviet Union. He was a reformer, and he'd risked his political career by denouncing Joseph Stalin and the abuses he'd committed. By releasing thousands of political prisoners and posthumously absolving others who had been persecuted under Stalin, Khrushchev attracted the suspicion of hard-line apologists and intellectuals who for years had denied reports of widespread abuse. His government was still a long, long way from resembling an open and free society, but Khrushchev— much more than his predecessors and rivals in Moscow—at least seemed willing to take a few steps in that general direction.

His theatrical initial announcement of the downed U-2 had milked the shoot down for political gain, without question, but in a sense he'd granted Eisenhower the benefit of the doubt. Khrushchev had been careful to attribute the U-2's incursion to "aggressive forces," probably inside the Pentagon, instead of laying the blame at the president's feet.

But now that the Americans had continued the lie, the CIA tried to anticipate how he'd react. A personality profile and psychological assessment drafted by the CIA around this time acknowledged that Khrushchev was "plainly less doctrinaire" than some of his comrades and easily underestimated. The document described his early years this way:

> From all appearances he was an impetuous, obtuse, rough-talking man, with something of the buffoon and a good deal of the tosspot in him.
>
> Before long, however, events would show that there was a great deal more to Khrushchev than the appearance suggested and that behind the exterior lay a shrewd native intelligence, an agile mind, drive, ambition, and ruthlessness. His own colleagues probably sold him short initially, but they undoubtedly knew from experience that he could not have escaped Stalin's murderous judgment if he had been witless or foolishly impulsive.
>
> It now is clear that he had other qualities which had only limited opportunity for expression under Stalin—resourcefulness, audacity, a good sense of political timing and showmanship, and a touch of the gambler's instinct.

After the State Department and NASA had repeated their lies about the U-2, Khrushchev knew he was holding the trump card, and it was time to throw it down. On Saturday, May 7, Khrushchev returned to the Supreme Soviet and delivered another speech, this one even more explosive than the first, and it seemed full of the cunning mentioned in the CIA psychological assessment.

"Comrades," he said, "I must let you in on a secret. When I made my report two days ago, I deliberately refrained from mentioning that we have the remnants of the plane—and we also have the pilot, who is quite alive and kicking!"

The Great Hall erupted in cheers. At the American embassy, Llewellyn Thompson's spirits sank as he watched the jubilation on state television.

Khrushchev seemed both outraged and overjoyed as he waited for the applause to die down. "We did this quite deliberately, because if we had given out the whole story, the Americans would have thought up still another fable. And now, just look how many silly things they have said: Lake Van, scientific research, and so on. Now when they learn that the pilot is alive, they will have to think up something else. And they will!"

Khrushchev explained that Powers was in good health—he had never felt dizziness nor experienced oxygen problems—and he had admitted to being an employee of the Central Intelligence Agency. To erase any doubts, Khrushchev listed details about Powers's detachment in Turkey and said the Kremlin had recovered the photos that Powers had taken from the plane, waving some prints of airfields and military installations in front of the crowd. He also said they'd recovered the recordings of signals from Soviet ground radar stations that the U-2 had captured. "Incontestable evidence of spying," he said.

Khrushchev reported that the plane had been equipped with a self-destruct unit, but because Powers feared the device might kill him, he didn't deploy it. "But this diabolical machine was not the only precaution taken," Khrushchev said. "To cover up his crime, the pilot was told that he must not be captured alive by the Soviets." Khrushchev held up a photograph of a small, sharp object. "He was to jab himself with this poison pin, which would have killed him instantly. What barbarism! Here it is! The latest achievement of American technology for killing their own people!" He then said that Powers also carried a pistol with a silencer. "Why a noiseless pistol? Not to take air samples, but to blow out someone's brains!" The idea that the U-2 was a weather plane, and not a CIA spy tool, was an insult to the intelligence of any thinking person, he suggested. "The whole world knows that Allen Dulles is no great weatherman!" Prosecuting Powers for espionage was the natural course of justice, he said.

Yet once again, Khrushchev seemed to offer Eisenhower an escape hatch, giving him a clear opportunity to blame the military and the CIA for the flight and, perhaps, preserve the possibility of the Paris Summit. "I remember the talks I had with Americans," Khrushchev said. "They impressed me very much. I still believe that those who met me want peace and friendly relations with the Soviet Union. But apparently the Pentagon militarists and their monopolist allies cannot halt their war efforts. I am quite willing to grant that the President knew nothing about the fact that such a plane was sent into the Soviet Union. . . . But this should put us even more on guard."

At the U.S. embassy, Thompson sent a cable to Washington that included his personal assessment of Khrushchev's mind-set—"I believe he was really offended and angry, that he attaches great importance to stopping this kind of activity, and that he believes this will put him in an advantageous position at the Summit. There is no doubt we have suffered a major loss in Soviet public opinion and probably throughout the world." Thompson succinctly outlined Washington's predicament: "Judging by the display which Khrushchev made of evidence in the Supreme Soviet today, I would doubt that we can continue to deny charges of deliberate overflight. Khrushchev has himself stated the dilemma with which we are faced: should we deny that the President himself had actual knowledge of this action?"

## "i'd like to resign."

Eisenhower was distressed, though not entirely serious, when he mumbled those words to his secretary, Ann Whitman, as he walked into the Oval Office Monday morning.

Ike was in a fix. All day, advisers offered conflicting advice on how to handle Khrushchev's revelation. His brother Milton Eisenhower, who was the president of Johns Hopkins University, told him that he should take advantage of the lifeline Khrushchev had thrown him and deny knowledge of the flight. But to continue to lie and blame the fiasco on others struck Eisenhower as slimy and hypocritical. It would also reinforce his image as a disconnected lame duck. And what if Khrushchev somehow came back with proof that each of the previous U-2 flights

had been personally authorized by the president? Eisenhower's legiti-
macy as a leader on the world stage would be destroyed.

On Monday afternoon, Eisenhower met with his National Security
Council in the Cabinet Room and decided that he had no choice but to
own up to the facts and suffer the consequences. "We will now just have
to endure the storm," he said.

# CHAPTER 9

# Secrets and Lies

Look, Senator, this is modern-day espionage. In the old days I could send you out or send a spy out and if he was caught, disavow him. But what do you do when you strap an American-made plane to his back, Senator?

—PRESIDENT EISENHOWER, TO A GROUP OF
CONGRESSIONAL LEADERS, MAY 1960

Barbara Powers's two CIA handlers kept her inside an informational bubble during her flight back to New York, saying very little. But during the car ride to her mother's house in Milledgeville, Georgia, the men stopped the car at a drugstore. When Barbara hobbled inside, she saw her husband's picture staring out at her from the newspaper rack. These were the first concrete details she'd received about her husband's fate.

The homecoming wasn't smooth. Her mother, Monteen Allen, had been drinking before they arrived, and soon Barbara was numbing her own nerves with whiskey. On May 10, her handlers helped her prepare for her first encounter with the news media. They told her that it might be good for a doctor to visit her shortly before the reporters showed up; he might be able to give her something to help her settle down.

"I've already had *that* kind of medicine," Barbara said, assuring them that she'd self-medicated with a little liquor. It didn't put them at ease. They hoped the doctor might prescribe her a more stable sedative—something less likely to loosen her tongue in unpredictable ways—and they urged her not to have another drink. Soon, a prominent Milledgeville physician, Dr. James Baugh, arrived and gave her a pill.

A Lockheed public relations man greeted reporters and shepherded them toward the lawn of her mother's house, where the press conference would be held. Wearing a black dress and still walking with crutches,

Barbara eased herself down on a bench glider in front of a leafy hedge. Her mother sat next to her. A short microphone stand was placed on the ground in front of them, near Barbara's plaster-wrapped leg, which was still healing from her dancing injury in Adana.

Milledgeville was a small town then, and the town's favorite daughter—the writer Flannery O'Connor, who spent most of her life there—once advised its parochial denizens, "When in Rome, do as you done in Milledgeville." The CIA was worried that Barbara might do exactly that when confronting the international press, and they wanted to preempt the possibility that she might turn into the brash, outspoken spitfire she'd always been.

The CIA men, both from Bissell's department of security, had instructed Barbara to tell the reporters, emphatically, that she did not believe that her husband was a spy. It was a baffling fib. For anyone who'd been reading the papers that week—and she'd been reading everything she could get her hands on—there could have been no doubt he'd been a spy.

Yet she did what they told her to do, pretending to be an unquestioning, blindly subservient wife—a role that the world had seemed to be pushing on her for years, and one that she'd successfully resisted. But now she discovered she could fake it pretty well, maybe because helpful instructions reminding her exactly how she should act were all around her. In *The New York Times* that week, between the articles she read about her husband, she could find a banner advertisement for *Ladies' Home Journal* that contained a message for young women just like her: it suggested that they should spare no effort to cherish their husbands, because a wife could never tell when an unforeseen tragedy might snatch her man away forever. "There is, truly, no relationship like marriage," the ad asserted. "Someone chose you . . . gave you the gift of status . . . and the only attempt at understanding that will again come your way. . . . Keep him as long as you can. You'll never have it so good again."

For the public, she inhabited the role of the docile spouse convincingly; when the reporters looked at her on that bench glider in her mother's backyard, they saw a young woman who seemed to possess no thought in her head other than a selfless compassion for Frank. Back in Turkey, if anyone asked her what her husband did for a living, she liked to respond with tongue planted firmly in cheek: "He's making flights over Outer Slobbovia and making love to the naked daughter of an Arab chieftain." Now she seemed to lack a mind or a mouth of her own, and the reporters described her with exactly the sorts of adjectives the CIA men must have prayed for: "pretty," "attractive," "striking," and "quiet."

"How did you break your leg, Mrs. Powers?" someone asked during the press conference.

*Dancing with another man after we'd both had too many drinks in Adana.* The truth wouldn't do; the CIA had already given her a cover story, and she parroted their line word for word.

"It was a water-skiing accident," she told the reporters.

Afterward, she felt tainted, as if she'd been inducted into a disreputable club—"the Double-Talk Fraternity," she called it. The group seemed to be growing every day, making room for everyone from pilots' wives to the president of the United States.

EISENHOWER'S ADMISSION OF RESPONSIBILITY for the U-2 was unprecedented in two ways: it was the first time a president admitted to lying to the American people, and it was the first time the United States formally acknowledged that it spied on other nations. Previously, American spying had been cast by the government as a purely defensive pursuit, an enterprise concerned solely with counter-espionage, even though the CIA for years had been trying to influence foreign affairs through secret, proactive operations, like the coup Bissell helped organize in Guatemala in 1954. The U-2 incident destroyed the fiction that spying was, somehow, *beneath* America, and to some of the reporters who had swallowed the cover stories—and those in the public who'd believed them—reality proved equal parts embarrassing and unnerving. "Newsmen discovered, to their horror, that they had participated in a lie," the *New Republic* observed. "Moral Leadership of U.S. Harmed," read a headline in the *San Francisco Chronicle.* And in the *New York Herald Tribune,* the editors wrote, "For the general public it was a disquieting surprise. Part of our strength in the world lies in our belief, of which we seek to convince others, that our motives and methods are invariably pure."

This was America's moment to take stock of the very *idea* of spying, to hold it to the light, to decide if it was something that could be sanctioned in good conscience. Before Powers's flight went down, espionage in America had usually been cast as something other countries did, and when Americans thought of spies, they almost always had foreign accents. They could be Russians, or Brits, or Turks, but if they were Americans, then they were usually people like Julius and Ethel Rosenberg, sneaky turncoats working for the other side. If Americans were forced to cite an example of a homegrown spy, there was only one publicly acknowledged example available to them to reference: Nathan Hale, who had gone behind enemy lines on Long Island to spy on the British during the Revolutionary War. In all the years since the country had gained its independence, even after the OSS and the CIA were created, the country had never confirmed the identity of another spy.

Through interviews and a televised address, Eisenhower did his best to sell espionage to the American people as a necessary evil—a "distasteful and disagreeable" prerequisite of life in the twentieth century. If the Russians were doing it, then America would be foolish not to counter their agents with its own spies.

In mid-May, both Eisenhower and Khrushchev traveled to France for the Paris Summit, and to no one's surprise it didn't go well. Khrushchev fumed and gesticulated and blamed the Americans; Eisenhower countered that it was the Soviets' fetish for secrecy that had forced him to approve the spy flights in the first place. Khrushchev demanded an apology from Eisenhower, but the president said he would never apologize for protecting his citizens. The arguments over the apology—or lack of one—sank the summit.

For the better part of a year, the summit had been hyped as a chance to inject some warmth into the Cold War and to hammer out a lasting peace. Because expectations had been so high, the meeting's failure felt all the more portentous.

Most Americans were ready and willing to blame Khrushchev for the diplomatic failure, but the corrosive residue of the White House's embarrassing lie remained. T. Keith Glennan, the NASA administrator who had helped the White House and the CIA advance the bogus cover story, wrote in his diary after the summit collapse, "We have been turned up to the rest of the world as just another ordinary nation, mouthing platitudes and moralities but indulging in a variety of activities of doubtful character."

FOR WEEKS POWERS HAD BEEN PESTERING his captors, asking them if they might spare him a few pieces of paper and a pen or pencil so he could write a letter home. On May 26, they relented, delivering writing materials to his cell.

"My dearest Barbara," he wrote at the top of the page:

> I want you to know that I love you and miss you very much. I did not realize how much until I found myself in this situation. Not knowing when, if ever, I will see you again, has made me realize how much you mean to me. I have had plenty of time to think since I have been here and plenty of time to regret past mistakes.
>
> I am sincerely sorry to cause you the suffering you must have had before you found out that I am still alive. I am also sorry to be the cause of any suffering or pain that you may be having because of the situation that I am presently in.

A guard stopped by his cell and asked him if he wanted to take his daily walk. He declined, wanting to finish the letter. He'd endured hundreds of hours of interrogations already, was wrung out to the point of exhaustion, and now he struggled to articulate his thoughts, to express the fear, the apprehension, the guilt. He lit another cigarette, the latest in a never-ending chain. The smoke had filled the corners of the cell and pressed ever closer.

> Barbara, I don't know what is going to happen to me. The investigation and interrogation is still going on. When that is over there will be a trial. I will be tried in accordance with Article 2 of their criminal code for espionage. The article states that the punishment is 7 to 15 years imprisonment and death in some cases. Where I fit in I don't know.

He gave a few details of the crash. The smoke curled from his cigarette and stung his eyes. In America, a few newspaper articles had painted him as some sort of all-American Boy Scout who never smoked (a patent untruth) and didn't drink (even worse). Now he couldn't get enough of the Laika cigarettes—named after the dog that had been locked into *Sputnik 2*—and smoked himself into a fog within his unventilated cell. It was too much. He roused the guard and said he changed his mind: he'd take him up on the offer of that walk outside, after all.

He put down his pen and cleared his head in the prison yard, soaking up his meager daily allotment of sunshine and fresh air. Then it was back to the smoky cell and the sheet of loose leaf paper he'd left on the small table:

Darling you are in charge of everything now. You have those Power of Attorneys so use them as you see fit. Everything is in your hands and I trust to your judgment. I don't want to hear anything about what you do with the money you and I saved, use your own good judgment and do what you think is best but don't bother me with your decisions. You are on your own now and I don't know for how long. Just be careful and maybe we can still buy a house some day. It is a pleasant thought, owning our own home, especially as I sit here in my cell thinking about it.

Well Darling, it is dark outside now and I guess I had better go to bed. I have written a lot more than I thought I could. At first I didn't seem to think of what to write but it kept coming out.

Barbara, once again I say I am very sorry for everything. I hope that you are all right and I want you to know that I love you very much. I am sending you, with this letter,

All my love.

Days later, Barbara spotted the Milledgeville mailman striding up her mother's street, a smile on his face, and she knew that the letter he was waving over his head was from her husband.

It came none too soon. Since the press conference, she'd taken to wearing dark sunglasses and hiding from reporters, and to counter the stress, she had continued to turn to alcohol. Her uncle Joe kept her well supplied with potent home brews, and if she overdid it, he'd be the one to toss her in the shower stall, douse her with water, dry her off, and nurse her back to sentience. Barbara's mother wasn't nearly so nurturing. She drank just as much as Barbara, if not more, and ever since Frank's CIA salary was published in the newspaper, she'd regularly been hitting up her daughter for loans. After Barbara had been abroad for several years, her homecoming had allowed her to see, as if for the first time, how rocky the household she'd grown up in had always been. The life she'd known before her husband had joined the CIA was long gone, and some of her oldest friends and relatives now seemed like strangers.

Her mother's full name, if you included the surnames she'd inherited from husbands, was Monteen Lillian Beck Spain Moore Brown

Allen. Jack Spain, her first husband, had simply vanished one day; Barbara didn't know a thing about him. Etsul Moore, Barbara's father, died young of a heart attack. Then came Raymond Brown, a man her mother had met at the Anchorage, a faith-based alcoholism rehabilitation center in Albany, Georgia. They were married for three years, until he was admitted to the state psychiatric hospital. Her fourth husband was Melton Allen, who, shortly after the wedding, also did a thirty-day stint in the psychiatric hospital and was treated for alcohol abuse. Although the two of them were still legally married, they lived apart. Alone in the house together, Monteen and Barbara had plenty of opportunities to butt heads.

Barbara ripped open the letter from Frank, the words swimming on the page as her eyes welled up. Nothing in her life was simple anymore. Maybe it never had been. She read to the end of the letter, then started again at the top. She must have read it twenty times, lingering over each page, until she'd committed the words to memory. At 9:00 that evening, she stuffed the letter back in an envelope, put a stamp on it, and dropped it back in the mail, where it would be delivered to an address the CIA had provided her.

She hated to let it go, but her handlers had demanded to see any letters that came her way from overseas, just in case Frank or anyone else had tried to embed a coded message into the text.

They didn't find any secret messages in the letter, only the scared and lonely confessions of a man who feared he might never see his wife again.

ANALYSIS OF THE LETTER DIDN'T END with a simple reading. The CIA persuaded the air force medical office to provide representative samples of Powers's handwriting from before his capture. They sent the samples, as well as the recent letter to Barbara, to two New York clinical psychologists—Molly Harrower and Matilda Steiner—who were considered experts in Rorschach tests and handwriting analysis. Harrower and Steiner weren't informed whose handwriting they were looking at, but together they concluded that the person had definitely undergone some sort of transformational trauma. "The most important deduction arrived at by the analysis of the before and after handwriting was that more than likely some type of organic psychiatric change of significant degree in the subject had taken place in the interim between the writings," a CIA report stated. "Such a change could result from such things as brain injury, electroshock, cerebral infection, or vascular deprivation and psychochemical application."

Some in the CIA regarded the analysis as distressingly ominous, and they concluded that little that Powers might say from this point on could be taken at face value.

KELLY JOHNSON HAD ALWAYS BEEN EXTRAORDINARILY loyal to people he liked, and he'd always liked Frank Powers. As speculation swirled around Powers, and people began to question everything from his piloting skills to his honesty, Johnson's instinct was to stick up for the pilot, whom he'd met four years earlier. He bristled when he heard people who didn't know Powers disparage him with uninformed gossip.

The same thing had happened back when Johnson had worked with Amelia Earhart. After she went missing, people began publicly casting doubt on her ability in the cockpit, mixing speculation with generous doses of misogyny. Johnson, on the other hand, professed his admiration for her and her skills as a top-notch pilot. And years later, in the mid-1950s, when some people began speculating that she might have been on a spy mission, overflying Japan to photograph military installations, Johnson dismissed the stories as baseless; she'd only had a Brownie camera with her, and even if she'd nonsensically carried a heavier and higher-powered camera, there were no openings in the aircraft that would have allowed aerial photos. Everyone who could legitimately be called an expert in aviation knew a grim truth: groundbreaking pilots often met disastrous ends, and when it happened, there was nothing sinister or conspiratorial about it; it was, unfortunately, the nature of the business.

But now he was in the spying business, where nothing was so clear-cut.

In the weeks after Powers was captured, the U-2 program needed an official face, someone who could answer the American media's technical questions about the plane and be trusted not to say too much about anything else. The job went to Johnson. Aside from Powers himself, he was the only person connected to the U-2 program whose name was revealed to the public after the incident.

The CIA decided to exploit Johnson's interactions with the media to its advantage. When the Soviets released the first photographs of the U-2 wreckage more than a week after Powers's capture, agency analysts were frustrated by the pictures, which offered few visual clues to help determine exactly how the plane was brought down. If an authority like Johnson cast doubt on the veracity of the images of the wreckage that the Soviets had released, perhaps Khrushchev's government would respond by releasing *more* images.

Johnson gamely cooperated with the CIA's requests. During a Monday morning press briefing in California, he told reporters, "After spending the best part of the weekend analyzing the photographs with my technical people, I am convinced that the Russians, for some reason, have released the pictures of some other airplane crash." He displayed an enlarged picture of the wrecked plane and told the assembled journalists that he—the man who knew the structural specifications of the U-2 better than anyone else—believed the plane the Russians were showing off wasn't a U-2 at all. He pointed to a section of the wing in the foreground of the photo; the tapering of the metal, he said, was all wrong. The structural patterns of the beams and ribs shown in the photo, moreover, also appeared to belong to another plane. In fact, he said that he couldn't identify a single part in the wreckage photo that matched a U-2. Johnson speculated that the photographed wreckage was of a Soviet Beagle. On behalf of the CIA, he tossed out an idea that was designed to irritate Khrushchev's tender Soviet pride: he suggested it wasn't his military that was responsible for downing the plane, but rather just dumb luck.

"I do not believe they shot down the U-2 by either a missile or another aircraft," Johnson said. "If they have the U-2, it is because some mechanical or oxygen failure caused it to descend far below its normal cruising altitude."

The ploy worked. The very next day, the Soviets released more pictures of the wreckage that clearly proved that it was a U-2 and also provided clearer shots of the tail damage and fuselage. "This is more like it," Johnson said, inspecting the pictures. "This is definitely not the same wreckage shown in the first pictures released by the Russians." However, when reporters asked him if he now thought the Russians had, in fact, shot the plane down with a missile, Johnson declined to comment, leaving a vacuum of expert opinion that was quickly filled by conspiracy theories.

THE NEW ISSUE OF *AVIATION WEEK* FEATURED a bold, two-page article by its editor in chief titled "Lockheed U-2 over Sverdlovsk: A Study in Fabrication," which claimed to correct the "welter of official lies pouring from Moscow and Washington." The magazine stated definitively that the U-2 hadn't been shot down by an anti-aircraft missile. Instead, Powers had descended to a relatively low altitude, the article surmised, before he was *somehow* forced to the ground.

The magazine's conclusions, which were widely repeated throughout the U.S. press, seemed to contradict the story that Powers was telling in Moscow. Also, an article in Moscow's *Krasnaya Zvezda* (Red Star), an official publication of the defense ministry, reported that Powers had told his interrogators that he'd been flying at the U-2's maximum cruising altitude when he bailed out. He hadn't hit the U-2's self-destruct button, because he knew the explosive charge would kill him, he said. The Soviets also claimed that his ejection seat mechanism bore a tag that indicated it hadn't been inspected since 1956, and after-crash tests indicated the mechanism wouldn't have worked even if Powers had tried to use it. If Powers had followed the CIA's instructions by hitting both the self-destruct button and ejecting as he'd been trained, therefore, he would have been trapped in his seat while the plane exploded, sacrificing his life and saving the U.S. government a lot of embarrassment and an international crisis. "Powers apparently knew his bosses' habits very well," the Soviets reported.

Most people at CIA headquarters dismissed the reports as propaganda—cheap shots to try to make the Americans appear so sinister that they'd booby-trap the plane to kill their own man (in truth, they didn't believe there was any chance of survival, so such measures would have been redundant). Some officers played off the Soviet reports and poked fun at Kelly Johnson, teasing him for being an evil mastermind bent on killing pilots, but Johnson didn't find the humor in it. He considered Powers's downing a tragedy, one that he probably felt more responsibility for than those who were ribbing him did.

Johnson hoped that his continued cooperation with the CIA— particularly his efforts to goad the Soviets into giving up more information about the shoot down—might ultimately help the captured pilot who'd risked his life for his country. But the ploy had an unintended effect: it increased public skepticism about Powers's character. If the designer of the U-2 himself doubted that the U-2 had been shot down at high altitude, didn't that mean that Powers had likely defied his orders to stay out of reach? Why would he have done that?

What if Powers had been on the side of the Russians all along? If he had descended to a safer altitude before bailing out, as the NSA report suggested, could that mean that he had planned a defection to the Soviet side all along? What if the plane hadn't been touched by a missile at all? What if Powers and the Kremlin had engineered his defection to appear as if it had been an accident, and what if America was falling straight into their trap?

Could *anyone* involved in this bizarre story be trusted?

INSIDE A SENATE HEARING CHAMBER in the summer of 1960, workmen draped heavy gray blankets against the doors to prevent anyone outside from overhearing the session that was about to start. Allen Dulles took a seat in front of the foreign affairs panel and settled in for an all-day briefing.

His testimony, which was kept secret for decades, portrayed the shoot down as an aberration, wholly unrepresentative of a U-2 program that should be considered a shining success, not an embarrassment. If contradictory stories came out of Moscow during Powers's trial, for example, the information should be taken with many grains of salt. "By that time they will have had a more thorough opportunity for a complete brainwashing operation which might produce a mixture of truth and fiction," he said.

Eisenhower, who had met privately with many of the same lawmakers days before, had also defended his decision by praising the U-2 itself, labeling it "nothing short of remarkable." Although the press criticized the CIA roundly, a different view was taking shape among Washington insiders with security clearances. Instead of pointing the finger of blame at the agency, many of them seemed to hold the architects of the U-2 program in even greater esteem *after* the failed mission.

No one seized on this apparent contradiction more swiftly and decisively than Richard Bissell. Instead of exercising more restraint after Powers was shot down, he was emboldened to take more risks.

That summer, after his promotion had given him more authority than ever before, he steered the CIA into uncharted waters. In June, while he monitored the U-2 fallout, he turned much of his attention toward Fidel Castro's Cuba. He asked Dr. Sidney Gottlieb, his special assistant for scientific matters, to come up with a list of toxic agents that could "incapacitate or eliminate" a man. Shortly thereafter, another CIA scientist was given a box of cigars—"Fidel's favorite brand," it was said—and proceeded to "contaminate a full box of fifty cigars with botulinum toxin, a virulent poison that produces a fatal illness some hours after it is ingested," according to the 1967 CIA inspector general's report. "[Name redacted] distinctly remembers the flaps-and-seals job he had to do on the box and on each of the wrapped cigars, both to get at the cigars and to erase evidence of tampering. He kept one of the experimental cigars and still has it. He retested it during our inquiry and found that the toxin still retained 94% of its original effectiveness. The cigars were so heavily contaminated that merely putting one in the mouth would do the job; the intended victim would not actually have to smoke it."

Also that summer, Bissell approached Colonel Sheffield Edwards, in the Office of Security, to see if he "had assets that may assist in a sensitive mission requiring gangster-type action" against Fidel Castro. The American Mafia had been deeply involved in gambling interests in Cuba since the 1930s, but it had lost its influence on the island after Castro took over and shut down the American casinos. Weeks after Bissell's request, an undercover CIA liaison named Robert A. Maheu, a former FBI agent, met with Johnny Roselli—"a high-ranking member of the 'syndicate'"—and offered him $150,000 to "remove" Castro. "It was to be made clear to Roselli that the United States Government was not, and should not, become aware of this operation," according to a CIA memo that remained classified for more than four decades. Roselli was hesitant to get involved, but nine days later he introduced Maheu to a friend—"Sam Gold," who was in fact Salvatore "Sam" Giancana, and his friend Santo Trafficante. "The former was described as the Chicago chieftain of the Cosa Nostra and successor to Al Capone, and the latter, the Cosa Nostra boss of Cuban operations," the CIA reported. Both men were on the Justice Department's list of ten most wanted criminals. With Maheu acting as a middleman, the CIA produced six highly lethal pills to deliver to Giancana, who said he knew of a man named Juan Orta who might be able to slip one into Castro's food or drink. But Orta reportedly got cold feet, and the plan was eventually abandoned.

At the same time Bissell was exploring the possibility of killing Castro, via either CIA operatives or the Mafia, he was also overseeing arms deals to deliver untraceable rifles and ammunition to opponents of Rafael Trujillo, the right-wing dictator of the Dominican Republic. The CIA feared that Trujillo's brutality was creating the conditions for a Communist uprising, much as had happened in Cuba. In June, Bissell's office began working to coordinate a drop of weapons "for the removal of key Trujillo people from the scene," according to CIA memos exchanged at the time.

He wasn't limiting his focus to Latin America, however. That same month—June 1960—Bissell also began entertaining ideas of how to deal with Patrice Lumumba, the prime minister of the Republic of the Congo, which had just gained independence from Belgium. By July, the new country was gripped by chaos, and Lumumba's enemies in the Katanga Province of the country had gone so far as to declare themselves independent of his rule. Lumumba turned to the Soviets for help, and soon supplies and support technicians were being airlifted into Africa in Russian planes. A CIA cable from a field officer that summer read, "Embassy and station believe Congo experiencing classic Communist effort takeover government."

Bissell was sailing on the *Sea Witch* when Dulles drafted a cable based on a meeting he'd had with Eisenhower the previous day. "In high quarters here it is the clear-cut conclusion that if [Lumumba] continues to hold high office, the inevitable result will at best be chaos and at worst pave the way to Communist takeover of the Congo with disastrous consequences for the prestige of the UN and for the interests of the free world generally. Consequently we conclude that his removal must be an urgent and prime objective and that under existing conditions this should be a high priority of our covert action."

Years later, Bissell would ask himself whether there was any chance that he might have misinterpreted the meaning of that cable. "Does this authorize assassination or doesn't it?" Bissell asked. "That is in the eye of the beholder. . . . I believe, however, that if you had asked Eisenhower what he was thinking at that moment he probably would have said, 'I sure as hell would rather get rid of Lumumba without killing him, but if that's the only way, then it's got to be that way.' Eisenhower was a tough man behind that smile."

Bissell called Dr. Sidney Gottlieb again and asked him to pick out a poison to use against an unspecified African leader who had been targeted for removal by "the highest authority." Gottlieb came up with several: tuberculosis, rabbit fever, undulant fever, anthrax, smallpox, and sleeping sickness. Bissell and Gottlieb settled on one that would be sufficiently fatal and indigenous to Africa. Bissell then dispatched

Gottlieb to deliver the poison to Africa, arming him with rubber gloves, hypodermic needles, gauze masks, and a fresh alias—"Joseph Braun," from Paris.

Getting a field officer to follow through with the assassination plan wasn't easy. The CIA officer Gottlieb met with in Congo wasn't excited about the plan, and considered it impractical. Bissell then turned to a spy named Justin O'Donnell, who rejected the idea on moral grounds, claiming his Roman Catholic faith prevented him from murdering another. Finally, Bissell settled on a CIA "asset" in Africa code-named WI/Rogue, who was described as a "soldier of fortune" who "carries out any assignment without regard to danger." Bronson Tweedy, the CIA station chief, described him this way in a cable to Washington:

> He is indeed aware of the precepts of right and wrong, but if he
> is given an assignment which may be morally wrong in the eyes
> of the world, but necessary because his case officer has ordered
> him to carry it out, then it is right, and he will dutifully undertake
> appropriate action for its execution without pangs of conscience. In
> other words, he can rationalize all actions.

He was perfect. But while the plan was still being hatched, Lumumba went into hiding. He was eventually seized by his political rivals, flown to the Katanga Province, and killed, leaving Bissell and his crew with clean hands, if not clean consciences.

WORKING OUT THE MORAL CALCULUS of spying consumed Edwin Land after he learned of the shoot down. By early June, after the U-2 and its repercussions had monopolized the cover of *Time* for five straight weeks, he was ready to stand before a group of more than seven hundred newly minted graduates of MIT to share his thoughts on the subject.

Land removed the mortarboard cap from his head and straightened his papers atop the lectern. It was stuffy in the gym; the predicted storms had turned out to be empty threats, and many of the students, sweating under their robes, were second-guessing the decision to move the ceremony indoors. Land's expression was stern and serious, and the tone of this speech matched it.

America and the Soviet Union were locked in a showdown that couldn't be overstated. "The next five years could be crucial in deciding the fate of the United States and of all Western culture," he warned. The winner of the battle, he said, would be the side that chose honor over unscrupulousness, and truth over lies.

The U-2 crisis, he said, was an instructive example. When the State Department and NASA lied about the U-2 program after the plane went missing, he said, they had made a grave mistake. When the lies began to unravel, Eisenhower and the State Department could have continued to lie and deny, and such a decision to embrace dishonesty, he said, might have forever tainted America. But by acknowledging the truth and accepting the embarrassment that came with it, Land said, the president and his staff had redeemed themselves and salvaged the nation's credibility, just in time.

"The heavy hand of honesty fell upon their shoulders, made them its servants, made them suddenly know the fate of the world for all time depended on speaking truth at that moment," Land told the crowd. Eisenhower, he said, had recognized an essential truth: "There is no place in the Western mind for the dogma that a nation, because it serves many individuals, may and should engage in deceptions that would be repugnant to them separately."

It was as direct a refutation of Jimmy Doolittle's theory as had ever been articulated in a public forum. "Our techniques for influencing the rest of the world cannot be rich and flexible, like the techniques of our competitors," Land said. "We can be dramatic, even theatrical. We can be persuasive. But the message we are telling must be true."

It was an interesting speech, but the graduates in the audience must have been somewhat puzzled by Land's passion. They had no idea that Land had any special insight into the matter; his involvement in the U-2 project had never been disclosed, and he didn't mention it during his address. To the graduates, he was simply an entrepreneur and scientist, and his thoughts on spying and the U-2 were no more informed than their own.

If they *had* known that Land, in fact, was the father of the U-2, his speech might have seemed rife with contradictions. What about a lie of omission? Wasn't that another form of dishonesty?

Apparently not, according to the ethical calculation that Land had worked out. The only way that his graduation address could be reconciled with his actions was to assume that lying outright wasn't equal to *hiding* the truth. It was a fragile distinction, but as he continued to work secretly for the CIA, the full weight of his conscience rested on it.

. . .

OLIVER POWERS—MINER, SHOEMAKER, fourth-grade graduate—
wasn't the least bit intimidated by elites who enjoyed the sort of elevated
social status he'd never experienced. Frustrated about the confusion
surrounding the fate of his son, he fired off a telegram directly to the
White House, addressing it to President Eisenhower himself.

I WANT TO KNOW WHAT ALL THIS IS ABOUT MY SON FRANCIS G.
POWERS THAT IS GOING ON AND I WANT TO KNOW NOW. ANSWER.

He was equally blunt in the letter he sent to Khrushchev, urging
him to be fair to his boy. "I understand Mr. Khrushchev used to be a
coalminer," he said. "Well, so was I for fifteen years. So, if we cannot
talk to one another any other way, maybe we can as one coalminer to
another." Oliver quickly began working on a plan to go over to Moscow
himself so he could talk sense into the Soviets and convince them his
boy did nothing wrong. When he visited a federal building in Abing-
don, Virginia, to apply for a passport, he told a reporter that he figured
the Russians might agree to let Frank go in exchange for him. "I would
like to go to see my boy if they'll permit me to get there, and take his
place," Oliver said.

Around the same time, Oliver Powers learned that a man named
Rudolf Abel was sitting in an Atlanta prison, accused of being a Soviet
spy. Oliver contacted a local lawyer, and they wrote to Abel in prison,
asking him if he might consider swapping places with Frank—a spy
trade, one for one. Abel could go back to his handlers in Russia, and
Frank could come home.

Abel got the letter and forwarded it to his American lawyer, James
Donovan, who'd defended him during his spy trial in 1957. All along,
Abel had insisted he was an East German—not Russian—and he asked
Donovan to forward Oliver's request to his wife in Leipzig. The CIA
figured that Abel's "wife," Hellen, was actually his Soviet KGB handler.
Donovan wrote to Hellen later that month, and Oliver promptly secured
a visa from the Soviet embassy in Washington to try to lobby for the
trade in person, with Khrushchev himself, if that was what it took.

The CIA heard of Oliver's plans and quickly tracked him down, urging him to cut all contact with Abel until the agency told him it was
okay to proceed. The CIA also persuaded him to postpone his trip to
Moscow.

But the agency couldn't keep him in rural Virginia for long. Once the Soviets announced that Frank's trial would begin in August, Oliver and Barbara, both determined to see Frank in the flesh, began making separate arrangements for what would become the most unpredictable and thoroughly dysfunctional family trip that the CIA had ever tried to monitor and control.

# CHAPTER 10

## *The Verdict*

If they hear him tell his story, and if they're fair, they'll know he's a good boy like he's always been. We'll have him back with us soon.

—OLIVER POWERS

In July, Powers met the lawyer who would be defending him in his Soviet trial. His name was Mikhail Griniev, and in 1954 he had defended the former chief of Stalin's secret police squad from charges of treason. He lost that case, and his client was executed. Griniev then defended twelve of the chief's underlings, losing all twelve cases. Four of those men were given harsh sentences; the other eight were killed.

Powers didn't like his chances.

At first he thought he might refuse to testify, until Griniev told him that the right to remain silent didn't apply in the Soviet Union; silence would be held against him. Unless he wanted to die, he had to testify, and he had to risk looking like a spy who buckled under pressure. "If it appeared to the world that I had told everything, it was a risk I'd have to take," Powers later wrote. "I knew that the President, the CIA, and others involved in the U-2 program would know better."

When he looked over his seventeen-page indictment, which summarized the information he'd given during his interrogations, Powers was disappointed to spot no mention of "Collins," his recruiter; he had hoped that the name would be included, which would have been a message to the CIA that he hadn't revealed everything. When it came time to take the stand, Powers decided that he'd make a point to emphasize Collins's role in his recruitment, and he again would also emphasize that he was shot down at the plane's "maximum" altitude—sixty-eight thousand feet. That would, he hoped, reassure the CIA that he had concealed the truth about the plane's performance specifications, remaining loyal to its code of secrecy.

The weeks before the trial passed slowly, and he killed time by fantasizing about his testimony and reading whatever books his handlers could find in English—*Gone with the Wind,* the Bible, and a translation of Mikhail Sholokhov's epic novel, *And Quiet Flows the Don.* In July, he ripped open his mail to learn that both his parents and Barbara had been granted visas to come to Moscow for the trial.

Part of him was happy, because he desperately wanted to see them. But something struck him as odd. It was clear from the letters that his parents and Barbara were traveling separately. His wife had never been particularly close to his parents, but it surprised him that given the circumstances they wouldn't be coming together as a united family. He had a sinking feeling that an unwelcome melodrama was about to descend on Moscow.

AS FAR AS BARBARA KNEW, her trip to Moscow was arranged and paid for by the Virginia Bar Association, which had provided two lawyers—Alexander Parker and Frank Rogers—to aid in Powers's defense. In fact, the CIA was secretly footing the bill, hoping that Parker and Rogers would keep Barbara on a tight leash throughout the trip and, if possible, take advantage of any familial access to Powers so they could debrief him on the agency's behalf. The CIA also paid the travel expenses of Barbara's mother and Milledgeville's own Dr. Baugh, who was assigned to keep her away from alcohol and sedate her if she got too excited.

The CIA wanted to handle the arrangements for Frank's parents, too, but they had other plans. Oliver had signed a deal with *Life* magazine, promising the editors an exclusive story about the trial in exchange for $5,000 and travel expenses for himself, his wife, Frank's sister, and the family doctor, who was supposed to monitor Ida, Frank's mother, who had a weak heart. Oliver also got the magazine to pay the airfare of a lawyer from his hometown of Pound, Virginia, a man who had collected affidavits from local residents vouching for Frank's character. Oliver hoped to present those statements to the Kremlin.

Barbara snapped when she heard of the arrangement with *Life.* To her, it seemed as if his parents were trying to profit from Frank's misfortune. The CIA had hoped she'd travel with the entire extended family and their friends, to project an image of familial harmony, but the ill will was far too strong now. She and her people would travel separately from Oliver and his party.

Barbara boarded a Sabena airlines flight to Moscow, via Brussels, at

Idlewild Airport on August 12. Flying over the Atlantic, she sat next to a thirty-year-old correspondent from CBS Radio named Sam Jaffe. He had been assigned to cover the trial, and the two of them struck up an easy friendship over drinks as they flew over the Atlantic.

Barbara didn't know it, but Jaffe was more than a journalist. Back in 1952, he'd been a young radio scriptwriter at the United Nations in New York when the FBI asked him to give them periodic reports on any Russians he happened to run across. When he snagged the assignment to cover the Powers trial, he told the FBI field office in New York, and he soon got a lunch invitation from the head of the local CIA office, who showed up at the restaurant with an agency psychologist. The two CIA men instructed Jaffe to watch Powers closely at the trial for any signs that he might have been brainwashed. He should also try to capture whatever insights he could about Powers's relationship with Barbara, who presumably might be allowed to visit her husband privately while in Moscow.

"Sam is one helluva guy," Barbara later wrote, apparently unaware that he had been working for anyone other than CBS. "He really helped me by loaning me his ear while I poured out my troubles to him during the flight."

Barbara met with Oliver's group, but both sides did little to hide their disdain. The CIA managed to get the whole family to pose for a picture together, but when they suggested a joint dinner, Barbara "categorically rejected" the invitation. "Barbara's lawyers said their party would have nothing to do with Oliver Powers' group because of latter's undercutting tactics," Ambassador Llewellyn Thompson wrote in a memo to the CIA two days before the trial. The *Life* contract, and the thought of the money Oliver was set to receive on behalf of the family, continued to irritate her, he suggested. "Unlike them, Barbara had rejected all offers of publicity tie-ups."

Oliver, both in the presence of journalists and in private, was spouting bile at whoever would listen to him. While Barbara attempted to distance herself from him, "Oliver Powers stormed in with tirade about ineffectual policies of US government, stating we should break relations with USSR for its failure [to] live up to agreement by not allowing us to see his son," Thompson's memo stated. "Threatened to leave before trial if he got no (undefined) satisfaction. Said would rip up things back home if no swap arranged for his son after trial." Thompson added that

Oliver "berated Barbara" and told him that he loved his son more than she did. "I don't know why *you* even bothered to come," he told her. Thompson ended his memo by observing that Oliver was probably "either shrewd or completely bewildered."

Barbara was eventually driven to the Sovietsky hotel, and she checked into the same room that Vice President Nixon had stayed in during his visit to the Soviet Union a year before, back when tensions seemed to be easing and the Paris Summit still glowed brightly in a hopeful future. Sam Jaffe slipped into a room four doors down from Barbara's. He was the only journalist who'd managed to snag a room on that particular floor of the hotel, which was reserved for luxury suites.

Shortly after they settled into their rooms, Barbara invited Jaffe to come over to share some Russian vodka. She didn't bother with glasses, grabbing the bottle by the neck and swigging. Even though the CIA had hired Dr. Baugh to try to keep her sober, Jaffe—another civilian secretly employed by the government—was working directly against that aim in an effort to cozy up to her. According to notes that Jaffe later sent to the FBI, in Moscow he spent "almost every night in the company of Barbara Powers in her room drinking."

IN THE DAYS BEFORE THE TRIAL, Powers's attorney, Griniev, met with him in Lubyanka prison to go over his defense. His case, essentially, rested on the idea that he was only following orders and that more senior officials in the U.S. government—all the way up to President Eisenhower—were ultimately responsible for the flight. As Griniev explained this, he paused and looked Frank deep in the eye.

"Could I ask you this question?" Griniev said. "Is everything you have said during the investigation the truth?"

It wasn't, completely. He'd lied about the maximum elevation of the U-2, for example, as well as the number of overflights he'd made. Griniev eyed Frank very closely as he answered. "Everything that I said, with the exceptions of any opinions or guesses on my part, were the truth."

"Will you say this at trial?"

He said he would, and something about the exchange allowed him to calm down a little. By adding that little caveat about guesses or opinions, Powers felt as if he were giving his conscience a little space to breathe. Griniev stressed that it would be important for him to convince the court that he'd been truthful because, according to Article 33 of the

Soviet criminal code, a sentence could be softened if a person truthfully cooperated during questioning, admitted his guilt, and offered "sincere repentance."

The day before the trial, a blue pin-striped suit was delivered to his cell. It was at least two sizes too big, but he'd have to wear it for the trial. Griniev told him that his family had made it to Moscow, and he gave him a gift package from them. It contained a few handkerchiefs, along with a card.

The following day, August 17, wasn't just the first day of Powers's trial; it was also his thirty-first birthday.

THE NIGHT BEFORE THE TRIAL, Barbara couldn't sleep. She had sent a telegram to Lubyanka prison earlier that day, asking to be allowed to see her husband before the trial, but she'd received no reply. She paced the suite of her room at the Sovietsky and eventually invited Sam Jaffe over. Her nerves were a wreck. Again she chugged vodka straight from the bottle, and he listened as she spilled inside details about her marriage, a union that seemed to weaken with each swallow. Frank had chased women all over Turkey, she told him—a claim that might, or might not, have been true. She said she had grown so resentful of him that she hadn't even wanted to come to Moscow at all. Just when she seemed thoroughly embittered, ready to denounce her marriage with finality, she'd get flooded with emotion and insist that she needed to see her husband, immediately, even if it was well past midnight.

"Call a cab," she told Jaffe.

Jaffe later said he felt conflicted about the trust Barbara seemed to invest in him, but he didn't talk her out of it; instead, he went along with her demands, making a few telephone calls, speaking a few words of Russian that she didn't understand, then leading her downstairs to hail a taxi. He slid into the car next to her, and together they rode through Moscow's rain-wet streets.

It was nearly 3:00 a.m. when they arrived at the prison gates.

Jaffe stepped out of the car, and Barbara seemed to lose her nerve. She stayed in the backseat, sobbing. After a couple minutes of standing in the rain, he got back in the taxi. "Let's go back to the hotel," he said softly.

After the trial, the FBI distributed a report to top bureau officials based on Jaffe's information—a document that was to be kept strictly confidential "due to the fact that it may reveal the identity of the informant," a CBS reporter. The report stated that the two of them returned to her room at the Sovietsky directly after their pilgrimage to Lubyanka:

> There she told the informant that she was not in love with her husband and did not have any intention of staying in the Soviet Union. Barbara Powers grabbed the informant and started kissing him, but he repelled her. He told her that she could not talk that way and could not divorce her husband at this time. He told her that she would be accused of "deserting a sinking ship" and that she should not even mention this.
>
> The informant said that on this occasion, he could have been intimate with Barbara Powers, but he was not. He said that on many occasions when he was in Barbara Powers' company, she was in her pajamas, and he could probably have been intimate with her if he so desired, but at no time was he intimate with her.

THE TRIAL WAS HELD INSIDE the Hall of Columns, an expansive auditorium where Tchaikovsky had once played and where both Lenin and Stalin had lain in state. Enormous marble pillars supported an impossibly high ceiling, and fifty-one glass chandeliers blazed overhead. About twenty-two hundred people packed the room, all of them seated on plush red velvet bench cushions. It reminded Powers of Carnegie Hall.

On an elevated dais in the center of a large stage, three judges sat in high-backed chairs. Behind them on the wall hung an enormous golden state seal, with a hammer and sickle in the center. At stage right, a desk was prepared for Roman Rudenko, the prosecutor. About forty feet across from him sat Griniev, Powers's attorney. A glass case on the stage held items that would be introduced as evidence: his wallet, cigarettes, pieces of the plane, parachute, and oxygen mask.

Powers was led to the stage and the murmuring audience hushed. He took his position behind Griniev inside a waist-high wooden enclosure, a "prisoner's dock" that some reporters described as looking like a child's playpen. He gazed out at the crowd; his mother and father were seated in the rear of the courtroom, and Barbara didn't say a word to them as she slipped into her seat next to them. Wearing a black silk dress and a velvet cloche hat, she wept when she caught a glimpse of her husband. She dropped her head, covering her eyes with her white-gloved hands.

As the judge began speaking to Powers, the crowd settled into their seats, and Powers did the same within his enclosure. "Defendant," the presiding judge quickly bellowed. "You are obliged to stand when the court addresses you."

He again rose to his feet as the judge read the full, four-thousand-word indictment, and a translator repeated everything for his benefit. "Do you understand the charge brought against you?" the judge asked him.

"Yes."

"Accused Powers. Do you plead guilty of the charge?"

"Yes, I plead guilty."

The trial lasted for two days, and it rehashed the same material that Powers had gone over during his weeks of interrogations. They reviewed the specifications of the plane, his recruitment, and his experience of the shoot down. He repeated that he was flying at the plane's maximum altitude when he lost control of the plane. "So you were shot down from this altitude?" the prosecutor said.

"It was at that altitude that I was struck down by something," Powers said.

"You say you were struck down by *something*?"

"I had no idea what it was," he said. "I didn't see it."

Much was made of the poison pin and the pistol he'd been carrying. Powers calmly fielded the questions, and he admitted that he was sorry for what he'd done and sorry he'd renewed his contract with the CIA and hadn't simply quit.

"Why are you sorry now?" the prosecutor asked.

"Well, the situation I am in now is not too good," he said. He had heard that the Paris Summit had been a failure, he told him, and many people were blaming his flight. "There was, I suppose, a great increase in tension in the world, and I am sincerely sorry I had anything to do with this."

Several times, Griniev, his own attorney, seemed to contradict Powers's testimony by implying that the United States knew in advance that the flight would be shot down. Griniev also implied that Powers had told him that his American bosses had mistreated him and that he'd been surprised by the good treatment he'd received in the Soviet Union. At one point, Powers had told Griniev that he didn't expect to return to the United States—meaning that he assumed he'd be executed in Moscow. But when Griniev mentioned his statement during the trial, he left out the part about an assumed execution; Powers feared that some people might think he meant that he'd stay in Russia even if the court let him off the hook.

During the closing statements, the prosecutor announced that he wouldn't insist on the death penalty but was instead asking the judge to condemn Powers to fifteen years in prison. But he made it clear that it wasn't just Powers who should be judged guilty: those at the CIA, Lockheed, and any other corporations who helped put the U-2 in the sky—Bissell, Johnson, and Land, in other words—were also being tried in absentia. "Here is a vivid example of the criminal conspiracy of a major American capitalist company, of an espionage and reconnaissance center, and of the military of America," the prosecutor stated.

When it was Powers's turn to speak, he tried to emphasize his remorse, hoping it might alleviate the punishment.

"I realize that I have committed a grave crime and I realize that I must be punished for it," Powers said. "I realize the Russian people think of me as an enemy. . . . I plead to the court to judge me not as an enemy, but as a human being who is not a personal enemy of the Russian people, who has never had any charges brought against him in any court, and who is deeply repentant and profoundly sorry for what he has done."

The judges deliberated for nearly five hours. During that lull, hundreds of journalists paced the building, hungry for updates, and the Soviet government took advantage of their impatience. Radio Moscow announced that this was a day filled with "joyous news" for the Soviet Union: just hours before, the country successfully launched a new, five-ton spaceship into orbit, this one carrying two live dogs and circling the earth once every 90.6 minutes. Soon, TASS, the state-run news agency, was distributing pictures of the two dogs and the capsule. The news spread among the international news crews waiting at the Powers trial, and reports of the launch appeared the next day in newspapers throughout the world.

As it happened, those two little dogs had company up in the ether. The Americans—at the very same time—were secretly capping a feat in space that would prove far more significant.

ON THE FINAL DAY OF THE TRIAL, the satellite that Edwin Land and Richard Bissell had spent three years trying to develop was reentering the atmosphere after completing seventeen orbits around the earth.

Since 1959, they had tried thirteen times to successfully operate a spy satellite, and thirteen times they had failed. The plan called for a metal capsule attached to a parachute to detach from the satellite when it reentered Earth's atmosphere, delivering a batch of photos to the CIA. But something always went wrong. One satellite misfired on the launchpad. Three broke down before achieving orbit, and a few more spun out into uncontrollable flight paths. One capsule ejected prematurely from the satellite. A couple of times the cameras operated for a brief moment, then mysteriously stopped working. Twice the retro-rockets— the thrusters that slowed the satellite's reentry into the atmosphere, to prevent it from burning up—malfunctioned. Bissell labeled the experience "a most heartbreaking business." By 1960, the monthly meeting to review the status of the program had been informally dubbed "Black Saturday."

The U-2 had been a Sunday stroll in comparison. Land blamed the various military bureaucracies for slowing down the development of the satellite, and in August he spearheaded an effort to reorganize the operation. He and Killian came up with an idea for a new government agency—the National Reconnaissance Office—that would be in charge of designing and purchasing spy satellites. On the second day of the Powers trial, Land invited Bissell to an all-day meeting in his Polaroid offices in Cambridge to help draft the proposal for the agency that he planned to present to Eisenhower and the National Security Council the following week.

That same day, as Land and Bissell rehearsed the presentation in Cambridge, yet another would-be spy satellite—the fourteenth one— was launched into orbit. At the moment that Powers was standing on the stage in the Hall of Columns, delivering testimony and listening to the evidence against him, the American spacecraft was zooming more than a hundred miles over the Soviet Union, completely unseen, taking pictures of an enormous swath of country. The camera featured a twenty-four-inch focal length, panoramic lens—a design suggested by Land's advisory group, selected by Bissell, and built by Itek, the Boston-based company that had been a spin-off of the U-2 project. Several other companies, including Lockheed, had produced other components on the pioneering spacecraft.

At 12:46 p.m. on the nineteenth, after passing over the restricted territory of the Soviet Union seven times, the satellite ejected its capsule over Kodiak, Alaska. Anticipating that ejection, Captain Harold E. Mitchell had taken off from Hickam Air Force Base in Hawaii in a C-119 airplane—a Flying Boxcar, as the planes were called—to try to snag it before it splashed into the Pacific Ocean.

When the capsule was at an altitude of about sixty thousand feet, a parachute was released to slow its descent. Mitchell, who was being directed by a ground crew calculating its trajectory, first spotted the orange and silver parachute in the air about four thousand feet above him, when it was at an altitude of perhaps fifteen thousand feet. The eighty-four-pound capsule was gold, about the size and shape of a kettledrum, and it reflected the sunlight as it fell. Mitchell's plan was to fly the plane right over it, and when he got close enough, his crew on the C-119 would open the plane's beaver-tail doors, extend several catch poles from the plane, and snag the chute as they passed.

On his first pass, they missed it by about six inches. Mitchell circled and tried again; this time, the plane was about two feet too high as it passed over the chute. Mitchell looked down and saw that a deck of stratus clouds had massed at about 7,500 feet, and he knew he only had one more chance before the capsule disappeared from sight. He rolled and brought the plane around again. As he eased the belly of the plane over the floating capsule, he felt a slight tug. His altimeter read 8,506 feet. In his headset, he heard a crewman say, "Good hit, Captain! We've got her in tow!"

When he landed, Mitchell was feted as a hero, and a beer keg was tapped in the hangar. Ecstatic phone calls were being placed all around the country—to air force command centers, to the CIA, and to Land's office in Cambridge. The event would make newspapers all over the country as a significant step in the space race, but none of the reports mentioned the real reason U.S. leaders were in such a celebratory mood: about twenty pounds of ultralightweight film were inside that capsule.

The film was in good shape, and it was flown to Sunnyvale, California. From there, it was taken to the Kodak developing center in Rochester, New York, before the images arrived at the U-2 photointerpretation center above the Ford shop in Washington. The photointerpreters were overwhelmed: the U-2 flights had revolutionized the CIA's data collection operations, but the intelligence gathered by the satellite was dizzying. In one day, it had photographed about 1.6 million square miles of Soviet and Eastern bloc territory, revealing sixty-four Soviet airfields and twenty-six new surface-to-air missile sites. The first satellite flight, they soon discovered, captured more tactically useful information in a single flight than all of the previous U-2 flights combined. The satellite photos weren't perfect; they weren't quite as sharp as the U-2's images, and a bright line obscured some of them. The U-2 could better avoid cloud cover and could be deployed nearly instantly, on an as-needed basis. However, the idea of the two tools—the U-2 and the satellite—working in tandem thrilled Land and the entire photointerpretation division at the CIA.

Land hustled to Washington and attended two back-to-back meetings. The first was in the Oval Office. Land unreeled a duplicate spool of the satellite's images across the carpet in the center of the room. "Here's your pictures, Mr. President," Land said.

Eisenhower was just as stunned as the photointerpreters had been. Land assured him that it was only the beginning. With the proper resources, he told the president, the technicians would be able to improve the resolution of the satellite's cameras by as much as 100 percent by Christmas. Eisenhower told Land to make it happen; he'd make sure the resources fell into place.

Fifteen minutes later, Land was in a meeting with the members of the National Security Council. They, too, were ecstatic. Land presented the plan for the new National Reconnaissance Office that he, Bissell, and others had worked on in Cambridge. The plan was instantly approved.

It was a triumph, but one with a bittersweet edge to it. How could Land celebrate this new chapter in America's aerial espionage program on the same day Frank Powers was reaping his punishment in Moscow?

POWERS STOOD WITHIN HIS ENCLOSURE and gripped the wooden rail as the judge read the verdict: guilty. He was sentenced to ten years of confinement, with the first three years to be served in prison and the remainder in a labor camp.

The crowd burst into applause, cheering the fact that the American "air pirate" would pay for his crime. Powers didn't have much time to contemplate the sentence; he was led off the stage and told that he could briefly visit his family members before he was taken back to his prison cell.

He was brought into a room outside the main hall, where a table of desserts and caviar was laid out in the center of the floor. Barbara and her mother stood alongside his father, mother, and sister. He began crying as soon as he laid eyes on them.

It was strangely awkward for all of them to finally be together in the same room. They chatted about minor things—the news back home, messages from aunts and uncles, Eck von Heinerberg's adjustment to life as Milledgeville's most well-traveled dog. They talked about the sentence, parsing its implications. Barbara suggested that she could try to get a job at the American embassy in Moscow to be close to him. He was skeptical of the plan. He knew that he'd soon be transferred to another prison; even if it was in Moscow, which wasn't certain, he didn't trust that the Soviets would actually let her visit him.

The meeting lasted an hour. Over the next two days, a Saturday and Sunday, Powers was left alone in his cell. Until that Friday, he had been mentally preparing for a death sentence. The thought of a decade in Soviet custody now, strangely, seemed worse. He spent the weekend brooding, slipping into a black mood.

On Monday, he was ushered to the Supreme Court building for a final visit with his parents and sister before they returned home to Virginia. With Soviet guards standing by, Oliver talked cryptically of "other efforts" he was pursuing to get him out of prison, but Powers had no idea what he was talking about. When they left, Barbara and her mother entered. They assured him the U.S. embassy wasn't giving up on him, and it had even assembled a small library of fifty paperback books for him. Soviet law permitted each visitor to receive one seventeen-pound package per month, and Barbara quickly compiled a list of things he might need: shaving cream, American cigarettes, instant coffee, sugar, and all the reading material he could get. Barbara's mother left the room, and Barbara was allowed to stay a few minutes longer. She told him that two lawyers had accompanied her on the trip so that they could talk to him. Powers understood this meant that the CIA had hoped to secretly debrief him, but the Soviets hadn't allowed the lawyers to join Barbara in the room. Barbara also mentioned that his father had made a deal with *Life* to sell his story. Barbara seemed bitter when she said it, and the tension between her and his parents suddenly began to make sense.

A guard abruptly announced that their time was up, and Barbara was led out of the room. The interpreter then surprised Frank by saying, "There's an American here who would like to see you."

Was it someone from the embassy? Or could the agency have succeeded in sneaking someone in? Powers was eager to find out and told the interpreter to send the person in.

A flush-faced, middle-aged man entered the room. He introduced himself as Vincent Hallinan—a name he assumed that Powers had heard before. Hallinan seemed surprised when Frank said he hadn't, because, as Hallinan took pains to emphasize, his candidacy in the U.S. presidential election in 1952 had generated lots of press coverage. To prove it, Hallinan pulled out a folder and showed Powers a sheath of old newspaper clippings about his run as the nominee of the Progressive Party.

Hallinan left out some details, like the fact that he'd been disbarred in San Francisco after being found in contempt of court during a trial in which he defended an accused Communist; that incident also earned him six months in McNeil Island prison. After his 1952 presidential run, he was sentenced to eighteen months in prison for tax evasion. It seemed that now Hallinan had been invited by the Soviet government to serve as an official American legal witness to the trial.

Hallinan talked for almost forty-five minutes, stopping only to light another in a never-ending chain of cigarettes. He told Powers that he should consider himself fortunate to have been given such a fair trial and such a light sentence. "You'll be okay," Hallinan assured Powers, telling him that he'd spent some time in prison himself and fared well enough.

Powers might never have heard of him, but the CIA and the U.S. embassy in Moscow had been paying close attention to Hallinan since he left California. During the trial, American observers spotted him sitting in a box inside the Hall of Columns that was reserved for diplomats and other dignitaries, and they noted that when the verdict was announced, he joined in the applause. A cable to the State Department in Washington noted that Hallinan had approached Barbara several times at the hotel, and he'd tried to persuade Sam Jaffe to film a joint interview of himself and Barbara. The lawyers who'd accompanied Barbara intervened, quashing the plan.

Hallinan told Powers he should take advantage of the opportunity to learn the Russian language and to closely observe the Soviet system of government and keep an open mind about it. "They bring up some good points—something you might like to think about," he told Powers.

Before he left, Hallinan asked him if there were any messages that he'd like for him to deliver to his employers in the U.S. government. Powers thanked him, but he decided it was probably wise to decline the offer.

THE SUMMER HAD BEEN MILD IN WASHINGTON, but in late August the temperatures started pushing into the mid-nineties, which gave Joe Alsop a good excuse to invite Bissell to his house for a few cold drinks. Not that he really needed an excuse. Senator John F. Kennedy, who'd won the Democratic nomination for president that same month, would be there, too, and Joe thought he and Bissell should meet.

Alsop had been one of the few voices in the media who'd been kind to the CIA since Powers had been shot down. His first column after the incident was headlined "The Wonderful News," because he believed the revelation that the United States had been spying on the Soviets from above for four years gave the United States a distinct advantage in the spy-versus-spy game that the Cold War was becoming. While other journalists pilloried the agency for getting caught, Alsop praised it. "No sensible American can fail to admire the courage and good sense of his fellow citizens, as yet unnamed, who originated this project," he wrote. All of his criticism was reserved for Eisenhower's White House, which Alsop blamed for botching the aftermath. The U-2 incident, Joe wrote, convinced other Western powers that "America's present leadership is bumbling and maladroit."

Kennedy had been saying much the same thing on the campaign trail, and he was sticking to the idea that America might be falling behind the Russians in the missile gap. He wouldn't go so far as to say that Eisenhower was deliberately keeping vital information secret from the American people, but he continued to hammer the president for what he termed a relaxed attitude toward America's defense. "I am not sure that the president is aware of the seriousness of the situation," Kennedy said that summer.

That sort of talk was right up Alsop's alley, of course; he'd been saying the same thing for years. Throughout that summer, Joe didn't attempt to hide his affection for both Kennedy and his wife, Jackie. In fact, he'd bonded with her first. The Kennedys lived about half a mile down the street in Georgetown, and he and Jackie, who was pregnant at the time, often got together to chat about anything and everything—Givenchy dresses, jewelers, maternity fashions, literature, and, sometimes, politics. After one lunch in which Jackie was joined by Bobby Kennedy, she scribbled a quick thank-you to Alsop for making her pregnancy bearable: "The most voluptuous daydream to which I treat myself is reliving every sip and bite—noisettes + mushroom rice + caviar + champagne— I have a feeling my brother-in-law is doing the same." Jackie even credited Alsop with convincing her she could handle life as a First Lady. She'd been envisioning herself as the mother of two very small children, with a husband she'd rarely get to see, and she'd sink into a mild depres-

sion at the very thought. Later, after she'd come to terms with the idea
of moving to the White House, she wrote to Joe, "You said, 'It's the only
game that's worth the candle.' Because YOU told me that—I thought
about it every day—and gradually came to agree with you. And that was
when the happy time started."

Now, in the months before the 1960 election, Alsop had become
something of an unofficial adviser to the Kennedys. Over dinner one
evening, Bobby Kennedy casually asked Alsop who he thought might
make a good new head of the CIA. Alsop was taken aback. Joe had never
considered the head of the CIA a political appointee that changed from
one administration to the next, and he hadn't entertained the notion
that Kennedy might get rid of Allen Dulles, who seemed more sym-
pathetic to Democrats than to Republicans anyway. Alsop argued that
Dulles had done a fine job, and the stability that comes with continuity
surely had some value. "Well," Bobby said, "what about the new face
that the administration wants to present to the world?" Alsop dismissed
the notion. "That matters much less than the continuity and good men
receiving their desserts."

That said, Alsop figured that Kennedy should probably get to know
the man whom many considered Dulles's logical successor, and he knew
they'd probably get along well. Both were extremely sharp thinkers, both
were great conversationalists, both were passionate sailors, both knew
how to enjoy themselves at a party, and both were unafraid to be ruth-
less when the situation called for it.

Alsop had praised Bissell's toughness to Kennedy, and, sure enough,
when the two men met at the house on Dumbarton Street, they got
along well. But Bissell was in an awkward position. He was still working
closely with the current administration, and he felt a loyalty to Eisenhower, even though he'd voted against him in two presidential elections.
It wasn't at all certain that Kennedy would defeat Vice President Nixon,
and until he won, Bissell couldn't tell him that new images from the spy
satellite had strongly disputed the idea of a missile gap.

As Bissell chatted with Kennedy, he liked what he was hearing. Unlike
other Democrats—including Adlai Stevenson, who'd lost to Eisenhower
in both 1952 and 1956—the young senator from Massachusetts seemed
more of a hawk than a dove when it came to the Communist bloc. Bissell believed the KGB would do anything, no matter how underhanded,
to score even the smallest of points in the Cold War—Joe Alsop's experience in Moscow had taught him that. Eisenhower—old Speedy Gonza-

les himself—was too cautious to effectively counter the Russians, Bissell thought, whereas Kennedy seemed as if he'd be "far less inhibited in trying to do something about it," Bissell wrote to a friend in 1960. He found himself hoping that Kennedy would beat Nixon. "My guess is that Washington will be a more lively and interesting place in which to live and work," Bissell predicted.

After the initial meeting at Alsop's house, Kennedy called Bissell to arrange a more formal meeting. Bissell stressed to Kennedy that he was still working for Eisenhower, and therefore he wouldn't talk about any active cases or venture into classified territory. "I also told him truthfully (and perhaps a little inappropriately since I was part of the current administration) that I agreed with most of his philosophy," Bissell later wrote.

An example of the sort of bold thinking that Bissell imagined Kennedy might support was a plan he was working on at that moment: a CIA-led insurrection in Cuba to topple Fidel Castro's government. Shortly after Powers was shot down, Bissell directed a group of thirty-two recruits to hack out a training base and airstrips in the Guatemalan jungle. U.S. Air Force men, in civilian clothes, were sent to train Cuban pilots who might fly missions into Cuba. At first, Bissell believed that the pilots might simply help fuel an internal uprising, dropping weapons and supplies to anti-Castro opposition fighters still inside Cuba.

As the months wore on in 1960, and the election drew closer, Bissell began to entertain the idea of creating a small guerrilla army led by a core group of Cuban exiles trained in sabotage, infiltration, and communications. As Bissell and Dulles began tossing around ideas for such a plan, Eisenhower seemed to doubt their seriousness. "Boys," the president said, "if you don't intend to go through with this, let's stop talking about it."

Bissell couldn't put the plan out of his mind, however, and his office continued to recruit more Cuban exiles and conduct more exercises in Guatemala. In a few months, he hoped he might be able to tell John F. Kennedy all about it.

IT WAS SHORTLY AFTER NOON ON WEDNESDAY, five days after his trial had ended, and Powers was finishing his daily walk in the prison courtyard when an interpreter approached. "Would you like to see your wife again?" the interpreter asked.

The opportunity caught Powers by surprise. "Can I do it?"

The interpreter said that he and Barbara could meet that afternoon, alone, without guards standing by. Conjugal visits, it turned out, were a long-standing tradition in the Russian penal system. The interpreter explained that Powers would have this one opportunity to perform his "husbandly duties" before Barbara returned to the States.

A guard brought him the same pin-striped suit he'd worn during the trial, and he quickly changed. At about 2:30 p.m. he was driven across the city to another prison. He was led into a stark room that someone had spent a little time trying to make comfortable. Fruits and carbonated soft drinks had been set out on a small table. Drapes covered the windows. Sheets and blankets had been spread over a leather couch, which also held two pillows. The room's door had a peephole built into it, but a piece of paper was taped over it to prevent anyone from looking inside.

Down the hall, Barbara was led into another room, where a Soviet prison official told her that she and Frank would be granted three uninterrupted hours for the conjugal visit. "We must insist, however, that you do not abuse this privilege by giving anything to your husband," he said. She didn't understand how she could pass him anything, because she'd already surrendered her purse to the guards. He explained that the wife of a German colonel who'd been imprisoned recently had found a way. "She had a capsule in her mouth, containing a deadly poison," he explained. "When she kissed her husband she transferred the capsule to his mouth. The colonel bit into the capsule, and within a few minutes he was dead."

Barbara was shown into the room where Frank was, and the man said he'd return in about three hours, at six o'clock. He shut the door, leaving it unlocked. Frank walked over to the room's window and pulled back the drapes to look outside: it faced a blank brick wall. No one could look inside through the window or the door, but his eyes began quickly scanning the room, looking for hidden cameras. He didn't see any, but he assumed the room was bugged somehow.

He and Barbara stood close together, whispering. Frank hadn't been able to take a shower in twelve days, and she thought he smelled "like a billy goat." From Barbara, Frank thought he caught the faint whiff of alcohol before she began to undress.

"You do realize the guards may be watching," Frank told her. Barbara said she didn't care.

The knock on the door came, as promised, roughly three hours later, at six o'clock. By that time, according to Barbara, they had made love three times.

She bade him farewell, and he watched her walk down the hall with a guard and an interpreter, then disappear.

Two days later, on Friday, August 26, he grabbed his diary to scribble an entry. "I was told that Barbara and her mother left this morning," he wrote. "Feel all alone once more."

# CHAPTER 11

## New Frontiers

There just do come moments, and unfortunately quite a lot of them
in world affairs, where power has to be exerted. And I have long felt
that many of the criticisms that are leveled at this one agency of the
government are in fact the criticisms of those who hate to admit,
to themselves or anyone else, that power must sometimes be used.

—RICHARD BISSELL

At 1806 I Street in Washington sits an unmarked, redbrick, three-
story nineteenth-century row house. Two cast-iron steps lead to
a windowless front door, which opens onto a dark and narrow
entrance hall, only four feet wide. A red worn carpet leads toward the
front room, which is as cluttered and aggressively eclectic as a flea market, if that flea market happened to be run by an extraordinarily well-
traveled group of men who jealousy guarded their adolescent fantasies
of masculine adventure. The house is a warren of rooms and hallways,
and above almost every doorway hang swords, cutlasses, scimitars,
rapiers, or bayonets. The front and back parlors on the main floor are
stuffed to their exposed ceiling beams with all manner of souvenirs:
steer horns; ceramic figurines of bare-breasted sea maidens; spittoons;
countless tankards, flasks, and steins; African sculptures; stuffed fish;
tribal totem poles; a Prohibition-era license plate that reads "Repeal the
18th Amendment"; an old hand-cranked phonograph record player; a
suit of armor from Japan that's about five hundred years old. On one of
the crowded mantels sits a lidded ceramic vase labeled "Opium." Red
leather club chairs are scattered throughout the rooms. Nearly every
inch of the red-papered walls is covered with framed pictures—old portraits of mustached men, newspaper cartoons, and sailing ships. There's
a mounted head of a bighorn sheep and another of a Himalayan yak. A
banister staircase leads upstairs to a room full of Japanese scrolls, and
another with a table for card games. There's a men's room upstairs—

a crude affair, featuring a small urinal bolted to the corner where two walls meet and a bare dangling bulb. There is no ladies' room, because this hideaway is for men only. It's one of the, if not *the,* most exclusive and secretive private social clubs in Washington: the Alibi Club.

Inside the doors of a wooden cabinet is mounted the never-publicized list of all of the club's members since 1884, the year it was founded. The roster is strictly limited to fifty men at a time; a new member can be voted in only after an existing one dies. The list has always included some of D.C.'s most powerful, boldfaced names: senators, U.S. Navy admirals, Supreme Court justices. It's nonpartisan but has always leaned a little more toward Republicans of an internationalist bent than toward Democrats. After World War II, veterans of the OSS and, eventually, the CIA began to establish a foothold in the ranks of the secretive club. In the late 1950s and early 1960s, Allen Dulles was one of its most active members, a regular attendee of its Friday afternoon luncheons. Dulles had first learned that Powers was alive, in fact, only after someone managed to find him inside the Alibi Club, where he was eating.

In February 1961, Dulles reserved the club's dining room for an informal dinner meant to introduce about ten of the CIA's top officials to the dozen men who constituted new president John F. Kennedy's inner circle at the White House.

They gathered in the dining room in the back of the house, settling into the Windsor chairs that encircled an oval tavern table that could accommodate twenty-four place settings. The red brick near the fireplace appeared blackened from years of smoke and soot, and the light from the two hanging fixtures was dim, reflecting off the copper kettles that hung from the low dark rafters. Tankards and cups were hooked to nails in the wall, and blue-and-white glazed plates were stacked in the built-in china cabinet. To get things started, three rounds of martinis were served to each man (except Ted Sorensen, Kennedy's principal speechwriter, who never drank alcohol). The idea was that the CIA men would introduce themselves with short introductions and descriptions of their principal duties and in this way would introduce the White House to the senior personnel within the agency and also provide an overview of their priorities.

Out of all the CIA men sitting around the table, Bissell was probably the most familiar to Kennedy. Shortly after the election, on November 18, Bissell and Dulles flew to Florida to meet with him at the Kennedy family compound in Palm Beach. The three men sat around the swimming pool in suits, Dulles puffing on his pipe, and gave the president-elect his first intelligence briefing. Since the U-2 incident, relations with the Soviet Union had been chilly, and Khrushchev's influence in Cuba was now a primary concern. For Kennedy's benefit, Bissell sketched the still-developing plans to back a small paramilitary infiltration, led by Cuban exiles, that might spark the overthrow of Castro. Those plans had accelerated, and the CIA's army of Cuban dissidents grew much larger during Eisenhower's final months; by the time of the poolside meeting, the force had grown to nearly six hundred men. Bissell worried the whole plan would fall apart if they didn't move soon. "You can't *mañana* this thing," he told Kennedy that February.

Kennedy was reluctant to launch a major operation to try to unseat Castro so early in his term, but he liked Bissell's enthusiasm. Just before the inauguration, when one of the members of his transition team asked him who might be the most trusted member of the intelligence community, Kennedy offered Bissell's name. Around the same time, Chester Bowles, appointed by Kennedy to a top policy post in the State Department, tried to lure Bissell to work with him. Kennedy got wind of the plan and called Bowles.

"I hear you're trying to get Dick Bissell," Kennedy said.

"That's right," Bowles told him.

"You can't have him."

"Why not?"

"He's going to take Allen Dulles's job on July 1," Kennedy said.

One of Kennedy's first acts as president had been to reappoint the CIA director, but Dulles's career was clearly winding down. Dulles told the new president he was happy to stay on—for a little while, anyway. "Then," Dulles told him, "I think I probably ought to retire." His chronic gout was getting worse, and on most days he hobbled around the office in bedroom slippers. The skin around his face had loosened, making him look much older than his sixty-seven years. Lots of men prized his job, but after his success with the U-2 and spy satellite programs Bissell was viewed within the agency as Dulles's logical successor.

At the Alibi Club, Bissell could be confident that his ambitions to create a bolder, broader CIA would be enthusiastically received by the new White House. Bissell knew about Kennedy's meeting with Ian Fleming at Alsop's house, and he knew the president loved the romance of the James Bond novels; in fact, Kennedy included *From Russia with Love* as one of his ten all-time favorite books on a list published in *Life* magazine that March. "One could argue that Kennedy wanted to adopt the style of the novels into the working operations of the Agency," Bissell later reflected. If that was true, Bissell—as the head of covert planning—was the man Kennedy would need to do it for him.

At the Alibi Club's dining room table, Bissell seemed confident in the role he'd play for the new president as he stood to introduce himself.

"I'm your man-eating shark," he said.

SHORTLY AFTER HIS TRIAL, POWERS WAS TRANSFERRED to Vladimir Prison, a hulking redbrick complex next to the Trans-Siberian Railway about 150 miles east of Moscow. Every month, the American embassy sent a care package to him in cell 31, but the magazines he had requested—*Time, Newsweek, Life*—were removed before the package reached him. Instead, the prison provided him copies of *Pravda, L'Humanité* (the newspaper of France's Communist Party), the *Daily Worker,* and, occasionally, the *Nation.* But one day, the prison officer on duty neglected to snag the American magazines, and four copies of *Time* slipped through to Powers.

One of the copies included a reference to his case. The magazine reported that Robert Maynard Hutchins—a former Yale Law School dean, president of the University of Chicago, and head of the Ford Foundation—had cited Powers as a living example of how America's core values were in a state of decay. When Nathan Hale was captured as an American spy during the Revolutionary War, Hutchins noted, his famous last words to his British executioners had been "I only regret that I have but one life to lose for my country." Powers, on the other hand, had apologized to the Russians, pleading with them that they "judge me not as an enemy." Hutchins asked, "Should we be alarmed by the difference between the behavior of Airman Powers and of Nathan Hale?" He suggested the answer was self-evident. Powers's behavior was an ominous sign "that the moral character of America is changing," Hutchins wrote.

Powers was stunned. He'd spent months suffering in a Soviet prison, unsure at times whether he'd live or die, and now people back home were questioning his valor? He might have been thoroughly demoralized had he not been so baffled by the reaction. "I wonder what in the world he is talking about?" he wrote in a letter to Barbara. "I hope I am not being accused of changing the moral character of America."

He didn't know the half of it. Hale had spent the past two centuries in peaceful obscurity, but now he was an American hero, thanks to all the articles that compared him favorably with Powers, who had proven himself a "tower of jelly," as one editorial phrased it. The American public wanted its spies to appear daring and defiant, as they were in the movies. But Powers, as he was depicted in the press after the trial, was no James Bond.

Ian Fleming himself weighed in on the matter, labeling Powers's capture "one of the great espionage fiascoes of all time." When a reporter tracked him down in Jamaica and asked him what James Bond would have done in Powers's situation, Fleming didn't miss a beat: "I hope he would have taken his pill." And if Fleming were in charge of the CIA, how would he have responded to Khrushchev when he revealed that he'd captured Powers alive? "You say you've got a fellow called Powers in a U-2 plane and he's got all this equipment, valuable, and a lot of money and gold on him," Fleming said, imagining the scenario. "Well, this is absolutely wonderful, because this fellow is an escapee from detention from our NATO base in Turkey, and he's a no-good, and he's stolen this money, stolen this plane, and we understand he's got a girlfriend in Paris—he's making for Paris. Now we quite understand that this man has infringed Soviet sovereignty in air space and we quite appreciate that he's got to suffer all the rigors of Soviet law. Please send us back our plane and the remains of our belongings and so on and so forth. As for this fellow Powers, well, he deserves all he gets."

FOR MONTHS, ANALYSTS AT THE CIA had been picking apart every statement that Powers had made during his trial, scouring the letters he was sending to Barbara, digging through his old air force personnel files, interviewing pilots who'd served with him—all in hopes of determining whether they could trust him or not.

Now, almost a year after the shoot down, Oliver Powers was still pushing for a swap of his son for Rudolf Abel, the Soviet spy in U.S. custody. Some in the CIA, particularly those who worked in Bissell's U-2 office, were convinced that he had remained loyal to America, and likely had held on to his most sensitive secrets, such as the identities of other CIA employees and the detailed performance specs of the U-2. But Powers's backers in the agency faced formidable opposition in the figure of James Jesus Angleton, the head of the agency's counterintelligence unit. Angleton believed that if Powers hadn't defected outright, purposefully parachuting into Russia, he had almost certainly folded like a flower as soon as he was captured, spilling every secret he knew. The evidence that cast doubt on Powers's trustworthiness—the handwriting analysis, the NSA report that suggested he had inexplicably changed his flight plan—raised too many questions. In Angleton's mind, Powers was a compromised asset, and trading him for Abel—a man who after three years was still concealing his real name, as well as everything else of intelligence value—was madness.

With the possible exception of Bissell, no one had more influence with Dulles than Angleton. For several years he'd enjoyed "no-knock" access to the director's office, able to come and go as he pleased. In the mid-1940s the two men had worked together for the OSS, where Angleton impressed nearly everyone as an elegant thinker.

During his college years at Yale, Angleton had edited multiple literary magazines and published verse in both English and French, earning the praise of some of the world's most respected modernist poets, including William Carlos Williams and E. E. Cummings. Through them, Angleton struck up a correspondence with T. S. Eliot and Ezra Pound. In the early days of World War II, Pound was investigated for anti-American statements, and the FBI called on Angleton, then at Harvard studying law, to quiz him about Pound's loyalty. In a letter to Cummings, Angleton described how he toyed with the witless FBI investigator, distracting him by talking about literary theory, thereby protecting Pound from a simpleminded philistine, yet the FBI's version of the encounter labeled Angleton as cooperative and helpful. Somehow, Angleton had managed to convince both sides that he was, essentially, on their team. Later, when he entered the spy world, the art of detecting loyalty—of looking beyond outward appearances to determine what side a person was *really* on—became nothing less than an obsession for Angleton.

As the head of the counterintelligence division, he was tasked with ferreting out double agents, and some of his colleagues worried that the skepticism that made him so good at the job was veering toward outright paranoia. Dr. Jerrold Post, a CIA psychologist, later observed that Angleton had a tendency to see the sinister in the benign, and once his mind latched onto a dark version of the truth, it rarely let go. "Jim spoke in brilliant woven threads," said Post, who based his observations on numerous encounters over many years. "It was a web being spun out of logic by a remarkable individual. Jim talked about disparate events which had occurred all over the world, and then he tied them all together. There was a Messianic quality in his presentation of the facts and in the clarity of his truth. For a moment, I was caught by the sheer spell of Jim's logic. Only afterwards did it all fall apart and I realized it was craziness. He had turned possibility into certainty."

Angleton's uncharitable opinion of Powers seemed to be hardening into a rigid conviction, and he began to actively campaign against the idea of trading him for Abel. In one interagency memo he wrote, "Operationally speaking, the trade would be an exchange of everything for nothing. Powers has told all he knows and is of no further use to the Soviets except as a pawn—as he is being used in this matter. On the other hand, Abel has conducted himself in a highly professional manner. He remains resistant; he has refused to give information, even such information as his true identity. He is a person of high caliber and a potential source of information of great value, provided the proper pressures can be brought to bear. His release and deportation would be a major victory for the Soviets."

WHILE POWERS LANGUISHED IN PRISON, Edwin Land seemed to be juggling a million different things. He was running a major American corporation, taking a lead role in secret government spy programs, and—on top of it all—preserving time in his schedule for free, unrestricted brainstorming sessions that might lead to even more innovations. To outsiders, his personal relationships, including those with close friends and his immediate family, often seemed to fall lower on his list of priorities.

The story of how he came up with the idea of the Land camera—an anecdote that by 1961 had already acquired the gloss of myth—was a revealing glimpse into his relationship with his family. In 1943, he and his wife, Terre, had been on vacation in Santa Fe, New Mexico, when Land paused to snap a photograph of their three-year-old daughter, Jennifer. Immediately, the girl asked to see the picture he'd just taken. It was impossible, of course; photography and instant gratification simply didn't mix in those days. But as the family walked together past the adobe shops of downtown Santa Fe, Land's mind drifted away from his daughter and his wife, and he fixated on a puzzle the girl had inadvertently planted in his mind. Why shouldn't she be able to see a picture right after it was taken? "Within an hour, the camera, the film and the physical chemistry became so clear to me," he later said. What his wife and kids were doing or saying during that hour was never mentioned when he recounted the story.

His wife, Terre, grew accustomed to his flights of thought, but she never completely got used to them. She couldn't deny that his daydreaming had done wondrous things for their family: Polaroid was perfectly positioned to take the 1960s by storm, and news articles would soon list Land as the third-richest American alive, trailing only Jean Paul Getty and Howard Hughes. But few outside the family could appreciate the price that Land's intensity exacted on the family. He seemed to work around the clock guiding Polaroid and its expanding line of products into the future, and somehow he managed to squeeze even more hours out of his days to do his secret work for the government. Terre, however, clearly saw the disadvantages that came with living with the celebrated thinker. "There are occasions when I'll be talking to him directly and I know that he is not listening to me," she said, in a rare interview with a newspaper reporter in 1960. "His mind is miles away. But all I have to say to him is 'Polaroid' and immediately I have his full and complete attention." She tried to persuade him to take more time off, to spend some of their money on vacations, and in early 1960 she persuaded him to take the family to Montego Bay, Jamaica, for ten days. He agreed, but brought along one of Polaroid's top scientists so they could bat around some ideas. A few months later, in the spring of 1961, their daughter Jennifer graduated from Smith College, a private school in Massachusetts. Land dutifully attended the ceremony, but, characteristically, he arrived late, much to Terre's annoyance. By this time, Terre had grown accustomed to being away from him for months at a time, spending her winters in Tucson, Arizona. Land, meanwhile, bought a four-wheel drive for the Boston winters—just in case a snowstorm threatened to keep him from the office.

No matter how obvious was the strain on his family, Land remained devoted to his personal creative ideal, and he could go on and on rhapsodizing about it. "If you dream of something worth doing," he said, "and then simply go to work on it, and don't think anything of personalities, or emotional conflicts, or of money, or of family distractions; if you just think of, detail by detail, what you have to do next, it is a wonderful dream." Other people couldn't share in this wonderful dream; they could only shatter it. "You don't want to drive the family car or go to parties. You wish people would just go away and leave you alone while you get something straight. Then you get it straight and you embody it, and during that period of embodiment you have a feeling of almost divine guidance. Then it is done, and, suddenly, you are alone and you have to go back to your friends and the world around you and to all history, to be refreshed, to feel alive and human once again." Even so, he often seemed to let slip the small, routine attentions on which close personal relationships rely. He had a large extended family, but his method required them to play by his rules, and few could meet his required standards of compliance. He didn't keep in touch with any of his eighteen cousins, not even those who lived very close to him, and he explained away his distance to a nephew by saying, "My work is my life."

His friendships, likewise, were managed on his terms. If they somehow eroded his sense of purpose, he simply let those friendships die. And in 1960 and 1961, his relationship with Richard Bissell began to wither.

In the early days of the U-2, they seemed to be in lockstep, both of them convinced that technology could be used to increase transparency and the open flow of information worldwide. But after Bissell took over the CIA's covert operations directorate in late 1960, his views seemed to change. When Bissell began steering the CIA toward using technology to advance what he called "the art of political warfare," Land cast a critical eye. He questioned Bissell's commitment to the U-2 and the satellite programs, and he began to suspect that all the inspiration he himself was pouring into America's spy program was being compromised by Bissell's ideals, which were at odds with his own.

HE'D NEVER BEEN A CHURCHGOER, but Bissell faithfully followed his own Sunday ritual: each week, he'd put Bach's Mass in B Minor on the turntable and let the music wash over him, following the ebb and flow of the movements, losing himself for a little while. It was as if his brain had been clenched tight in problem solving all week, and this was his moment to let it relax, to soak up the music and renew. If the weather cooperated, sometimes he'd turn the record player up loud, open the back doors, and sit in the garden behind the house. A couple years earlier he'd planted bamboo stalks along the side of the yard to try to block out the noise from Thirty-Fourth Street and insulate his private garden, his refuge of tranquillity.

On Sunday, April 9, Bissell desperately needed some peace. The past couple weeks had been the most pressure filled of his life. Some nights, he wouldn't get home from the office until past midnight, and then he would be up early in the morning to go back; in the few hours between, the red telephone in the alcove dedicated to work calls might ring at any time. In just a few days, on April 14, the Cuban exile force was scheduled to storm the island's shore, and the planning was a tangle of complexities. The task had started out small—a side job he'd taken on in addition to overseeing the CIA's covert ops in more than fifty foreign stations around the world . . . in addition to managing the U-2 and satellite programs . . . in addition to keeping an eye on the agency's budget. The Cuban operation started with a CIA team of about forty full-time staff; in a matter of months that number had increased more than tenfold. The exile force, too, had ballooned from about four hundred men in January to about thirteen hundred in April. And now, days before the mission could *finally* be launched, on a bright spring Sunday custommade for Bach in the backyard, Bissell got an unexpected telephone call on the red phone: Jacob Esterline and Colonel Jack Hawkins, two CIA operatives helping Bissell with tactical planning, said they were coming over to the house. Everything was falling apart, they told him. The whole mission should be scrapped.

A few months before, Hawkins had been the one who outlined the project's objectives in a memo for Kennedy. An amphibious force would land on the Cuban coast, establishing a beachhead. They'd be able to do this with little resistance, because before they made land, a fleet of bombers would fly over the island and bombard all the Cuban military aircraft and naval vessels that might be in a position to respond to the covert invasion. "It is expected that these operations will precipitate a general uprising throughout Cuba and cause the revolt of large segments of the Cuban Army and Militia," Hawkins wrote. But the success of the mission depended in large part on those preliminary air bombardments, he wrote. "If this is not done, we will be courting disaster."

Kennedy that spring ordered his Joint Chiefs of Staff to evaluate the plan, and their summary indicated it had "a fair chance of ultimate success"—a vague summary that Bissell chose to interpret optimistically. But senior members of the State Department and a few members of Kennedy's own staff urged caution. Arthur Schlesinger, Kennedy's special assistant, worried that if anyone found out that the United States backed the invasion, the president would be in the same impossible position Eisenhower had been in after Powers was shot down. "If we admit involvement," Schlesinger wrote, "we admit action taken in violation of the basic characters of the hemisphere and of the United Nations. If we justify such violation by pleading a higher law, we place ourselves thereafter on the same moral plane as the Soviet Union. If we deny involvement, few will believe us; and we invite a repetition of the U-2 episode, which made us look absurd before the world."

Bissell, however, had pointed out that inaction could be just as humiliating. The troops of exiles would have to be disbanded if not used soon. "Its members will be angry, disillusioned and aggressive," Bissell predicted, "with the inevitable result that they will provide honey for the press bees and the U.S. will have to face the resulting indignities and embarrassments."

Kennedy believed action had to be taken; it was simply a question of what kind of action. Soviet weapons and fighter planes were pouring into Cuba, and the longer the United States waited, the stronger Castro would get, and then the leader would go from a mere nuisance to a genuine, existential threat for the United States. If Castro ever got his hands on nuclear weapons, the proximity of the threat to the United States could shift the entire balance of the Cold War. But Kennedy agreed with Schlesinger: plausible deniability was a key to the whole operation. When Bissell walked him through the invasion plans, the president was both impressed and unnerved by its ambition. "Too spectacular," he said. "It sounds like D-Day. You have to reduce the noise." If the exiles seemed *too* powerful, if their air raids and beach landings seemed too formidable, no one would believe that the Americans weren't pulling the strings.

To Bissell, making a big noise was the whole point; the assault had to shock Castro's soldiers inside Cuba into thinking they had no chance of winning, forcing them to switch sides and join the inevitable victors, the exiles. But to reduce the noise level, Bissell agreed to move the planned landing site to a much quieter stretch of coast about 130 miles southeast of Havana. The site was called the Bahía de Cochinos, or the Bay of Pigs.

Kennedy committed to the plan on April 4, and Bissell met with the Joint Chiefs of Staff to go over the details. However, one of the joint chiefs—the marine commandant—was unable to attend, and sitting in for him as a replacement was the air force's vice-chief: Curtis LeMay.

Even now, more than six years after the CIA was chosen over the air force to lead the U-2 project, the tension between the two groups was palpable, particularly between LeMay and Bissell. In late 1960, Bissell had asked for more air force support in planning the air raids; his requests went unanswered, and he eventually had to call on the Air National Guard for help instead. Now, less than two weeks before the operation, LeMay dismissed Bissell's notion that air strikes were essential to the mission.

"I was shocked," Bissell later wrote. "We all knew only too well that without air support the project would fail."

Now, the Sunday before the troops were to be sent, Bissell's two key deputies—Esterline and Hawkins—were standing on his front porch, demanding an emergency meeting. He calmly ushered them into his living room, where they got right to the point: the mission was doomed, and Bissell should call it off while there was still time.

The question of air support worried both of them. Hawkins, a marine colonel, had been incensed when told of LeMay's opposition to air strikes: if any senior marine had been in that meeting, Hawkins said, air support would have been labeled a priority. He also worried that the last-minute change of landing sites was unwise. Just inland from the Bay of Pigs stretched a dense, nearly impenetrable swamp. One of Bissell's original ideas was that if the troops encountered any problems holding their position after they landed, they could retreat to the Escambray Mountains, where they could hide out and continue to launch guerrilla-style attacks on Castro's forces. But with the swamp in the way, those mountains would be very hard to reach.

Esterline and Hawkins told Bissell that if he didn't call off the operation, they'd resign.

This was exactly what Bissell *didn't* need: key members of his team bailing out on him when the going got tough. He restrained his temper, calmly considered what they were saying, and told them that he agreed with them: the mission had been compromised, no doubt. But it was too late to scrap everything now, he argued, and asked them to stay. The two men agreed, Hawkins later wrote, on one condition: that Bissell "take immediate action" to convince Kennedy that strong air raids were an absolute necessity.

The next day, Hawkins traveled down to Nicaragua for one last review of the paramilitary forces, and two days later he sent a cable to Bissell's office. "My observations of the last few days have increased my confidence in the ability of this force to accomplish not only initial combat missions but also the ultimate objective of Castro's overthrow."

The next day, Bissell showed Kennedy a copy of Hawkins's message. The planned air strike was now less than twenty-four hours away, and Kennedy seemed reassured. As an aside, he asked Bissell how many planes were going to be involved in the first strike. Sixteen, Bissell answered.

That was too many, Kennedy decided.

"As far as I know, he made this decision without consulting either the Joint Chiefs or the Secretary of Defense," Bissell later wrote. "I was simply directed to reduce the scale and make it 'minimal.' He left it to me to determine exactly what that meant, and I responded by cutting the planned sixteen aircraft to eight."

KELLY JOHNSON, STILL THE ONLY MEMBER of the U-2 development team who'd been publicly identified, assumed the Soviets were watching him. The CIA had instructed him in the basics of evasion and escape. He began taking different routes to work each day and grew wary of strangers. Even during the best of times, his anxiety burned holes in his stomach, and now he began sleeping with an automatic pistol next to his bed.

He continued to refine the U-2, but much of his work now centered on finishing a prototype for its planned successor, the supersonic A-12, which was designed to fly nearly three miles higher than the U-2. Bissell wanted the first A-12 ready to fly by the end of 1961, but a shortage of titanium meant that supply shipments were running up to nine months late. On April 18, 1961, Johnson flew to Washington to brief Bissell on the unwelcome developments. He didn't know Bissell already had all the bad news he could handle.

When Johnson walked up to the porch of the big house in Cleveland Park that Tuesday night for dinner, Annie Bissell welcomed him inside. Richard was working late, she said, and wouldn't be able to eat with them. So Annie and Johnson dined together, enjoying each other's company, unaware that across town at the CIA offices in Quarters Eye, Bissell was watching his career fall apart.

THE FIRST AIR STRIKE, LAUNCHED DAYS BEFORE the brigade was supposed to land on the beach, failed to wipe out Castro's fighter planes, and it didn't knock his runways out of commission, either. Bissell hoped another round of preliminary strikes would do the job, but Kennedy called them off. That meant the forty-plus air strikes designed to weaken Castro's response to the amphibious landing had been reduced to a mere eight.

"Goddamn it, this is criminal negligence," barked Hawkins, slamming a fist on a table. By the time the brigade landed on the beach, it was clear that they were sitting ducks. At 1:45 that Tuesday afternoon, April 18, the commander of the brigade radioed a desperate message to his CIA overseers: "We are under attack by two Sea Fury aircraft and heavy artillery. Do not see any friendly air cover as you promised. Need jet support immediately."

By Tuesday evening, things had only gotten worse. Bissell requested an emergency meeting with Kennedy, who'd been attending a 10:15 p.m. reception to honor members of Congress. Bissell got a ride to the White House, where he met Kennedy, who was still dressed in white tie and tails. They convened in the Cabinet Room at about two minutes before midnight, joined by Vice President Lyndon Johnson and other key members of the administration.

All day Bissell had been urging Kennedy to order warplanes from an aircraft carrier to provide cover to the brigade; it was the only way to salvage the mission, he said. The chief of naval operations, Admiral Arleigh Burke, supported Bissell's request, believing the navy F-4s could wipe out Castro's attackers. But Kennedy, still worried about keeping America's role in the operation a secret, nixed the idea.

"Burke, I don't want the United States involved in this," Kennedy said.

"Hell, Mr. President," Burke responded, "but we *are* involved."

The reports grew grimmer by the minute, and by 3:46 a.m., when the meeting broke up, it was obvious that Kennedy was facing the first full-blown crisis of his presidency. Around 4:00 a.m., Kennedy took a walk alone around the South Lawn of the White House, his hands thrust deep in his pockets. Aides who saw him later said he appeared to be on the edge of tears.

Castro's forces eventually captured 1,189 members of the brigade. America's hand in the fiasco was thoroughly exposed. Some politicians began calling for the CIA to be subject to congressional oversight, and others argued it should be completely dissolved.

For Bissell, it was an unmitigated catastrophe.

• • •

EDWIN LAND WAS FURIOUS WHEN HE FOUND OUT that as many as fifteen U-2 missions had been launched over Cuba to support the failed Bay of Pigs invasion. To him, it violated the very spirit of the plane. He vented his frustrations with James Killian, arguing that Bissell had, in a way, betrayed them by allowing the U-2 to be used as a tool for aggressive paramilitary action.

"Both Land and Killian looked upon science and technology almost as a religion, something sacred to be kept from contamination by those who would misuse it for unwholesome ends," stated an in-house CIA history written years after the incident. "Into this category fit the cover operations and 'dirty tricks' of Dick Bissell's Directorate of Plans."

Even with Eisenhower gone, Land still had the ear of the White House. In a memo circulated among Kennedy's staff shortly after the election, Land was listed among candidates the president should consider appointing as his scientific adviser. "Land has more prestige and perhaps greater breadth than any of the others," the memo stated, but quickly added a caveat: he'd probably never leave Polaroid for a full-time White House job. But Land agreed to serve as "consultant-at-large" for the President's Science Advisory Committee, and in the days after the Bay of Pigs invasion he became a founding member of the President's Foreign Intelligence Advisory Board.

Kennedy created the board in the days after the failed Cuban operation, writing an executive order and asking his brother Attorney General Bobby Kennedy to handle the matter "on an urgent basis." The group would oversee the nation's intelligence agencies and, Kennedy hoped, prevent him from ever stumbling into another Bay of Pigs. Kennedy chose Killian to chair the group of eight. Killian and Land agreed that its first orders of business should include stripping the CIA of the authority to launch paramilitary maneuvers and moving the U-2 and the satellite reconnaissance programs away from Bissell and putting them under a new office within the agency. They believed that Bissell had been an effective manager of the U-2 program in the early days, but his increasingly elaborate forays into covert actions had left him distracted and overextended.

Maybe they shouldn't have worried that Bissell had too much on his plate. *The New York Times,* in an article that explained the mission of the new advisory board, included this tidbit of gossip: "It is regarded as virtually certain now that Allen W. Dulles, the C.I.A. director, and Richard

M. Bissell Jr., a deputy director who was in general charge of the Cuban operation, will be leaving the agency, perhaps this autumn."

EARLY FRIDAY MORNING after the Bay of Pigs disaster, Kelly Johnson, back home in Encino, grabbed his morning newspaper and read another article about the Cuban debacle. Bissell's name was right there in black and white. The fall guy.

Unlike Land, Johnson didn't see any problem with Bissell using the U-2 in the operation. His visit to Washington that week convinced him that Bissell was working harder than anyone, doing what he believed was right for his country, and now Bissell was getting crucified for it. Johnson grabbed a pen and a piece of paper and began scribbling out a note:

> Dear Dick,
>     I want to drop you a line to state my thanks and admiration for the terrific job you did last week while I was in Washington. I've been told of your one man stand against most terrific odds last Tuesday nite and morning during the very critical hours of the Southern Crisis. . . . Seeing the frustrations, the terrible needless obstructionism on the part of our so-called "defense department" when they really were asked to do so little to give a shove to make the whole thing a success—makes me deeply concerned for our nation's safety when the chips are really down. If there is anything I can ever do to help carry part of your load don't hesitate for an instant to call me. I've thought continually of your problems of the last week to see what we can do here to assist. . . . Thank Anne for the fine dinner Tuesday and accept a grateful U.S. citizen's thanks for your splendid efforts on our behalf.
>     Sincerely,
>     Kelly

Bissell was touched by this gesture; Johnson was one of just a handful of people who wrote to take his side. This had been the most unpleasant week Bissell had ever experienced—"even worse than the first week of May 1960," he wrote in a reply to Johnson. He was taking a pounding in the press, and he suspected that Kennedy was cursing his name to everyone in the White House. The worst part was that Bissell suspected he probably deserved it. "I certainly feel I have served my country ill," Bissell wrote to Johnson. "I deeply appreciate your remarks; it was kind of you to take the trouble to write them down. I hope the next time I see you some of these clouds will have begun to roll away."

But the following Sunday, Bissell's mood remained dreary and dark. He put an opera on the turntable, turned the record player up loud, walked outside, and sat in his garden, alone.

# BOOK FOUR

# Icarus Reborn

I've never been certain whether the moral of the
Icarus story should only be, as is generally accepted,
"Don't try to fly too high," or whether it might also be
thought of as, "Forget the wax and feathers, and do a
better job on the wings."

—STANLEY KUBRICK

# CHAPTER 12

# *Trade-Offs*

With the Bay of Pigs disaster, I gave up any hopes for clemency.

—FRANK POWERS

In 1961, Barbara got a job at a restaurant in Milledgeville, a rowdy place on the edge of town called the Log Cabin. The owner, Charlie Deason, also ran a roadhouse and a catering business, and he told her he could use some help keeping his books.

The Log Cabin became a refuge. She'd hang out at the bar, chatting with customers, even when she wasn't on the clock. Deason was in his mid-forties, with a wife and a grown daughter, and he seemed to take a protective interest in Barbara.

One day, Charlene, Deason's daughter, was searching for her father, and someone told her she might find him at Barbara's house. Charlene and her husband stopped by for a surprise visit. They marched in the front door and found Deason was barefoot, wearing only an undershirt and pants, which he quickly zipped up. Barbara was wearing only a housecoat. Both of them appeared to be drunk.

Barbara insisted she and Charlie were just good friends and that they weren't "indecent," as Charlene claimed. Her denials couldn't stop rumors from spreading around town. Even Barbara's mother seemed to believe Charlene's interpretation of the encounter.

All the while, Dr. James Baugh, the physician the CIA had assigned to be Barbara's "spokesman" during the Moscow trip, chronicled her behavior in periodic updates to the agency. Baugh's task, according to the CIA's internal summary of events, was "to keep her out of the public eye (and out of jail)." As the summer of 1961 unfolded, it became a nearly impossible job.

On June 22, a Milledgeville police officer spotted a car driving erratically. He pulled it over and found Barbara at the wheel. She was arrested for drunk driving, fined, and released. The incident didn't slow her down a bit. Several weeks later, in September, Barbara walked into the house to find her mother, brother, and sister waiting for her. On Dr. Baugh's urging, they had decided to stage an intervention.

"Barbara, I'm going to ask you to do something that might sound a bit scary, but believe me, it's for your own good," her brother, Jack, said.

She needed psychiatric help, he told her, and a stint in the state psychiatric hospital might do her some good. Barbara couldn't believe what she was hearing. They thought *she* was crazy? She told them that *they* were the crazy ones for thinking they were any better off than she was. She flatly refused to check herself in. Jack said he was sorry to hear it, but in that case they'd simply have her committed against her will.

The Baldwin County sheriff was already parked outside. Jack picked up the phone, made a call, and within minutes three doctors were at the house to perform a quick evaluation of her. Dr. Baugh filed the petition to send her to the hospital. The papers stated, "We do find Barbara M. Powers to be incapable and incompetent of managing her affairs and liable to have a guardian appointed, and to be committed to University Hospital, Hervey M. Cleckley Building, Psychiatric Center, Augusta, Georgia." Her brother retained a CIA-cleared attorney to be her legal adviser.

The psychiatrist she was sent to was Dr. Corbett H. Thigpen, a minor celebrity who four years earlier had co-authored the best seller *The Three Faces of Eve,* which was quickly made into a movie starring Joanne Woodward as the title character, a woman with multiple-personality disorder. Corbett's psychiatric ward was divided into two sections: one for patients deemed able to handle the relative freedoms of recreation and social mixing, and a second reserved for those requiring stricter supervision. Barbara was assigned to the second one.

Barbara liked Thigpen, and she later claimed that he'd given her a clean bill of mental health after several weeks of observation. The CIA record painted a darker picture:

> The psychiatrist in charge at the Clinic, Dr. Corbett Thigpen, diagnosed Barbara as psychopathic. However, she was released from the hospital in her mother's care on 30 October. On 18 November she was recommitted after a bout of drinking which ended in delirium tremens, was treated, again released in a week to her mother. Doctors at the clinic in consultation with an Agency

team of CI and legal staff were in agreement that Barbara Powers would never change her activities or interests and that her behavior would continue to follow the pattern set thus far. The Agency team therefore concluded that should Barbara attempt to seek revenge against the Agency by talking to the press or in other ways, there was little that could be done to prevent her taking such action.

Agency officials also worried that word of Barbara's struggles might filter back to Powers in prison and that his concern for her well-being might throw him into a state of helpless desperation. If that happened, they feared, he might decide to reveal more classified secrets to the Soviets in hopes of clemency and the chance to try to reclaim his marriage and personal life. Even some of those most skeptical of Powers's loyalty inside Angleton's counterintelligence division began to think an exchange—Abel for Powers—might be wise.

It was wholly unintentional, but Barbara had made a tragic sacrifice: the dramatic deterioration of her mental health had helped resurrect her husband's prospects for freedom.

THROUGHOUT 1961, ATTORNEY JAMES DONOVAN had maintained sporadic contact with Rudolf Abel's "wife" in Berlin, who he assumed was a Soviet agent. On September 11, Donovan got a letter from her saying she'd visited the Soviet embassy in Berlin to discuss the matter of a spy swap. "I gathered from our talk that there is only one possible way to achieve success," the letter stated, "that is simultaneous release of both Francis Powers and my husband, which can be arranged." The final clause suggested that the Soviets were ready and willing to surrender Powers, and in Washington officials in the CIA and State Department started to lobby Attorney General Bobby Kennedy for official approval.

Powers was oblivious to all of this, and with each passing day he seemed to sink a little deeper into a pessimistic rut. The idea of spending years confined in a cell, thousands of miles from everyone he loved, felt unbearable. "I am sure I will never stay for ten years," he wrote in his prison diary. "Will do something drastic first." He had hoped the new presidential administration might pursue his release more enthusiastically than Eisenhower's had, but after the Bay of Pigs debacle, which he'd read about in Soviet news reports, he figured the chances of an agreement had never been more of a long shot. Frank doubted that Kennedy ever spared a thought about him. "I am afraid I will never be a Kennedy supporter in the future," Frank wrote in his diary.

He cursed the naïveté that had led him to assume the government actually cared about his well-being. "Before I was captured I had a great tendency to accept things as they were, not questioning the policies of the United States, since I knew we had intelligent people in our government whose job it was to make decisions for the benefit of the country as a whole," he wrote in September 1961. "I realized that they were more intelligent than I, and if they did something I thought strange, it was only because I did not know all the reasons for the action, and I accepted it as right and proper. But now I realize there is more to it all than I saw at first."

Barbara's letters were sporadic; sometimes she'd send two in one week, and other times more than a month would pass without a word. At first he suspected the Russians were holding her letters, but prison officials insisted they weren't; she simply hadn't written to him, they said.

He had no clue how bad things were at home until October 13, when he got a letter from Barbara's mother saying she'd been committed to the mental hospital. He was shocked. Barbara's most recent letter was dated September 18—just four days before the intervention—and she'd given no hints that anything was wrong. Her mother's letter included few details, and he quickly fired off a response, begging for the full story. The next day, he confessed to his diary, "I am very upset and cannot get it out of my mind. If only I knew exactly what was going on, I think I would feel much better. I am sure that a great deal is my fault."

His thoughts were hijacked by a black desperation, the very kind that the CIA feared might splinter his resolve. Frank entertained the possibility of writing a personal letter to the Kremlin to propose some sort of deal; maybe they'd let him briefly visit Barbara if he promised to come back and remain their prisoner. But how would the Soviets benefit from that? "I know it is stupid," he wrote in his journal, "but I am grasping at straws."

IN LATE 1961, THE NEW CIA HEADQUARTERS was nearly complete, and several departments had already moved to the new site in Langley, Virginia.

The building was a colossus, an H-shaped mass of pale concrete and glass that contained 1,135,000 square feet. After the U-2 incident elevated the agency's public profile, it had become something of a parlor game in Washington to guess how many people might work in the new complex. It was reported that one senator on Capitol Hill learned from the new building's architects that the designers used a rule of thumb that allotted 98.5 square feet to each employee; he did the math and estimated that the CIA must have exactly 11,533 locally based employees. Whatever the real number, it had become clear to everyone in Washington that the intelligence business had become an industry unto itself. By the fall of 1961, even before the south wing of the complex was finished, traffic heading to the new headquarters was already snarled at rush hour on the Chain Bridge across the Potomac.

On November 28, President Kennedy made an unannounced visit, arriving by helicopter. In a ceremony attended by hundreds of agency employees, Kennedy pinned the National Security Medal on Allen Dulles's lapel. "It is not always easy," Kennedy said during the event. "Your successes are unheralded, your failures are trumpeted. I sometimes have that feeling myself."

The next day, Dulles officially resigned. His departure had been pending for months; after the Bay of Pigs, he knew he'd have to go. But in the months before he left, Dulles still held out hope that his old protégé, Richard Bissell, might be able to salvage a career inside the agency. Even after the debacle in Cuba, many in the CIA were convinced that it would be a shame to lose Bissell, who'd been such a central part of the agency and knew as much about its inner workings as anyone. Dulles and McGeorge Bundy, a special assistant to Kennedy, worked that summer to counter a rival faction within the CIA that wanted Bissell fired, and they proposed a new role for him—founding a unit that would be in charge of "unorthodox" paramilitary operations, including guerrilla warfare.

It wasn't an easy sell. A CIA postmortem on the Bay of Pigs was being prepared at the same time, and it laid the lion's share of the blame on Bissell's shoulders. By the fall of 1961, Bissell felt as if the Kennedy brothers wanted him to prove his worth, to convince them that he deserved a shot at redemption. That November, Bissell told Samuel Halpern, a CIA colleague, that "he had recently been chewed out in the Cabinet Room in the White House by both the President and the Attorney General for, as he put it, sitting on his ass and not doing anything about getting rid of Castro and the Castro regime." Halpern asked Bissell what "getting rid of Castro" meant. Bissell told him that the Kennedys hadn't spelled it out, in specific terms, but they didn't need to: it was clear to him that they were talking about an assassination.

Days later, on November 16, Bissell called upon a veteran agency operative, William Harvey, for help. Bissell's previous plans to entangle the Mafia in a plot to kill Castro had gone nowhere, but now he instructed Harvey to get in touch with Roselli, the CIA's initial contact in the criminal underworld. Bissell wanted to know if Roselli might be able to resuscitate the possibility of a mob hit on the Cuban leader—just in case the Kennedys ever decided extreme measures were necessary.

The Mafia plot ultimately fizzled, again, which was fine with Bissell. Years later, after the CIA's Mafia connections became public, Bissell brushed off the episode as a minor distraction. But it didn't change the fact that he still hadn't succeeded in "getting rid of Castro," which is what the Kennedys seemed to consider his primary objective.

In the final months of 1961, Bissell began contemplating a career outside the CIA. President Kennedy had offered him the option of staying on, suggesting that he might take command of the newly formed Directorate of Science and Technology, where he could continue to work with Land and Johnson.

Bissell appreciated the offer, but it felt like a demotion, as if Kennedy were trying to rein him in. The thrill of covert action had seeped into his blood. In a note to his daughter, Ann, he wrote, "I have a horror of hanging on here to a job that is not at the center of things, as so many people do."

ON NOVEMBER 29, 1961, KENNEDY APPOINTED John McCone, a wealthy California industrialist, to become the new director of the CIA. McCone had been the head of the Atomic Energy Commission in the final years of the Eisenhower administration, and he arrived with a dim view of both Powers and the U-2 program in general. More than a year earlier, just after Powers was shot down, he'd said that he suspected the pilot had purposefully defected to the Soviet Union. And when he first began making the rounds at Langley, McCone treated Bissell's aerial reconnaissance division with a narrow-eyed skepticism. "What are you people doing in the airplane business?" he asked.

Days before McCone took over, Dulles's deputy director, Charles Pearre Cabell, wrote a letter to Secretary of State Dean Rusk saying the CIA now supported the idea of swapping Abel for Powers. During the first week of January 1962, Bobby Kennedy formally signed off.

That week, the CIA and officials at the State Department met to formally draft a plan, although McCone and others within the agency still weren't completely sold on the idea. "Our friends at the CI Staff [James Angleton's counterintelligence division] did everything they could to torpedo that exchange," recalled John N. McMahon, a CIA official who later became the agency's deputy director. "I can remember several officers in State speaking against the exchange. I pointed out that President Kennedy authorized the exchange, and I wanted the names of those that were against it. The objections disappeared."

James Donovan, the lawyer for Abel, got in touch with Abel's "wife," whom he arranged to meet in Berlin. He flew to Germany on February 2, and for the next four days negotiated the terms of a swap with Soviet embassy officials. One of them was Ivan Schischkin, a man who introduced himself as an embassy undersecretary but whom the CIA knew as the chief of Soviet espionage for all of Europe.

The Soviets suggested that in exchange for Abel they could give up Frederic L. Pryor, a Yale student who'd recently been arrested in the Communist-controlled East Zone of Berlin and whose parents were in West Germany lobbying hard for his release. Donovan balked, insisting that Powers's release was the key to a deal. Talks appeared to be progressing, and Abel was flown to Berlin on February 8 in case everything quickly came together. Schischkin then angered Donovan by suggesting they had decided to hold on to Powers and instead give the Americans Marvin Makinen, a University of Pennsylvania graduate who in 1961 was arrested in Russia for taking pictures of Soviet military installations. Donovan threatened to return to America and take Abel with him. Finally the Soviets relented, agreeing to give up Powers and throwing Pryor into the deal for good measure. It was all set: during a secret rendezvous on a bridge uniting East and West Germany, Abel and Powers would trade places.

BY EARLY 1962, POWERS HAD BEEN in custody for nearly twenty-one months. At all hours of the day, he heard a high-frequency ringing in his ears. Sometimes he'd be shaken by frightening heart palpitations, and recently his eyesight seemed to be going a little haywire, as if there were blind spots—washed-out patches—in the center of his vision. Maybe it was a vitamin deficiency, or maybe it was just nerves. He lay awake at night wondering if he could ever salvage anything resembling a normal life with Barbara. If a few weeks passed without a letter from her, he began to suspect she'd forgotten about him; maybe she'd moved on with her life, and maybe he should just accept that. On January 28, he'd written in his diary, "I must admit I am becoming more and more afraid of what the future holds for me. Am I man enough to face all the things I may have to face, including a divorce? Divorce, much as I hate the idea of it, is fast becoming the only answer to Barbara's and my problems. I must truly admit I do not know how well I will face up to things. I hope it works out so that I am proven wrong in all my thoughts. But that hope is slim."

Then, on the evening of February 7, a KGB colonel and an interpreter paid him an unexpected visit.

"How would you like to go to Moscow tomorrow morning?"

He wasn't sure what they meant.

"Without guards," the interpreter added.

His spirits soared, but he tried to conceal his excitement. "Why? What's happening?" They were coy, just telling him to be ready to leave early. He didn't allow himself to fully believe he was being released until the next morning, when prison officials turned over the belongings that they'd been holding throughout his imprisonment. He dug through his things—the wallet, the identification cards—and, for the first time since he was captured, slipped on his wedding ring.

POWERS SPENT TWO NIGHTS IN MOSCOW, still in the custody of Soviet guards, before he was flown to East Germany on Friday, February 9. The next morning dawned misty and cold. Powers was awoken early and shepherded into a car that drove him to the Havel River, which ran between West Berlin and East Germany. Wearing a fur hat and a heavy coat, Powers stood with Schischkin and several other Soviet officials at the foot of the Glienicke Bridge. Barriers on each side of the bridge restricted passage, but Powers could see several indistinct figures standing at the other end, across the river. Donovan and Abel were there, as was Joe Murphy, a U-2 pilot who'd met Powers back at Area 51 and was on hand to verify his identity.

At about 8:20 a.m., the barriers lifted. Schischkin and the other Soviet officials walked toward the center of the bridge, where they met Donovan and Murphy. Soon both Abel and Powers joined the group. A KGB man who'd been with Powers stepped close to Abel, asked him to remove his glasses, and verified that he was the right man. Then Murphy stepped toward Powers and attempted to do the same.

"Gee, it's good to see you," Powers told Murphy. He recognized him as an acquaintance, though he was having trouble coming up with his name.

"You know who I am, don't you?" Murphy said.

Powers took a guess. "You're Bill."

He had confused Murphy with another U-2 crew member he'd met in Peshawar. Murphy tried to clear things up by asking the follow-up questions he'd been given in case Powers didn't remember his name.

"What was the name of your high school football coach?" Murphy asked.

Powers remembered that he'd filled out an air force form years ago with the answers to questions like this, but in the excitement of the moment he couldn't pull the answer from his memory. So Murphy dug deeper into his list of questions, and Powers nailed each one of them. His wife's name was Barbara, his mother's name was Ida, and his dog was Eck von Heinerberg.

"You're Francis Gary Powers," Murphy said with a smile.

They lingered on the bridge for about half an hour, making small talk and waiting for a radio message to verify that Pryor, the American student, had been turned over to American officials at a secondary location.

"Next time you come to see us," Schischkin told Powers, "come as a friend."

"Next time I'll come as a tourist," Powers replied.

Finally, someone shouted that Pryor had been released. At 8:52 a.m., Powers was officially a free man.

He flew back to Wiesbaden, where he, Donovan, and Murphy hopped onto the Lockheed Super Constellation that was usually reserved for the air force's commanding general in Europe.

On board over the Atlantic, Powers ate a green salad, potatoes, and a steak, medium rare. "You know," he said, "a couple weeks ago in my cell, I dreamed one night about a martini." He drank several of them as the jet flew over the Atlantic, back home.

# CHAPTER 13

## Together and Apart

The tenacity with which human beings, and governments, can stick to a fixed notion, even in the face of overwhelming proof to the contrary, is quite incredible.

—FRANK POWERS

Someone from the CIA called Barbara at home in Milledgeville early on the morning of February 10 to let her know Frank was on his way home. The news caught her off guard; she'd been out of the asylum for more than three months, but she had no idea the negotiations had even been under way. She quickly called a hairdresser for an emergency styling, but before she could leave the house, reporters were knocking on the door. The sudden attention set her on edge, and she poured herself a couple of drinks. Her brother, Jack, came over and tried to keep the reporters at bay, but someone from the *Chicago Tribune* managed to get through on the telephone. Jack said that Barbara likely wouldn't be traveling immediately to meet Frank because she "was just getting over an attack of influenza and [didn't] feel up to making the trip today." In truth, her family was pouring hot coffee into her, trying to sober her up for the imminent reunion. She was finally ready to go just before five o'clock that afternoon. She and Jack walked out of the house, through a cluster of newspaper photographers, and drove to Atlanta, where they caught a midnight flight to Washington.

In the early hours of morning, they checked into the Dupont Plaza Hotel—the same place where Frank, eight years before, was grilled by the CIA during his induction tests. After three or four hours of sleep, CIA employees whisked them into a car and raced through the streets of Washington, running red lights as reporters followed in pursuit. At a private hangar at a local airfield they climbed aboard a charter plane, which flew them to Maryland's Eastern Shore, where Frank was waiting at a site called Ashford Farm.

It was a sprawling Georgian mansion set on more than sixty acres of rolling land along the Choptank River, a tributary of the Chesapeake Bay. The CIA had purchased the twelve-room manor in 1951, using it as a safe house for defectors and spies. Staffed by CIA cooks and servants, the house was enormous—about eighty-seven hundred square feet, with seven bedrooms. A high wire fence ringed the property, and a couple of German shepherds stood guard.

The blue Chevy station wagon carrying Barbara turned onto the one-lane access road and slowly made its way to the circular drive out front. Snow was falling on the mansion's peaked roofs, and smoke billowed out of one of the chimneys.

Inside, Frank was trying to relax, struggling to quiet his mind. That morning, when one of the CIA guys asked him how he felt, he admitted he was nervous. He gave Frank a tranquilizer, which made him feel a little better by the time his parents showed up late that morning. Just before Barbara arrived, his parents were led away so the couple could enjoy their reunion alone.

From the second-floor landing, he saw her standing at the bottom of the carpeted staircase. She looked different—older. She'd gained nearly thirty pounds, he guessed, and her face was masked in thick makeup. It was clear to him that she'd suffered during his imprisonment, perhaps faring worse than he. But for the moment, he pushed all of that out of his mind, and they embraced, relieved to be back in each other's arms.

She was the only member of the family who was allowed to stay with him at Ashford Farm. That night and the following day, they caught up on a year-and-a-half of news and gossip, and every now and then she'd slip hints of her resentment toward the CIA into the conversations. Her anger was sharp and quick, and it didn't take Frank long to realize that it ran very deep.

The CIA told the couple that they would keep them secluded for several days, away from the press and other relations, while the agency subjected Frank to a full debriefing. Neither he nor Barbara could leave the house, they said.

Frank didn't know what to think of the quarantine. All the people he'd spoken with had insisted they were overjoyed that he was finally free, so why were they still treating him like a prisoner?

That day, Frank took a walk through the snow outside the house with Joe Murphy. "Tell me something," he asked Murphy. "If I wanted to leave right now—just pack my bag and walk out—could I do it?"

Murphy considered it for a moment. "I don't think so."

ON FEBRUARY 12, ONE OF THE CIA OFFICERS inside the safe house got a phone call. "Some reporter's on to our location," he said. "We're going to have to move." The day before, the White House had released a photograph of Powers, and two exterior doors were clearly visible in the background. The former owners of Ashford Farm identified the doors—specifically the colonial hinges and latches on them—as belonging to the mansion, and the news found its way into the *Baltimore Sun*.

The next morning, two men from the Associated Press snuck through the gate and got close enough to peer through a window of the house; all they could really make out were a couple of filing cabinets before they were confronted by a CIA security officer in a sour mood. "This is government property. I am sure you are aware that you are not welcome here. You know which way you came in, and you can get out the same way."

Actually, the reporters had arrived too late: Frank and Barbara were already gone. The CIA had driven them under the cover of night to another safe house outside Gettysburg, Pennsylvania, close to former president Eisenhower's farm. The drive had been slow going; about five inches of snow and freezing rain fell on Maryland that night, and road crews shoveled cinders onto the icy highways to prevent drivers from losing control.

At the new safe house in Pennsylvania, Frank and Barbara settled into the routine they'd be forced to observe for nearly three weeks: he spent his days undergoing intensive interviews with CIA debriefers, while Barbara sat reading in front of a fireplace, trying to combat her desire to drink.

It was still snowing on the morning of Valentine's Day when a helicopter settled down on the grounds near the safe house. Two men hopped out. One was Jim Cunningham, who'd helped recruit Powers into the U-2 program and who'd been his case officer and main contact in Bissell's office from the beginning. Alongside him was Kelly Johnson, who'd been summoned from Lockheed to visit a pilot he hadn't seen since Area 51.

Inside, Johnson found Powers getting ready for a marathon question-and-answer session, a debriefing designed to help the agency try to sort out what really happened when his plane went down. Both of them sat at a table where a reel-to-reel tape recorder had just begun to spin, and Cunningham joined them.

"Kelly and I came up today simply to sort of associate ourselves with you again," Cunningham said, "and not to conduct any kind of detailed discussion necessarily of the aerodynamics. But since Kelly built it, I can't think of any better guy to ask you some of the questions that I know have been on his mind over these past few years, a good many of which I think we had from the beginning, as a function of what we saw in the press and what we heard from the other side. Kelly, do you think you would like to pursue the line of questioning at this point?"

Actually, Johnson *did* plan to get into a detailed discussion on the aerodynamics of the crash, but before he went there, he wanted to lighten the mood. Powers was clearly nervous; he'd said as much when he first sat down for the debriefing. "Well," Johnson began, "I want to start off with saying I'm awfully glad to see you again, Frank."

"Thank you."

"We certainly did our best to try to study what happened when the famous May Day came around," Johnson explained. "We've taken May 1 off our calendar—from now on, we go directly to May 2."

For the next couple hours, Johnson guided Powers through the whole story of his flight, from takeoff to the moment he was captured. He quizzed him about the plane's responsiveness, the automatic-pilot troubles, the altitude readings, the electrical systems, his fuel levels, the flight plan, the weather. When Powers described the orange flash of light and the slight bump he felt before losing control, Johnson zeroed in on the specifics. Was he sure the flash was orange? (Yes.) Did it originate in front of, or behind, the plane? (Seemed to fill the whole sky.) Could he have been at a lower altitude, and perhaps the orange light of the sun was reflecting off a white cloud? (No.) Was he sure the plane fell straight down and he hadn't leveled at a lower altitude before he jumped? (Yes, it came straight down.)

Johnson was impressed. Everything Powers said was consistent with the laws of physics and the specs of the airplane. When Frank described when and how the wings tore off, the way the plane spun in the air, the forces pressing against him in the cockpit, the loose feeling of the yoke in his hands, it all rang true to Johnson's ear.

Johnson then pulled out some pictures of the U-2 wreckage that had been released by the Soviets. He indicated the points of damage to the wings and the tail and traced that damage back to some of the sensations that Powers had felt in the air. "One thing that I was very—have always been mystified about—I've not seen anything of a horizontal tail in these pictures," Johnson said. It appeared as if part of the tail section of the plane had been knocked off, yet the tail wasn't completely destroyed. Johnson shared his theory that the missile fired at him might have been a near miss, damaging the tail without obliterating it—a guess that struck Powers as plausible.

As Frank described exactly what he saw as he came down, Johnson snapped up every detail. When they got around to discussing the ejection seat mechanism, Frank mentioned that he'd been worried his legs would have been severed from the force of an ejection because he was pushed too far forward in his seat. Johnson told him he shouldn't have worried. "I mean, there's so much acceleration at the start of it that their legs get snapped back in," Johnson explained. Other pilots, too, had expressed the same fears to him before, but they didn't understand its design. "They might hit their toes on the board, but . . . that's better than not getting out."

The Soviets, it seemed, didn't understand the design of the seat, either. Way back in May 1960, when the photos were first released, Johnson had spotted something wrong. "It's fishy because they took it apart and misassembled it," he now told Powers.

"They told me during the investigation that it was rigged up so that if I pulled the ejection seat it would have blown up immediately," Powers said, recalling his interrogations with the Soviets, who had insisted that whoever had made the plane had wanted to make sure he never survived a crash. "They were trying to kill—"

"This is absolutely not true," Johnson insisted.

"Well, I know that," Powers said. "I didn't believe it for a minute."

Cunningham jumped in. "I think we gave you a little ribbing on that as I remember, Kelly."

"Quite a little, as a matter of fact," Johnson said.

Powers would go on to endure hour upon hour of questioning for nearly three weeks. As he rehashed everything—his routine in prison, the layout of the prison cells, the descriptions of the people he met, the specifics of his interrogations—he noticed a theme emerging: it seemed as if his CIA questioners weren't concerned about getting to the truth of things as much as they were with establishing that they couldn't be blamed for anything. Many times, he had the feeling that they didn't believe him, that they suspected he was trying to hide something. The exception to all of this was this one day spent going over the crash with Johnson. Of all the people who questioned him, the Lockheed designer never seemed to doubt that his story was true.

Near the end of that debriefing with Johnson, as Cunningham was asking Powers about how much the Soviets seemed to know about the cameras and the film in the U-2, Johnson broke in to interrupt him. "Jim, I must leave in a few minutes," he said. "I'd like to change the course of conversation." Johnson had heard enough. "Frank, I wanted to tell you that I don't know what your plans are, or what life will come," Johnson said, "but if you decide you want to come back to work, we've got places where, I think, we can give you something to do. Perhaps, if you'd want to work down in our Marietta, Georgia, plant, close to where your wife is, or some other place. If you'd give Jim a ring, I'd like to do what I can to get you back into this thing."

Powers was touched. "That's very nice of you," he said. "I have no idea what the future's going to be like."

It was nearly impossible for him to imagine anything beyond the moment. When he returned to Barbara at the end of the day, she desperately wanted a drink. He was in no position to preach to her about recreational drinking, but this seemed to go far beyond that. He tried to persuade her to talk to the doctor inside the safe house, to admit to him her cravings. Even as she begged Frank to ransack the house in search of a beer, Barbara refused to admit that she had a problem.

RICHARD BISSELL DIDN'T MAKE IT to the debriefing sessions. On February 17, the same day Frank was scouring his memory to describe the windows in Lubyanka, Bissell submitted his formal resignation to the CIA.

Earlier that winter, the agency threw a going-away party for Allen Dulles in the Alibi Club, toasting him over dinner and presenting him with a silver tray emblazoned with the CIA's logo. It marked the end of an era. Now it was Bissell's turn to say good-bye. John McCone, Dulles's successor, opened up his home in northwest Washington to host Bissell's own farewell, and he invited most of the senior agency men who'd served with Bissell since 1954. It was a nice gesture, if not a genuine one. In early 1962, McCone confided to a *New York Times* reporter that he considered Bissell "a dreamer" who was lacking in administrative skills. And when Bissell had declined President Kennedy's suggestion that he lead the planned Directorate of Science and Technology, McCone hadn't seemed at all disappointed. "The Agency's loss will be great," he told Bissell, "but from your point of view, I think you're wise."

McCone wasn't a popular choice among the agency's old guard, given that he had little intelligence experience. But the new administration was unafraid to stoke conflict, as if Kennedy viewed disagreement as a healthy prerequisite of solid decision making. Perhaps no one illustrated that notion more vividly than did Kennedy's latest appointment to the Joint Chiefs of Staff—General Curtis LeMay. The air force general's rise to the Joint Chiefs was a result of the Bay of Pigs, which convinced Kennedy that the panel needed new blood. The president seemed to believe that LeMay would be able to fit into the group and work with others, but his predecessor on the Joint Chiefs, General Thomas White, knew LeMay as a man "with almost no social graces" and a natural disregard for opposing viewpoints. LeMay, for his part, had often complained that White had been too open-minded and quick to compromise. "I never believed in that," LeMay said. "I thought if you believed in something, God damn it, you got in there and fought for it." But LeMay clashed so hard and so quickly with others in Kennedy's inner circle that Secretary of Defense Robert McNamara declined to attend his swearing in at the White House.

Within McCone's CIA, the friction wasn't quite as bad, but some couldn't help feeling as if the office were in the midst of a purge. McCone had picked Richard Helms to succeed Bissell as the head of clandestine operations, sending a clear signal of a new direction. If anyone could have been considered Bissell's nemesis within the agency, it had always been Helms. In the beginning of their relationship, Helms believed that Bissell paid too much attention to technology and not enough to flesh-and-blood spies. In the past two years, however, Helms had complained that Bissell had become reckless and too enamored with paramilitary actions. During the Bay of Pigs planning, Helms made sure to remain distanced and, ultimately, uncontaminated by the operation; when Bissell outlined the invasion plans during meetings, Helms would sit in silence while, as one CIA official later recalled, "often inspecting his well-manicured fingernails." Helms, who'd sarcastically saddled Bissell with the nickname "Wonder Boy," had been disappointed when Dulles in 1958 put Bissell in charge of clandestine operations, but now, in Helms's view, McCone had corrected the oversight.

At McCone's house that evening, Bissell listened as his colleagues raised their glasses in his honor and showered him with praise. Helms, as Bissell later recalled in a letter to his daughter, offered a "particularly gracious toast."

THE OFFICERS WHO DEBRIEFED POWERS—all of them labeled "experts" in interrogation by the CIA—unanimously believed he was telling the truth. But John McCone wasn't content to take their word for it. He decided that a panel of three judges—a board of inquiry—should decide whether he had "complied with his obligations as an American citizen."

The board reviewed the transcripts of sixteen tape recordings of Powers's recent debriefings, studied the transcript of his trial in Moscow, and examined numerous other exhibits. For six days they grilled Powers and more than twenty other witnesses—CIA officers, psychologists, U-2 pilots, counterintelligence officers, and NSA analysts. At the end of the ordeal, they subjected Powers to a polygraph test. He recognized the man who administered the test; it was the same man who'd given him his first lie detector test in the Dupont Plaza Hotel years earlier.

"Do you have any funds deposited in a numbered Swiss bank account?"

"Did anything happen in Russia for which you could be blackmailed?"

"Are you a double agent?"

Powers passed the test. When the board evaluated all the evidence presented during the hearings, the only evidence it found that contradicted Powers's story was the report compiled by the NSA, which had been based on the intercepts of Soviet radar signals and chatter. "In the course of presentation of the evidence to the Board the obvious possibility of confusion and error was pointed out," the panel reported. "It is the conclusion of the Board that the evidence establishes overwhelmingly that Powers' account was a truthful account." Nothing he did— from the information he surrendered during his Soviet interrogations, to his decision not to use his poison pin, to his inability to destroy the aircraft—suggested he had acted against his duties as a CIA employee or as an American.

A congressional panel followed up by reviewing the board's conclu-

sions, questioning Powers, McCone, and others in the CIA. Several lawmakers praised Powers for his service to the country, but a few remained
skeptical. Representative Frank J. Becker, a Republican from New York,
believed the board had erred by clearing Powers's name. He scoffed at
the notion that Powers was unsure whether a Soviet missile directly hit
the U-2 or not, and he suggested Powers was a traitor for failing to hit
his self-destruct button. "Nothing but a whitewash," Becker said of the
board's conclusions. "A lot of Powers' statements sound fantastic to me.
There appears to be a lot of cover-up going on."

Many in the CIA were eager to move on, but McCone wasn't ready to
let Powers off the hook. McCone asked the air force's Office of Special
Investigations to conduct yet another separate investigation of Powers,
and he prevented the pilot from interacting with the news media and
telling his side of the story. President Kennedy called McCone and told
him to let it go.

The CIA dropped the issue, but others quickly picked it up. Ian Fleming again slammed Powers's actions, writing in a column in London's
*Sunday Times* that he didn't believe Powers had been downed by a missile. Fleming wrote, "I have strong views about the Powers Case. It will
go down in history, I think, as one of the classical espionage cases, classical in the sense of its majestic mishandling."

Walter Cronkite of CBS News aired a report that cast a highly critical
eye on the "pardon" that had been granted Powers, and he cited the erro-
neous NSA intercept reports—the ones that had unwittingly confused
Powers's U-2 and the Soviet fighter planes that were chasing him—as
evidence. Cronkite muddled matters even more when he mistakenly
reported that Powers himself had been radioing in his altitude readings
during his overflight; in fact, Powers had maintained radio silence. At
the end of his report, Cronkite posed a series of rhetorical questions to
his TV audience:

> What is behind the apparent discrepancy between the radio
> conversation with Powers during his flight and the story he told
> in Moscow and Washington, the fairly swift catastrophe at 68,000
> feet as against the gradual, 80-minute descent from 68,000 to
> 40,000 feet? Why, as Congressman Becker asks, if Powers was
> under instructions to cooperate with his captors, did the CIA wait
> almost two years to say so? And why, finally, has the CIA persisted
> in keeping Powers under wraps, out of range of the understandable

public curiosity and indeed public interest? The CIA, to whom we put these questions today, has declined any further comment, and until these questions are answered, the books will remain open on the Powers Case.

AFTER THE DEBRIEFINGS AND INTERROGATIONS, the pressure was building on Frank and Barbara. Both of them had been secluded for more than a month, shielded from the public eye, and they were going stir-crazy. Finally, after the congressional hearing, the CIA allowed them to travel.

Frank took off for Pound, Virginia, where he visited the family home for the first time since 1953. Barbara, meanwhile, returned to Milledgeville to collect her belongings, most of which she'd left with her mother.

The press caught up with Frank in Pound and snapped pictures of him horseback riding. About eight hundred people showed up to the county's National Guard Armory for a welcome ceremony, which seemed to include every politician in southern Virginia. From the podium, Frank sheepishly expressed his thanks, and later tried to deflect the questions from newsmen who wanted to know what he'd thought of the people who doubted his patriotism. "A lot of people were saying a lot of words about something about which they knew nothing," he said.

They asked him what he planned to do with his life now, and he said he wasn't sure—an honest answer. The CIA had offered him a job, something low-key in its training division, until he figured out a more permanent solution. Every now and then he thought of Kelly Johnson and the offer he'd made during the debriefing back at the safe house. But before he could begin to contemplate the future, he needed to get a better handle on the present.

Frank left Pound and drove to Milledgeville, where he picked up Barbara. They loaded the Mercedes with several suitcases and drove back to Alexandria, Virginia, where the CIA had helped them find an apartment just across the Potomac River from Washington.

Frank took the desk job at Langley and tried to fit into life in the greater Washington area. Shortly after they got back, some friends threw a party for him at a crab shack in Popes Creek, Maryland, about forty miles south of Washington. While Barbara mixed with the crowd, a friend of his put a drink in front of him, and he politely refused it: after two years of forced sobriety, he said, he was learning to take it easy on the alcohol. "I was handed a martini on the airliner back to the States, and I really felt it," he said.

Barbara was enjoying herself. Someone put on some music—"The Twist," a fad that had swept America during the past two years, and one that Frank had completely missed. She rushed to the table and grabbed Frank's arm, dragging him onto the floor. He humored her for a minute and then retreated to the table, leaving her without a partner. "That dance just doesn't feel right," he said. "I guess I haven't been back long enough."

It was a variation of a scene that repeated itself during those first weeks inside their Alexandria apartment. Barbara wanted Frank to take her out on the town, to restaurants and clubs, but he preferred staying in; it was too stressful for him to always be on the lookout for the press, he told her. "My God," she snapped back, "I've been ducking them for *two years!*"

When she made long-distance calls to Milledgeville, he suspected her of infidelity. He grumbled that he was treated better in prison than he was by her at home. One evening that April, he warned her that if she didn't cut back on her drinking, he'd make sure she got medical help. Later that same night, in their apartment, she swallowed twenty-eight capsules of Nembutal, a barbiturate.

Frank found her unconscious on the living room floor at about 3:00 a.m. Failing to rouse her, he called an ambulance. She was rushed to a hospital in Alexandria, where she was admitted in "very serious" condition. For more than three hours, doctors tried to revive her, but they couldn't. She was then transferred to Georgetown University Hospital, where the following evening she finally regained consciousness. CIA officers visited the hospital and urged the doctors to keep her records closed to the public. In the hospital registry, the reason for her visit was listed as "acute gastrointestinal upset." But they forgot to visit the Alexandria hospital, which listed her as suffering from a "medication reaction," and reports of the overdose made it into newspapers a couple days later. Still, the family tried to protect her and Frank. The *New York Post* contacted two of Frank's sisters, who told the paper that their brother blamed the episode on some spoiled oysters she ate from their refrigerator. According to the *Post,* the sisters "denied reports that the couple had not been getting along well lately."

Shortly after she recovered, Barbara returned to Milledgeville to see her family, while Frank traveled to the West Coast on CIA business. On the way back, he had a stopover in Phoenix, where he planned to see some old friends. Just as he got off the plane, he was paged: TWA had a message for him. When he reported to the airline counter, he was given a local telephone number to call. The CIA employee he eventually reached told him there'd been a problem in Georgia. Barbara had caused some sort of disturbance at a drive-in restaurant in Milledgeville, and the police had been called. At the time of her arrest, Barbara had been with Charlie Deason, her old boss at the Log Cabin restaurant.

He'd had enough. He traveled to Milledgeville and delivered an ultimatum: she could check herself into a clinic for alcoholism, promise never to see Deason again, and return to Alexandria; or she could stay in Milledgeville.

The CIA, she believed, had ruined her life, and she didn't want anything more to do with the agency. She stayed in Georgia, and Frank filed for divorce later that summer.

EDWIN LAND WASN'T FOND OF the new CIA director, a feeling shared by many of the scientists who'd collaborated with the government over the years. James Killian was so dismayed when McCone was appointed that he threatened to resign from the President's Foreign Intelligence Advisory Board.

There was a lot of history between McCone and the scientists, and it stretched all the way back to the persecution of J. Robert Oppenheimer and the disagreements surrounding nuclear disarmament that followed the stripping of his security clearance. In 1956, McCone had been a trustee at the California Institute of Technology when several scientists on the faculty issued a statement supporting a nuclear test ban. McCone responded by attacking them, claiming that they were trying "to create fear in the minds of the uninformed that radioactive fallout from H-bomb tests endangers life." McCone complained that the scientists had been "taken in" by Soviet propaganda, and he reportedly lobbied to get the scientists fired. Two years later, when McCone was appointed to the Atomic Energy Commission, he denied that he tried to fire them, but he defended his attacks, saying that the scientists had abused their positions by trying "to inject themselves into a political discussion" instead of sticking to the technical matters relating to their scientific specialties.

Land, of course, wasn't one to shy away from mixing his science with ethics, and shortly after McCone was named director, he and Killian injected themselves into politics with unabashed directness. In the summer of 1962, the CIA's most recent National Intelligence Estimate was again leaked to the press—not to Alsop this time, but to *The New York Times*'s Hanson Baldwin. Through his work on the U-2, Land had formulated an informal doctrine that steered him through the covert world: always tell the truth if confronted about a secret, but try very hard to avoid those confrontations in the first place. The media leak frustrated Land, because it revealed many of the secrets about the Soviet nuclear arsenal—information that he and others had worked for years to gather through the U-2 and satellite programs. He wasn't alone; both Kennedy brothers were enraged, and they instructed the FBI to try to ferret out Baldwin's source. In early August, Land, Killian, and Clark Clifford—all members of the President's Foreign Intelligence Advisory Board—visited the White House with a proposal: have the CIA investigate leaks.

"Given the damaging nature of this," Killian told Kennedy, "it justifies you in taking very drastic and unprecedented procedures to prevent it in the future." The board suggested that the CIA create a permanent team dedicated to investigating media leaks. The team would secretly shadow journalists like Joe Alsop, Hanson Baldwin, and Chalmers Roberts of *The Washington Post,* and it would compile lists of their sources. Clifford said, "I think it would be mighty interesting to know who Alsop sees, and who Chalmers Roberts sees, and the rest of these fellows. Let's then begin to get up a file on these different men. . . . To my knowledge it's never been done before and it is long overdue."

Land, Killian, and Clifford were suggesting that the CIA spy on American citizens, an activity that is specifically prohibited in the agency's charter. The Kennedys seemed to like the idea. After the meeting, the CIA tapped the phone lines of multiple reporters for several months through Operation Mockingbird, a program that wasn't revealed for decades—years after Land, Killian, and Clifford were dead.

Land's idealism had been repeatedly challenged since he'd first set out to redefine American spying. If it was true that any problem could be solved through the power of dedicated focus, as he maintained, it was also true that the resulting solutions often spawned problems of their own. Land's work with the CIA, which he treated as a crusade to defend an open society, was built upon a necessary compromise: secrecy. The complications and contradictions that resulted from that foundational tradeoff, in which he sacrificed a part of the very ideal he was working to protect, only intensified as surveillance technology—a phenomenon he helped create—gained wider acceptance throughout the government. Land never spoke about the ethical contortions that were required of him to support Operation Mockingbird, but clearly his internal debate concerning the morality of espionage had undergone an evolution: he still adamantly opposed using covert technologies for violent or aggressive purposes, but he no longer seemed to ask himself *if* ethically suspect intelligence gathering was acceptable; it was *when* it was acceptable.

THE CIA CONTINUED TO REFINE its aerial surveillance program, and in 1962 new stereoscopic cameras on the spy satellites dramatically improved the picture quality, making the images three times sharper than they'd been just a year before. That didn't mean the U-2 was obsolete. If the government had a specific target area it wanted to glimpse at a specific time, the satellites weren't ideal; it was difficult to preplan their orbits to ensure that they passed over those areas at the right time, when cloud cover was light. For those reasons, U-2s were flying regularly over Cuba in 1962 to keep an eye on the Castro regime.

Meanwhile, in California, Kelly Johnson and his team at Skunk Works were still trying to perfect a successor to the U-2 that might fly faster, higher, and with less chance of a shoot down. Johnson floated an idea to the CIA that he believed might solve the sorts of complications that the Powers incident had created. In 1962 he suggested the creation of a modified version of the A-12, the supersonic reconnaissance plane he was still trying to perfect. It would be an unmanned drone, one that could be launched off the back of a moving A-12 and then fly for up to three thousand miles at more than three times the speed of sound and at heights of eighty-seven thousand to ninety-five thousand feet. Like the U-2, it would carry a camera in a Q-bay, but the drone was designed for one-way trips. After photographing its targets, the drone would eject the film, which would be snatched in air by a JC-130 Hercules—just like how the film canisters from the satellites were collected. The drone would then self-destruct, destroying all evidence of its existence.

On October 10, 1962, Johnson was instructed by the CIA to commence work on the drone project, the agency's first foray into the world of what are now known as unmanned aerial vehicles, or UAVs. Inside Skunk Works, Johnson and a small team of designers went to work in a walled-off corner of the shop. It wasn't the first drone ever developed; crude unmanned aircraft had been used as ramming torpedoes as early as World War I, and short-range "radioplanes" were developed soon after. But Johnson's D-21, as it was eventually designated, was by far the most advanced UAV developed to date, and it was the first one designed for spying.

Johnson was on his own when it came to bringing the project to fruition, perhaps because—yet again—there were no precedents for the work he was doing. "The drone is developing without much discussion between Headquarters and ourselves," he wrote in his log. "I think I know what they want, but no one has spelled it out."

For the current fleet of U-2s, Skunk Works was still a vital maintenance center, and Johnson's roster of engineers and test pilots now numbered in the hundreds. Around the same time that he began working on the drone, Johnson got a call from a CIA friend suggesting that he make room for one more on his payroll: Frank Powers.

Powers had been unhappy with his desk job at Langley, and after he split with Barbara in late May, he'd been itching for a change. He remembered what Johnson had told him during the debriefings at the safe house in Pennsylvania, and he asked a friend to call Lockheed to see if the offer of a job was still on the table.

Johnson's loyalty to Powers was undiminished. The pilot didn't know it, but Johnson had actually submitted a report to the government after the debriefings earlier in the year in which he wrote of Frank, "I will gladly contribute to a fund for decorating this officer for the fine job he did under the most difficult circumstances."

In September 1962, the two of them met at Skunk Works to discuss options. Before Powers had a chance to say that he hoped he might be able to get back in the cockpit, Johnson offered him a job as a test pilot flying U-2s.

Frank flew back to Washington and resigned from the CIA. He drove back to California in the gray Mercedes, which he'd recovered from Barbara, and rented a new apartment in Burbank. He reported for his first day of work on October 15, 1962, just five days after Johnson had gotten the approval to begin work on the drone. When Johnson greeted him that morning, the plan was that Frank would test the work of the engineers at Skunk Works by flying the U-2s that had been sent back to Lockheed for upgrades or repairs.

Neither Powers nor Johnson realized that in Washington, that same day, CIA photointerpreters were laying eyes on a fresh batch of incredibly disturbing U-2 images taken over Cuba. Within days, those photos would ramp up the tensions between Washington and Moscow to all-time highs, until the world itself seemed to tremble on the brink of destruction.

## CHAPTER 14

# Endgame

Optimism is a moral duty.

—EDWIN LAND

B y the late summer of 1962, rumors reached Washington that Khrushchev was up to something sinister in Cuba. Scattered reports from refugees suggested that the Soviets were moving lots of strange, heavy equipment onto the island. For most of August and September, the spy satellite images were obscured by heavy cloud cover. At the same time, the CIA and air force administrators who were now jointly running the U-2 program were skittish; in early September, a U-2 was lost over Communist China, believed shot down by the same kind of Soviet-made rocket—the S-75 Dvina—that had downed Powers. Nervous that a U-2 incursion over Cuba could damage relations with Khrushchev beyond repair, Washington held off on overflights. But by October the rumors were getting louder, and President Kennedy okayed an overflight of Cuba, the first one since August. For four days, the weather got in the way of a flight, but on the morning of October 14 air force major Richard Heyser took off in a U-2 from McCoy Air Force Base in Orlando, Florida, for a quick run over San Cristóbal, in Cuba's Pinar del Río Province.

He entered Cuban airspace at 7:37 a.m. on October 15, and it took him only six minutes to make a pass across the island. He headed directly back to Orlando, where the film from the plane was carted onto another aircraft and flown to a photo-developing center in Suitland, Maryland. Shortly after 10:00 a.m. technicians began developing the film, printing duplicate positives, and spooling it into film cans for delivery. A U.S. Navy truck carried the film to the CIA photointerpretation center, still housed in the grungy Ford building on K Street, and two armed guards rushed it into the building before noon.

The eight cans of film were split among three separate photointer-pretation stations, where analysts bent over their light tables with mag-nified stereoscopes. Their eyes passed over sandy beaches, tall marsh grasses, sugarcane fields, baseball diamonds, sprawling fincas, bustling towns, and railroad lines. At one of the tables, two of the analysts spot-ted something strange: six unusually long objects that appeared to be covered with canvas. Vince DiRenzo, a CIA analyst with an expertise in missile systems, took a closer look. He consulted file images of the same area that had been taken on previous missions, and he determined the objects were newly installed. The interpreters noticed that there was a lot of activity on the roads leading to the site: a convoy of ten trucks, for example, appeared to be heading there. DiRenzo knew that the Soviets had S-75 Dvina ground-to-air missiles on the island—the ones capable of shooting down U-2s—but this looked like a different kind of missile site. The six objects covered by canvas each measured about sixty-five feet, about twice as long as the S-75 Dvina.

The analysts went back to the archives and pulled more images, including shots taken at May Day and other military parades in Moscow. DiRenzo reviewed the pictures of several different kinds of missiles, and he came across a full side view of the SS-4, a mid-range ballistic missile capable of carrying nuclear warheads to targets more than a thousand miles away—close to the distance between Cuba and Washington. He paused as he stared at the picture. "That sure looks like it," he said.

The analysts worked all afternoon, taking more precise measure-ments and zeroing in on the suspicious sites. Around 5:00 p.m., they shared their findings with Art Lundahl, the head of the department who'd founded the office back in 1956. "I think I know what you guys think they are," Lundahl said, "and if I think they are the same thing, and we are both right, then we are sitting on the biggest story of our time."

After examining the images, Lundahl was convinced. He ordered the office to work through the night, and he immediately placed a call to Ray Cline, McCone's deputy director of intelligence at the CIA.

"Are you fellows sure?" Cline asked.

Word that a crisis might be building began to spread around Langley and the State Department. As the night wore on, the photo analysts real-ized things were even worse than they'd first suspected. It appeared that the missiles had been shipped as road-mobile units, which meant they could be ready to fire very quickly. Around the sites they discovered fueling and communications equipment, already in place. Later in the evening, one of the analysts called out, "I've got something new."

"What does it look like?"

"They look like boats."

Boats? In the middle of the island? In fact, they were launcher erectors, and soon the analysts realized they had found a second cluster of mid-range ballistic missiles. By 10:30 p.m., they had found a third site. The analysts worked through the morning, and by dawn a set of enlarged images was being labeled and mounted on briefing boards for President Kennedy.

Lundahl and Cline took the boards to the White House at about 8:00 a.m., but President Kennedy's agenda was jammed. Wally Schirra, one of the original Project Mercury astronauts who'd just completed a six-orbit journey around Earth, was visiting with his family, and the earliest opening on the president's schedule was 11:45 a.m. While they waited, Lundahl showed the photos to Bobby Kennedy in an office in the basement. As Lundahl walked him through the images, the attorney general began pacing the room, slamming his fist into his hand and cursing Khrushchev, who had repeatedly assured the Americans that he would never install offensive missiles in Cuba. "Oh shit!" he said. "Shit! Shit!"

The consequences of a full-scale nuclear war had reached obscene levels of grim absurdity. Back in 1954, when the U-2 was conceived, the Soviet nuclear program had inspired American leaders to consider military scenarios that were too horrible for extended contemplation; now the possibilities simply short-circuited the imagination. In late October 1961, the Soviets had exploded a hydrogen bomb on a remote archipelago above the Arctic Circle, creating the most powerful explosion mankind had ever produced. It was the rough equivalent of fifty million tons of TNT, and it released about 1,570 times more energy than the atomic bombs in Hiroshima and Nagasaki combined. The mushroom cloud was forty miles high, and its cap was nearly sixty miles wide. Everything within a 34-mile radius was completely destroyed, and windowpanes were broken as far as 560 miles away. It no longer sufficed to suggest that the stakes of a nuclear war were high. Millions could die in a catastrophe too grisly to contemplate.

Around 11:50 a.m., Lundahl carried the briefing boards upstairs to the Cabinet Room and set up an easel near the fireplace. The president had been warned about the photos, and he appeared calm as he settled into his leather-upholstered chair at the middle of the long table. As Lundahl grabbed his pointer to start his presentation, someone burst through the door and into the room.

It was Caroline, the president's four-year-old daughter. "Daddy, daddy," she said, "they won't let my friend in." Kennedy rose from his chair. "Caroline, have you been eating candy?" he said. When she didn't answer, he smiled, put his arm around her shoulder, and began to lead her out of the room. "Answer me—yes, no, or maybe."

When he returned a few seconds later, his smile had left him, and his expression—grim, preoccupied—would remain largely unchanged for the next thirteen days.

EARLY IN THE EVENING OF OCTOBER 16, Joe Alsop busied himself around the house, preparing for a dinner party. Bunny Mellon, the wife of millionaire philanthropist Paul Mellon, that day had delivered a large box of flowers to the house, and Alsop artfully scattered them through the house, arranging them just so. He got decorating help from the former Susan Mary Patten, the widow of Joe's college roommate, Bill Patten. The couple had been Joe's guides to the social scene in Paris during the weeks before his fateful trip to Moscow in 1957, and after Bill died, Susan Mary moved back to Washington. In 1961, she and Joe surprised all of their friends by getting married.

After the Soviets tried to blackmail him, Alsop had followed the advice of Chip Bohlen, the U.S. ambassador who'd helped him flee Moscow, by keeping the incident—and his homosexuality—a secret. Susan Mary was under no illusions, however. Their unconventional marriage had nothing to do with sex; they simply loved being around each other.

The dinner party that evening was to celebrate none other than Chip Bohlen, to whom Joe had felt deeply indebted ever since Moscow. Bohlen had returned to the United States, but President Kennedy recently appointed him to be the next ambassador to France. Bohlen was scheduled to depart for Paris the next day, and this was his send-off. Joe and Susan Mary had carefully curated a small guest list, inviting the French ambassador and his wife, as well as Isaiah Berlin, the Oxford University historian and political philosopher. The key invitee of the evening, however, was President Kennedy himself, whom Alsop had urged to attend as a favor to Bohlen.

John and Jacqueline showed up after the others, and immediately Alsop realized that something wasn't quite right. Normally, JFK was a scintillating guest—smiling, talkative, quick with a joke, and a fiend for gossip. But Joe found him unusually quiet on this night and oddly stone-faced. Alsop knew the president was facing pressure. Just the day before, Alsop himself had published a column arguing that Kennedy was spending too much time making stump speeches about social welfare and the economy and ignoring the one thing everyone in America really cared about—Cuba and the Soviet Union.

Since the Bay of Pigs, Kennedy's critics complained that he was paralyzed by indecision when it came to the Soviet threat. The Berlin Wall had been built the previous summer, completely cutting off East Germany from the West, and Kennedy did nothing to intervene with its construction. If the Soviets put nukes in Cuba, would Kennedy do anything to stop them? Alsop wasn't the only one who wanted to know the answer. That morning, on October 16, a headline on the front page of *The New York Times* said, "Eisenhower Calls President Weak on Foreign Policy." Kennedy's dour mood at the dinner party must have been related to the criticisms, Alsop believed.

Before dinner, the president grabbed Chip Bohlen and led him into the courtyard garden, where they whispered out of earshot of the others. Kennedy was urging Bohlen to delay his trip to Paris. As someone who'd spent years in Moscow and who knew Khrushchev fairly well, Bohlen would be a valuable addition to a core team of experts the White House was rapidly assembling, and Kennedy needed all the help he could get as he discreetly tried to figure out how to respond to the developing missile crisis. Bohlen, who was told about the U-2 photos that day, didn't like the idea of deferring his trip. The Russians would be sure to notice the delay, and perhaps it would help tip them off that the missile sites had been detected. As they spoke among the azaleas and philodendrons, Alsop noticed that it appeared less a conversation than a dispute, but he couldn't make out anything they were saying.

Throughout all four courses of dinner, Kennedy barely spoke. When dessert was finished, the guests split into two groups; the ladies stayed inside, while the men retreated to the courtyard. The conversation in the garden was too stiff and formal for Alsop's taste, and it seemed as if Kennedy's obvious discomfort were infecting the whole party. Finally, talk turned to nuclear war, and everyone looked to the president. Alsop knew that Kennedy often liked to defuse the tension around such discussions by lightheartedly assessing the odds of a nuclear confrontation in the same way a gambler sized up a horse race, usually estimating the chances of war at one in five. But something had shifted. On this night, Kennedy remarked that the chances of an H-bomb war breaking out in the next decade were "somewhere near even."

Everyone's face fell. Alsop glanced at Hervé Alphand, the French ambassador, and saw that he'd "turned the color of an uncooked biscuit." Joe, who prided himself on being difficult to shock, was stunned to silence.

GENERAL CURTIS LEMAY WAS IN EUROPE on October 16 when an emergency call summoned him back to Washington. He reported to the White House, where he holed up in the Cabinet Room with other senior members of Kennedy's national security team.

During his first year on the Joint Chiefs, LeMay was viewed with suspicion—if not downright hostility—by the president's staff. Ted Sorensen, who was Kennedy's speechwriter and one of his closest aides, called LeMay "my least favorite human being." The general's unflagging hawkishness seemed to know no bounds, and Robert McNamara, the secretary of defense, believed he knew why. "LeMay's view was very simple," said McNamara, who had served as a lieutenant colonel under the general in World War II. "He thought the West, and the U.S. in particular, was going to have to fight a nuclear war with the Soviet Union, and he was absolutely certain of that. Therefore, he believed that we should fight it sooner rather than later, when we had a greater advantage in nuclear power, and it would result in fewer casualties in the United States."

In the first days of the Cuban missile crisis, the president's advisers outlined several possible courses of action. Chip Bohlen, who delayed his departure to France by a couple days, lobbied for a diplomatic solution. Others suggested the navy could create a blockade of ships around the island, preventing the Soviets from delivering any more missile supplies and demanding that the missiles on the ground be dismantled. LeMay's was the loudest voice advocating a full-scale bombardment of the missile sites, followed by a military invasion of the island.

After the first missile sites were found, the president ordered additional U-2 flights over Cuba. On the morning of October 19, new images were delivered to the Cabinet Room just as the Joint Chiefs of Staff and the president were gathering around the table. Additional missile sites had been discovered, and these included intermediate-range ballistic missiles, which were capable of hitting targets nearly twenty-eight hundred miles away, or twice as far as the others that had been found. That would have threatened nearly every major U.S. city. Kennedy grabbed the latest intelligence report. "Let's see," he said, and began reading aloud. "Two of these missiles are operational now . . . missiles could be launched within eighteen hours of the decision to fire . . . yields in the low megaton range."

Kennedy was visibly shaken, and LeMay was chomping at the bit to seize the moment. The only option was a full-on assault. If the United States responded with anything less, Khrushchev would believe he could get away with anything. "If we don't do anything to Cuba," LeMay told Kennedy, "then they're going to push on Berlin and push real hard because they've got us on the run." A blockade, he suggested, was cowardly. "This is almost as bad as the appeasement at Munich."

It was a loaded reference, and LeMay knew it. Before World War II, the president's father, Joseph Kennedy, had been the U.S. ambassador in London, and he had advocated a policy of appeasement, or negotiation, with Adolf Hitler. The president had been trying to shed himself of that paternal baggage ever since, and in 1940, just after graduating from Harvard, he'd even published a book—*Why England Slept*—that attempted to put the issue in context. Everyone at the table knew Kennedy was sensitive to criticisms about appeasement, and LeMay's comment was a slash at the jugular.

After a silent pause, LeMay made the case for a first strike. By his reckoning, the military could be ready for an attack by dawn on October 21, although two days after that would be optimal. "I think that a blockade, and political talk, would be considered by a lot of our friends as being a pretty weak response to this," LeMay said. "And I'm sure a lot of our citizens would feel that way, too. You're in a pretty bad fix, Mr. President."

Kennedy looked at the general. "What did you say?"

"You're in a pretty bad fix."

"Well, you're in it right with me," Kennedy said. "Personally."

The president left the meeting and told his assistant that LeMay and the others advocating aggression had one advantage over him. "If we listen to them and do what they want us to do, none of us will be alive later to tell them that they were wrong," Kennedy said.

Moscow continued to insist that it had no offensive weapons in Cuba, a statement the U-2 photos had proved was a lie. As Kennedy and his team continued to weigh their options, the military readied its nuclear bombers, and troops were sent to southern bases for possible emergency deployment.

On the evening of October 22, Kennedy sat in front of a television camera inside the Oval Office and addressed the American people, who'd been alerted that day that an announcement of critical importance was forthcoming. More than 100 million Americans, the largest audience that had ever watched a presidential address, tuned in as Kennedy spent the next eighteen minutes outlining the crisis. He explained that he had decided to try to stop the ongoing offensive buildup by implementing a "strict quarantine"—a naval blockade—on all equipment shipped to Cuba.

For the next five days, the world braced for war. The Soviets doubled down on the fiction that all of their missiles on the island were defensive, not offensive. On October 25, additional surveillance images showed that the Soviets were continuing to assemble the missile bases, and Kennedy responded by authorizing the loading of nuclear warheads onto U.S. aircraft. The American military was ordered to stand by on DEFCON 2—one step short of nuclear war.

For the next two days, the Americans struggled to read the Soviets' intentions, and vice versa. Kennedy began discussing the possibility of a back-channel deal: if the Soviets agreed to dismantle the missile sites in Cuba, the United States would do the same to nuclear missile sites that it maintained in Turkey and Italy. But on October 27—a day that would later be dubbed "Black Saturday"—everything changed when a U-2 was shot down over Cuba.

Responsibility for the U-2 flights had officially been transferred from the CIA to the air force two weeks earlier. A U-2 piloted by air force major Rudolf Anderson took off from Orlando on the morning of October 27, and when Anderson neared Banes, Cuba, he was killed after a Soviet SA-2 downed the plane. At about 5:40 that afternoon, Secretary McNamara was sitting in the Cabinet Room when he was handed a note.

"A U-2 was shot down," he said.

Kennedy tensed. "Well now," he said, "this is much of an escalation by them, isn't it?"

"Yes, exactly," McNamara responded. Khrushchev had announced earlier that the Soviets wouldn't fire on American planes unless those planes fired first. This seemed like a dangerous shift in Soviet strategy.

McNamara immediately began planning when they might be able to launch an air attack in retaliation. As Bobby Kennedy later wrote, "The noose was tightening on all of us, on Americans, on mankind."

Paul Nitze, the assistant secretary of defense, said, "They've fired the first shot." News of a second emergency—this one *also* involving a spy plane—reached Washington in the early afternoon when Curtis LeMay told McNamara he'd just received an alarming message.

"A U-2 has been lost off Alaska," LeMay said.

After taking over the day-to-day operations of the U-2 flights from the CIA earlier in the month, the air force continued to conduct missions in the Arctic to collect radioactive air samples as a way to monitor distant Soviet missile tests, and it seemed that no one thought to suspend those flights during the missile crisis. Now the unthinkable was happening at the worst possible moment: A pilot on a routine sampling mission had made a serious navigational error, and now he was more than 1,000 miles off course and hundreds of miles into Soviet territory. To Khrushchev and his military commanders, the presence of an American plane flying over their territory during the most tensely charged moment of the Cold War could be interpreted as a clear sign of aggression. It was impossible to predict how Khrushchev's forces would react.

The Soviets detected the wayward U-2, and several MiG fighters began pursuing it. The Strategic Air Command in the U.S. also monitored the action, and a pair of F-102 fighter-interceptors soared toward the wayward U-2. The MiGs were unable to reach the spy plane, and the American pilot, running dangerously low on fuel, was eventually able to drift out of the country and land safely at a U.S. radar station in the Arctic.

It was yet another close call in a day full of them. Arthur Schlesinger, the president's special assistant and "court historian," later described that Saturday as "the most dangerous moment in human history."

TIMES SQUARE WAS EXCEPTIONALLY QUIET that Saturday. But at 5:30 p.m., the sound of footsteps and chanting could be heard growing louder, coming from the north. About three hundred people, most of them college students dressed in toggle-button coats and Levi's, were marching down Forty-Second Street, holding signs that read "No War over Cuba." "One, two, three, four! We don't want another war!"

When they reached the Avenue of the Americas, a line of fifty police officers met them and ordered them to turn around. Times Square had been declared off-limits all week to large gatherings, the police said.

These had been strange days. A Catholic priest in the city told the *New York Herald Tribune* that confessions had tripled. At Fifty-Fifth Street and Broadway, construction crews had detonated a small batch of explosives during a street excavation. Inside a restaurant, the lunchtime diners tensed, their forks frozen still for a moment in front of their mouths, as if making sure they were still alive. Inside a Horn & Hardart Automat on Seventh Avenue, one man complained about the sorry state of the potholed pavement outside; another man at his table calmly finished lighting a cigar, held it in his hand, and declared, "There's liable to be a lot more holes in the streets pretty soon, and it will take quite a few years to fix them."

A test of the civil defense sirens, normally held at noon on Saturdays, was canceled that day, for fear that people would mistake it for the real thing. Governor Nelson Rockefeller was out of town, meeting with other governors in Washington to discuss emergency preparedness. Days before, the city's police department asked "all able-bodied men" to register as auxiliary civil defense officers, and the state's director of civil defense told everyone else to do whatever they could to protect their homes against nuclear fallout. "Not everyone can come up with a masonry fallout shelter in the next few days," he said, "but everyone should be able to improvise some kind of protection."

In Washington, colorful identification cards were handed out to high-ranking government officials, which would be their tickets onto helicopters that would fly from the White House lawn to "the Hideout" in the mountains of West Virginia; the IDs had been printed with gold threads across the fronts to prevent counterfeiting. The 2857th Test Squadron, a helicopter squadron based in Harrisburg, Pennsylvania, had been given protective uniforms and instructions about how to evacuate the president in case of a Soviet strike; they would land on the White House lawn, crowbar their way into a bunker under the building, cover Kennedy in a radiation suit, and rush him out of Washington. In the underground lair at High Point, plastic flowers decorated the tables in the cafeteria, and a therapeutic mattress was installed in the presidential bedroom especially for Kennedy's ailing back.

. . .

ON SUNDAY MORNING, AT 9:09, a Teletype message arrived in the White House and at the CIA delivering news of an announcement that had been broadcast four minutes earlier from Radio Moscow, the official organ of the Kremlin:

> Moscow Domestic Service in Russian at 1404GMT on 28 October, Broadcast a message from Khrushchev to President Kennedy stating that the USSR had decided to dismantle Soviet missiles in Cuba and return them to the Soviet Union 28 October 908a-FRR/HM.

Khrushchev had backed down. It turned out that he hadn't authorized the shoot down of the U-2 over Cuba, and he'd been angry when he learned of it. Just after he sent a message to Kennedy, he sent a message to the commander of the Soviet Group of Forces on Cuba: "We consider that you acted too hastily in shooting down the American U-2 spy plane, at a time when an agreement was already emerging to avert an attack on Cuba by peaceful means." Khrushchev also sent a private message to Kennedy expressing his dismay over the fact that America had allowed a U-2 to stray into Soviet territory. "One of your planes violates our frontier during this anxious time we are both experiencing when everything has been put into combat readiness," Khrushchev wrote. "Is it not a fact that an intruding American plane could be easily taken for a nuclear bomber, which might push us to a fateful step?"

That Sunday, it was difficult to appreciate how close the two superpowers had come to war. But the crisis had been averted. Curtis LeMay, for one, couldn't believe it was over, and he was loath to scrap the plans for an air strike. "It's the greatest defeat in our history," he grumbled. "We should invade today."

Most everyone else in the White House was in the mood to celebrate. "I feel like a new man now," President Kennedy told his personal assistant after Khrushchev's announcement. "Do you realize that we had an air strike all arranged for Tuesday?"

In a way, Kennedy *was* a new man after the Cuban missile crisis. In news accounts—many of which failed to mention that the deal he struck with the Russians included the American dismantling of missiles in Turkey and Italy—he was cast as a resolute leader who went eyeball to eyeball with the enemy and didn't blink. In the months that followed, a hotline was established between Washington and Moscow to make sure that if anything like this ever happened again, a nuclear strike might be averted by quicker and easier communications between the two superpowers. The crisis also spurred a series of disarmament talks that resulted the following year in both countries signing the Limited Nuclear Test Ban Treaty. The Cold War didn't end, but it never again matched the levels of intensity that it had reached between 1954 and 1962.

After the crisis, Kennedy singled out the U-2 program for particular praise. The downing of the plane over Cuba and the temporary loss of another over the Soviet Union had almost triggered disaster, but without the images the spy planes had delivered, he believed, a full-scale arming of the island would have proceeded, perhaps shifting the balance of the Cold War for good. In a letter sent to the CIA, he lauded the program, writing, "The magnitude of their contribution can be measured, in part, by the fact that the peace was sustained during a most critical time."

It was now possible to argue that the U-2 had actually fulfilled the purpose for which it was conceived: it had detected a serious and impending threat to the United States *before* that threat had fully materialized.

William Colby, a CIA officer who would later become the agency's director, said, "One of the most important consequences of the missile crisis was on the morale of the Agency: it soared."

Years before, when the very first U-2 images from the Soviet Union had arrived in Washington, Frank Wisner, the CIA's former head of covert intelligence, had guessed that a single photo from the spy plane might be worth a million dollars to America. But he'd said that before Powers had been shot down and before all of the tensions his capture had sparked. In late 1962, Ray Cline, the deputy director of the CIA, decided to revisit the question in light of the crisis the country had just endured. Cline asked Robert Kennedy and McGeorge Bundy, a presidential adviser, how much a single U-2 photograph—the one that proved there were missiles in Cuba—might have been worth to the United States. Both Bundy and Kennedy suggested that Wisner's previous estimate had been far too modest. Cline recalled, "They each said it fully justified all that the CIA had cost the country in all its preceding years."

# Epilogue: Landings

The CIA was sixteen years old when former president Harry Truman decided he no longer recognized the intelligence service that he'd created. "I never had any thought that when I set up the CIA that it would be injected into peacetime cloak and dagger operations," Truman wrote in a 1963 op-ed published in *The Washington Post*. He recommended scaling back the agency's activities, and he said getting rid of paramilitary and interventionist activities, such as the attempted operation at the Bay of Pigs, should be the first step. The CIA, he suggested, had somehow moved away from the business of protecting freedoms and had gotten into the business of eroding them. "We have grown up as a nation, respected for our free institutions and for our ability to maintain a free and open society," Truman wrote. "There is something about the way the CIA has been functioning that is casting a shadow over our historic position and I feel that we need to correct it."

A collective unease over the agency's role only intensified during the Vietnam War, and it peaked in the mid-1970s, when the U.S. Senate's Church Committee held hearings that exposed many of the most secretive, and scandalous, operations in CIA history. Led by Idaho senator Frank Church, the panel grilled current and former agency officials, including Richard Bissell, and for the first time the government formally revealed its attempts to assassinate foreign leaders, including Castro and Lumumba. The hearings also exposed a long-running program by the CIA and the FBI to surreptitiously open and photograph hundreds of thousands of pieces of mail sent to and from U.S. citizens. Public backlash was swift, and congressional outrage led to a series of reforms, including the establishment of the Senate Select Committee on Intelligence—an oversight body that was first proposed in the aftermath of the U-2 incident.

The Church Committee was particularly interested in the idea that technological spying might be a double-edged sword. From the days of Edwin Land's brainstorming sessions back in 1954, technology had radically enhanced the CIA's ability to gather intelligence, and also to abuse its power. Church warned that if Americans ever elected a president prone to totalitarian urges, the marriage of espionage and technology might prove too powerful a force to contain. "If this government ever became a tyranny, if a dictator ever took charge in this country," Church warned, "the technological capacity that the intelligence community has given the government could enable it to impose total tyranny, and there would be no way to fight back because the most careful effort to combine together in resistance to the government, no matter how privately it was done, is within reach of the government to know."

The U-2, which underwent several redesigns over the years, remained an important technological component of the American spy program, and it generated little controversy after the early 1960s. But decades later, the emergence of unmanned aerial vehicles—indirect offspring of the U-2 program—intensified the ethical dilemmas surrounding American surveillance, creating opportunities for more pervasive spying and even remote-controlled air strikes.

In 2006, the U.S. government announced that after fifty full years of spy flights the U-2 would finally be retired. It was drone technology, it said, that would make the phaseout possible.

The U-2s were still regularly used to spy over countries like Iran and North Korea, but the Pentagon believed the new UAVs, like the Northrop Grumman RQ-4 Global Hawk, would allow it to save billions each year by eliminating the pilot program and other U-2 costs. The government announced that the spy plane's last flights would occur sometime around 2010.

There was just one complication: in side-by-side comparisons with drones over Afghanistan, the U-2 consistently produced better intelligence. Military intelligence officials reported that the film used in the old U-2 cameras provided such high-resolution images they could track the footprints of insurgents, and they could even pick out land mines from thirteen miles in the air. What's more, the U-2's extreme altitude capabilities allowed the planes to sweep up Taliban members' electronic telephone signals that would otherwise have been blocked by high mountain peaks. Increasingly, the United States began using the U-2 as its principal intelligence-gathering vehicle in Afghanistan, while Predator and Reaper drones used that intelligence to fire missiles and launch strikes. Congress, as a result, postponed the U-2's retirement, and each time a phaseout has been proposed since, it has ultimately been rejected.

In 2017, the air force reported that the unpredictable and unconventional nature of the war against the Islamic State had made the U-2 more valuable than ever. "We plan to keep the platform well into the future," said air force major general James Martin during the annual budget briefing at the Pentagon in 2017.

The spy tool that its founders had envisioned as a temporary solution to a lack of Cold War technology—a "melting technology" that likely had a very short window of effectiveness—had become the most durable intelligence-gathering machine in American history, flying thousands of missions and producing millions of square feet of photographic images.

EDWIN LAND'S CONTRIBUTIONS TO THE CIA in general, and the U-2 and satellite programs in particular, remained unknown to the general public throughout the rest of his life. Within the agency, however, he had become something of an icon. In 1963, the CIA formally inaugurated its Directorate of Science and Technology, which, as a matter of official policy, put technological innovation on an equal footing with human operations. More than two decades later, after the office had become an integral part of the CIA, the agency published a classified history of the office that concluded, "The existence of the Directorate of Science and Technology must ultimately be considered a monument to the wisdom of Edwin H. Land and James R. Killian, Jr."

Meanwhile, his fame as a corporate innovator continued to grow. In 1963, Polaroid introduced Polacolor film, and Land set his sights on redefining the concept of instant photography that he'd invented nearly two decades before. The early Polaroid cameras required the user to peel apart the prints and let the chemicals dry before they could be freely handled, but now Land was working on something he called the "one-step" camera that ejected a finished print that would develop on its own, with no peeling or drying. The first prototype of the camera was called the U-2, an acknowledgment of his "other life," which was an open secret among the scientists inside the Polaroid labs. Land even brought in his old friend James Baker—the Harvard astronomer who had helped him conceive of the spy plane—to design the camera's lens. By the early 1970s, the camera had gone through numerous evolutions—the U-2 gave way to the U-3, then to the U-4. When it was ready in 1972, the camera incorporated more than three hundred transistors to control its automated functions and represented the work of dozens of engineering, manufacturing, and research teams—"a tremendous technological symphony," as Land called it. The camera was introduced as the Polaroid SX-70, and it was a sensation. *Business Week* magazine compared the complexity of Polaroid's achievement with the Apollo moon landing, and *Fortune* wrote that "the mere production of the SX-70 must already be counted as one of the most remarkable accomplishments in industrial history." Land in 1972 was pictured with the camera on the covers of both *Time* and *Life* magazines, and the company's value soared. Within a decade, the company's sales had more than quadrupled, and Land's status as one of America's richest men solidified.

The country, however, was changing rapidly. The generational transformation that had begun in the early 1960s had flowered into the countercultural and antiwar movements, and their spirit of social activism challenged the status quo of America's military-industrial complex—an elite that Land, as a bridge between corporate America and the government, had helped establish. He publicly empathized with the student and protest movements, and he tried to assert himself as the rare corporate leader who actually encouraged his employees to express their social and political consciences as the 1960s wore on. When the United States invaded Cambodia in the spring of 1970, and after Ohio National Guardsmen killed four student Vietnam War protesters and wounded nine more at Kent State University, Land invited workers at Polaroid to tell the government what they thought about it; if they sent telegrams to the White House, he announced, he'd pay to transmit them all to Washington. About twenty-five hundred of his employees took him up on the offer.

Later that same year, it was publicized that Polaroid film was used to produce the pictures included in the passbook that every black citizen in South Africa was required to carry, and Polaroid employees began leading protests outside the company headquarters in Cambridge. The company's initial response was one of confusion and denial in the face of the demonstrations: Polaroid had no plant, employees, or direct investments in South Africa, and Land downplayed the company's connection to the regime. After the protests grew more intense, the workers' message finally got through to Land. "Polaroid is considered a great and generous company," he said at a meeting to discuss the issue. "Shouldn't we use that power?" Polaroid became the first major American company to publicly condemn South African apartheid, which it criticized in advertisements placed throughout the international press, and it prohibited its film from being used in the passbook program.

All the while, Land continued his clandestine work with the U.S. government, but that relationship had begun to strain by the early 1970s.

President Richard Nixon's inner circle put Land's name on one of its "Enemies Lists," and when the Watergate scandal broke, Land resigned from his post as a presidential science adviser, a position he'd held in one capacity or another since 1954. "I visited just after he had been listed as one of Nixon's '200 enemies,'" the Cambridge University optics professor F. W. Campbell later recalled. "I congratulated him. He replied that he was particularly honoured as it was the only honour he had received without working for."

The contradiction that would always run through the center of the CIA—the idea of a secretive agency inside a free and open society—would also mark Land's personal life, and he never fully reconciled his ideals of openness and transparency with his classified life and the necessary cover-ups. Before he died in 1991, he used his fortune to privately endow the Rowland Institute for Science, now part of Harvard University, which is a monument to the free flow of information and ideas, funding experimental work in chemistry, physics, biology, and other sciences. He donated many of his scientific papers and notes for future generations to sort through, but the secrecy he'd embraced in the 1950s stuck with him until his dying days. He ordered that all of his personal papers and almost all of his personal correspondence be destroyed, which it was.

As the digital age took hold, Polaroid ceded the vanguard of American technology to computer companies, yet Land's example loomed large. Steve Jobs, in an interview with *Playboy* in 1985, tried to outline the sort of company he wanted Apple Computer Inc. to become: one that valued "troublemakers" who weren't afraid to follow their own paths. Jobs offered an example to illustrate his point. "You know, Dr. Edwin Land was a troublemaker," he said. "He dropped out of Harvard and founded Polaroid." Land was the sort of person Jobs aspired to be, one who constantly pushed for innovation and seemed unwilling to surrender a vital part of his integrity in the process. Jobs made sure he met Land, making a pilgrimage to Polaroid to see firsthand the empire he'd created.

"The man is a national treasure," Jobs continued. "I don't understand why people like that can't be held up as models. This is the most incredible thing to be—not an astronaut, not a football player—but *this*."

RICHARD BISSELL HAD WATCHED the Cuban missile crisis unfold from the strangely unfamiliar position of the sidelines. James

Killian had helped him land a job at the Institute for Defense Analysis, a nonprofit that had been formed a few years earlier to strengthen relations between the Pentagon and university scientists. Bissell started in March 1962, a couple weeks after he left the CIA, and by June he'd been promoted to become the organization's president, but he discovered that the job simply lacked the adrenaline rush of covert operations. During the height of the Cuban missile crisis, he wrote a letter to his son Winthrop, who was away from home at a boarding school. The crisis hadn't really touched him, Bissell wrote. "Most of my friends in the government have been so busy that they have not even been free for lunch. All in all, I feel very much an outsider."

Much as he tried, he never really got back on the inside. At IDA, he immediately tried to establish new, more objective quality-control assessments for military weapons and aircraft systems, insisting that the analysis be performed by high-level scientists and technological experts. But almost immediately, Bissell ran into a hauntingly familiar nemesis— Curtis LeMay. The general was still occupying a position on the Joint Chiefs—a job he'd hold until 1965, when his repeated clashes with President Johnson and Secretary McNamara over the Vietnam War (LeMay demanded more bombing) forced him into retirement. Along with the other joint chiefs, LeMay regarded Bissell's reforms at IDA as existential threats to the Pentagon's autonomy and its budgets. The Joint Chiefs complained to Secretary of Defense Robert McNamara, and eventually word of the conflict was leaked to the press. *Newsweek* reported that Bissell had started at IDA "just in time to become a handy target for the deep and increasing hostility of the military to the ascending role of the civilian policy makers." In a letter to his son Richie, written just after Kennedy was assassinated, Bissell expressed the anguish he felt over the loss, and he added, "Just to compound matters, my office crisis has finally been resolved—at my expense. The decision is that I shall leave IDA, probably in about six months' time. . . . It may mean that we leave Washington entirely, if I find an attractive opportunity elsewhere."

What he was looking for, really, was a job that re-created the excitement and the energy he felt when he was leading the U-2 program. The further away from the CIA he got, the more Bissell looked back upon that project with fondness and pride, seeing it as the capstone of his government career. He mended his relationship with Edwin Land, who had been disappointed in Bissell's emphasis on covert actions during his final years in the CIA. When Bissell was searching for opportunities in late 1963, Land offered him a position at Polaroid in Massachusetts. Bissell considered it but ended up taking another job that would allow him to move his family to his hometown of Hartford, Connecticut, and would thrust him back into the world of airplane manufacturing, which he missed. He became the director of marketing and economic planning for United Aircraft, a company whose Pratt & Whitney subsidiary had produced the engine for the U-2.

He would spend a decade there, a period he'd later summarize as "unfulfilling." Later he became a management consultant, and he served as a board member of the Covenant Mutual Insurance Company, which was run by Joe Alsop's younger brother John.

As he got older, his reputation rested mostly on the fact that he was considered the architect of a failure, the Bay of Pigs. He was often asked about his role in the operation, and his take on it never changed: it was a regrettable failure and he was willing to take his share of responsibility for it, but it sure would have been nice to have gotten the air support the operation required.

He would come to terms with the fact that his life was often judged only by what he did between the years of 1954 and 1962, a period that he said provided him with "successes and regrets and a legacy that still has not been put to rest historically and perhaps never will be." Just before he died in 1994, he tried to take stock of it all: "When I look back on my life, I think it can be said that I was something of an opportunist. I had no grand plan for advancing myself or any offices to which I particularly aspired. I did want to lead a challenging life and, if I could, participate in the key issues and events of my time. To attain this end, I seized those opportunities that came my way and made the most of them. Some of my accomplishments I am very proud of, others less so, but I take pride in knowing that I did my best."

In late 1963, just before he left Washington with a sense of defeat, when few people jumped to Bissell's side to defend him publicly, the one notable exception was Joe Alsop.

"If any member of the general public recalls the name of Richard M. Bissell, it will probably be because of the Bay of Pigs," Alsop lamented in a column written just before his friend left Washington. But Bissell's true legacy, Alsop argued, was one that the public would likely never fully appreciate: the secret success of the U-2 and satellite programs.

which continued to prove that America had a tactical advantage over the Soviets. That information, Alsop said, was worth far more than any historian or military analyst would ever be able to calculate.

"Such then is the debt owed to Dick Bissell," Alsop wrote. "As he happens to be this reporter's oldest friend, the debt is here acknowledged with pride."

KELLY JOHNSON EMERGED FROM THE CUBAN MISSILE crisis with a long to-do list. The U.S. government urged him to keep trying to perfect a successor to the U-2, a faster and higher-flying aircraft that could evade the sorts of missiles that brought down the spy planes over Sverdlovsk and Cuba.

Johnson's first attempt—the supersonic A-12, or "Archangel"—was manufactured for two years, between 1962 and 1964, and it flew missions from 1963 to 1968. Eventually, that plane morphed into the SR-71, yet another Skunk Works innovation, and one that would continue to fly missions around the world until 1998. The plane flew at speeds in excess of Mach 3 (three times the speed of sound), and its radical shape and radar-evasion components made it virtually invulnerable to the sorts of missiles that downed Powers. During its more than thirty years of operational missions, not a single SR-71 was ever shot down.

He also continued to work on the D-21 drone for several years— an extremely challenging and problematic engineering project that, nevertheless, was secretly deployed over Chinese nuclear testing sites from 1969 to 1971. The success rate of the missions was low: only four out of twenty-one attempted flights were successful, and only moderately so. The drone project was formally discontinued around the same time that President Richard Nixon was working to normalize relations with China. Johnson certainly understood the decision, but the news still disappointed him. "It was a sad occasion for all," he wrote. "We will probably see the day when we will greatly rue the decision taken to scrap the program." The perceived failure of the D-21 delayed the full-scale deployment of drones by the CIA for many years, but Johnson's pioneering drone was a forerunner of the high-performance UAVs that the agency would embrace about four decades later over the skies of Afghanistan and throughout the Middle East.

Lockheed, thanks mostly to Johnson and partly to the U-2, by the early 1960s had become a unique corporate partner to the U.S. government. The relationship was so close, and so guarded from public transparency, that the company at times seemed to be an arm of the nation's intelligence and military services. From the early 1960s on, this raised alarm bells for those who believed the military-industrial complex that Eisenhower had first named in 1961 might be growing out of control and the secret flows of money that escaped public notice might possess the power to corrupt. "To slip the immense power of the purse, under the blanket of security, from the many in Congress to an elite few—no matter how dedicated and responsible they may be—is perilous to our form of government," wrote the *Chicago Tribune* in an editorial about Lockheed's secret projects in 1964.

But none of those apprehensions seemed to slow Johnson down. The months after the Cuban missile crisis were particularly active for him, in part because he was still the only public face of the U-2 program, and seemingly everyone wanted to congratulate him on his achievement. In 1963 the Air Force Association gave him the Theodore von Karman Award, its highest honor, for his work on the U-2, "thus providing the Free World with one of its most valuable instruments in the defense of freedom." The very next year, the organization presented him with the same award, once again. President Lyndon Johnson in 1964 invited him to Washington to receive the Presidential Medal of Freedom, which he received alongside other honorees including Walt Disney, T. S. Eliot, Helen Keller, Edward R. Murrow, Carl Sandburg, and John Steinbeck. Two months later, President Johnson invited him back to the White House's Rose Garden to present him with the Collier Trophy, an annual prize awarded for "the greatest achievement in aeronautics or astronautics in the country." Less than two years later, he was beside President Johnson yet again to collect the National Medal of Science.

Perhaps the most unusual of the ceremonies Johnson attended was one held on April 20, 1963. Those who had participated in the U-2 program, including many of its early pilots, were being awarded the Intelligence Star for Valor, one of the CIA's highest honors. It was an unusual ceremony mainly because of one conspicuous absence that no one failed to notice: Francis Gary Powers had not been invited to attend.

POWERS FOUND OUT ABOUT THE CEREMONY from his pilot friends, even though they'd been told not to mention it to him. He took it as a snub, a blatant slight, and it stung. Ever since he'd returned to America, he'd had the feeling that people still questioned his loyalty. They'd smile and assure him they knew he'd done nothing wrong whe⁻

he was shot down, but he could never quite quell the feeling that they might be saying something different behind his back. The CIA eventually awarded him the Intelligence Star, in 1965, and asked him not to publicly reveal the award. The medal, instead of being a source of pride, would always be a reminder of suspicions he believed he never deserved.

These had been tumultuous years for him. Early in 1963 he had to return to Milledgeville for his divorce hearings, where he and Barbara had relived the worst parts of their relationship. Charlene Justice, the daughter of Charlie Deason, took the stand to tell the story of walking in on Barbara and her father in various states of undress. Frank told the judge Barbara's alcohol abuse was at the root of their problems, insisting that from their days together in Adana, Turkey, drinking was a daily habit for her. "For many years, during the time that I lived with her, I cannot remember a single day that went by that she didn't have at the very minimum, one, and most of the time, more than one drink," he testified. "When I say more than one, that could be anything from two to fifty." Barbara countered that he was drinking right alongside her, and she testified that his experience with the CIA had changed him and he no longer resembled the man she had married. "He's not the same," she said. "He took all his bitterness out on me." Barbara, certainly, had emerged from the U-2 drama a different woman, hollowed by the pressures of a life connected to the CIA, but she got very little sympathy from the government or from her and Frank's old friends from the U-2 program, from whom she distanced herself. A jury granted Powers the divorce, and it also ordered him to pay her $5,000 in a lump-sum alimony, plus her attorney fees.

Powers returned to California and continued to work alongside Johnson, flying U-2s sent back to California for repairs or modifications. Before he'd moved to California, just after he split up with Barbara, he had begun dating Claudia Edwards Downey, or Sue to her friends. She was a psychologist at the CIA, working at Langley, and throughout 1963 the two of them maintained a long-distance relationship. By the end of that year, Sue retired from the CIA, and they were married in Virginia. Four months later, Barbara married a man named William Reynolds, also from Milledgeville.

Powers and Sue had a child, Francis Gary Powers Jr., in 1965, and he became the legal father to another daughter that Sue had from a previous marriage. They bought a house in the Verdugo Mountains, which overlooked the runway at the Burbank Airport. Sue learned how to recognize the sound of the U-2 engine, and she'd run to the living room window and wave, hoping to catch his eye when he took off or landed.

Every so often media interview requests would come into Lockheed's office for Powers, but the company's public relations department shielded him from them. It didn't take long for the public to forget his face, and he was able to move around the Los Angeles area without being recognized. Once, in 1965, a writer from *Esquire* showed up at the door of his house and was let in, where he found Powers in a gold velour chair, sipping a gin on the rocks. He'd stopped smoking a year before and had been struggling to keep his weight down ever since, careful to stay fit enough to keep his job with Johnson. He only allowed himself drinks on the weekends, he said, never during the week.

"I love flying and I want to stay with it as long as I can," Powers said. "After that, well, I've got a little ol' fishing hole staked out in Virginia. And I'd like to play some golf and travel. There are so many places I'd like to see in this country."

Things didn't really work out that way. He wanted to write a book about his experience, but the CIA didn't like the idea and steered him away from the project. Powers grew increasingly bitter with the agency, believing that it was preventing him from moving on with his life and making some money out of telling the story from his point of view. In 1969 he finally signed a book deal. Around the same time, Kelly Johnson informed him that he had to let him go. When NASA passed him over for a job, he complained to Johnson, who in turn wrote in a private memo, "I am very unhappy with Powers . . . and consider him extremely ungrateful for what Lockheed and I personally have done with him." Johnson never publicly criticized Powers, and always stood up for his actions in the U-2, but their relationship was strained after Powers left Lockheed.

Powers struggled to find another job and supported himself and his family with the publication of the book and a series of lectures. In 1972 he landed a job with the KGIL radio station in Los Angeles, which hired him to fly a Cessna over the city and report on traffic. Four years later he began to fly a helicopter for KNBC TV. On August 1, 1977, he had finished covering a brush fire in Santa Barbara when his chopper, which was hovering over a softball field, began to sputter and dip. Power-

crashed to the ground and was killed instantly. Later, some of the boys playing softball on the field said they were certain that the pilot of the helicopter had purposefully swerved the aircraft to avoid hitting them.

The police determined that Powers had run out of fuel. Later it was revealed that the helicopter's gas gauge had long been considered faulty, and whenever it reached "empty," it actually still had fuel left in the tank. According to Powers's friends and colleagues, the gauge had been repaired the night before, but no one had told Frank.

By the end of his life, Powers's views of the CIA and his role in the U-2 saga were marked by a complex ambivalence. It was difficult for him to judge anything the CIA did in simple, binary terms: the agency's actions were rarely just good or bad, but instead were usually a muddy mixture of both. Anyone who entered that world had to make peace with that. Later in life, Powers seemed to feel at times that his life had become a cautionary tale, a real-life example of what's sacrificed when good ideas and the best intentions are subsumed within a murky, governmental labyrinth where secrecy was sometimes an end unto itself.

Years after he disappeared from the daily headlines, he tried to summarize what the U-2 drama had taught him. "While the lack of accurate intelligence may be one of the greatest threats to our national survival, it is not the only one," Powers wrote. "Sometimes in our rush to achieve an objective we overlook our reason for pursuing it. It would be tragic if, in the process of trying to protect our government, we forgot that it was founded upon the concept of the worth of the individual."

# Acknowledgments

Of all the people that deserve thanks for helping me with this book, the librarians and archivists—the unsung heroes of narrative nonfiction—might as well come first. The staff at the Dwight D. Eisenhower Presidential Library, the John F. Kennedy Presidential Library, and the Library of Congress were, without exception, welcoming and helpful. Archivist Valoise Armstrong at the Eisenhower Library in Abilene, Kansas, deserves to be singled out for her tireless patience and encouragement while guiding me through the protracted process of filing declassification requests for redacted and withheld materials. The staff at the National Archives Records Administration building in College Park, Maryland, helped me navigate their trove of declassified CIA documents, many of which were—mercifully—released online in early 2017. In Evanston, the staff at the Northwestern University Library, particularly all those tasked with re-spooling all the microfilm reels I abused, provided me with a welcoming home away from home, where much of the writing and documentary research for this book was completed.

The Association of Former Intelligence Officers helped me get in touch with several retired officers who'd been part of the U-2 program, including Tony Bevacqua, a former U-2 pilot and a roommate of Francis Gary Powers, and the late Stanley Beerli, who helped lead the program during its early years. Dino Brugioni offered insights into the world of photointerpretation, as well as personal recollections of some of this book's main characters. Sergei Khrushchev and his wife, Valentina, graciously welcomed me into their home in Rhode Island and shared memories of the period covered in this book from the Soviet perspective. Richard Bissell's children, Ann and Richard, were generous and valuable windows into their father's life, as was David C. Acheson, one of Bissell's closest friends and whose life in Washington intersected with numerous other figures in the book. Charles Sibert, who was stationed in Adana in the late 1950s, helped me piece together a vivid picture of the base there. I'd also like to thank the members of the Alibi Club, who opened several of their doors and cabinets to me, helping me recapture some of the atmosphere of a side of Washington that's rarely seen.

I'm deeply indebted to my agents, Larry Weissman and Sascha Alper, for their counsel, encouragement, and friendship. At Doubleday, I've been lucky to work with several skilled editors: Melissa Danaczko championed the book from its conception through its early drafts, and Kris Puopolo and Daniel Meyer ably steered it toward publication. Others at Doubleday who contributed their time and talents include Ingrid Sterner, Bette Alexander, Lorraine Hyland, Iris Weinstein, Michael Windsor, Charlotte O'Donnell, and Sarah Engelmann. My editors at Bloomberg—Robert Blau and Flynn McRoberts, particularly—backed this project without reservation, and they helped me carve out the time necessary to finish it.

Finally, this book simply wouldn't exist if my family hadn't been wholeheartedly supportive. I will never be able to thank Mei-Ling, Sofia, and Violet enough for giving me this, along with so much else.

# Notes

## PROLOGUE

3   It's a warm spring day: The descriptions and actions recounted throughout New York in the prologue were drawn from news reports, period advertisements, weather reports, and archival photographs from May 1960. That material can be found in the following publications: "Nation Takes Cover in Air-Raid Alert," *New York Times*, May 4, 1960, 1; "Seventh Nation-Wide Civil Defense Drill Reported Generally Successful," *New York Times*, May 4, 1960, 48; "Public Must Obey Raid Alert Today," *New York Times*, May 3, 1960, 41; "Civil Defense Drill Briefly Halts Business and Baseball, but Politics Are Unaffected," *Wall Street Journal*, May 4, 1960, 7; "Sirens to Wail, TV Radio to Go Off for Defense Drill," *Chicago Tribune*, May 3, 1960, A1; "Life on W. 42nd Street: A Study in Decay," *New York Times*, March 14, 1960, 1; "Supermarket with Ramps Planned," *New York Times*, Dec. 29, 1959, 10; David W. Dunlap, "Architect Once Envisioned a Guggenheim of Groceries," www.nytimes.com, March 11, 2015.

4   On the observation deck: The city's central siren at 30 Rockefeller Plaza was upgraded several times after World War II, and in addition to the articles cited above, descriptions of its evolution can be found in "Chopped Air: The World's Loudest Siren," *New Yorker*, Sept. 20, 1952, and "A Six Bladed Rotary Chopper," *New Yorker*, May 19, 1943.

5   The recording depicted a prudent family: "CONELRAD 1960" promotional 45 rpm record, New York State Civil Defense Commission, General C. R. Huebner, director.

5   They estimate that had Soviet jets: "Governor Thanks Workers in Alert," *New York Times*, May 5, 1960, 14.

6   with the exception of a park: In addition to the newspaper reports cited above, information about the protests was taken from Garrison, *Bracing for Armageddon*, 98; "College Suspends 53 Drill Critics," *New York Times*, May 15, 1960, 14.

6   The members of the National Security Council: Description of the meeting and the members' deployment comes from "Memorandum: Discussion at the 443rd Meeting of the National Security Council," May 5, 1960, Dwight D. Eisenhower Presidential Library, Abilene, Kans.

7   The sprawling underground lair: "Interim Standing Operating Procedures for Emergency Use of the Classified Location," U.S. National Archives, Records Group 396, Declassified P 95 Records, box 6, Folder: Special Facilities Branch. Additional information came from Ted Gup, "The Doomsday Blueprints," *Time*, Aug. 10, 1992, 35; Graff, *Raven Rock*; "Memorandum for the Record: Trip to High Point," CIA-RDP72-00450, June 1959, declassified Oct. 2006.

8   "Just think, what would be the reaction": "Statement by Chairman Khrushchev to the Supreme Soviet on 5 May 1960 Concerning Shootdown of U-2," *History of the Office of Special Activities (OSA) from Inception to 1969*, declassified in March 2016.

10  "It constituted nothing less than a revolution": George J. Tenet, "The U-2 Program: The DCI's Perspective," *Studies in Intelligence* (Winter 1998–99).

10  "Even now at times": Ovid Demaris, "Going to See Gary," *Esquire*, May 1966, 88.

## CHAPTER 1: THE IDEALIST

13    "If you are able to state a problem": Robert Reinhold, "Land Achieves His Dream with New Polaroid SX-70," *Life,* Oct. 27, 1972, 48.

13    Just before 3:30 p.m.: "Soviet Jet Bombers," CIA declassified draft document, April 27, 1954.

13    He walked to the white parapet: Descriptions of the embassy are from various sources including Harrison Salisbury, "Kremlin Offers U.S. 10-Story Site for Its New Embassy in Moscow," *New York Times,* Aug. 23, 1952, 1; Stanley Johnson, "U.S. Occupies a Lot of Moscow," *Washington Post,* Dec. 26, 1954, E3.

14    Just six weeks earlier: Details of the test and its effects come from Thomas Kunkle and Byron Ristvet, "Castle Bravo: Fifty Years of Legend and Lore—A Guide to Off-Site Radiation Exposures," Defense Threat Reduction Agency Analysis Center, Jan. 2013; Titus, *Bombs in the Backyard.*

14    a bold headline at the top: William Lawrence, "H-Bomb Can Wipe Out Any City, Strauss Reports After Tests," *New York Times,* April 1, 1954, 1.

15    "It was symbolic": Hanson Baldwin, "The Bomb and a Battle," *New York Times,* April 1, 1954, 21.

15    President Eisenhower was on edge: Descriptions of the establishment of the TCP are from Hewlett and Holl, *Atoms for Peace and War;* Killian, *Sputnik, Scientists, and Eisenhower.*

16    "I hope very much": Golden, *Science Advice to the President,* 315.

16    As a boy, Land had grown fascinated: For the best account of Land's early life, see McElheny, *Insisting on the Impossible.*

17    The camp's founder, Barney "Cap" Girden: Descriptions of the camp and Girden from ibid., 21–23; Andrew H. Malcolm, "Our Towns: Returning to a Camp That Lives Only in Memories," *New York Times,* Oct. 6, 1992; Diane Winston, "Camp Days Live Again at Nostalgic Reunion," *New York Times,* Nov. 28, 1979, 58.

18    "De Tocqueville enjoyed pointing out": Edwin Land, "Generation of Greatness: The Idea of a University in an Age of Science," Ninth Annual Arthur Dehon Little Memorial Lecture at MIT, May 22, 1957.

18    When General George S. Patton complained: Wensberg, *Land's Polaroid,* 72.

18    When the Coast Guard dogs: For information on Land's wartime work on goggles for both men and dogs, see McElheny, *Insisting on the Impossible,* 127; Harris Ewing, "Sunglasses at War: His Lenses Pierce Fog, Banish Glare," *New York Herald Tribune,* May 7, 1944, SM26; William E. Jones, "Fighter Pilots Wear Red Lenses at Night," *Boston Globe,* Nov. 28, 1944, 10.

18    When American soldiers in the South Pacific: William L. Laurence, "Synthetic Quinine Produced, Ending Century Search," *New York Times,* May 4, 1944, 1; Jay Franklin, "Synthetic Quinine Evolved Here," *Boston Globe,* May 3, 1944, 1.

18    a new type of radiation "dosimeter": "Device Measures Radiation Dosage," *Baltimore Sun,* Nov. 16, 1950, 1.

18    "The man is a whirlwind": Hyde to his parents, May 28, 1945, reproduced in "A Symposium in Honor of Edwin Land," *Bulletin of the American Academy of Arts and Sciences* 45 (1992): 23–52.

18    Land decided to leave Cambridge: Gregory W. Pedlow and Donald E. Welzenbach, *The Central Intelligence Agency and Overhead Reconnaissance: The U-2 and OXCART Programs, 1954–1974,* CIA declassified history, released June 2013, 29; Donald Welzenbach, "Din Land: Patriot from Polaroid," *Optics & Photonics News,* Oct. 1994, 25.

19    "Home screens are getting bigger": Barbara Berch Jamison, "And Now Super-colossal Headaches," *New York Times,* Jan. 10, 1954, SM20.

19    Hitchcock didn't like the idea: Hitchcock's struggles with 3-D are outlined in several biographies, including Spoto, *Life of Alfred Hitchcock*.

19    "It's a big, gross, hulking monster": Barbara Berch Jamison, "3-D Spells 'Murder' for Alfred Hitchcock," *New York Times,* Oct. 11, 1953.

20    "Tremendous new problems": Ibid.

20    in 1953 the company had a backlog: S. Shane, "Depth," *New Yorker,* May 16, 1953, 26.

20    "As is the case of any product": "Inventor Sure 3D Is Here to Stay," *Los Angeles Times,* Nov. 1, 1953, 15.

20    He attended a special media screening: "Polaroid Corp. President Sees Improved 3D," *Box Office,* Sept. 26, 1953, 22.

20    "a witless and hackneyed trifle": Bosley Crowther, "3-D Film and 2 Imports," *New York Times,* Oct. 1, 1953.

20    Land believed the public's waning interest: "VistaVision, Paramount Wide Screen Race Entry, Has 1st Public Showing," *Wall Street Journal,* Aug. 25, 1954.

20    But his heart wasn't in it: Olshaker, *Instant Image,* 36.

21    A study by the Harvard Business School: Ibid., 30.

21    "My motto," Land said: Brugioni, *Eyeball to Eyeball,* 13.

21    The forty-two members: "Report of the Technological Capabilities Panel of the Science Advisory Committee," Department of State, RD Files, Lot 71, D-171; Richard V. Damms, "James Killian, the Technological Capabilities Panel and the Emergence of President Eisenhower's 'Scientific Elite,' " *Diplomatic History* 24, no. 1 (Jan. 2000): 57–58.

21    Killian managed to snag a few rooms: Descriptions of offices and building from Killian, *Sputnik, Scientists, and Eisenhower,* 85; John DeFerrari, "The Eisenhower Executive Office Building, America's 'Greatest Monstrosity,' " *Streets of Washington,* Sept. 29, 2014.

22    Striding through those halls: Richard Garwin, "Impressions of Edwin H. Land," *Optics & Photonics News,* Oct. 1994, 24; Dino Brugioni, interview with author, 2015.

22    He'd silently slip into a chair: R. Cargill Hall, "Interview with William O. Baker," *NRO History,* May 7, 1996.

22    "Land could overcome his shyness": George Ehrenfried, "Working with Edwin Land," *Optics & Photonics News,* Oct. 1994, 56–57.

22    "Land is an authentic genius": Killian, *Sputnik, Scientists, and Eisenhower,* 87.

22    He told Killian he wanted his group: Pedlow and Welzenbach, *Central Intelligence Agency and Overhead Reconnaissance,* 29.

23    He considered intellectual inquiry: Land's views on intellectual inquiry are explored in many of his public speeches, and also in Olshaker, *Instant Image,* 131.

23    "You are handling so many variables": "The Third University of Utah Research Conference on the Identification of Creative Scientific Talent," held June 11–14, 1959, report published by University of Utah Press, 19.

23    The other major, industrialized nations: Olson, *Fair Play.*

23    "If Anglo-Saxon civilization stands for anything": Beverly Gage, "The Strange Politics of 'Classified' Information," *New York Times Magazine,* Aug. 22, 2017, 15.

24    by 1950 employed about five thousand people: Staffing estimates from Raleigh, *Agency.*

24    It quickly became clear to Land: Pedlow and Welzenbach, *Central Intelligence Agency and Overhead Reconnaissance,* 29.

25    "It is shocking to learn the extent": "Report of the Technological Capabilities Panel of the Science Advisory Committee," 23.

25    Oppenheimer had led the Manhattan Project: Oppenheimer's evolving views on nuclear weapons are traced in Bird and Sherwin, *American Prometheus.*

26  "Some people in the Air Force": Ibid., 451.
26  "offense is the best defense": Joseph Alsop and Stewart Alsop, "Rethinking the Problem of Defense Against Atomic Attack," *Baltimore Sun,* March 22, 1953, 18.
26  Thomas Finletter . . . was convinced: Bird and Sherwin, *American Prometheus,* 445.
26  "More probably than not": Ibid., 478.
27  "While I cannot take the time": Stone, *Perilous Times,* 331.
27  "There's enough to draw": Paul V. Craigue, "McCarthy Drops Furry, Plans Look at MIT," *Boston Globe,* Dec. 16, 1953; "MIT, Senate Probers Hold Secret Meeting on Project Lincoln," *Boston Globe,* Dec. 15, 1954, 1.
28  "If it is a question of wisdom": Robert Coughlan, "Dr. Edward Teller's Magnificent Obsession," *Life,* Sept. 6, 1954, 63.
28  Many scientists who knew Oppenheimer: Numerous newspaper articles chronicled the scientists' support of Oppenheimer and opposition to Teller and McCarthy, including Elie Abel, "Services Accused on Science Policy," *New York Times,* July 29, 1954.
28  "He impressed me in these meetings": Killian's testimony is transcribed in *United States Congressional Serial Set,* 11745:37.
29  "Not just their talents are required": Joseph Alsop and Stewart Alsop, "What Is Security?," *Washington Post,* June 4, 1954, 12.
29  Killian described an atmosphere: *United States Congressional Serial Set,* 11745:37.
29  "We would go in and interview": Pedlow and Welzenbach, *Central Intelligence Agency and Overhead Reconnaissance,* 29.
30  LeMay sketched out an air force strike plan: Rhodes, *Dark Sun,* 566.
30  "Dawn might break over a nation": Ibid.
30  "All war is immoral": Ibid., 22.
30  "He was the finest combat commander": Hornfischer, *Fleet at Flood Tide,* 374.
30  LeMay in 1948 took over the Strategic Air Command: LeMay, *Mission with LeMay,* 473.
30  LeMay had personally alerted Edward Teller: Rhodes, *Dark Sun,* 344; Chuck Hansen, "The Bomb, Part 2," *Bulletin of the Atomic Scientists,* Sept. 1995, 52–53.
31  LeMay carried that same aggressive swagger: LeMay's resistance to Lockheed's proposals are chronicled in Pedlow and Welzenbach, *Central Intelligence Agency and Overhead Reconnaissance,* and Pocock, *U-2 Spyplane.*
31  "This is a bunch of shit": Pocock, *U-2 Spyplane,* 14.
31  That summer, Land paid a visit: Pedlow and Welzenbach, *Central Intelligence Agency and Overhead Reconnaissance,* 29–30.
32  "We don't do market surveys": Fierstein, *Triumph of Genius,* 3.
32  "I will never let anyone tell me": Bonanos, *Instant,* 15.
32  Doolittle's classified report: James H. Doolittle, "Report on the Covert Activities of the Central Intelligence Agency," July 1954, declassified and provided to the Senate Select Committee on Intelligence on Aug. 6, 1976.
32  Doolittle was one of aviation's true pioneers: For an overview of his achievements, see Groom, *Aviators.*
32  "It is now clear": Doolittle, "Report on the Covert Activities of the Central Intelligence Agency," 3–4.
33  "that there are historic principles": Land's quotation is from "The Public Television Act of 1967: Hearings Before the Subcommittee on Communications," *Hearings of the 90th U.S. Congress* (Washington, D.C.: U.S. Government Printing Office, 1967), 167.
33  By pursuing an espionage strategy: Land's views on the moral foundations of democracy and America are explored in ibid. and numerous other statements made throughout his career and chronicled in McElheny, *Insisting on the Impossible.*

33    In early 1952, while Land was working: "Beacon Hill Report: Problems of Air
      Force Intelligence and Reconnaissance; Appendices B and C," Project Lincoln,
      MIT, 1952, declassified May 2014.

34    "I think I have the plane": Donald E. Welzenbach and Nancy Galyean, "Unortho-
      dox: Airplane and Man," *Studies in Intelligence* 32 (1988), declassified Sept. 2009.

## CHAPTER 2: THE MAN WHO COULD SEE AIR

35    "I understood that I was essentially": Johnson, *Kelly*, 188.

35    It explained that the reason: Miller, *Lockheed Martin's Skunk Works*, 73–75.

35    LeMay had asked Lockheed to design: Johnson, *Kelly*, 195.

36    Back in February, Johnson had heard: The story of Johnson's early involvement
      in the U-2 project is outlined in Pedlow and Welzenbach, *Central Intelligence
      Agency and Overhead Reconnaissance; History of the OSA*, 224; and Miller, *Lock-
      heed Martin's Skunk Works*, 72.

36    The new plane wouldn't fly: Miller, *Lockheed Martin's Skunk Works*, 73.

37    "no more devoted citizen": Polenberg, *In the Matter of J. Robert Oppenheimer*,
      139.

38    "All right, Mr. Secretary": Welzenbach, "Din Land," 23.

38    "I think Talbott may have had": Ibid., 24.

38    "a good fighting Irish name": Most details of Johnson's youth and early life at
      Lockheed come from his autobiography, *Kelly*.

39    "a wonder for lightness and power": Victor Appleton, *Tom Swift and His Sky
      Racer* (New York: Grosset & Dunlap, 1921).

40    "Dear Johnson, You will have to excuse": Johnson, *Kelly*, 24.

41    "That damn Swede": Rich and Janos, *Skunk Works*, 114.

41    Land's house, at 163 Brattle Street: Details of Land's house come from contempo-
      rary newspaper reports and from "Cambridge Then—from the Cambridge His-
      torical Society," *Homeowner's Guide: A Quarterly Newsletter from Charlie Allen
      Restorations*, Jan. 2009.

41    Johnson had always been proud: Johnson, *Kelly*, 34; recent views of the ranch
      house at 16801 Oak View Drive can be viewed at www.zillow.com.

42    he looked less like Popeye: Some of the most vivid descriptions of Johnson can
      be found throughout Rich and Janos, *Skunk Works*.

42    the family cook keep fresh casseroles: Robert Lenzner, "Land: The Man Behind
      the Camera," *Boston Globe*, Oct. 17, 1976, B1.

42    The scientist had transformed: Garwin, "Impressions of Edwin H. Land," 24.

42    Land's team wasted no time: Details of Land's early work with Johnson are out-
      lined in Pedlow and Welzenbach, *Central Intelligence Agency and Overhead
      Reconnaissance*; Miller, *Lockheed Martin's Skunk Works*, 76.

42    James Baker, the MIT astronomer: Edwin Land to Allen Dulles, Nov. 5, 1954;
      Miller, *Lockheed Martin's Skunk Works*, 81.

43    He had rung up Henry Yutzy: Welzenbach, "Din Land," 25.

43    "Oh, it's the bane of my existence": McElheny, *Insisting on the Impossible*, 44.

44    One evening in October: Welzenbach, "Din Land," 26.

44    Dulles had been a traditional: Details of Dulles's early life are from Grose, *Gen-
      tleman Spy*.

44    "When he comes to the Great Game": Rudyard Kipling, *Kim* (London: Penguin
      Books, 1987), 177.

45    "He might without disrespect": Ambrose, *Ike's Spies*, 177.

45    "good, comfortable, predictable": Grose, *Gentleman Spy*, 318.

45    he rented a west-facing hotel room: McElheny, *Insisting on the Impossible*, 64.

46    Land was discouraged: Pedlow and Welzenbach, *Central Intelligence Agency and
      Overhead Reconnaissance*, 30–36.

46   That Sunday morning, Eisenhower: Details of the sermon are from "Eisenhower Hears an Appeal for Religion in Political Life," *New York Times,* Nov. 1, 1954, 33; "Ike Attends Episcopal Services; Minister Discusses Oppenheimer," *Bridgeport Telegram,* Nov. 1, 1954, 45.

46   Adlai Stevenson . . . led the national campaign: "Stevenson Calls G.O.P. Drive 'Ugly,'" *New York Times,* Oct. 24, 1954, 57.

46   "Almighty God, the source of all wisdom": "Ike Attends Episcopal Services," 45.

47   "bitterness in Washington": "Eisenhower on Air," *New York Times,* Nov. 2, 1954, 1.

47   "By golly, sometimes you sure get tired": "Clackety-Clack Tires President," *Albuquerque Journal,* Nov. 3, 1954, 15.

47   Eisenhower welcomed Land and James Killian: Welzenbach, "Din Land," 26.

48   "If we are successful": McElheny, *Insisting on the Impossible,* 301.

48   Killian later wrote: Killian, *Sputnik, Scientists, and Eisenhower,* 82.

48   "The plane itself is so light": "A Unique Opportunity for Comprehensive Intelligence," a letter from Edwin Land to Allen Dulles, Nov. 5, 1954, declassified April 6, 1988.

49   Land told Dulles that he could build twenty planes: Welzenbach, "Din Land," 26.

49   John Tukey . . . sat behind the wheel: Ibid., 27.

50   "We'll let those SOBs get in": Beschloss, *Mayday,* 105.

50   "Kelly," Gardner said, "begin clearing out that hangar": Ibid.

## CHAPTER 3: THE MYSTERIOUS MR. B.

51   "I took to covert action": Thomas, *Very Best Men,* 186.

51   "It is extremely difficult": Miller, *Lockheed Martin's Skunk Works,* 77.

51   "Rich," Johnson said, "this project is so secret": Rich and Janos, *Skunk Works,* 117.

51   "You've just had a look": Ibid.

52   "We don't dress up": Rich and Janos, *Skunk Works,* 114–15.

52   "Working like mad on airplane": Miller, *Lockheed Martin's Skunk Works,* 78.

53   "I actually observed guys flushing": Rich and Janos, *Skunk Works,* 128.

53   "What guy?" he deadpanned: Ibid., 130.

53   Richard Bissell was born with crossed eyes: Descriptions of Bissell's early years come from Bissell, *Reflections of a Cold Warrior.*

53   "Take up the White Man's Burden": Kipling's poem was first published in the *New York Sun,* Feb. 10, 1899.

54   "good sense from the expansion": Agathangelou and Ling, *Transforming World Politics,* 73.

54   It was strange, Twain observed: Mark Twain, "To the Person Sitting in Darkness," *North American Review,* Feb. 1901.

54   It was an airy castle: Descriptions of the house from letter to Clatter Valley Road Society, May 6, 1981, Correspondence Series, box 12, Richard M. Bissell Jr. Papers, Eisenhower Presidential Library.

55   "stole the defense's papers": Thomas, *Very Best Men,* 91.

55   One day, a young man in a dark suit: Ibid., 92.

55   "open to charges of serious irresponsibility": Joseph Alsop, "America First—the Capital Parade," *Washington Post,* May 28, 1941.

56   Bissell stood on a stage: Mark Wortman, "The Forgotten Antiwar Movement," *Yale Alumni Magazine,* July/Aug. 2016.

56   "by far the most successful": Duffy, *Lindbergh vs. Roosevelt,* 156.

56   He created his own database: Herken, *Georgetown Set,* 50.

56   One of his fans was James Killian: Jacobson, *Area 51,* 50.

56   He moved into a house: Bissell, *Reflections of a Cold Warrior,* 76.

56  He resisted until one evening in 1953: The story of Bissell's recruitment comes from multiple sources, including Bissell, *Reflections of a Cold Warrior,* 79; Thomas, *Very Best Men,* 91; and Herken, *Georgetown Set,* 51.

56  Bissell became Dulles's "special assistant": Bissell, *Reflections of a Cold Warrior,* 91.

57  "I want you in a meeting": Details of Bissell's assignment to the Pentagon are detailed in ibid., 95; Beschloss, *Mayday,* 84–85.

57  "Where is this money": Bissell, *Reflections of a Cold Warrior,* 96; "Interview with Richard M. Bissell," June 1, 1977, Bissell Papers.

58  "You fellows who spend all of your time": "Connally Blasts U.S. Aid to Asia Nations," *Salt Lake Tribune,* July 31, 1951, 15.

58  Bissell listened calmly: For the rest of his life Bissell would passionately defend the work of the Marshall Plan, continuing a pattern he began in 1951; see "Marshall Plan Bows Out mid Self-Applause," *Chicago Tribune,* Dec. 30, 1951.

58  Office of Policy Coordination: "National Security Council Directive on Office of Special Projects," June 18, 1948, RG 273, Records of the National Security Council, National Archives and Records Administration.

58  "When future historians look back": "Marshall Plan Bows Out mid Self-Applause."

59  "Well, the Director of Central Intelligence": "Interview with Richard M. Bissell," June 1, 1977.

59  The parcels were addressed to CLJ: The story of Johnson's setting up a phony manufacturing company is included in several recently declassified histories of the program, including Pedlow and Welzenbach's *Central Intelligence Agency and Overhead Reconnaissance,* and the name of the fictional company has been recorded in various sources as CMJ, C&J, and—by Johnson himself—CLJ Manufacturing. I have gone with CLJ because Johnson's explanation (the name stood for his initials, Clarence Leonard Johnson) seems most likely.

59  "We discussed at length": Miller, *Lockheed Martin's Skunk Works,* 81.

60  The CIA's Los Angeles office: All security measures are detailed in "Chapter 7: Security and Cover," in *History of the OSA,* 542–44.

60  Inside, he found two personal checks: Pedlow and Welzenbach, *Central Intelligence Agency and Overhead Reconnaissance,* 57; Johnson, *Kelly,* 123.

61  "Six more inches?": Pedlow and Welzenbach, *Central Intelligence Agency and Overhead Reconnaissance,* 69.

61  "Let me remind you": Rich and Janos, *Skunk Works,* 126.

61  Johnson calculated that each pound: Pedlow and Welzenbach, *Central Intelligence Agency and Overhead Reconnaissance,* 164.

61  "suffered from the unusually heavy": Johnson, *Kelly,* 157.

61  "Having terrific struggle with the wing": Miller, *Lockheed Martin's Skunk Works,* 128.

62  They called it the U-2: The story of the U-2's name is recounted in multiple sources, including ibid., 81.

62  Joe Alsop would rise in the morning: Herken, *Georgetown Set,* 91–92; box 129 (General Correspondence through March 1958), Joseph and Stewart Alsop Papers, Manuscript Division, Library of Congress.

63  "Charming," he judged those houses: Herken, *Georgetown Set,* 90.

64  Alsop, the Bissells, and a handful: Ann H. Bissell, interview with author.

64  the best friend of Bissell's oldest child: Richard Bissell III, interview with author.

64  "enormous military value": Stewart Alsop, "Debate on the Satellite," *New York Herald Tribune,* May 25, 1955, 20.

64  "A tempest in a teapot": Thomas, *Very Best Men,* 105.

64  Bissell knew that perhaps: Ibid.

65  "Close the goddam door": Rich and Janos, *Skunk Works,* 131.

65  For two days, he buzzed over Death Valley: The details of the site selection of

Area 51 come from a variety of sources, including *History of the OSA,* 649–53; Beschloss, *Mayday,* 93; Pocock, *U-2 Spyplane,* 27: Bissell, *Reflections of a Cold Warrior,* 102; Jacobson, *Area 51,* 50–52; Rich and Janos, *Skunk Works,* 131.

66    "very illegally," Johnson noted: Rich and Janos, *Skunk Works,* 131.

66    "Physical security of this site": "The Test Base Site," declassified CIA memo, transmitted April 26, 1955.

67    "Mr. Bissell pleased": Rich and Janos, *Skunk Works,* 132.

67    "the bomber gap": Alsop wrote numerous columns outlining his views on the bomber gap between 1954 and 1956, and a representative example is Joseph Alsop, "Killian and Porkkala," *New York Herald Tribune,* Sept. 21, 1955, 20.

67    Stewart Alsop traveled to Moscow: Stewart Alsop, "In the Moscow Skies," *New York Herald Tribune,* June 27, 1955, 14; Stewart Alsop, "The Big Show," *New York Herald Tribune,* July 10, 1955, A3.

68    As early as 1946, the Alsop brothers: Herken, *Georgetown Set,* 66.

68    "the spectacle of the Minority Leader": Joseph Alsop and Stewart Alsop, "Why Has Washington Gone Crazy?," *Saturday Evening Post,* July 29, 1950.

68    "morally perverted and degenerate": Transcript from *The Congressional Record,* 96:11979.

69    "We were brought up": Alsop, interview with Barbara Newman, 1979, Bissell Papers.

69    "almost ladylike interest": Merry, *Taking on the World,* 26.

69    an emergency trip to San Francisco: Herken, *Georgetown Set,* 421.

69    the FBI sent a report to an aide: Theoharis, *From the Secret Files of J. Edgar Hoover,* 314–15.

69    "All I can say is, Mr. Bohlen": Bohlen, *Witness to History,* 211.

70    "Senator McCarthy asked whether I thought": FBI memo from Hoover to Tolson, Lad, and Nichols, March 18, 1953.

70    "I know what's in Bohlen's file": "Dulles Denies Overriding Security Chief," *Troy (N.Y.) Times Record,* March 21, 1953, 3.

70    "There is no doubt in my mind": Bissell, *Reflections of a Cold Warrior,* 79.

70    started a file on *him*: Memo from Hoover to the Executive Office of the President, "Subject: Former HSA Employees," Office of the Director for Mutual Security, July 30, 1953, released in 2016 through the Freedom of Information Act and posted in the archives of www.muckrock.com.

71    Remington was accused: The Remington case and Bissell's role in it are explored in May, *Un-American Activities.*

71    "These men are believed to be": See Hoover, "Subject: Former HSA Employees."

71    When Joe published a column in 1955: Joseph Alsop, "Killian and Porkkala," 20.

71    President Truman had established: Gage, "Strange Politics of 'Classified' Information," 15.

72    FBI agents lurked in cars: Herken, *Georgetown Set,* 318.

72    a drunk driver ran a red light: Johnson, *Kelly,* 155; Rich and Janos, *Skunk Works,* 133.

72    "Airplane essentially completed": Miller, *Lockheed Martin's Skunk Works,* 78.

72    On July 24, in the predawn darkness: First days at Area 51 chronicled in *History of the OSA,* 649–53; Beschloss, *Mayday,* 93; Pocock, *U-2 Spyplane,* 27; Bissell, *Reflections of a Cold Warrior,* 101–2; Jacobson, *Area 51,* 50–52; Rich and Janos, *Skunk Works,* 131.

73    "I almost crapped": Rich and Janos, *Skunk Works,* 134–36.

74    "Goddam it, LeVier, what in hell happened?": Ibid.

74    "No ill effects": Cable-048 (IN 31046) to ADIC, Aug. 2, 1955.

74    "Kelly, it flies like a baby buggy": Rich and Janos, *Skunk Works,* 136.

75    "Tony, you did a great job today": Ibid.

75    The Bissell house on the corner of Newark: The accounts of the Bissell house

are from author interviews with Bissell's children Ann and Richard, as well as Thomas, *Very Best Men.*

76   "*real* perfume," Ann Bissell later recalled: Author interview.

76   "unsettling in its coolness": The comment came from Richard Helms, reported in Thomas Powers, *Man Who Kept Secrets,* 95.

## CHAPTER 4: THE HUMAN ELEMENT

78   "I have never thought of myself as a spy": Francis Gary Powers, *Operation Overflight,* 3.

78   Radium Springs Casino: Descriptions of the casino are taken from period newspaper advertisements and a copy of its promotional brochure.

79   "I was told to ask": Francis Gary Powers, *Operation Overflight,* xii.

80   Bissell's office, with help: Details of the recruitment process are taken from an interview with James Cunningham in front of the Board of Inquiry, Feb. 19, 1962, declassified in 2003.

80   "if properly approached": TS-103563, June 13, 1955, sent from Bissell for the Chief of Staff, USAF.

80   Six of the potential recruits: Cunningham Board of Inquiry interview, Feb. 1962.

80   Powers had performed well: Details of Powers's training and performance come from Francis Gary Powers, *Operation Overflight,* 17–19; interview with Colonel Leo Geary, Board of Inquiry, Feb. 1962, declassified in 2003.

81   he was labeled "possibly counterphobic": "What's Expected in the Powers Trial," *U.S. News and World Report,* vol. 49, p. 56.

81   "Was not sure at time": The information came from a document labeled "Personal History," dated April 9, 1956, which was read in a closed session before the Board of Inquiry in Feb. 1962.

81   "gallus-snappin', snuff-dippin', moonshine-lovin' ": Barbara Powers, *Spy Wife,* 15.

82   "That's my oldest daughter": Details of the courtship come from ibid., 14.

82   In his roommates' eyes: Tony Bevacqua (Powers's roommate in Albany), interview with author.

83   "Could you be patient, dearest one": Barbara Powers, *Spy Wife,* 17.

83   "Now don't you keep flying away": Ibid.

84   "I'm in," Powers said: Francis Gary Powers, *Operation Overflight,* xv.

84   "You won't have many volunteers": Brugioni, *Eyes in the Sky,* 105.

84   "It would seem that you would be able to recruit": Ibid.

84   "In order to have a second string": Declassified memo titled "Status Report on Project," TS-142630, Nov. 19, 1955.

84   "It's been decided to use only American pilots": Rich and Janos, *Skunk Works,* 142.

85   "because of the extensive knowledge": "Memo to Project Director from Cover Officer," SAPC-6734, June 5, 1956.

85   the CIA concluded that the U-2's cover story: TS-143237, "Memo for Project Director from D/Admin," March 7, 1956; *History of the OSA,* 570.

85   "The need for more detailed information": National Advisory Committee for Aeronautics, "NACA Announces Start of New Research Program," press release, May 7, 1956.

86   He urged Bissell to accompany: "Memorandum: Subject: Conversation with Colonel Andrew J. Goodpaster, Dr. James Killian, and Dr. Edwin Land," June 21, 1956, TS-143448, declassified Aug. 2000.

86   "a much bolder action": "Memo for the Record," Nov. 6, 1956, declassified through CIA CREST program Aug. 2001.

86   "It was left that we would think": Ibid.

86   Lockheed's Burbank campus during World War II: Dino Brugioni, interview

with author; Breuer, *Deceptions of World War II;* Lockheed Aircraft Corporation, *Of Men and Stars* (Burbank, Calif.: Lockheed Aircraft Corporation, 1957).

87   He had known Doolittle: Johnson, *Kelly,* 25.

87   bogus contracts identifying them as "Flight Test Consultants": Bissell, "Memorandum for Contracting Officer from Project Director," TS-143292, April 12, 1956.

88   The phony manual included photographs: Rich and Janos, *Skunk Works,* 153.

88   "What do you call it?": The dialogue and descriptions of the scenes inside the hotel come from Francis Gary Powers, *Operation Overflight,* 11–12, supported by period advertisements of the hotel with descriptions of the rooms and furnishings.

89   The place was run by William Randolph Lovelace II: Biographical material and the early history of the clinic come from "Lovelace Then and Now," a special section produced by the *Albuquerque Journal,* Sept. 21, 1986.

90   The clinic's specialists conducted: The results were published twenty years later in C. S. White, "Biodynamics of Airblast," Defense Nuclear Agency, Washington, D.C., July 1, 1971.

90   Randy Lovelace tapped Dr. Donald Kilgore: Pocock, *U-2 Spyplane,* 35.

90   Kilgore hopped on a TWA flight: Ackman, *Mercury 13,* 35.

90   "the brownest, dustiest place": "Lovelace Then and Now."

90   Luft knew something about adventure: "Nanga Parbat Disaster Told: Only One German Survivor," *North-China Herald and Supreme Court & Consular Gazette,* June 30, 1937, 561.

91   By the end of a full week at Lovelace: Bevacqua, interview with author; Francis Gary Powers, *Operation Overflight,* 13.

92   "Why don't we just stuff Kotex": Rich and Janos, *Skunk Works,* 137.

92   "grab the ball and run": *History of the OSA,* 672.

93   the shuttle carried thirteen passengers: The air crash is detailed in a variety of documents declassified in 2016, including "Subject: Shuttle Crash," a report by Colonel O. J. Ritland, Nov. 17–19, 1955; *History of the OSA,* 550–59. Additional details from Plaskon, *Silent Heroes of the Cold War Declassified.*

93   "added an emotional overtone": *History of the OSA,* 572.

93   "A complete veil of secrecy": Plaskon, *Silent Heroes of the Cold War Declassified,* 35.

93   One item they failed to find: The story of the lost briefcase came out with the 2016 declassification of *History of the OSA,* 558.

94   one of the biggest risks he'd face: The physical risks described come from www .nasa.gov.

94   The air force partnered with a clothing manufacturer: Pedlow and Welzenbach, *Central Intelligence Agency and Overhead Reconnaissance,* 62.

94   "exactly like a too-tight tie": Francis Gary Powers, *Operation Overflight,* 17.

95   eight other recruits: *History of the OSA,* 786.

96   Perhaps the trickiest part: The descriptions of flying a U-2 come primarily from Bevacqua, interview with author; Francis Gary Powers, *Operation Overflight,* 19–20; Pocock, *U-2 Spyplane,* 34.

97   He felt "a special aloneness": Francis Gary Powers, *Operation Overflight,* 19.

97   On April 14, 1956, Richard Bissell: The details of the emergency landing come from Bissell, *Reflections of a Cold Warrior,* 107; "Interview with Richard M. Bissell," June 1, 1977; Pedlow and Welzenbach, *Central Intelligence Agency and Overhead Reconnaissance,* 79.

98   he was working out of "Quarters Eye": The descriptions of the CIA offices in Quarters Eye come from numerous sources including Brugioni, interview with author; Mickolus, *Stories from Langley.*

98    First, Bissell moved it out: The descriptions of the E Street office come from
      Beschloss, *Mayday*, 90; "Independent Offices Appropriation Bill for 1943," *Hear-
      ings, Seventy-Seventh Congress* (Washington, D.C.: U.S. Government Printing
      Office, 1943).

98    his own "private duchy": Beschloss, *Mayday*, 90.

99    "No one saw copies of cables": Ibid.

99    the U-2 project was generating: *History of the OSA*, 511.

99    "Bissell's Narrow-Gauge Airline": Pedlow and Welzenbach, *Central Intelligence
      Agency and Overhead Reconnaissance*, 72.

99    "Amusingly enough," Bissell later recalled: "Interview with Richard M. Bissell,"
      June 1, 1977.

99    "not evil but mischievous": The descriptions of Bissell's younger years from Bis-
      sell, *Reflections of a Cold Warrior*, 3–9, and Thomas, *Very Best Men*, 92.

100   "marked a man a fuddy-duddy": Stewart Alsop, *Stay of Execution*, 151.

100   "Why bother with the rule": Taubman, *Secret Empire*, 123.

100   "Allen Dulles knew less of what went on": Beschloss, *Mayday*, 90.

101   his temper flared: Thomas, *Very Best Men*, 189.

101   "It's going to be better": Taubman, *Secret Empire*, 125.

101   Edwin Land was spending a lot of time: Brugioni, interview with author.

101   "open twenty-four hours a day": *Antecedents and Early Years, 1952–56*, vol. 1 of
      *National Photographic Interpretation Center*, Directorate of Intelligence Histori-
      cal Series, Dec. 1972 (declassified in 2012).

102   "On these we could easily count": Eisenhower, *Waging Peace*, 600.

102   something he called the Minicard: Details of the Minicard system come from
      Brugioni, *Eyeball to Eyeball*, 125; A. W. Tyler, "American Documentation," *Jour-
      nal of the Association for Information Science and Technology* 8, no. 4 (Oct. 1957):
      243–333; *History of the OSA*, 421; Ernest P. Taubes, "The Future of Microfilm-
      ing," *American Archivist* 21 (April 1958): 153–55.

102   "capable of a level of information manipulation": *History of the OSA*, 421.

103   "make a new science": Ian Menzes, "Itek Is the Wonder Child of Space-Age
      Industries," *Boston Globe*, May 7, 1959, 56.

103   the company's "cryptic name": Richard P. Cooke, "Taking Chances," *Wall Street
      Journal*, July 15, 1959, 1.

103   "My daddy was killed yesterday": "Lad's Show and Tell Quiets Third Graders,"
      *Reno Gazette Journal*, May 21, 1956, 16.

103   "The aircraft disintegrated over a wide area": "Remembering CIA's Heroes:
      Agency Pilots in the U-2 Program," www.cia.gov, posted May 14, 2008.

103   His family got a payout: The pilots' insurance plan and the debate over coverage
      are chronicled in *History of the OSA*, 727–28.

104   "They were particularly concerned": "Subject: Report of Discussions with Pilots,"
      memorandum for Special Assistant to Director for Planning and Coordination,
      March 13, 1956, declassified Jan. 2006.

104   "The pilots' equipment": *History of the OSA*, 731–32.

105   the normal rules of human conduct: Bissell acknowledged that he shared Doo-
      little's feeling during an interview for a television documentary called *The Sci-
      ence of Spying*, which aired in 1965 on NBC.

105   "The Farm" was the nickname: Details of the facility and the training regimen
      come from "Subject: Drivers Survival Training," declassified memorandum,
      Aug. 7, 1956; Ted Gup, "Down on 'the Farm': Learning How to Spy for the CIA,"
      *Washington Post*, Feb. 19, 1980, 1.

106   "Instructions for use": "Subject: Transport, Storage, Issuance, and Operation
      Instructions for Utilization of a Certain Device," declassified memorandum, July
      23, 1956, TS-158358, declassified Sept. 2002.

107 "It should also be mentioned": "Memorandum for Chief of Operations, Subject: Supply of L Tablets on Hand in Project CHALICE," Sept. 8, 1960, CHAL-1178; "Memorandum: Subject: Transport, Storage, Issuance, and Operational Instructions for Utilization of a Certain Device," July 23, 1956.

107 "It would be impossible": Eisenhower, *Waging Peace*, 600.

107 "a *complete* given, a *complete* assumption": Beschloss, *Mayday,* 8.

107 "I'm going to catch hell": Ibid.

108 "The recently released testimony": Joseph Alsop and Stewart Alsop, "Partridge and LeMay," *Washington Post,* June 10, 1956, 2.

108 "We've got to think about": Taubman, *Secret Empire,* 176.

108 "Suffice it to say here": Eisenhower to Richard Leo Simon, April 4, 1956.

109 Bissell and Johnson came up with: Rich and Janos, *Skunk Works,* 155.

109 Barbara Powers was given a typewritten note: Barbara Powers, *Spy Wife,* 23–24.

109 "deeply resentful of the censorship": "Memorandum for the Record: Subject: AQUATONE Contracts," Aug. 22, 1956, declassified through CIA CREST program.

110 "to fight this insidious, mysterious thing": Barbara Powers, *Spy Wife,* 24.

110 "Mrs. Powers was a very cooperative employee": Ibid., 25.

110 on June 20, 1956, a U-2 flew: Details surrounding the first operational U-2 flight, and the dialogue quoted in relation to the event, are taken from Pedlow and Welzenbach, *Central Intelligence Agency and Overhead Reconnaissance,* 117–19; Beschloss, *Mayday,* 121; Bissell, *Reflections of a Cold Warrior,* 111–12.

## CHAPTER 5: IN PLAIN SIGHT

115 "One of the best ways to keep a great secret": From Edwin Land's address to Polaroid employees at Symphony Hall, Boston, Feb. 5, 1960, as quoted in McElheny, *Insisting on the Impossible,* 198.

115 by ten o'clock thousands of people: "Thousands Mark 4th in Outings, Shows Here," *Washington Post,* July 5, 1956, 1.

115 a new, comfortably isolated complex: Many of the details of the construction plans come from "The CIA Campus: The Story of Original Headquarters Building, Searching for a Permanent Home," www.cia.gov, posted May 22, 2008.

115 "Well, Allen," Bissell said: Thomas, *Very Best Men,* 167.

116 The best aerial tracking machine: Pedlow and Welzenbach, *Central Intelligence Agency and Overhead Reconnaissance,* 7.

116 a "wasting asset" or a "melting technology": "AQUATONE/OILSTONE PROJECT," CIA memorandum, May 3, 1957.

116 It was the perfect day: The physical details and quotations from the party come from archival photographs and various printed sources, including Bohlen, *Witness to History,* 15; B. J. Cutler, "Top Reds Toast U.S. at 4th of July Party," *New York Herald Tribune,* July 5, 1956, 1; "Big Soviet Brass Toasts Success of Geneva Talks," *Abilene Reporter-News,* July 5, 1955, 38. Some newspapers at the time reported that Bohlen didn't attend the party, but was represented by his wife; archival photos and firsthand accounts clearly contradict those reports.

118 Soviet radar operators: Sergei Khrushchev, *Nikita Khrushchev and the Creation of a Superpower,* 156–59.

118 "We have to create air defenses": Ibid.

118 About thirty thousand feet: The details of the photo development process come from "Cover Story for Photo Intel," CIA memorandum, Dec. 1, 1955; *Antecedents and Early Years, 1952–56.*

119 There was plenty *not* to like: Brugioni, interview with author.

119 "Where a choice be necessary": Brugioni, *Eyes in the Sky,* 121.

120    Bissell and Dulles stood in front: Rich and Janos, *Skunk Works*, 165; Bissell, *Reflections of a Cold Warrior*.

120    "East German radar picked it up": Bissell, *Reflections of a Cold Warrior*, 112.

120    Frank Wisner, the head of covert intelligence: Dino Brugioni, "The Million-Dollar Photograph," *Studies in Intelligence* 23 (Summer 1979).

121    After a good long look: Brugioni, interview with author; "Interview with Richard M. Bissell," June 1, 1977.

121    Soviet ambassador Georgi Zaroubin: Details of the Soviet complaint come from various sources including Pedlow and Welzenbach, *Central Intelligence Agency and Overhead Reconnaissance*, 121; *History of the OSA*, 834; Dana Adams Schmidt, "Moscow Charges U.S. Air Incursions by Military Craft," *New York Times*, July 11, 1956, 1.

121    "According to precisely verified data": *History of the OSA*, 834.

122    "the invented overflights": Department of State press release No. 398, July 19, 1956.

122    *The New York Times* repeated the U.S. view: Edwin L. Dale, "Soviet Air Charge Is Rejected by U.S.," *New York Times*, July 19, 1956, 1.

123    "Airfields previously unknown": Memorandum for Project Director, "Subject: Suggestions re the Intelligence Value of Aquatone," July 17, 1956, declassified Aug. 2000.

124    The first bottle of scotch: Suhler, *From Rainbow to Gusto*, 12–13.

124    "By noon," Johnson noted in his diary: Ibid.

125    "For the past six weeks": Ibid., 1.

125    Land explained that it was a simple precaution: Ibid., 14.

126    Adana, in southern Turkey, was a bustling city: The descriptions of the city and the base come from numerous sources, including author interviews with individuals stationed at the base in the 1950s, including Charles Sibert and Stanley Beerli; *History of the OSA*, 853–56; Francis Gary Powers, *Operation Overflight*, 43–50.

126    About 130 men accompanied: *History of the OSA*, 853.

126    "delayed completion of facilities": Ibid., 856.

127    "Your wife," Perry explained: Francis Gary Powers, *Operation Overflight*, 42.

127    she called the number: Barbara Powers, *Spy Wife*, 26.

128    a thirty-three-year-old captain: The information about Jackson comes from ibid., xx; "Funeral Services Set Tomorrow for Captain Jackson," *Mexia Daily News*, Feb. 28, 1958, 1; "Plane Crash Victims Identified," *Weirton Daily Times*, Feb. 19, 1958, 6; "Capt. R. B. Jackson Among Lost," *Mexia Daily News*, Feb. 18, 1958, 1.

128    a Boy Scout troop from Nevada: *History of the OSA*, 558.

129    "The compromise of the project's security": Ibid.

129    "You're taking all the fun": Thomas, *Very Best Men*, 168.

129    From a high window above the Ford shop: Brugioni, *Eyes in the Sky*, 163.

130    "augmented by an ancient": *Antecedents and Early Years, 1952–56*.

130    "Rented to the CIA": Ibid.

130    "More difficult to cope with": Ibid., 60.

130    Bissell got on a plane to visit: Ibid., 50; Francis Gary Powers, *Operation Overflight*, 229.

131    He intercepted her before she could flush: Barbara Powers, *Spy Wife*, 37; Francis Gary Powers, *Operation Overflight*, 229.

132    "One of the ways": Joseph Alsop, "Ike's Great Test," *Boston Globe*, Aug. 25, 1956, 12.

133    "There is something rancid": Merry, *Taking on the World*, 306–7.

133    "troubadours of the most aggressive circles": Herken, *Georgetown Set*, 204.

133    "you and your government may well hold": Alsop to Zaroubin, Aug. 8, 1956.

133  "The rest of this long conversation": "Memo to Robert Armory," Nov. 8, 1956, Joseph and Stewart Alsop Papers.

134  "rich, dark strawberry red": Joseph Alsop, "A Party at the Kremlin," *Boston Globe,* Jan. 16, 1957, 1.

134  an enormous fur hat: Several details of Alsop's trip to the U.S.S.R. come from his letter to M. Paul, March 27, 1957, box 129, Alsop Papers, Library of Congress.

134  Alsop found himself seated next to a man: The details of the encounter come from Alsop's recounting of the event in "Subject: Joseph Alsop," memorandum from Allen Dulles to J. Edgar Hoover, April 1, 1957, declassified May 1999.

## CHAPTER 6: ROCKET MEN

137  "You can't put your foot": "Clarence L. Johnson," *Los Angeles Times,* Dec. 22, 1990, 8.

137  Before Joe Alsop arrived: Details in this section are from Alsop's memo, as related in "Subject: Joseph Alsop," memorandum from Dulles to Hoover, April 1, 1957.

139  "JOSEPH ALSOP C/O ASTORIA HOTEL": "Telegram from Davis: PRAVI- TELSTVENNAIA MOSCOU 05/21 33 21 1100Z," Joseph and Stewart Alsop Papers.

140  "I have been an incurable homosexual": "Subject: Joseph Alsop," memorandum from Dulles to Hoover, April 1, 1957.

140  Alsop stayed in Paris: Information about his itinerary and activities after his U.S.S.R. trip comes from Alsop's letters to Bohlen, April 1957, box 129, Joseph and Stewart Alsop Papers.

140  Hoover stated that the information: Yoder, *Joe Alsop's Cold War,* 156.

141  "The Russian trip was an immense success": Letter from Joseph Alsop, March 27, 1957, box 129, Joseph and Stewart Alsop Papers.

141  By early 1957, the U-2 photointerpreters: Brugioni, *Eyes in the Sky,* 227–30; *Antecedents and Early Years, 1952–56.*

141  the Alsop brothers, who had reported: Joseph Alsop and Stewart Alsop, "The Race We Are Losing in Russia," *Saturday Evening Post,* April 28, 1956, 25.

141  "In the long haul, our safety": Gladwin Hill, "America's Survival May Hinge on Attaining Space Superiority, Missiles Chief Asserts," *Atlanta Constitution,* Feb. 20, 1957, 2.

141  "The United States has one leg up": Lloyd Norman, "America's 3,200-Mile Rocket!," *Chicago Tribune,* Jan. 27, 1957, G22.

142  "The Soviets have been cagey": Chalmers M. Roberts, "Outer Space . . . Ike Hints of Reining Missiles," *Washington Post,* Jan. 12, 1957, 7.

142  "still a long way behind": John W. Finney, "Man Could Fly to Moon by 1982," *New York Times,* Feb. 8, 1957, 46.

142  Wernher von Braun, a former Nazi scientist: *National Photographic Interpre- tation Center,* vol. 2, Directorate of Intelligence Historical Series, Dec. 1972 (declassified in 2012), 102–7.

143  "You get all this information": Ibid.

143  "Nobody's to know who you are": Suhler, *From Rainbow to Gusto,* 18.

143  In 1956, the CIA had reported: Burrows, *Deep Black,* 155.

144  classified as *above* top secret: Miller, *Lockheed Martin's Skunk Works,* 109; "A Comparison of US and USSR Capabilities in Space," CIA confidential memoran- dum, Jan. 1, 1960.

144  "produced a veritable bonanza": *Antecedents and Early Years, 1952–56,* 169.

145  *"Ladies and gentlemen, we are bringing to you":* NBC radio clip is excerpted in *The Fever of '57: The Sputnik Movie,* directed by David Hoffman, MVD Enter- tainment Group, 2012.

145    comparing it to the discovery of America: Dickson, *Sputnik: The Shock of the Century,* 117.
145    "The Russians can now build": Hardesty and Eisman, *Epic Rivalry,* 76.
145    "The Russians are now on their own": Ibid.
146    "Why doesn't somebody go out there": Burrows, *This New Ocean,* 205.
146    "Let's quit acting as if nothing has happened": The quotation is taken from "Sputnik-2 Panic and Paranoia in 1957," a compilation of television video news clips posted on the YouTube site of the Dan Beaumont Space Museum, Nov. 23, 2011.
146    Rabi introduced Edwin Land: "Memorandum of Conference with the President," Oct. 15, 1957, DDE diary, staff notes, box 27, Eisenhower Presidential Library.
146    "He said that the country": Ibid.
147    "By the end of the afternoon": McElheny, *Insisting on the Impossible,* 326.
147    his desktop reverted to its natural state: Thomas Powers, *Man Who Kept Secrets,* 5.
148    he delivered a presentation: "The Stimulation of Innovation," Nov. 15, 1957, report prepared by Richard Bissell and declassified by the CIA in 2004.
148    "it was quite clear": "Diary Notes," Dec. 20, 1957, declassified by the CIA in 2003.
148    "You just can't do away": Beschloss, *Mayday,* 144.
148    Powers's contract was set to expire: Francis Gary Powers, *Operation Overflight,* 45.
148    Bissell came up with an idea: *History of the OSA,* 869.
149    "We could at least give it one more try": Francis Gary Powers, *Operation Overflight,* 46.

CHAPTER 7: TO THE SUN

150    "In this age, in this country": Land, "Generation of Greatness."
150    "We offered them such high rent": Barbara Powers, *Spy Wife,* 55.
150    New buildings were springing up: Details of Adana base come from Charles Sibert, interview with author; Francis Gary Powers, *Operation Overflight,* 64.
151    "Its wings actually do flap": Barbara Powers, *Spy Wife,* 60.
151    Johnson's crew added the device: "Memorandum for the Director, Subject: Emergency Equipment for Pilots," Nov. 8, 1956, declassified through CIA CREST program, Sept. 2001.
151    But the designers hadn't realized: Francis Gary Powers, *Operation Overflight,* 44, 62.
152    they could afford to throw: Barbara Powers, *Spy Wife,* 60–66; Francis Gary Powers, *Operation Overflight,* 46.
152    "I'm afraid I've got to publish it": Beschloss, *Mayday,* 234.
153    "The aircraft has no announced military application": "Planes Worth Modeling—Lockheed U-2," *Model Airplane News,* March 1958, 34.
153    "It is time to say quite bluntly": Joseph Alsop, "Untruths on Defense," *Washington Post,* Aug. 1, 1958, 19.
154    "We had the dope": Beschloss, *Mayday,* 154.
154    "We're fed up": Dialogue from Merry, *Taking on the World,* 363.
154    "A prominent American journalist": Herken, *Georgetown Set,* 243.
155    "The munitions makers": Taubman, *Secret Empire,* 278.
155    "God help the nation": Beschloss, *Mayday,* 153.
155    "making science as popular as baseball": Seaborg, *Chemist in the White House,* 22.
156    "every king and princeling": Kistiakowsky, *Scientist at the White House,* 151.
156    "The President and Mrs. Eisenhower hope": Foerstner, *James Van Allen,* 161.
157    The *Washington Post* ran an article: Marie Smith, "At White House Dinner, Outranked Scientists Outnumber Military," *Washington Post,* Feb. 5, 1958, 3.
157    Bissell kept an "R.B.A.F." coffee mug: Beschloss, *Mayday,* 147.

157  a nickname drenched in jealousy: Ibid., 155.
157  These were long, hard days: Ann H. Bissell and Richard Bissell III, interviews with author.
158  "We do not think that Castro": "Ex-CIA Head Said Castro Was No Communist," *Boston Globe,* March 28, 1982, 4.
158  "the overthrow of Castro": "Memorandum for Director of Central Intelligence, Subject: Cuban Problems," Dec. 11, 1959, declassified by CIA in Dec. 2006.
159  "Everybody else has been nice to him": Numerous details and dialogue from Khrushchev's visit come from archival footage shown in "Cold War Roadshow," a film produced by PBS's *American Experience,* aired Nov. 18, 2014, and also Carlson, *K Blows Top.*
160  Khrushchev's son, Sergei, asked his father: Sergei Khrushchev, interview with author.
160  "My military leaders come to me": Dialogue from Nikita Khrushchev, *Reformer,* 517.
161  "The clouds of war": Beschloss, *Mayday,* 223.
161  the *Sea Witch,* a fifty-seven-foot yawl: The descriptions of the *Sea Witch* and Bissell's relationship with it come from a variety of sources, including Richard Bissell III, interview with author; Wyden, *Bay of Pigs.*
161  "My friends . . . question my commitment": Bissell, *Reflections of a Cold Warrior,* 88.
162  "Goddammit," he said: Wyden, *Bay of Pigs,* 11.
162  Ian Fleming arrived in Washington: Pearson, *Life of Ian Fleming,* 296; John Cork, "The President's Bond Girl," Nov. 2, 2016, www.ianfleming.com.
162  Jackie, in fact, had gotten Allen Dulles hooked: "Memo to Mrs. John F. Kennedy from Allen Dulles," Nov. 17, 1959, declassified by the CIA in 2003.
163  "We talked of new tools": Allen Dulles, "Our Spy-Boss Who Loved Bond," *Life,* Aug. 28, 1964, 19.
163  "Ridicule, chiefly," Fleming replied: Pearson, *Life of Ian Fleming,* 296.
163  compiled some ideas for bold schemes: Grose, *Gentleman Spy,* 495.
163  "discrediting Castro personally": "Report on Plots to Assassinate Fidel Castro," May 23, 1967, released in sanitized form by the CIA in 1997.
164  "[Name redacted] recalls a scheme": Ibid.
164  "No operation is to be carried out": Taubman, *Secret Empire,* 303.
165  a flying maneuver called "zoom climbs": Pedlow and Welzenbach, *Central Intelligence Agency and Overhead Reconnaissance,* 162.
165  The new jet generated: Ibid.
166  On the morning of April 27: Francis Gary Powers, *Operation Overflight,* 76–79; additional details of the flight preparations and flight come from "Debriefing of Francis Gary Powers," Feb. 13, 1962, tapes 1–16, declassified in 2003.
166  he inhaled pure oxygen: Francis Gary Powers, *Operation Overflight,* 53.
167  At 5:20 a.m., about forty minutes: *History of the OSA,* 891; Pedlow and Welzenbach, *Central Intelligence Agency and Overhead Reconnaissance,* 176.

CHAPTER 8: FALLEN ANGEL

173  "It was like a poker game": Francis Gary Powers, *Operation Overflight,* 93.
173  telephone next to Nikita Khrushchev's bed: The details from the Soviet perspective on May 1 come from Sergei Khrushchev, interview with author; Sergei Khrushchev, *Nikita Khrushchev and the Creation of a Superpower,* 370–80; "Description of 1960 Shoot-Down of Powers' U-2," 90UMO530A Moscow, KRASNAYA AVEZDA, April 27, 1990, 90–93.
174  "They flew over again": Dialogue from Sergei Khrushchev, *Nikita Khrushchev and the Creation of a Superpower,* 369.

175    "The target has discharged chaff": Ibid., 374.

175    Powers had peered down: Descriptions of the flight are from Francis Gary Powers, *Operation Overflight*, 58–70; "Debriefing of Francis Gary Powers."

177    "Radar operators report that the target": Sergei Khrushchev, *Nikita Khrushchev and the Creation of a Superpower*, 374.

177    As Safronov and other pilots: "Description of 1960 Shoot-Down of Powers' U-2," 90–93.

179    "What do you mean": Sergei Khrushchev, *Nikita Khrushchev and the Creation of a Superpower*, 377.

179    Safronov, they decided, crashed: "Description of 1960 Shoot-Down of Powers' U-2," 90–93.

181    "Are you an American?": All descriptions and dialogue come from Francis Gary Powers, *Operation Overflight*, 70–73; "Debriefing of Francis Gary Powers."

182    "Why was this flight": Francis Gary Powers, *Operation Overflight*, 78.

183    "Bill Bailey didn't come home": Whittell, *Bridge of Spies*, 179.

183    "It's a goddamn national emergency!": Ibid.

183    "I don't know whether": Ibid.

184    Amelia Earhart's technical adviser: Johnson, *Kelly*, 42.

185    "That's that," he told a small group: Rich and Janos, *Skunk Works*, 160.

185    the National Security Agency manned: Aid, *Secret Sentry*, 53–55.

185    NSA operators monitored this electronic chatter: Michael L. Peterson, "Maybe You Had to Be There: The SIGINT on Thirteen Soviet Shootdowns of U.S. Reconnaissance Aircraft," article that originally appeared in the NSA's *Cryptologic Quarterly*, declassified Nov. 2009.

186    "One of our reconnaissance planes": Beschloss, *Mayday*, 34.

186    "A NASA U-2 research airplane": "Statements by National Aeronautics and Space Administration, May 3," *Department of State Bulletin*, May 23, 1960, 817.

187    It was five o'clock in the morning: Barbara Powers, *Spy Wife*, 67.

187    "I just can't leave him here": Ibid.

189    "Probably in the club": "Debriefing of Francis Gary Powers."

189    May 5 got off to an odd start: Beschloss, *Mayday*, 42–55.

190    Thompson made his way: Details drawn from "Telegram 2715," May 5, 1960, transmitted by Thompson, Department of State, Central Files, 716.5411/5-560.

191    "The pilot hit the silk": Ibid.

191    "About one hour after takeoff": "NASA Statement of May 5," *Department of State Bulletin*, May 23, 1960, 817.

192    "to prevent the building up": Beschloss, *Mayday*, 57.

192    "These Congressional fellows": Ibid.

192    "There was absolutely no": "Transcript of Press and Radio News Briefing, Thursday, May 5, 1960," DPC-104, released by CIA CREST program on May 13, 2004.

193    "From all appearances he was an impetuous": "Khrushchev—a Personality Sketch," OCI No. 2391/61, document declassified by CIA in Dec. 2006.

194    "Comrades," he said, "I must let you in": Beschloss, *Mayday*, 58–59.

194    "We did this quite deliberately": Ibid.

195    "I believe he was really offended": Ibid.

195    "I'd like to resign": ACW Diary Series, box 11, Eisenhower Presidential Library.

196    "We will now just have to endure the storm": Grose, *Gentleman Spy*, 487.

## CHAPTER 9: SECRETS AND LIES

197    "Look, Senator, this is modern-day espionage": Beschloss, *Mayday*, 309.

197    "I've already had *that* kind of medicine": Barbara Powers, *Spy Wife*, 77.

197    A Lockheed public relations man: "U-2 Pilot's Wife Denies He Spied," *New York Times*, May 11, 1960, 3.

197  Wearing a black dress: "Mrs. Powers Can't Believe He's a Spy," *New York Herald Tribune*, May 11, 1960, 1.

198  "There is, truly, no relationship": Advertisement for *Ladies' Home Journal, New York Times*, May 10, 1960.

198  "He's making flights": Barbara Powers, *Spy Wife*, 57.

199  "How did you break your leg": Ibid., 78.

199  "Newsmen discovered, to their horror": Beschloss, *Mayday*, 231–34.

199  "Moral Leadership of U.S. Harmed": "Moral Leadership of U.S. Harmed," *San Francisco Chronicle*, May 8, 1960, 1.

199  "For the general public": "Spy Plane Incident and Disarmament," *New York Herald Tribune*, May 12, 1960, 2.

200  "distasteful and disagreeable": Brugioni, *Eyes in the Sky*, 352.

200  "We have been turned up": Beschloss, *Mayday*, 307.

201  "My dearest Barbara": Barbara Powers, *Spy Wife*, 85; "Letter from Powers to Barbara Powers," May 26, 1960, Eisenhower Presidential Library.

202  Barbara spotted the Milledgeville mailman: Barbara Powers, *Spy Wife*, 84.

203  "The most important deduction": *History of the OSA*, 1016.

204  The same thing had happened: Johnson, *Kelly*, 45.

205  Johnson gamely cooperated: Ibid., xx.

205  "After spending the best part": Miles Marvin, "U-2 Designer Retains Faith in Value of Plane," *Los Angeles Times*, May 11, 1960, 1.

205  "I do not believe they shot down the U-2": Ibid.

205  "This is more like it": "New Picture of U-2 Seen as Authentic," *Los Angeles Times*, May 12, 1960, 2.

206  "welter of official lies": "Lockheed U-2 over Sverdlovsk: A Study in Fabrication," *Aviation Week*, May 16, 1960, 12.

206  "Powers apparently knew his bosses' habits": "Spy Thought Jet Failed," *Chicago Tribune*, May 11, 1960, 9.

206  He considered Powers's downing a tragedy: "Debriefing of Francis Gary Powers."

207  "By that time they will have had": "Statement for the Senate Foreign Relations Committee," May 31, 1960, Eisenhower Presidential Library.

207  "nothing short of remarkable": Taubman, *Secret Empire*, 314.

207  He asked Dr. Sidney Gottlieb: Details from "Report on Plots to Assassinate Fidel Castro," May 23, 1967, released in sanitized form by the CIA in 1997.

208  "had assets that may assist": "Memorandum for Executive Secretary, CIA Management Committee, Subject: Family Jewels," May 16, 1973, declassified 2007.

208  "It was to be made clear": Ibid.

209  "for the removal of key Trujillo people": Theoharis, *Central Intelligence Agency*, 170–71.

209  how to deal with Patrice Lumumba: Bissell, *Reflections of a Cold Warrior*, 143–44.

209  "Embassy and station believe Congo": Madeleine Kalb, "The CIA and Lumumba," *New York Times Magazine*, Aug. 2, 1981, 7.

209  "In high quarters here": "Telegram from the Central Intelligence Agency to the Station in the Congo," Central Intelligence Agency Files, Job 79–00149A, DDO/IMS Files, box 23, folder 1, African Division, Senate Select Committee, vol. 2.

209  "Does this authorize assassination": Bissell, *Reflections of a Cold Warrior*, 144.

209  Gottlieb came up with several: Kalb, "CIA and Lumumba," 7.

210  "soldier of fortune": *Congressional Series of United States Public Documents* (Washington, D.C.: U.S. Government Printing Office, 1975), 259.

210  "He is indeed aware": Ibid.

210  Land removed the mortarboard cap: The details from the MIT commencement come from author interviews with MIT Class of 1960 members Norman

Vadner, Jorge Rodriguez, John Beckett, Alan Shalleck, Albert Tobin, Tony Phillips, Robert Stengel, Richard Dattner, Larry Alley, Tom Thiele, Dan Mitchell, David Svahn, and David Klahr; "The Commencement Address," *MIT Technology Review,* July 1960, 30–34; Francis Burns, "U-2 Spying Should Continue, Dr. Killian Tells MIT Grads," *Boston Globe,* June 11, 1960, 3.

211   "Our techniques for influencing": "Commencement Address," 32.

212   "I WANT TO KNOW": Beschloss, *Mayday,* 253.

212   "I understand Mr. Khrushchev": "Pilot's Father Appeals to Khrushchev," Associated Press, May 9, 1960.

212   "I would like to go see my boy": "Spy Pilot's Father Seeks to Die for Son," *Los Angeles Times,* May 17, 1960, 11.

212   Oliver Powers learned that a man: For more about the negotiations concerning Abel, see Giles Whittell, *Bridge of Spies: A True Story of the Cold War* (New York: Broadway Books, 2010).

## CHAPTER 10: THE VERDICT

214   "If they hear him tell his story": Carl Mydans, "For the Prisoner's Family: Ordeal in a Strange Land," *Life,* Aug. 29, 1960, 17.

214   "If it appeared to the world": Francis Gary Powers, *Operation Overflight,* 125.

215   the CIA was secretly footing the bill: *History of the OSA,* 1021–30.

216   correspondent from CBS Radio: Beschloss, *Mayday,* 329; "Correspondent Sam Jaffe and the Web of Uncertainty That Entangled Him," *Baltimore Sun,* Feb. 17, 1985, 2L.

216   "Sam is one helluva guy": Barbara Powers, *Spy Wife,* 98.

216   "Barbara's lawyers said their party": "TELEGRAM from Moscow to Secretary of State," No. 393, Aug. 14, 1960, 4:58 p.m.

216   "Oliver Powers stormed in with tirade": Ibid.

217   "almost every night in the company": "Memorandum to Director, FBI, from SAC, New York, Subject: Francis G. Powers Espionage Trial, Miscellaneous Information Concerning," NY 105-42639, Oct. 10, 1960.

217   "Could I ask you this question?": "Debriefing of Francis Gary Powers."

218   "Call a cab": Barbara Powers, *Spy Wife,* 97.

219   "There she told the informant": Beschloss, *Mayday,* 331.

219   About twenty-two hundred people: Details from Francis Gary Powers, *Operation Overflight,* 124–30; "U-2 Pilot's Trial Opens in Moscow," *New York Times,* Aug. 17, 1960, 1.

221   "I realize that I have committed": Quotations in this section from Francis Gary Powers, *Operation Overflight,* 128–29.

221   the country successfully launched: Walter Sullivan, "Russians Orbit a Satellite Carrying 2 Dogs and TV," *New York Times,* Aug. 19, 1960, 1.

221   they had tried thirteen times: Details on tests are from Kevin C. Ruffner, ed., *Corona: America's First Satellite Program* (CIA History Staff, Center for the Study of Intelligence, 1995); Albert D. Wheelon, "Lifting the Veil on Corona," *Space Policy* 11, no. 4 (1995): 249–60; "Interview with Lt. Col. Harold E. Mitchell," Los Angeles Air Force Base SMC/HO Oral History Program; Taubman, *Secret Empire,* 295.

222   "a most heartbreaking business": Bissell, *Reflections of a Cold Warrior,* 139.

223   "Good hit, Captain!": Mitchell interview.

224   "Here's your pictures": McElheny, *Insisting on the Impossible,* 336–37.

224   It was strangely awkward: Francis Gary Powers, *Operation Overflight,* 178.

225   "There's an American here": Ibid., 163; "Debriefing of Francis Gary Powers."

226   Hallinan talked for almost forty-five minutes: Hallinan's visit was also reported

in "TELEGRAM 527 from Moscow to Secretary of State," Aug. 24, 1960, 2:39
p.m., C-15417, declassified March 1998.
226    "They bring up some good points": Ibid.
227    "No sensible American": Joseph Alsop, "On Folk Dancing," *New York Herald
Tribune,* May 25, 1960, 18.
227    "America's present leadership": Joseph Alsop, "World Peril Mounts; U.S. Must Be
Strong," *Boston Globe,* May 20, 1960, 11.
227    "I am not sure that the president": Marvin Miles, "Kennedy Displays Confidence
Here," *Los Angeles Times,* June 1, 1960, B1.
227    "The most voluptuous daydream": Jacqueline Kennedy to Joseph Alsop, box 130
(General Correspondence 1958–68), Joseph and Stewart Alsop Papers.
228    "You said, 'It's the only game' ": Ibid.
228    "Well," Bobby said, "what about the new face": "Oral History," box 268 (Oral History Interviews), Joseph and Stewart Alsop Papers.
229    "far less inhibited": Bissell, *Reflections of a Cold Warrior,* 159–60.
229    "I also told him truthfully": Ibid., 160.
229    "Boys," the president said: Ambrose, *Ike's Spies,* 311.
229    "Would you like to see your wife again?": Francis Gary Powers, *Operation Overflight,* 163.
230    Barbara was led into another room: Some details of the visit from "TELEGRAM
from Moscow to Secretary of State," C-16349, Aug. 25, 1960, 2:57 p.m.
230    "We must insist, however": Barbara Powers, *Spy Wife,* 112.
230    smelled "like a billy goat": Ibid., 113.
231    "I was told that Barbara": Francis Gary Powers, *Operation Overflight,* 164.

CHAPTER 11: NEW FRONTIERS

232    "There just do come moments": *Science of Spying.*
232    At 1806 I Street in Washington: Descriptions of the Alibi Club are taken from
the author's personal observations inside the club, as well as conversations with
members. Additional details are from the club's National Register of Historic
Places registration form 10-900, Sept. 20, 1994; Marjorie Hunter, "A Historic
Excuse for a Club," *New York Times,* Jan. 9, 1985, 20.
233    In February 1961, Dulles reserved: Wyden, *Bay of Pigs,* 94–95.
233    on November 18, Bissell and Dulles flew to Florida: Bissell, *Reflections of a Cold
Warrior,* 162; Wyden, *Bay of Pigs,* 68; Rasenberger, *Brilliant Disaster,* 100.
234    "I hear you're trying to get": Wyden, *Bay of Pigs,* 96.
234    "I think I probably ought to retire": Rasenberger, *Brilliant Disaster,* 99.
235    "One could argue that Kennedy": Leonard Klady, "007: Bonding Fact and Fiction," *Los Angeles Times,* July 26, 1987, K3.
235    "I'm your man-eating shark": Wyden, *Bay of Pigs,* 95.
235    Powers was transferred: Francis Gary Powers, *Operation Overflight,* 167–68.
235    "Should we be alarmed": Ibid., 214.
235    "I wonder what in the world": Ibid.
236    "tower of jelly": Ibid.
236    "one of the great espionage fiascoes": Ian Fleming, "Gary Powers and the Big Lie,"
*Sunday Times,* March 11, 1962, 4.
236    "I hope he would have taken his pill": "The Powers Case," broadcast on CBS TV,
March 9, 1962, produced by CBS News Special Program Unit, Studio 42, New
York.
236    the figure of James Jesus Angleton: Biographical details of Angleton are drawn
from Mangold, *Cold Warrior;* Holzman, *James Jesus Angleton, the CIA, and the
Craft of Counterintelligence;* Macintyre, *Spy Among Friends.*

237    "Jim spoke in brilliant woven threads": Mangold, *Cold Warrior,* 34.

238    "Operationally speaking, the trade": "Memo to DCI from James Angleton, Chief, Counter Intelligence Staff, Subject: Exchange of Rudolf Abel for Powers," June 30, 1961, included in *History of the OSA.*

238    The story of how he came up: McElheny, *Insisting on the Impossible,* 163.

238    "Within an hour, the camera": Ibid.

239    "There are occasions when": Ibid., 216.

239    "If you dream of something": Edwin Land, "Addiction as a Necessity and Opportunity," *Science* 171, no. 3967 (1971): 151–53.

240    "My work is my life": *Biographical Memoirs* (Washington, D.C.: National Academies Press, 1999), 77:198.

240    He questioned Bissell's commitment: Absher, Desch, and Popadiuk, *Privileged and Confidential,* 53–55.

240    he'd put Bach's Mass in B Minor: Ann H. Bissell, interview with author; Thomas, *Very Best Men,* 267.

241    "It is expected that these operations": Rasenberger, *Brilliant Disaster,* 106.

241    "a fair chance of ultimate success": Ibid.

242    "If we admit involvement": Ibid., 164.

242    "Its members will be angry": Ibid., 130.

242    "Too spectacular," he said: Ibid., 138.

243    "I was shocked": Bissell, *Reflections of a Cold Warrior,* 175.

243    "My observations of the last few days": Rasenberger, *Brilliant Disaster,* 184.

244    "As far as I know": Bissell, *Reflections of a Cold Warrior,* 183.

244    He began taking different routes: Johnson, *Kelly,* 128.

244    On April 18, 1961, Johnson flew to Washington: Robarge, *Archangel;* "Memorandum for the Record, Subject: Oxcart," April 4, 1961, declassified Oct. 2006.

244    Annie and Johnson dined together: Clarence L. Johnson to Richard M. Bissell Jr., April 21, 1961, Correspondence Series, Bissell Papers.

245    "Goddamn it, this is criminal negligence": Bissell, *Reflections of a Cold Warrior,* 185.

245    "We are under attack": Rasenberger, *Brilliant Disaster,* 273.

245    "Burke, I don't want the United States": Ibid., 282.

246    "Both Land and Killian looked upon": Donald E. Welzenbach, "50 Years of the CIA's DS&T: Origins of a Directorate," *Studies in Intelligence* 56, no. 3 (Sept. 2012): 74.

246    "on an urgent basis": Absher, Desch, and Popadiuk, *Privileged and Confidential,* 55.

246    "It is regarded as virtually certain": "Killian Unit Maps Revision of C.I.A.," *New York Times,* July 2, 1961, 9.

247    grabbed his morning newspaper: Johnson to Bissell, April 21, 1961.

247    "I want to drop you a line": Ibid.

247    "even worse than the first week of May 1960": Richard M. Bissell Jr. to Clarence L. Johnson, April 25, 1960, Correspondence Series, Bissell Papers.

248    He put an opera on the turntable: Thomas, *Very Best Men,* 267.

## CHAPTER 12: TRADE-OFFS

249    "I've never been certain": Kubrick's quotation is from his acceptance speech upon receiving the D. W. Griffith Award from the Directors Guild of America, as cited in: James Naremore, *An Invention Without a Future: Essays on Cinema* (Berkeley and Los Angeles: University of California Press, 2014), 214.

251    "With the Bay of Pigs disaster": Francis Gary Powers, *Operation Overflight,* 284.

251    Barbara got a job at a restaurant: Barbara Powers, *Spy Wife,* 121. Some details

from "Charlie Arthur Deason, Aug. 1, 1942–Oct. 4, 2012," obituary from Williams Funeral Home & Crematory, Milledgeville, Ga.

251 "to keep her out of the public eye": *History of the OSA*, 1030.

252 "Barbara, I'm going to ask you": Barbara Powers, *Spy Wife*, 125–27.

252 "We do find Barbara M. Powers": Ibid.

252 "The psychiatrist in charge at the Clinic": *History of the OSA*, 1031.

253 "I gathered from our talk": Donovan, *Strangers on a Bridge*, 369.

253 "I am sure I will never stay": Francis Gary Powers, *Operation Overflight*, 167.

254 "I am afraid I will never be a Kennedy supporter": Ibid., 220.

254 "Before I was captured": Ibid.

254 "I am very upset": Ibid.

254 "I know it is stupid": Ibid., 223.

255 "It is not always easy": "Remarks upon Presenting an Award to Allen W. Dulles," Nov. 28, 1961, American Presidency Project, www.presidency.ucsb.edu.

255 they proposed a new role for him: Robert S. Allen, "CIA Post Poses Tough Problems for President," *Los Angeles Times*, Sept. 26, 1961, B4.

255 "he had recently been chewed out": "Testimony of Richard Bissell," Church Committee Boxed Files, NARA Record 157-10011-10017.

256 "I have a horror of hanging on here to a job": Thomas, *Very Best Men*, 272.

256 "What are you people doing": Richelson, *Wizards of Langley*, 38.

257 "Our friends at the CI Staff": "An Interview with Former DDCI John N. McMahon," *Studies in Intelligence*, Feb. 8, 2007, declassified June 2010.

258 "I must admit I am becoming": Francis Gary Powers, *Operation Overflight*, 222.

258 "How would you like to go to Moscow": Ibid.

259 "Gee, it's good to see you": Ibid., 237.

259 "You know," he said, "a couple weeks ago": Ibid., 239.

## CHAPTER 13: TOGETHER AND APART

260 "The tenacity with which human": Francis Gary Powers, *Operation Overflight*, 368.

260 Someone from the CIA called Barbara: Details of Barbara's reactions and reunion from *History of the OSA*, 676; Barbara Powers, *Spy Wife*, 128–30.

260 "was just getting over an attack of influenza": "U-2 Pilot's Parents Leave for Reunion," *Chicago Tribune*, Feb. 11, 1962, 2.

260 At a private hangar: "Mrs. Powers' Flight Cloak-and-Dagger Saga: Tight-Lipped Guards Brush Off Newsmen, Take U-2 Pilot's Wife to Secret Destination," *Los Angeles Times*, Feb. 12, 1962, 2; William Anderson, "Powers Arrives Back in U.S. and Rendezvous with Family," *Chicago Tribune*, Feb. 12, 1962, 2; Larry Rue, "Powers Free: Flies Home: Return of U-2 Pilot Cloaked in Secrecy," *Chicago Tribune*, Feb. 11, 1962, 1.

261 It was a sprawling Georgian mansion: Ann Hughey, "The House That Hid the CIA's Secrets," *Wall Street Journal*, Aug. 26, 1981, B1; Francis Gary Powers, *Operation Overflight*, 235–40; Barbara Powers, *Spy Wife*, 136.

262 "Tell me something": Francis Gary Powers, *Operation Overflight*, 247.

262 "Some reporter's on to our location": Ibid., 248.

262 The former owners of Ashford Farm: "Confirm Powers on Shore," *Frederick (Md.) News*, Feb. 14, 1962, 1.

262 "This is government property": Ibid.

262 The drive had been slow going: "Snow, Sleet Strike State," *Gettysburg Times*, Feb. 14, 1962, 11; Francis Gary Powers, *Operation Overflight*, 250.

262 a helicopter settled down: Dialogue and descriptions of the interview sessions from "Debriefing of Francis Gary Powers."

263    "Kelly and I came up today": Ibid.

265    When he returned to Barbara: Francis Gary Powers, *Operation Overflight*, 250–53.

265    going-away party for Allen Dulles: "Diary Notes, DD/S," CIA-RDP76, Oct. 24, 1961, declassified Aug. 2000.

265    John McCone, Dulles's successor, opened up his home: David Robarge, *CIA History: John McCone as Director of Central Intelligence, 1961–65*, monograph produced by CIA, Washington, D.C., declassified April 2015. Some sources have reported that Bissell's farewell party was held at the Alibi Club, but the monograph and other CIA memos contradict this.

265    McCone confided to a *New York Times* reporter: Ibid.

266    "The Agency's loss will be great": Ibid.

266    "with almost no social graces": Kenneth Williams, ed., *LeMay on Vietnam* (Washington, D.C.: Air Force History and Museums Program, 2017).

266    "I never believed in that": Ibid.

266    "often inspecting his well-manicured": Thomas Powers, *Man Who Kept Secrets*, 103.

267    "particularly gracious toast": Thomas, *Very Best Men*, 272.

267    "complied with his obligations": "Report of Board of Inquiry," Feb. 27, 1962, sanitized copy declassified March 1978.

267    "Do you have any funds": Francis Gary Powers, *Operation Overflight*, 280.

267    "In the course of presentation": "Report of Board of Inquiry," Feb. 27, 1962.

268    "Nothing but a whitewash": Warren Rogers Jr., "Public Image of Powers Comes Full Circle," *Tennessean* (Nashville), March 9, 1962, 18; "Powers Case Is Criticized," *Baltimore Sun*, March 8, 1962, 1; Warren Rogers Jr., "When a 'Goat' Becomes a Hero—a Lonely Cry of Whitewash," *New York Herald Tribune*, March 8, 1962, 4.

268    "I have strong views": Fleming, "Gary Powers and the Big Lie," 4.

268    "What is behind the apparent discrepancy": "Powers Case."

269    The press caught up with Frank: "Virginia Hill Country Residents Warmly Welcome Powers Home," *St. Louis Post-Dispatch*, March 12, 1962, 2.

269    "A lot of people were saying": "Powers Goes Home to Virginia Hills," Associated Press, March 13, 1962.

269    a party for him at a crab shack: Walter Wingo, "Powers Is Just Another U.S. Worker Here Now," *Washington Daily News*, April 1, 1962, 1.

270    "That dance just doesn't feel right": Ibid.

270    "I've been ducking them for *two years!*": Barbara Powers, *Spy Wife*, 153.

270    Frank found her unconscious: "Mrs. Powers' Condition Now Reported Good," *Washington Star*, April 21, 1962, 2; "Pills Fell Wife of U-2 Pilot," *New York Mirror*, April 21, 1962, 4; "Police Plan Talks with Mrs. Powers," *Washington Star*, April 22, 1962, 3; Robert Young, "Wife of U-2 Spy Pilot Victim in Drug Mystery," *Chicago Tribune*, April 21, 1962, 1.

270    "denied reports that the couple": Milton Viorst, "CIA Hushes Facts on U-2 Pilot's Wife," *New York Post*, April 23, 1962, 3.

271    Edwin Land wasn't fond: Kistiakowsky, *Scientist at the White House*, 21.

271    "to create fear in the minds": Chalmers Roberts, "McCone Selection Criticized by Some," *Washington Post*, Oct. 23, 1961, 10.

272    "Given the damaging nature": Naftali, *John F. Kennedy*, 191.

272    Operation Mockingbird: "Memorandum for Executive Secretary, CIA Management Committee, Subject: Family Jewels."

273    making the images three times sharper: Bruce Berkowitz, *The National Reconnaissance Office at 50 Years: A Brief History*, monograph produced for the Center for the Study of National Reconnaissance, Chantilly, Va., Sept. 2011.

273 Johnson floated an idea: Miller, *Lockheed Martin's Skunk Works*, 135–37.
274 "The drone is developing": Robarge, *Archangel*; Graham, *Complete Book of the SR-71 Blackbird*, 42.
274 "I will gladly contribute": Johnson, *Kelly*, 129.


## CHAPTER 14: ENDGAME

276 "Optimism is a moral duty": Fierstein, *Triumph of Genius*, 8.
276 Richard Heyser took off in a U-2: Details of the flight and operation are from Sherman Kent, "The Cuban Missile Crisis of 1962," *Studies in Intelligence* (Spring 1972), declassified March 2007.
277 The eight cans of film: Brugioni, *Eyeball to Eyeball*, 216, 223.
277 "That sure looks like it": This and subsequent dialogue among photointerpreters come from ibid., 220–28.
278 "Oh shit!" he said. "Shit! Shit!": Thomas, *Robert Kennedy*, 209.
279 "Daddy, daddy," she said: Dobbs, *One Minute to Midnight*, 3.
279 Joe Alsop busied himself: Joseph Alsop, *I've Seen the Best of It*, 447–49.
280 a headline on the front page: Tom Wicker, "Eisenhower Calls President Weak on Foreign Policy," *New York Times*, Oct. 16, 1962, 1.
281 "turned the color of an uncooked biscuit": Joseph Alsop, *I've Seen the Best of It*, 449.
281 "my least favorite human being": Robert Dallek, "JFK vs. the Military," *JFK in His Time and Ours*, a special issue of the *Atlantic Monthly*, Aug. 2013.
281 "LeMay's view was very simple": Talbot, *Brothers*, 78.
282 "Let's see," he said: Dobbs, *One Minute to Midnight*, 21.
282 "If we don't do anything": Ibid.
283 A U-2 piloted by: Kent, "Cuban Missile Crisis of 1962."
283 "A U-2 was shot down": Dialogue from Thomas, *Robert Kennedy*, 227.
284 "the most dangerous moment": Schlesinger made the judgment in his preface to a 1999 reissue of Kennedy, *Thirteen Days*.
284 But at 5:30 p.m., the sound of footsteps: Robert A. Poteete, "New York City— Under the Bomb," *New York Herald Tribune*, Oct. 25, 1962, 1; Tom Wolfe, "6,000 Pacifists March Through Midtown—and Anti-Castro Fists Fly," *New York Herald Tribune*, Oct. 29, 1962, 10; Tom Wolfe, "How Activation Came to AF Reserve," *New York Herald Tribune*, Oct. 30, 1962, 10; George E. Sokolsky, "These Days Always Cuba," *Washington Post*, Oct. 15, 1962, 13.
285 "Not everyone can come up": Barrett McGurn, "Police Plea—All Able Men for CD Work," *New York Herald Tribune*, Oct. 26, 1962, 19.
285 In the underground lair at High Point: Dobbs, *One Minute to Midnight*, 317.
286 "Moscow Domestic Service": Kent, "Cuban Missile Crisis of 1962."
286 "We consider that you acted": Dobbs, *One Minute to Midnight*, 326.
286 "It's the greatest defeat": Ibid., 335.
286 "I feel like a new man now": Ibid., 334.
287 "The magnitude of their contribution": Kennedy to John McCone, Jan. 9, 1963, as quoted in "Artifacts Commemorate CIA's Role in Cuban Missile Crisis," www .cia.gov.
287 "One of the most important consequences": Brugioni, *Eyeball to Eyeball*, 566.
287 "They each said it fully justified": Helms, *Look over My Shoulder*, 216.


## EPILOGUE: LANDINGS

289 "I never had any thought": Harry S. Truman, "CIA Trickery Perils U.S., Warns Truman," *Boston Globe*, Dec. 22, 1963, 1.
289 the U.S. Senate's Church Committee: See *Hearings Before the Select Committee*

to *Study Governmental Operations with Respect to Intelligence Activities, United States Senate, Ninety-Fourth Congress, First Session,* vol. 7 (Washington, D.C.: U.S. Government Printing Office, 1976).

289   "If this government ever": Statement by Frank Church on *Meet the Press,* Aug. 1975, www.NBCUniversalArchives.com.

290   the U-2 would finally be retired: Pamela Hess, "Pentagon to Retire U-2 Spy Plane," UPI, Jan. 4, 2006.

290   in side-by-side comparisons: Christopher Drew, "U-2 Spy Plane Evades Retirement," *New York Times,* March 21, 2010, B1.

290   "We plan to keep the platform": "Air Force Kills Retirement Date for U-2 Spy Plane," *DOD Buzz Online Defense and Acquisition Journal,* May 23, 2017, www.military.com.

291   "The existence of the Directorate": Welzenbach, "50 Years of the CIA's DS&T," 74.

291   "a tremendous technological symphony": Fierstein, *Triumph of Genius,* 34.

292   "the mere production of the SX-70": Ibid.

292   Land invited workers at Polaroid: Olshaker, *Instant Image,* 199.

292   "Polaroid is considered a great": Eric J. Morgan, "The World Is Watching: Polaroid and South Africa," *Enterprise & Society* 7, no. 3 (Sept. 2006): 520–49. Additional information is from Robert C. Maynard, "Polaroid's Challenge: Racism or Morality?," *Washington Post,* Jan. 17, 1971, B2; Donald White, "Polaroid: A Corporate Guinea Pig," *Boston Globe,* Jan. 31, 1971, 1; Thomas Oliphant, "Shifting of Its Gift Jolts Polaroid," *Boston Globe,* Dec. 30, 1970, 3.

293   "I visited just after he had been listed": F. W. Campbell, "Edwin H. Land," *Biographical Memoirs of Fellows of the Royal Society* 40 (1994): 195–219.

293   "You know, Dr. Edwin Land": David Sheff, "Playboy Interview: Steve Jobs," *Playboy,* Feb. 1985, 43.

294   "Most of my friends": Bissell, *Reflections of a Cold Warrior,* 232.

294   "just in time to become": Ibid., 234; "A Secret Operative," *Newsweek,* Nov. 12, 1963, 19.

294   "Just to compound matters": Bissell, *Reflections of a Cold Warrior,* 235.

294   He mended his relationship: Ibid., 239; "Memorandum: Wheelon vs. McMillan: Dr. Land's Advice," Feb. 16, 1965, declassified by CIA, April 2005.

295   a period he'd later summarize as "unfulfilling": Bissell, *Reflections of a Cold Warrior,* 239.

295   "successes and regrets and a legacy": Taubman, *Secret Empire,* 329.

295   "When I look back": Bissell, *Reflections of a Cold Warrior,* 244–45.

295   "If any member of the general public": Joseph Alsop, "A Debt Is Owed," *Washington Post,* Dec. 23, 1963, 21.

296   The U.S. government urged him: Robarge, *Archangel.*

296   "It was a sad occasion": Miller, *Lockheed Martin's Skunk Works,* 141.

297   "To slip the immense power": "Warns Against Big Spending," Chicago Tribune Press Service, May 19, 1964.

297   "thus providing the Free World": "Clarence Leonard 'Kelly' Johnson," *Biographical Memoirs* (Washington, D.C.: National Academy Press, 1995), 67:234.

297   alongside other honorees: "Medalists Include Presidential Consultant, Folklore Expert," *Washington Post,* July 4, 1964, B2.

297   "the greatest achievement in aeronautics": "Top Airplane Designer Gets Collier Award," *Chicago Tribune,* Sept. 25, 1964, B4.

297   Powers found out about the ceremony: Francis Gary Powers, *Operation Overflight,* 296; "Gary Powers Decorated by CIA, Told Not to Wear, Discuss Medal," *St. Louis Post-Dispatch,* May 5, 1965, 2.

298   "For many years, during the time": "Powers of U-2 Divorces Wife on Drunk Claim," Los Angeles Times News Service, Jan. 17, 1963; Barbara Powers, *Spy Wife,* 157–58.

298 "He's not the same": "Powers Granted Divorce, Alimony Ruled for Wife," *Washington Star,* Jan. 16, 1963, 3; "Powers Wins Divorce Suit," *Baltimore Sun,* Jan. 17, 1963, 2.

298 Barbara married a man: "Powers' Ex Is Married," *New York Journal American,* Feb. 5, 1964, 14.

299 "I love flying": Demaris, "Going to See Gary," 90.

299 "I am very unhappy with Powers": Beschloss, *Mayday,* 398.

300 "While the lack of accurate intelligence": Francis Gary Powers, *Operation Overflight,* 319.

# Selected Bibliography

Absher, Kenneth Michael, Michael C. Desch, and Roman Popadiuk. *Privileged and Confidential: The Secret History of the President's Intelligence Advisory Board*. Lexington: University Press of Kentucky, 2012.

Ackman, Martha. *The Mercury 13: The True Story of Thirteen Women and the Dream of Space Flight*. New York: Random House, 2004.

Agathangelou, Anna M., and L. M. H. Ling. *Transforming World Politics: From Empire to Multiple Worlds*. London: Routledge, 2009.

Aid, Matthew M. *The Secret Sentry: The Untold History of the National Security Agency*. New York: Bloomsbury Press, 2009.

Alsop, Joseph. *I've Seen the Best of It: Memoirs*. New York: W. W. Norton, 1992.

Alsop, Stewart. *Stay of Execution: A Sort of Memoir*. New York: J. B. Lippincott, 1973.

Ambrose, Stephen E. *Ike's Spies: Eisenhower and the Espionage Establishment*. New York: Anchor Books, 2012.

Bamford, James. *Body of Secrets: Anatomy of the Ultra-secret National Security Agency*. New York: Anchor Books, 2002.

Beschloss, Michael. *Mayday: Eisenhower, Khrushchev, and the U-2 Affair*. New York: Harper & Row, 1986.

Bird, Kai, and Martin J. Sherwin. *American Prometheus: The Triumph and Tragedy of J. Robert Oppenheimer*. New York: Vintage Books, 2006.

Bissell, Richard M., Jr. *Reflections of a Cold Warrior: From Yalta to the Bay of Pigs*. With Jonathan E. Lewis and Frances T. Pudlo. New Haven, Conn.: Yale University Press, 1994.

Bohlen, Charles. *Witness to History*. New York: W. W. Norton, 1973.

Bonanos, Christopher. *Instant: The Story of Polaroid*. New York: Princeton Architectural Press, 2012.

Breuer, William B. *Deceptions of World War II*. New York: John Wiley & Sons, 2001.

Brugioni, Dino. *Eyeball to Eyeball: The Inside Story of the Cuban Missile Crisis*. New York: Random House, 1993.

———. *Eyes in the Sky: Eisenhower, the CIA, and Cold War Aerial Espionage*. Annapolis, Md.: Naval Institute Press, 2010.

Burrows, William E. *Deep Black: Space Espionage and National Security*. New York: Berkley Books, 1988.

———. *This New Ocean: The Story of the First Space Age*. New York: Random House, 1998.

Carlson, Peter. *K Blows Top: A Cold War Comic Interlude, Starring Nikita Khrushchev, America's Most Unlikely Tourist*. New York: PublicAffairs, 2009.

Dickson, Paul. *Sputnik: The Shock of the Century*. New York: Walker & Company, 2001.

Dobbs, Michael. *One Minute to Midnight: Kennedy, Khrushchev, and Castro on the Brink of Nuclear War*. New York: Vintage Books, 2009.

Donovan, James. *Strangers on a Bridge: The Case of Colonel Abel and Francis Gary Powers*. New York: Scribner, 1964.

Duffy, James P. *Lindbergh vs. Roosevelt: The Rivalry That Divided America*. Washington, D.C.: Regnery, 2010.

Dulles, Allen. *The Craft of Intelligence*. New York: Harper & Row, 1963.

Eisenhower, Dwight D. *The White House Years: Mandate for Change, 1952–1956*. Garden City, N.Y.: Doubleday, 1963.

———. *The White House Years: Waging Peace, 1956–1961*. Garden City, N.Y.: Doubleday, 1965.

Fierstein, Ronald K. *A Triumph of Genius: Edwin Land, Polaroid, and the Kodak Patent War*. Chicago: Ankerwycke, 2016.

Foerstner, Abigail. *James Van Allen: The First Eight Billion Miles*. Iowa City: University of Iowa Press, 2007.

Garrison, Dee. *Bracing for Armageddon: Why Civil Defense Never Worked*. Oxford: Oxford University Press, 2006.

Golden, William T., ed. *Science Advice to the President*. New Brunswick, N.J.: Transaction, 2003.

Graff, Garrett M. *Raven Rock: The Story of the U.S. Government's Secret Plan to Save Itself—While the Rest of Us Die*. New York: Simon & Schuster, 2017.

Graham, Richard. *The Complete Book of the SR-71 Blackbird: The Illustrated Profile of Every Aircraft, Crew, and Breakthrough of the World's Fastest Stealth Jet*. Minneapolis: Zenith Press, 2015.

Groom, Winston. *The Aviators: Eddie Rickenbacker, Jimmy Doolittle, Charles Lindbergh, and the Epic Age of Flight*. Washington, D.C.: National Geographic, 2013.

Grose, Peter. *Gentleman Spy: The Life of Allen Dulles*. New York: Houghton Mifflin, 1994.

Hardesty, Von, and Gene Eisman. *Epic Rivalry: The Inside Story of the Soviet and American Space Race*. Washington, D.C.: National Geographic, 2007.

Helms, Richard. *A Look over My Shoulder: A Life in the Central Intelligence Agency*. Novato, Calif.: Presidio, 2004.

Herken, Gregg. *The Georgetown Set: Friends and Rivals in Cold War Washington*. New York: Vintage Books, 2015.

Hewlett, Richard G., and Jack M. Holl. *Atoms for Peace and War, 1953–1961: Eisenhower and the Atomic Energy Commission*. Berkeley: University of California Press, 1989.

Holzman, Michael. *James Jesus Angleton, the CIA, and the Craft of Counterintelligence*. Amherst: University of Massachusetts Press, 2008.

Hornfischer, James D. *The Fleet at Flood Tide: America at Total War in the Pacific, 1944–1945*. New York: Bantam Books, 2016.

Jacobson, Annie. *Area 51: An Uncensored History of America's Top Secret Military Base*. Boston: Back Bay Books, 2012.

Johnson, Clarence L. *Kelly: More Than My Share of It All*. With Maggie Smith. Washington, D.C.: Smithsonian Institution Press, 1985.

Kennedy, Robert. *Thirteen Days: A Memoir of the Cuban Missile Crisis*. New York: W. W. Norton, 1999.

Khrushchev, Nikita. *Memoirs of Nikita Khrushchev*. Vol. 2, *Reformer*. University Park: Pennsylvania State University Press, 2013.

Khrushchev, Sergei. *Khrushchev on Khrushchev: An Inside Account of a Man and His Era*. Boston: Little, Brown, 1990.

———. *Nikita Khrushchev and the Creation of a Superpower*. University Park: Pennsylvania State University Press, 2001.

Killian, James R. *Sputnik, Scientists, and Eisenhower: A Memoir of the First Special Assistant to the President for Science and Technology*. Cambridge, Mass.: MIT Press, 1982.

Kistiakowsky, George B. *A Scientist at the White House*. Cambridge, Mass.: Harvard University Press, 1976.

Lashmar, Paul. *Spy Flights of the Cold War*. London: Sutton, 1996.

LeMay, Curtis D. *America Is in Danger*. New York: Funk & Wagnalls, 1968.

———. *Mission with LeMay*. With MacKinlay Kantor. Garden City, N.Y.: Doubleday, 1965.

Macintyre, Ben. *A Spy Among Friends: Kim Philby and the Great Betrayal*. New York: Crown, 2014.

Mangold, Tom. *Cold Warrior: James Jesus Angleton: The CIA's Master Spy Hunter*. New York: Simon & Schuster, 1991.

May, Ernest R., and Philip D. Zelikow, eds. *The Kennedy Tapes: Inside the White House During the Cuban Missile Crisis*. New York: W. W. Norton, 2002.

May, Gary. *Un-American Activities: The Trials of William Remington*. New York: Oxford University Press, 1994.

McElheny, Victor K. *Insisting on the Impossible: The Life of Edwin Land*. Cambridge, Mass.: Perseus Books, 1998.

McIlmoyle, Gerald, and Linda Rios Bromley. *Remembering the Dragon Lady: Memoirs of the Men Who Experienced the Legend of the U-2 Spy Plane*. Solihull, West Midlands: Helion, 2011.

Merry, Robert. *Taking on the World: Joseph and Stewart Alsop, Guardians of the American Century*. New York: Viking, 2010.

Mickolus, Edward, ed. *Stories from Langley: A Glimpse Inside the CIA*. Washington, D.C.: Potomac Books, 2014.

Miller, Jay. *Lockheed Martin's Skunk Works*. Leicester, U.K.: Midland, 1995.

Naftali, Timothy, ed. *John F. Kennedy: The Great Crises, July 30–August 1962*. New York: W. W. Norton, 2001.

Olshaker, Mark. *The Instant Image: Edwin Land and the Polaroid Experience*. New York: Stein and Day, 1978.

Olson, James M. *Fair Play: The Moral Dilemmas of Spying*. Washington, D.C.: Potomac Books, 2011.

Pearson, John. *The Life of Ian Fleming*. London: Bloomsbury Reader, 2013.

Plaskon, Kyril D. *Silent Heroes of the Cold War Declassified*. Las Vegas, Nev.: Stephens Press, 2009.

Pocock, Chris. *The U-2 Spyplane: Toward the Unknown: A New History of the Early Years*. Atglen, Pa.: Schiffer Military History, 2000.

Polenberg, Richard, ed. *In the Matter of J. Robert Oppenheimer: The Security Clearance Hearing*. Ithaca, N.Y.: Cornell University Press, 2002.

Powers, Barbara. *Spy Wife*. With W. W. Diehl. New York: Pyramid Books, 1965.

Powers, Francis Gary. *Operation Overflight: A Memoir of the U-2 Incident*. With Curt Gentry. Washington, D.C.: Potomac Books, 2004.

Powers, Thomas. *The Man Who Kept Secrets: Richard Helms and the CIA*. New York: Alfred A. Knopf, 1979.

Raleigh, John. *The Agency: The Rise and Decline of the CIA*. London: Sceptre, 1987.

Rasenberger, Jim. *The Brilliant Disaster: JFK, Castro, and America's Doomed Invasion of Cuba's Bay of Pigs*. New York: Scribner, 2011.

Rhodes, Richard. *Dark Sun: The Making of the Hydrogen Bomb*. New York: Simon & Schuster, 1995.

———. *The Making of the Atomic Bomb*. New York: Simon & Schuster, 1986.

Rich, Ben R., and Leo Janos. *Skunk Works: A Personal Memoir of My Years at Lockheed*. Boston: Back Bay Books, 1996.

Richelson, Jeffrey T. *The Wizards of Langley: The CIA's Directorate of Science and Technology*. Boulder, Colo.: Westview Press, 2002.

Robarge, David. *Archangel: CIA's Supersonic A-12 Reconnaissance Aircraft*. Washington, D.C.: Center for the Study of Intelligence, 2012.

Seaborg, Glenn. *A Chemist in the White House: From the Manhattan Project to the End of the Cold War*. Washington, D.C.: ACS Books, 1997.

Spoto, Donald. *The Life of Alfred Hitchcock: The Dark Side of Genius*. London: William Collins & Sons, 1983.

Stone, Geoffrey R. *Perilous Times: Free Speech in Wartime from the Sedition Act of 1798 to the War on Terrorism*. New York: W. W. Norton, 2004.

Suhler, Paul A. *From Rainbow to Gusto: Stealth and the Design of the Lockheed Blackbird*. Reston, Va.: American Institute of Aeronautics and Astronautics, 2009.

Talbot, David. *Brothers: The Hidden History of the Kennedy Years*. New York: Free Press, 2007.

Taubman, Philip, *Secret Empire: Eisenhower, the CIA, and the Hidden Story of America's Space Espionage*. New York: Simon & Schuster, 2003.

Theoharis, Athan, ed. *The Central Intelligence Agency: Security Under Scrutiny*. With Richard Immerman, Loch Johnson, Kathryn Olmsted, and John Prados. Westport, Conn.: Greenwood Press, 2005.

———. *From the Secret Files of J. Edgar Hoover*. Chicago: Ivan R. Dee, 1991.

Thomas, Evan. *Robert Kennedy: His Life*. New York: Simon & Schuster, 2000.

———. *The Very Best Men: Four Who Dared: The Early Years of the CIA*. New York: Simon & Schuster, 1995.

Titus, A. Costandina. *Bombs in the Backyard: Atomic Testing and American Politics*. Reno: University of Nevada Press, 2001.

Wensberg, Peter C. *Land's Polaroid: A Company and the Man Who Invented It*. Boston: Houghton Mifflin, 1987.

Whittell, Giles. *Bridge of Spies: A True Story of the Cold War*. New York: Broadway Books, 2010.

Wolfe, Tom. *The Right Stuff*. Thorndike, Maine: Thorndike Press, 1979.

Wyden, Peter. *The Bay of Pigs: The Untold Story*. New York: Simon & Schuster, 1979.

Yoder, Edwin M. *Joe Alsop's Cold War: A Study of Journalistic Influence and Intrigue*. Chapel Hill: University of North Carolina Press, 2011.

# Index

# ILLUSTRATION CREDITS